TRADING AT THE SPEEI

Trading at the Speed of Light

How Ultrafast Algorithms Are Transforming Financial Markets

Donald MacKenzie

PRINCETON UNIVERSITY PRESS

PRINCETON AND OXFORD

Copyright © 2021 by Princeton University Press

Requests for permission to reproduce material from this work
should be sent to permissions@press.princeton.edu

Published by Princeton University Press
41 William Street, Princeton, New Jersey 08540
99 Banbury Road, Oxford OX2 6JX

press.princeton.edu

First paperback printing, 2023
Paperback ISBN 9780691217789

The Library of Congress has cataloged the cloth edition as follows:

Names: MacKenzie, Donald A., author.
Title: Trading at the speed of light : how ultrafast algorithms are
    transforming financial markets / Donald MacKenzie.
Description: Princeton, New Jersey : Princeton University Press,
    [2021] | Includes bibliographical references and index.
Identifiers: LCCN 2020049217 (print) | LCCN 2020049218 (ebook) |
    ISBN 9780691211381 (hardback) | ISBN 9780691217796 (ebook)
Subjects: LCSH: Investments—Data processing. | Program trading
    (Securities) | Stock exchanges. | Algorithms. | Finance.
Classification: LCC HG4515.5 .M33 2021 (print) |
    LCC HG4515.5 (ebook) | DDC 332.640285—dc23
LC record available at https://lccn.loc.gov/2020049217
LC ebook record available at https://lccn.loc.gov/2020049218

British Library Cataloging-in-Publication Data is available

Editorial: Hannah Paul and Josh Drake
Production Editorial: Natalie Baan
Jacket/Cover Design: Karl Spurzem
Production: Erin Suydam
Publicity: Kate Farquhar-Thomson and Kate Hensley
Copyeditor: Steven Krauss

Jacket/Cover image: Shutterstock

This book has been composed in Adobe Text and Gotham

In memory of Alice MacKenzie Bamford (1988–2020)

CONTENTS

Figures

Tables

ACKNOWLEDGMENTS

I am enormously grateful to all the people who spoke to me, many of them multiple times, during my research for this book. Nearly all prefer to be anonymous, but their input was essential. George Lerner and Jean Czerlinski Whitmore played particularly important roles in helping me find crucial people to speak to. Taylor Spears kindly produced the maps in figures 1.3, 1.4, and 4.1. Frances Burgess heroically word-processed multiple versions of the chapters, and assembled the bibliography. Esje Stapleton and Neil Marchant between them transcribed hundreds of interview recordings, and the very high quality of their work was essential to the research. Dylan Cassar, Arjen van der Heide, Julius Kob, and Alec Ross also helped me enormously in constructing the chapters and figures. The research was supported financially by the ESRC (the UK Economic and Social Research Council: grant ES/R003173/1) and by the European Research Council (grant 291733, Evaluation Practices in Financial Markets), with some of the initial exploratory fieldwork also supported by ESRC grant RES-062-23-1958. Although all errors remain my responsibility, Princeton University Press's anonymous reviewers gave me some very helpful suggestions, as did Leo Melamed, Greg Laughlin, Mike Persico, Alex Pilosov, Stéphane Tyč, and a number of interviewees who need to remain anonymous. Huge thanks to all.

I have written this book with general readers, not just my academic colleagues, in mind. The writing style is, therefore, a little less formal than is normal in academic writing. I've also put my summary of the existing most directly relevant academic literature on the book's topic, high-frequency trading, into an appendix. I trust that my colleagues will understand that this decision is stylistic rather than the result of my underestimating my intellectual debt to them. The academic field of this book—the "social studies of finance," in other words the application to financial markets not of economics but of wider social-science disciplines (in my case, sociology and the social studies of science and technology)—is a friendly and collegial one, and that is a blessing.

Over the years, Peter Dougherty has kept encouraging me to write a book for Princeton University Press. When I was finally ready, Sarah Caro, Hannah Paul, and Natalie Baan handled the book with insight and efficiency, with Natalie kindly allowing me to unscramble mistakes I had made with the illustrations. Steven Krauss edited the book very sympathetically. Moyra Forrest has indexed most of my books, and I am very grateful to her for doing so again. During the research, I wrote about high-frequency trading and related topics both in the academic literature and the *London Review of Books*, and those articles are drawn on here, especially MacKenzie (2015, 2017a&b, 2018a&b, 2019a,b,c,d&e), MacKenzie and Pardo-Guerra (2014), and MacKenzie, Hardie, Rommerskirchen, and van der Heide (2020). I'm grateful to the copyright owners and my coauthors for allowing me to do this.

TRADING AT THE SPEED OF LIGHT

1

Introduction

Walk down Broad Street toward the southern tip of Manhattan, and you pass the imposing neoclassical façade of the New York Stock Exchange, police barriers, and—in normal times—tourists taking photographs. Throughout the twentieth century, that famous building, crammed with human traders, epitomized what "finance" meant. A couple of minutes' walk farther south, you would most likely pass 50 Broad Street without a second glance. It has a handsome frontage, and has been renovated internally, but is otherwise an ordinary Manhattan office building (see figure 1.1). In 1993, that stretch of Broad Street, then scruffy and neglected, struck a *New York Times* journalist as exemplifying downtown's decline.[1] More than in any other single place, though, what happened at 50 Broad Street in the 1990s and early 2000s transformed the world's financial markets. Now, just one trace of that role remains: inscribed in panels attached to the stonework above a storefront (which, despite the area's revival, has been empty for years) is the word "island."[2]

Island, launched in 1996, was an electronic venue for the trading of US shares. It was not the first such venue, but none of its predecessors had changed the financial system radically. Some had gone out of business; some had been assimilated into existing ways of doing things; some had succeeded modestly but had not come to occupy central roles. Island was different. Its computer system, packed into the basement of 50 Broad Street, consisted almost entirely of cheap machines of the kind you could have bought in a computer store, but it was blazingly fast by the standards of the 1990s. The

FIGURE 1.1. 50 Broad Street. Author's photograph.

interviewee I am calling AF told me that if Island's system received both a bid to buy shares and an offer to sell the same shares at the same price, it could execute a trade in a couple of milliseconds (thousandths of a second), a thousand times faster than the more mainstream electronic system to which it was most comparable, Instinet. To human eyes, trading on Island appeared instantaneous.

Just as consequential as Island's speed was that machines started to trade on it. There had been previous efforts to automate trading, but often they had not gone smoothly. It could be difficult for an automated trading system to interact seamlessly with exchanges' systems, which in the 1980s and 1990s were usually designed on the assumption that traders were human beings, not machines. Indeed, those who ran exchanges' early electronic trading systems often protected their human users from "unfair" automated competition by prohibiting the direct connection of computers to them. In the privacy of their offices, traders found ways to circumvent the

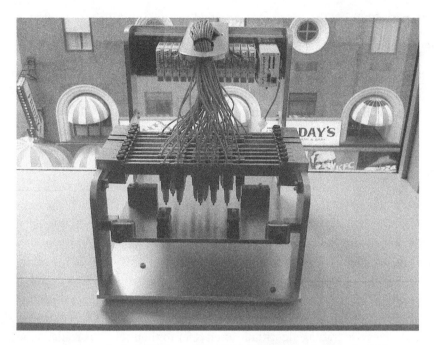

FIGURE 1.2. Lehman Brothers "Clackatron" (ca. 2002), used to strike the keys of an EBS (Electronic Broking Services) foreign-exchange trading keypad. Photograph courtesy of interviewee FL.

prohibition—sometimes even constructing robotic devices to hit the keys of terminals designed for human users (one such device is shown in figure 1.2)—but doing this was cumbersome.[3] Island, in contrast, was machine friendly from the outset. At its core was a set of "order books": electronic files, one for each stock, of the bids to buy the shares in question and of the offers to sell them. Every time Island's computer system executed a trade or received a bid, an offer, or a cancellation of an order, an electronic message was sent out via a continuous datafeed that traders' computers could use to maintain an up-to-date electronic mirror of Island's order books. It was also straightforward for those computers to send Island bids and offers in a fast, succinct, standardized electronic format.

As the machines that traded on Island got faster, the delays that were inevitable if their orders needed to be transmitted to lower Manhattan through hundreds of miles of fiber-optic cable became ever more salient. Dave Cummings, founder of the Kansas City high-frequency trading firm Tradebot ("Trading Robot"), told the *Wall Street Journal* in 2006 that he had come to realize that the 10 milliseconds it took a signal to get from Kansas

City to 50 Broad Street put his firm at a disadvantage: "We were excluded because of the speed of light" (Lucchetti 2006). Starting around 2002, the firms whose machines traded on Island began to move them into 50 Broad Street, at first informally (a web-services firm that had offices in the building hosted their computer servers) and then—in a formal, paid-for arrangement with Island—placing them in Island's computer room in the building's basement, next to Island's heart, the "matching engine": the system that managed its order books and executed trades.

What emerged in and around 50 Broad Street ("emerged" is the right word: no one planned it) is this book's topic: high-frequency trading, or HFT. The practice emerged before the name did; as far as I can tell, the term first came into use at the Chicago hedge fund Citadel in the early 2000s. HFT is "proprietary" automated trading that takes place at speeds far faster than an unaided human can trade and in which trading's profitability is inherently dependent on its speed.[4] (The goal of proprietary trading is direct trading profit, rather than, for example, earning fees by executing trades on behalf of others.) Although the human beings employed by HFT firms to design and supervise trading algorithms often refer to themselves as traders, the trading itself is actually done by those computer algorithms. Humans write the algorithms and (less often now than in HFT's early years) sometimes tweak their parameters during the trading day, but the decisions to place bids to buy and offers to sell are made by the algorithm, not the human being.

HFT algorithms trade both with each other and with other categories of algorithm, such as the "execution algorithms" used by institutional investors—and by banks or other brokers acting on behalf of these investors—to break up a large order to buy or sell shares (or other financial instruments) into much smaller, low-profile "child" orders.[5] HFT firms' algorithms also interact with orders placed manually by human beings, for example by those whom market participants refer to as "retail" (individual investors). Only a minority of retail orders, though, end up being traded on exchanges such as the New York Stock Exchange. Most are executed directly by what are sometimes called wholesalers (which are often branches of HFT firms), who pay the brokers via whom retail investors trade to send them these orders.[6]

HFT firms, in aggregate, trade on a giant scale. For example, as we will see in chapter 4, in just over two months in 2015, eight HFT firms traded Treasurys worth in total about $7 trillion. (Treasurys are the sovereign debt securities of the United States. A trillion is a million million.) The anonymity of most of today's trading makes it difficult in most cases to be certain just how much of it is HFT, but observers often estimate that HFT accounts for around half of all trading on many of the world's most important markets (see, e.g., Meyer and Bullock 2017; Meyer, Bullock, and Rennison 2018).

The HFT firms that are responsible for these huge volumes of trading are typically recently established and small. Only a small number date from before 2000, and even an HFT firm with no more than a few dozen employees can be a significant player. Consider, for example, Virtu, an HFT firm whose headquarters, as it happens, are just a few blocks away from 50 Broad Street. Virtu's primary activity is "market-making"—continuously posting both bids to buy shares or other financial instruments and slightly higher-priced offers to sell them—and it does this in more than 25,000 different instruments traded in 36 countries. It is responsible, for example, for around a fifth of all US share trading.[7] It rose to its dominant position, my interviewees report, while employing no more than 150 people (its headcount has risen recently because of its acquisition of two firms with more labor-intensive businesses).[8]

In particular niches, even firms with only a handful of employees can be important. In 2019, an interviewee calmly told me that his tiny European HFT firm was responsible for 5 percent of all the share trading in India. Some big banks used to be active in HFT, but their efforts were often less than fully successful; the rapid development of the fast, highly specialized software systems that are needed can be difficult in a large, bureaucratic organization. Banks are still engaged in market-making in some classes of financial instrument (such as those discussed in chapter 4: foreign exchange and governments' sovereign bonds), albeit often using systems that are slow by HFT standards, but large-scale use of other HFT strategies by banks was effectively ended by the curbs on banks' proprietary trading that followed the 2008 banking crisis.

The HFT firms I have visited differ widely. Some had offices in unremarkable or even scruffy buildings; others had spectacular views over Lake Michigan, Manhattan, or Greater London. The décor is generally bland, although as I sat waiting for an interviewee in one HFT firm's new offices, some of the owner's art collection was ready to be hung. The paintings were wrapped and unlabeled, but I'm told they are very fine: the owner has good taste and the firm has been highly successful. More often, though, HFT firms' premises could pass for those of a generic dot-com firm, and they usually have something of the relaxed feel of a software start-up. The employees of HFT firms are mostly young and—at least in the roles closest to trading—mostly male. Office kitchens, for example, often contain multiple boxes of breakfast cereal, stereotypically young men's food. I am happy to report, though, that the sexist pinups that sometimes used to disfigure trading floors are no longer to be seen. Almost no one in HFT routinely wears a business suit—it is common for me, as the visitor, to be the only person wearing a tie, and I've been told off for being overdressed—and the shouting and swearing that used to be heard on banks' trading floors is less common in HFT firms. That might, of course, be because of my presence, but interviewees tell me that such behavior is indeed less prevalent. As discussed below, I have visited firms only in the US and Europe. There, at least, white faces predominate, though often intermingled with those of South Asian or Chinese extraction, while African Americans, for example, seem rarer.

The internal organization of the HFT firms from which my interviewees come varies. Some operate as unified entities, without even the traditional individual P&L (a trader's profit or loss, the prime determinant of her/his bonus); one firm had a computerized "signal library"—an electronic compendium of data patterns useful to HFT algorithms—that was accessible to all its traders and software developers. Just as Lange (2016) discovered, though, other HFT firms are divided into strictly separate trading teams, with deliberate barriers to communication. One firm, for example, physically separates teams by placing a row of administrative staff between them, and in its main offices even plays white noise between the rows to reduce the chance of members of one team overhearing what is said by members of another. Another firm compartmentalizes its trading by dividing up its long, narrow trading room with white curtains that prevent members of one team from seeing what others are doing. At one compartmentalized firm, said a young trader (interviewee AC) who worked there, "you . . . could get in trouble for being in the next room talking to someone you're not supposed to talk to."[9]

High-frequency trading, however, does not actually happen in these rooms. Instead, it takes place in the computer datacenters of exchanges and other trading venues, which typically contain both the exchange's computer system and the systems of HFT firms and other algorithmic traders, of banks, of communications suppliers, and so on.[10] Exchanges' datacenters aren't generally found in city centers, but in suburban areas in which real estate is cheaper. The datacenters important to HFT are mostly large buildings, and indeed they usually look like suburban warehouses, with, for example, few windows. They are packed with tens of thousands of computer servers, typically on racks in wire-mesh cages (although sometimes the cages have opaque walls, so that a trading firm's competitors cannot see the

FIGURE 1.3. The "equities triangle" in New Jersey. The Nasdaq and NYSE (New York Stock Exchange) datacenters host the share-trading exchanges run by those groups; NY4 and NY5, which are in effect a single datacenter, host the share-trading exchanges run by the third of the exchange groups, the Chicago Board Options Exchange. (Locations in this and other maps are given only approximately.)

equipment it is using). The servers are interconnected by mile upon mile of cabling, typically running above the racks in what looks to an outsider like an incomprehensibly complex spaghetti of different types of cable. In aggregate, those servers consume very large quantities of electricity and generate large amounts of heat, making a powerful cooling system also a requisite. Normally, few human beings are to be found in these datacenters, just a small number of security and maintenance staff, along with (at least some of the time) engineers from exchanges, trading firms, or communications suppliers who may be visiting to fix problems or install new equipment.

No more than around two dozen datacenters globally host the bulk of the world's financial trading and the vast majority of its HFT. Most US share trading, for example, takes place in the four datacenters in northern New Jersey shown in figure 1.3. One is owned by what is now the New York

Stock Exchange's parent company, the Intercontinental Exchange. Another is leased by Nasdaq, traditionally the main rival to the NYSE as a trading venue for US shares. Two further datacenters (NY4 and NY5) host the systems of multiple trading venues, including the third main group of US stock exchanges, now owned by the Chicago Board Options Exchange. NY4 and NY5 are close together, and in practice are run as a single datacenter. Because of this, market participants often refer to the NYSE datacenter, its Nasdaq equivalent, and NY4/5 as the "equities triangle." (An "equity" is simply another word for a share.)

All of the most important US stocks are traded in all of these datacenters. That makes the automated trading going on in one share-trading datacenter a vitally important source of data for algorithms trading shares in the other datacenters: a vital class of "signal," as market practitioners would call it. A signal is a pattern of data that informs an algorithm's trading, for example by prompting it to bid to buy shares or offer to sell them, or perhaps to cancel an existing bid or offer. A signal of the kind used by HFT algorithms is typically a very short-lived pattern of information: in 2008–9 its duration was usually "less than 3–4 seconds" (Brogaard, Hendershott, and Riordan 2014: 2302). By 2015, a signal may have flickered into life for as little as 10 microseconds—in other words, 10 millionths of a second (Aquilina, Budish, and O'Neill 2020: 55). Another source of signals of this kind, which is of great importance to algorithms trading US shares, is what is going on in the share-index futures market, which is not in New Jersey but in a datacenter in the suburbs of Chicago; see figure 1.4. (A "future" is a standardized, exchange-traded contract that is economically close to the equivalent of one party undertaking to buy, and the other to sell, a set quantity of some underlying asset on a given future date but at a price agreed upon at the inception of the contract.) For reasons to be discussed in chapter 2, the prices of share-index futures in Chicago tend to move a tiny fraction of a second before the corresponding movements in the prices of the underlying shares in the New Jersey datacenters.

When I began my research, I imagined that the data patterns that informed trading by HFT algorithms would be quite complicated, and that those involved would have had to use sophisticated machine learning to discover those patterns. Although machine learning does play a role in the activity (there are examples of this in chapter 6), it is less central than I had assumed. In many ways the most crucial signals for HFT are the kind of relatively simple data patterns just discussed, patterns that often arise (as the following chapters will show) from the way trading is organized and regulated. Those

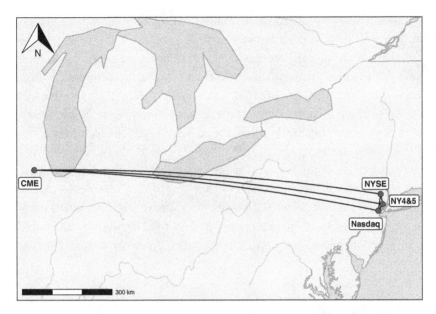

FIGURE 1.4. Geodesics from Chicago to the New Jersey share-trading datacenters. "CME" is the main Chicago Mercantile Exchange datacenter.

patterns are common knowledge in the sector, which means that how fast an algorithm can respond to a signal such as a price movement in share-index futures is vital to whether an algorithm's trading is profitable or loss-making.

Because HFT is, and has to be, very fast (we will see just how fast in the next section), the speed of transmission of signals among datacenters is crucial. That makes the geodesics among them the site of intense activity by communications suppliers, originally mainly using fiber-optic cables, but now using wireless links as well. (A geodesic, or great circle, is the shortest path on the surface of the earth between two given points.) Indeed, US share trading now takes place in what—were it not for the fact that no one planned it and it has no fully coherent overall design—could be called a large technical system, made up of the tens of thousands of machines in the datacenters whose locations are shown in figures 1.3 and 1.4, and of the communications links along the geodesics among these datacenters. Huge volumes of electronic messages (above all, reporting changes in exchanges' order books) flow through this system. The market-data-processing firm Exegy continuously measures the numbers of messages flowing through its equipment in NY4; at the time of writing, the peak recorded on its system was a burst equivalent to 105.3 million messages per second, at 2:39 p.m. on July 19, 2018.[11]

The core systems of automated trading can keep working with little direct human intervention. That became evident in March 2020, as lockdowns belatedly began in Western countries and it finally became clear to their financial markets just how serious the coronavirus epidemic was. Huge amounts of turbulent trading took place, and crucial markets were badly disrupted, including the market for the traditionally safest of safe assets, Treasurys, which as already noted are the sovereign debt securities of the United States. In April, the prices of oil futures even briefly became negative, as a result of the combination of reduced demand for oil and difficulties in storing it. Nevertheless, "the market's plumbing held up" (Osipovich 2020). The turmoil was not exacerbated by major failures of the infrastructures of automated markets. While there are certainly risks involved in automated trading (as discussed in chapter 7), this quiet achievement should also be recognized.

Material Political Economy

This book belongs in the "social studies of finance," the collective name for research on finance not by economists but in wider social-science disciplines such as anthropology, sociology, politics, and science and technology studies. That research has grown rapidly in the last twenty years, and includes, for example, research on HFT. Although my research builds on the work of many colleagues, this book's readers will not all be specialists, so I've put discussion of the existing literature on HFT (including the work of economists) into an appendix at the end of the book. I do, though, need to explain the approach this book takes to the analysis of HFT, which I call "material political economy." It is a single idea, not three ideas, but let me explain it by taking each of the words in turn: all three—"material," "political," and "economy"—are significant.

"Material" indicates a fundamental feature of this book. The previous section has already begun to sketch the material arrangements of today's US share trading. The chapters that follow (especially chapter 5, but not that alone) focus, in as great a depth as is relevant to the book's themes and as my research data allow, on HFT's materiality. Human beings' bodies are part of the material world—if you have any doubts as to whether a human body is material, wait until you have an aging one—and, as Borch, Hansen, and Lange (2015) discuss, the mundane materiality of human bodies is important to HFT. Consider what human eyes and brains can process and what they can't, because it's too fast; what one trader, interviewee OG, calls the "toilet test" (do you trust an algorithm sufficiently to leave it running unsupervised while you attend to bodily needs?); and what you may need to do to stay focused and awake in the long hours, especially overnight, in which there is often little activity in financial markets.

Nonhuman forms of materiality are, however, much more salient than human bodies in the chapters that follow. HFT is trading *by* machines (trading firms' computer servers and other equipment) *on* machines: all modern exchanges are, at their heart, computer systems. The characteristics of machines, and how those characteristics have changed through time, are hugely important to HFT. Materiality, though, does not refer only to solid objects. Light and other forms of electromagnetic radiation are just as material, and just as salient to HFT, as cables and silicon chips are. The reference to the speed of light in this book's title refers to the need in HFT for the fastest possible transmission of data and orders to buy or to sell.

I think of the materiality of HFT as "Einsteinian." By introducing the name of the celebrated physicist, I don't mean to imply that it's necessary to apply his theory of relativity to understand the aspects of HFT covered in this book, because I don't think that's so, except in limited respects.[12] Rather, the Einstein I invoke is the one portrayed by the historian of physics Peter Galison: an Einstein who was not just a theoretical physicist, but also an inspector in the patent office in Bern, Switzerland, familiar with the technologies of measurement and the practical problem of ensuring the synchronicity of clocks in different spatial locations—Einstein as what Galison (2003: 255) calls a "patent officer-scientist." (Clock synchronization, it is worth noting, is just as prominent a problem in HFT as it was in the railway networks of the late nineteenth and early twentieth centuries. One of my HFT interviewees, CQ, told me how his firm's trading had been badly disrupted by a failure of synchronization.) Einstein's thinking about practical, technological issues such as synchronization, Galison suggests, lay in the background of his development of the theory of special relativity, with its famous postulate that the fastest any signal can travel is the speed of light in a vacuum.

That limit is the fundamental material constraint on HFT. In the early years of HFT, transmission between datacenters was generally via laser-generated pulses of light in fiber-optic cables, but (as described in chapter 5) that gets you only around two-thirds of the way to Einstein's maximum signal speed, because light pulses in these cables are slowed by the materials from which their strands are made, which are specialized forms of glass. In contrast, a wireless signal sent through Earth's atmosphere travels at very nearly the speed of light in a vacuum. Because, however, wireless transmission for HFT requires radio frequencies that are in high demand, tailor-made radios, and antennas in specific locations (see chapter 5), it is much more expensive than the routine use of fiber-optic cable usually is. One interviewee, indeed, spoke of trying to avoid what he called "radio-frequency markets": those in which an HFT firm has no alternative but to use signals transmitted through the atmosphere.

One way of gauging the speed of HFT is the response time of an HFT firm's system: the delay between the arrival of a "signal" (a pattern of data that informs an algorithm's trading) and an action—the dispatch of an order or a cancellation of an order—in response to that signal. In March 2019, an interviewee told me that, although his own systems were slower than this, he had learned of the achievement of response times as low as 42 nanoseconds.[13] A nanosecond is a billionth of a second, and in a nanosecond, even light in a vacuum, or a wireless signal in the atmosphere, travels no more than around thirty centimeters, or roughly a foot.

That nanoseconds are important in HFT makes its world Einsteinian: for HFT, that no signal can travel faster than the speed of light in a vacuum is a practical constraint, not just a theoretical limit. For a signal to travel even as short a distance as a meter takes what is potentially an economically consequential amount of time, and that makes HFT exquisitely sensitive to the precise location of technical equipment and to how closely the path of a fiber-optic cable or wireless link hugs the geodesic between datacenters.[14] The materiality of HFT is, therefore, above all a *spatial* materiality. It's easy to think of what is sometimes called today's postmodernity as involving the shrinking of both time and space.[15] In an Einsteinian world, though, as time shrinks, space becomes ever more salient.

The computer specialists who work for HFT firms have to be materialists in their thinking and their practices. One such specialist with whom I chatted during a coffee break in a traders' conference in Amsterdam told me that he had had to unlearn the attitude that he had unwittingly picked up during his time as a computer-science student. He could not, as he had implicitly been taught, safely abstract away from the physicality of the hardware on which his algorithms run. A computer, from the viewpoint of HFT, is not an abstract information processor, but a material assemblage of plastic, metal, and silicon through which electrical signals flow, and making them flow as quickly as possible is a vital practical concern. When I use the word *algorithm* in this book, I don't mean the word in the dominant sense in which it is used in computer science: a "recipe" that achieves a goal or solves a problem in a finite number of precise, unambiguous steps, and which is abstract in the sense that it can be implemented in different programming languages running on different machines. Rather—and I am following my interviewees' predominant usage here—an algorithm is a recipe of this kind written in a particular programming language, running on particular physical hardware, and having material effects on other systems.[16]

I didn't begin my research on HFT with the concept of material political economy in mind. The notion evolved as I conducted my fieldwork, and it seems to me a useful way of framing the research and of capturing its findings. I don't want, however, to try to draw an ontological divide between "material" and "nonmaterial" phenomena, or to suggest that we should focus on the materiality of economic life and exclude everything else. Nor do I see "material political economy" as making redundant other ways of studying economic phenomena, such as "cultural economy" (du Gay and Pryke 2002), "cultural political economy" (Jessop 2009), or, for example, the various forms of "international political economy" pursued by scholars in politics. Even a quintessentially material business such as HFT is influenced by factors that we wouldn't ordinarily think of as "material": beliefs, metaphors, epistemic authority, legitimacy, and so on. (Ultimately, all of these factors come down to material phenomena: words or images on paper or in other media, and sometimes other physical objects; the soundwaves that encode speech, and so on, including material patterns of neural activity in human brains. However, while the materiality of "culture" in this sense is indeed sometimes important, it would be facile to argue on these a priori grounds that it should always be focused on.)

Consider legitimacy, for example. As I will shortly discuss, the history of HFT has been marked by systematic conflicts with trading's incumbents. Scandals that have undermined those incumbents' legitimacy—such as the Nasdaq scandal in the 1990s touched on in chapter 3—have been important in creating opportunities for the rise of HFT. Similarly, as will be described in chapter 6, a crucial internal divide in HFT is between "market-making" strategies (which, as already noted, involve continuously posting both bids and offers in order books that others can execute against) and "liquidity-taking" strategies, which involve executing against orders that are already present in order books. Market-making inherits the legitimacy of a traditional human role in markets, and some—although by no means all—of my interviewees regard it as a preferable, even a more moral, economic activity than liquidity-taking. It is true that the extent to which this preference shapes particular forms of trading, rather than simply being invoked to justify them, is questionable. After one of the leaders of an HFT firm emphatically presented its activity to me as market-making, another interviewee (who had recently left the firm) described that image as a "legitimatory" move rather than fully factual. However, that the role played by legitimacy is often ambiguous in this way certainly does not imply that it should be ignored. The materiality of human activity is inseparably bound up with questions of belief, the achievement (or loss) of authority, and so on, and to close one's eyes to this would be to pursue an impoverished form of research.

Material *Political* Economy

HFT's materiality is nevertheless crucial, and the approach I'm taking owes a great deal to the perspective—called actor-network theory—that has in recent years done most to place materiality at the heart of social sciences.[17] (Marxism was also originally a thoroughly materialist intellectual enterprise—that is certainly the case, for example, in the memorable passages on machinery in volume 1 of Marx's *Capital* [Marx 1976]—but twentieth-century developments, such as the rise of more philosophically oriented Western Marxism, in practice rather weakened this emphasis.)[18] In a lovely contribution to actor-network theory, John Law and Annemarie Mol (2008) discuss what they call "material politics." The idea is in essence simple, and it has antecedents—we will encounter one of them at the start of chapter 7, in research conducted in the 1930s by the historian Marc Bloch—but is elegantly laid out by Mol and Law. As they argue, it is possible to arrange the material world in different ways, and at least sometimes the issue of which of these ways becomes real has a political dimension. There are, for example, "roads not taken" in the development of technology, as the historian Ruth Schwartz Cowan (1983) points out, drawing the phrase from the poet Robert Frost: technologies that could have been developed but weren't, and not necessarily because they were simply less efficient than the successful alternative, but sometimes for reasons that have more to do with class, gender, and ethnic divides, state power, and so on.[19]

"Material politics" is a pivotal aspect of HFT. As already noted, the activity's history is characterized by incumbent-challenger conflicts, in which HFT firms have traditionally been in the role of challenger; some of those conflicts continue today. Conflicts of this kind are emphasized by the sociological perspective known as field theory, and elsewhere I've argued that the materiality of actor-network theory needs to be complemented by the field-theory emphasis on such issues, despite the occasional bitter clashes between the two perspectives.[20] Incumbent-challenger conflicts in finance are played out in multiple dimensions, but the material arrangements of trading are certainly one of those dimensions. In chapter 6, for example, we will discuss a material procedure ("last look") that has protected the incumbents in foreign-exchange trading from HFT firms' faster systems.

The divide, already mentioned, between "market-making" and "liquidity-taking" algorithms fuels much of today's material politics of HFT. The existing bids and offers that liquidity-taking algorithms execute against are, in most of the world's leading electronic markets, often those that have been submitted by HFT market-making algorithms, so that a good proportion of the profits made by liquidity-takers is most likely at the expense of the latter. As discussed in chapter 6, there is at least a degree of differentiation among trading groups and sometimes even entire firms in the extent to which they specialize in either market-making or liquidity-taking, and the material arrangements of trading can tilt the playing field in favor of one or the other. These arrangements are, therefore, a form of material politics.

More mundanely, HFT firms (even though small and often closely steered by their founders) are not immune from internal disharmony and office politics. For example, even in a compartmentalized HFT firm with strictly separate trading groups, there is usually a common technical and communications infrastructure, and how access to that infrastructure is shared among the groups can reflect what interviewee DC calls "a . . . political dynamic." When, for example, the firm for which he worked started to lease wireless bandwidth, "it was the politics of who gets to use that line. . . . It was such limited capacity, then people started really fighting over it." Since the trading groups in a compartmentalized firm have their own—possibly very different—approaches to HFT, the overall trading activity of such a firm may sometimes be shaped substantially by the outcomes of struggles of this kind.

"Politics" and "political" are, of course, elastic words. In this book, I use them mainly in their broadest sense, which refers to the full gamut of phenomena that shape and are shaped by actors' power and position, the status and respect they enjoy or fail to receive, their economic resources, and other factors. However, politics in the narrower sense of political parties, members of Congress, congressional committees, and so on, has also played a part in the development of HFT, especially via the interaction between the political system and the regulation of finance. (When writing about politics in the narrower sense, I will sometimes for clarity use the ordinary term "political system," although once again "system" suggests a coherence that is often absent.) The interaction between the political system and financial regulation takes a variety of forms, including, for example, differences among political parties in their typical attitudes to regulation. In the US, for instance, Democrats have generally preferred stricter forms of regulation, and Republicans often have deregulatory impulses. Politicians, furthermore, are often lobbied by financial-sector interests, and money from the financial sector can form an important part of campaign contributions to politicians (there is an example of this, and of its consequences, in chapter 2).

The tightness of the connections between financial regulation and the political system should not, however, be overstated. Again, sociological field theory is relevant. "Politics" and "regulation" (and, indeed, extending the point, "exchanges" and "trading") are all what sociologists such as Pierre Bourdieu and Neil Fligstein call "fields," or what the Chicago sociologist Andrew Abbott calls "ecologies." In other words, they are specific domains of social and economic life, characterized by differently positioned actors competing and collaborating to achieve rewards that are often specific to that field or ecology. (The key reward for politicians, for example, is usually votes.) Fields are often characterized by an implicit sense of what forms of behavior are legitimate, and there are sometimes explicit rules about what actors should and should not do. We should not, however, expect to find consensus. Rules often privilege some actors over others, and one form that competition can take is for challengers to seek to change a field's norms and rules.[21]

Although different fields thus differ in their specific dynamics, in their norms and rules, and in the rewards at stake, developments in one field can affect adjacent fields in important ways. One way is via what Abbott (2005) calls a "hinge": a process that generates rewards in more than one field or, in his terminology, more than one ecology.[22] As Abbott points out, though, the political system differs from many other fields or ecologies in that issues that are continuously important in those other fields (for example, licensing in nineteenth-century medicine; or the organization and regulation of trading) are salient only sporadically in the political system, because most of the time there are few directly political rewards for pursuing them. The hinges that link the field of politics (in the narrow sense) to the fields of finance—or, in Abbott's chief example, to the ecology of the professions—are thus often transient and contingent, even idiosyncratic. That does not mean, however, that they are unimportant. In chapter 2, for example, we will see how the lasting effects of one such idiosyncratic 1970s-era hinge have profoundly shaped automated trading in the US.

Material Political *Economy*

Why, though, do we need the third word, "economy"? Surely, everything to do with finance is self-evidently economic? The reason for emphasizing the economic (indeed, the monetary) aspects of finance is that they have often been given insufficient attention in the specialist area of the social sciences to which this book belongs. That area, to repeat, involves the application to the study of finance not of economics, nor of individualistic "behavioral finance," but of wider social-science disciplines such as anthropology and sociology. This specialism first crystallized in the late 1990s, and it's understandable that in its early years it usually focused not directly on money-making—perhaps implicitly seen as covered by existing scholarship, especially in economics— but on other aspects of finance of a kind more familiar in those wider disciplines. (I intend no criticism of my colleagues here—that was just as true of my own work in that period as it was of that of others—and some of them, especially Olivier Godechot, did pay attention to money-making; see, especially, Godechot 2007.)

What in particular has been neglected is what I think of as the "mundane" political economy of finance: the undramatic, everyday ways in which money is made, often individually fairly small amounts of money, but time and time again.[23] It is easy when one is new to the study of finance—as I was, twenty years ago—to focus on its dramatic aspects (finance's giant crises; the making or losing of huge sums; and so on), and ignore the undramatic. What was for me, therefore, a surprising side benefit of researching HFT is how often its development throws light on preexisting mundane ways of money-making. Money-making was and is often made possible by the occupancy of favorable positions in what practitioners call "market structure," by which they mean the way in which a market is organized, especially the formal and informal rules of the game that dictate matters such as who or what can trade with whom, and on what terms; how information flows; where its flows are blocked, and so on.[24] Precisely because the rise of HFT has often involved challenges to aspects of market structure such as these, it thereby renders them visible. Although sociological field theory has had no influence that I can detect on practitioners' use of the notion of market structure, it is perfectly reasonable to see market structures as the very core of the various fields that make up the financial system.

Let me give an example of a mundane but consequential aspect of market structure. As I've already mentioned, trading on Island was, and trading on the majority of the most crucial of today's electronic markets is, organized

BIDS TO BUY

$29.49	100	100	200
$29.48	50	30	
$29.47	100		
$29.46	50	100	100	100
$29.45	200		

OFFERS TO SELL

$29.54	100	200	
$29.53	50		
$29.52	40	50	
$29.51	50	50	200
$29.50	100	100	100

FIGURE 1.5. An order book. *Source:* author's interviews and observations of trading.

around "order books"—lists of the bids to buy and offers to sell the stock or other financial instrument being traded that have not yet been executed. (For a visual representation, designed for human eyes, of an order book, see figure 1.5.) On Island, and in most of the other electronic markets discussed in these chapters, order books are visible—in electronically mediated ways—to all the humans and machines trading on those markets. That, however, has not always been the case. As will be described in chapter 3, until the early 2000s a stock's order book on the New York Stock Exchange was largely private to the designated "specialist," the trader who coordinated trading in that stock. Initially, indeed, an NYSE order book was almost literally a book, made up of preprinted forms on which orders were handwritten by specialists or their clerks. An NYSE rule introduced in June 1991 required specialists to "share general information about their books with other floor traders on an informal basis when asked" (Harris and Panchapagesan 2005: 26). Prior to that, order books were—at least in principle—accessible only to specialists, their clerks, and NYSE officials.

An order book, whether handwritten or electronic, often contains information that is extremely helpful to trading. If, for example, the book contains many more bids to buy than offers to sell, it is reasonable to anticipate that prices are about to rise. (The balance between bids and offers and how that balance is changing—along with the sequences of executed trades—form a crucial class of "signals" for HFT.) The mundane issue of who or what has access to the order book can therefore be economically consequential.

Access, furthermore, is an inherently material process, an issue of which data flow to which computer systems and when, or—in the case of human traders—what they can and cannot see. As touched on in chapter 3, when the NYSE's order books were handwritten on paper, a trading-floor broker could sometimes catch a useful glimpse of a book's contents, because a specialist or a clerk had to open it to write down the broker's order. (A broker in a financial market is an intermediary who either executes trades on behalf of a customer—that is the main sense in which the term is used in the NYSE—or arranges trades between others.)

As the sociologist Mitchel Abolafia showed in his pioneering early 1990s ethnographic research on the NYSE, its specialists' exploitation of their central role in trading was constrained by phenomena of a kind familiar to academics in the social studies of finance like me: the NYSE's formal rules and its monitoring of specialists' trading, its informal trading-floor culture, and floor brokers' countervailing power (Abolafia 1996; see also Mattli 2019). Yet that conclusion needs to be balanced against the reality that the NYSE's market structure *did* give its specialists an informational advantage. Using three months of unusually detailed NYSE data (November 1990–January 1991, which is within the period of Abolafia's observations), Harris and Panchapagesan showed that the contents of order books were predictive of price movements, and they concluded that specialists "use this information in ways that favor them" (2005: 25). However, their data did not enable them to determine "[w]hether this advantage produces significant trading profits" (2005: 27) or whether such profits outweighed the risks inherent in the specialists' obligation to continuously "make a market," bidding even when there were few other buyers or offering to sell when there were few sellers.

The rise of HFT has eroded or eliminated a variety of older market structures, such as that of the NYSE's trading rooms, and created in their place a different set of mundane political economies. To put it in capsule form, the shift has been from structures whose pivot was *who* could see the order book (or its loose equivalents in other preexisting market structures) to structures in which money-making is affected crucially by *when* the order book can be "seen." The book is electronically visible to all, but how long it takes their systems to receive, process, and respond to order-book updates is a critical determinant of whether a trading firm makes or loses money. (There are exceptions to the visibility of order books even today, which include the trading venues called "dark pools."[25] If a dark pool has an order book—and not all do—it is not visible to participants. I have written about dark pools in an open-access article [MacKenzie2019d], but have decided not to discuss them in this book to avoid overcomplicating it.)

In HFT, the margin between making and losing money is slender. The profits of HFT are mundane in the sense that what can typically be earned on individual HFT trades is very small. Drawing on documents released at the time of the initial public offering of the shares of Virtu, the HFT firm discussed earlier in this chapter, Laughlin (2014) estimates that Virtu was on average earning trading revenues of 0.27 cents per share traded. He calculates that if it were typical of HFT at large, it would imply that HFT firms were earning revenues, in aggregate, of around $2.5 billion annually trading US shares; by comparison, the investment bank Goldman Sachs's total revenues in 2013 were $34.2 billion (Goldman Sachs 2014: 1). A quarter of a cent per share traded is mundane enough, but that quarter of a cent is considerably reduced when HFT firms' heavy expenses are taken into account.

Against, for example, Virtu's 2013 trading revenues of $624 million must be set operating expenses of $477 million, which included $195 million on brokerage, exchange, and clearing fees and $65 million spent on technology and communications links (Virtu Financial 2014: 73). I have found it difficult to get HFT interviewees to talk freely about the activity's profitability after fees and other expenses. It is a sensitive topic, because HFT firms quite often fail financially, and my impression is that the most common way in which they do so is not by losses in trading but when revenues from trading are swamped by expenses. Nevertheless, there seems to be some consensus among interviewees that 0.05–0.1 cents per share traded (or its rough equivalent in other asset classes) is a healthy rate of profits net of expenses. Even if that is an underestimate (and it may not be), it does indicate the narrowness of the economic difference in HFT between success—regular tiny profits on huge volumes of trades do add up[26]—and failure: the inability to earn revenues that exceed a firm's expenses.

Chapter 5 will discuss the technologies and communication links on which HFT firms spend so much money, and chapter 6 why they often have no alternative but to do so, but the question of fees is worth briefly discussing now because it throws light on another aspect of the mundane economics of HFT. One of this book's themes is that it is impossible to entirely separate out discussion of HFT, and its place in the "fields," or "ecologies," of trading, from analysis of the exchanges and other trading venues on which it takes place. Those venues form a distinct ecology. At least to a first approximation, exchanges compete with each other, not with HFT firms.[27] As discussed in chapter 3, however, Abbott's "hinges" are at work here. The mundane economics of exchanges (which are nowadays almost all profit-making commercial firms or subsidiaries of such firms) has become interwoven with the economics of HFT.[28] Many exchanges earn much of their income from HFT firms, not just in trading fees but also in fees for receiving the fastest versions of the streams of electronic-update messages necessary to mirror exchanges' order books, and for the "cross-connect" cables within datacenters through which those streams are transmitted. Incumbent exchanges therefore profit from HFT's speed race, which (as Budish, Lee, and Shim 2019 point out) may make them reluctant to materially reorganize trading to mitigate this speed race.

Once again, I must emphasize that I see attention to finance's mundane money-making as complementary to research on its more dramatic aspects such as financial crises, not as displacing it. (Indeed, crises often have their roots *in* mundane money-making.) Mundane money-making, though, should be an important topic for researchers in the social studies of finance because it is a vital determinant of what goes on: for example, which technological or organizational changes are readily adopted and which are resisted fiercely. My favorite, because sublimely mundane, example of resistance is what I think of as "the battle of the asterisk," but I save that example for chapter 7.

There is a second, quite different, argument for more research on finance's mundane money-making, implicitly revealed in a remarkable article by the economist Thomas Philippon (2015).[29] I've written about his article elsewhere—initially in the *London Review of Books* (MacKenzie 2016)—but the point is worth repeating: it sounds esoteric, but its implications are large. What Philippon has done is to measure the "efficiency"—the unit cost of financial intermediation—of the US financial system through time.[30] Strikingly, and quite surprisingly, his data, shown in figure 1.6, do not reveal any clear tendency for finance's efficiency to increase between the 1880s (the era of clerks writing in ledgers by pen, perhaps by gaslight) and 2012, in the epoch of HFT and the iPhone.

If Philippon's data are correct in suggesting that the unit cost of financial intermediation has changed little over this long period, why should that be so, given that the information and communication technologies that underpin finance have improved so radically? One possible answer is that most of those efficiency gains have been captured by mundane money-making within the financial system, and take the form of extremely high remuneration for elite employees of banks and other financial firms, along with (less reliably high) dividends and capital gains for the shareholders in those firms. If that is so, we have here a crucial component of societal inequality in income and wealth,

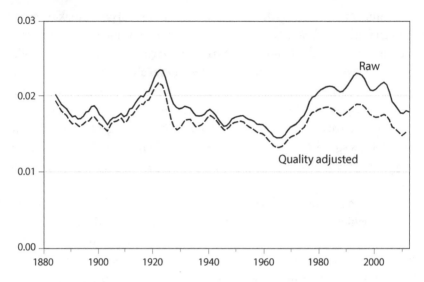

FIGURE 1.6. The unit cost of financial intermediation in the United States, 1884–2012. Data courtesy of Thomas Philippon. For details, see endnote 30 of chapter 1 and Philippon (2015).

because high rewards in the financial system have contributed palpably to that inequality in recent decades.[31] For example, between the 1940s and 1980s, workers in the US financial sector earned salaries similar to those in other sectors with comparable educational qualifications. Thereafter, their relative salaries rose markedly, so that eventually senior executives in finance were earning two and a half times more than their equivalents elsewhere (Philippon and Reshef 2012). Although there is no definitive proof, what may be involved in this dramatic change in the fortunes of the finance sector is an increase in what an economist would call "rent," defined by the commentator Martin Wolf (2019) as "rewards over and above those required to induce the desired supply of goods, services, land or labour."[32] In effect, the financial system may be exacting rents from the rest of the economy, and, of course, among the expected consequences of this would be slower growth of the wider economy.

Let me not raise false expectations about the chapters that follow: on no plausible calculation are the aggregate profits, salaries, and bonuses earned via HFT large enough to contribute in anything other than a minor way to overall inequality of income and wealth. Indeed, HFT's slender profit margins suggest that the automation of trading (and the associated changes in market structure) may actually have reduced, quite considerably, the substantial rents that trading's well-placed insiders could traditionally exact. Rent, though, may still be relevant to the mundane economics of HFT; that, at least, is the conclusion reached by the Chicago economist Eric Budish and colleagues (Budish, Cramton, and Shim 2015; Budish, Lee, and Shim 2019). Consider what happens when an unequivocal "signal" appears in the datafeed from an exchange: if, for example, the price of a share-index future traded on the Chicago Mercantile Exchange rises, or there is selling of Apple's shares on the NYSE, or the bids to buy Amazon's shares in a Nasdaq order book suddenly evaporate. As already noted, my interviews make clear that simple signals such as these are familiar to all high-frequency traders, and their appearance triggers a race to be first to respond to them. Traces of races of this kind can be found in London Stock Exchange electronic-message data from 2015 at an average incidence of around one race per minute for each of the 100 leading stocks on that exchange (Aquilina et al. 2020: 3–4). The algorithm that is fastest to detect and react to a widely employed signal of this kind can, at least on average, make money by "picking off"— that is, executing against—quotes that in the light of the signal are "stale," or out-of-date (or, if the algorithm is following a market-making strategy, it can avoid losing money by canceling its stale bids or offers). As Budish, Cramton, and Shim (2015) put it, "mechanical arbitrage opportunities are built into" the current material arrangements of trading, creating what they call "arbitrage rents" (Budish et al. 2015: 1548).

That usage of the notion of rent may appear abstract, but it translates into rents of a more familiar kind. The race to execute against or cancel stale quotes makes it possible for those who control the means of transmission (such as the "cross-connect" cables that link trading firms' servers to an exchange's computer system), or the locations that are crucial to speed, to charge heavily for access to them. These locations include, for example, racks within the datacenters in which exchanges' matching engines are located, and microwave towers or particular places on datacenter roofs that are especially favorable as sites for wireless antennas. HFT's Einsteinian materiality creates what interviewee DE calls "pinch points," and those who control pinch points can exact rent. (See chapter 6 for another race that takes place among market-making algorithms trying to reach the head of what is in effect a queue for electronic execution.)

Data Sources

I began the research for this book with exploratory interviews in 2010. High-frequency trading (since its inception, almost always a low-profile activity) had been in the news in the previous year, especially following a front-page story about HFT in the *New York Times* in July 2009, which began, "It is the hot new thing on Wall Street, a way for a handful of traders to master the stock market, peek at investors' orders and, critics say, even subtly manipulate share prices" (Duhigg 2009). I was intrigued. My initial interviewing involved little more than trying to find out more about HFT from people who I thought (sometimes rightly, sometimes wrongly) might be able to tell me more about it.

After those exploratory interviews, I focused on finding—first from published sources, and then by introducing myself to people at traders' conferences or obtaining referrals from earlier interviewees—current employees, former employees, and founders of HFT firms. There are no HFT firms in Edinburgh, Scotland, where I teach, and so to keep my travel from becoming wholly excessive, I concentrated on the four main centers of HFT worldwide: Chicago, New York, London, and Amsterdam. Although there is also HFT in a variety of other markets—Brazil, Canada, India, Singapore, Hong Kong, South Korea, Japan, and Australia, to name a few—I decided for this practical reason to focus my research on the US and Europe. I ended up interviewing 86 practitioners of HFT (see table 1.1), 22 of them more than once, including, for example, one whom I interviewed six times, one seven times, and one nine times. These repeat interviews were particularly useful, because in a first interview an interviewee would often present a somewhat idealized account of events or practices, and—embarrassingly often—I did not at first understand enough technically to be able to focus my questions properly. Multiple interviews with the same person helped me to develop my technical understanding and helped them to begin to trust that I would not misuse the information they gave me, making it possible for me to extend the conversation beyond topics that I had already learned were part of what interviewee AG called "High-Frequency Trading 101."

These interviews with employees or former employees of HFT firms did not follow any set format. They were more like conversations in which I tried to get interviewees to talk about the activity, not always successfully. (One of the most frustrating was a lunch in Chicago with two employees of an HFT firm who had both been traders in Chicago's famous "open-outcry" trading pits. They were more than happy to talk at any length about the pits, but steering the conversation toward HFT was much harder.) Gradually, largely by trial and error, and especially by having more than one meeting with the same person, I began to identify topics that were common knowledge among high-frequency traders. At the same time, I began to get a sense of the kind of thing that would count as an example of "secret sauce," and

TABLE 1.1. Interviewees

Founders, employees, or former employees of HFT firms (AA-DI)	86
Members or staff of exchanges, clearinghouses, and other trading venues (EA-HI)	87
Traders for investment-management firms (IA-IJ)	10
Manual traders (MA-ML)	12
Practitioners of other forms of algorithmic trading (OA-OY)	25
Regulators, lawyers, lobbyists, and politicians (RA-SE)	31
Suppliers of technology and communications links (TA-UF)	32
Researchers and market analysts (VA-VU)	21
Dealers, brokers, and broker-dealers (XA-YG)	33
Total	337

Note: Two-letter codes are used to preserve anonymity.

which interviewees would be reluctant to talk about, perhaps fearing losing their jobs if it became known that they had done so.

There is a fair amount of movement of staff among HFT firms, which makes common knowledge of the techniques of HFT quite extensive. "It's really hard to keep those special nuggets of information special for very long," says interviewee BD. Even without hiring a candidate, interviewing him or her can be a useful way of finding out how things are done at other firms, as well as an occasion on which the senior staff who conduct them can discover that what they have taken to be their "secret sauce" is actually common knowledge.[33] Examples of common knowledge include the three main classes of signal already touched on in this chapter: price movements in relevant futures contracts; the contents of order books; and (in the case of shares or other financial instruments traded on more than one exchange) trading and price movements on those other exchanges. These are all unequivocally part of AG's "High-Frequency Trading 101." In contrast, precisely how a firm's algorithms analyze the changing contents of order books has an element of secret sauce to it. I deliberately avoided asking overly detailed questions about this, and the only time an interviewee volunteered real detail was the last time I met him in his trading group's offices; the group had not been able consistently to earn revenues in excess of its expenses and was closing down.

Some of my interviews took place in cafes, restaurants, bars, or interviewees' homes; one memorable interview involved my taking off my socks, shoes, and trousers and helping an interviewee launch his jet ski into Lake Michigan.

However, many of my interviews with employees or founders of HFT firms took place in those firms' offices, and I was often taken around those offices before or after the interview. Such visits helped give me a sense of the "feel" of those firms, and sometimes conveyed other information as well. (For instance, on my second visit to one HFT firm I noticed that its large, impressively well equipped trading room, fully occupied on my first visit, had emptied out markedly. It was my first direct encounter with the economic precariousness of HFT. A year or so later the firm went out of business.)

Gradually, too, I came to realize that to understand HFT I had to interview more widely than in HFT firms. The opportunities for HFT and important aspects of how it is practiced depend on the rules and material configurations of exchanges and other trading venues, and those venues in turn are influenced, sometimes deeply, by the actions taken (and not taken) by government regulatory agencies. Exchange staff, regulators, lawyers, and others therefore became important categories of interviewee. Because those interviews mostly dealt with topics that were less sensitive, they were typically more straightforward than the interviews with high-frequency traders, and many fewer repeat interviews were required. (Of the 87 employees of exchanges, other trading venues, and clearinghouses that I spoke to, I interviewed only 6 more than once.) In addition, those most intimately familiar with the materiality of HFT's "signals" are often not employees of HFT firms but the specialized communications suppliers to those firms; thus I interviewed them as well. There was a great deal I needed to learn in this sphere; here too, another interviewee allowed me to interview him nine times. Overall, across all categories of interviewee (high-frequency traders, exchange staff, etc.), I conducted 358 interviews with 337 people; see table 1.1 and an endnote.[34]

There are no comprehensive, accessible lists of the relevant populations of high-frequency traders, exchange staff, and the like, so interviewees cannot be guaranteed to be representative, either statistically or in other ways. Despite my best efforts, I am almost certainly guilty of a "seniority bias" in those to whom I spoke. This is partly because relevant senior people are easier to identify, and partly because younger employees, especially in HFT firms, may feel they need to be especially wary of speaking to outsiders about their work. (At least one leading HFT firm explicitly bans its employees from doing so.) I tried wherever possible to interview female occupants of relevant roles, but despite this only 17 of my 337 interviewees are women. High-frequency trading and related fields tend to be male-dominated, but I suspect that seniority bias may also help account for this small proportion of women. About halfway through the interviewing, I became aware that my sample of high-frequency trading interviewees was biased toward specialists in market-making. My efforts to persuade larger numbers of specialists in liquidity taking to be interviewed were, however, only partially successful.[35]

Despite difficulties of this kind, there was much that emerged unequivocally from the interviews. As, for example, the interviews began to reveal the main classes of financial instrument in which HFT firms are active, it became clear that there are very large differences between those classes in how trading is organized, and sometimes also substantial differences between the US and Europe. Trying to understand and explain those differences then became one of the goals of the research. In this book, I focus on four classes of instrument—futures, shares, governments' sovereign bonds, and foreign exchange—that are all comparable in that they are simple and highly liquid. (The research also encompassed options and interest-rate swaps, but the greater complexity of these instruments makes them less directly comparable. Apart from chapter 6, in which the options market offers an extreme case of what is being discussed, I have not considered these markets, again to avoid overcomplicating the book.)[36]

Understanding and explaining how trading is organized requires taking a historical perspective, because its organization is "path dependent": how trading was organized in the past affects how it is organized today. Liquidity, for example, is "sticky," in the sense that once traders expect a trading venue to be the most liquid, it tends to remain so because they direct their trades there. (As we shall see, however, there are also "political economy" issues that create stickiness.) There is existing literature on the history of electronic trading to draw upon, notably an exemplary study by Fabian Muniesa of the automation of the Paris Bourse, and a fine book by Juan Pablo Pardo-Guerra on developments in the UK and US (see the appendix on the existing literature). Historically focused interviews were, however, still necessary, especially to cover the history of the trading of financial instruments other than shares, and to throw light on the more recent history of share trading. In unraveling these histories, I found I had to speak to incumbents—for example, to sovereign-bond and foreign-exchange dealers and to the inter-dealer brokers who arrange trades among those dealers—to understand their conflicts with HFT from their perspectives. (Dealers are intermediaries who trade on their own behalf as well as with clients.)

Most of my interviewees preferred anonymity, and quotations from them are identified only by two-letter labels (see table 1.1). Occasionally, I refer to something someone said that is especially sensitive or that might make it possible for an insider to HFT to guess to whom a label refers: no label is used in such cases. In the small minority of cases in which interviewees were happy for their names to be used, I do so. As far as possible, I tried to check what one person told me against what others had said. I also supplemented the interviewing by attending six traders' conferences (two in London, two in Chicago, and two in Amsterdam), along with an algorithmic-trading training course in New York, three events focusing on cryptocurrencies (see chapter 7), and a meeting attended by many employees of governments' debt-management offices. At such gatherings, it was often possible to chat informally with people whom I could not interview formally. I was also taken on tours of trading floors, including the two that still had genuinely significant roles: the main trading room of the New York Stock Exchange, which is important during the NYSE's daily opening and closing auctions, and the section of the trading floor of the Chicago Board Options Exchange which trades options on the Standard & Poor's 500 share-price index. (Face-to-face trading had, of course, to be suspended as the coronavirus epidemic peaked, and at the time of writing, in June 2020, it has restarted only partially.)

I'm not an economist, and this book does not try to answer the questions that economists have traditionally asked about HFT, such as whether it increases market liquidity or volatility; see the appendix on the literature on HFT. As described in the appendix, though, I have certainly gained insights from economists' research on HFT. That research is also sometimes helpful as a way of confirming that what interviewees report about the "signals" employed by their algorithms is indeed plausible.[37] Occasionally, too, the wider literature of financial economics (which now stretches back more than fifty years) provides historical evidence. For example, the first unequivocal evidence of the tendency of the share-index futures market to move before the underlying shares do is in Kawaller, Koch, and Koch (1987).

Some particular episodes discussed in this book were covered in the specialist press, and that too usefully complemented the interviews. I visited the archives of the New York Stock Exchange and the records of the Securities and Exchange Commission in the US National Archives, but more productive than either were records of one of the first firms to conduct an early version of what we now would call HFT: Automated Trading Desk, set up in Charleston, South Carolina, in 1989. (I was given access to those records by the firm's cofounder, David Whitcomb, and by another interviewee.) Four individuals important to the episodes discussed in the chapters that follow—Leo Melamed, former chair of the Chicago Mercantile Exchange; Iowa politician Neal Smith; the stockbroker and trader Donald Weeden; and

Dave Cummings, founder of the HFT firm Tradebot—have written auto-biographies, and I have occasionally drawn on these too in what follows.[38]

When you are studying a material activity, it helps to get a sense of the physical setting in which it occurs. As noted, HFT is conducted not in trading firms' offices, but in exchanges' computer datacenters. Visits to datacenters are not straightforward to arrange, but I was able to visit two and I walked past others, taking note, for example, of communications infrastructure such as the microwave towers described in chapters 2 and 5. In one sense, I didn't learn much from doing this. Simply walking around inside a datacenter, much less viewing it from outside, doesn't give you much insight into the computations performed there. It was, nevertheless, essential to do it. I was trying to understand a world, so to speak—the material world of HFT, the way it emerged, the conflicts surrounding it, its mundane economics, and so on—and seeing where HFT actually happens was a vitally important part of the process.

Synopses of Chapters

Chapter 2 focuses on the Chicago Mercantile Exchange (CME) and its transformation into one of the world's leading sites of ultrafast automated trading. The chapter describes the deeply conflictual process by which the buying and selling of futures shifted from Chicago's open-outcry trading pits to electronic trading, including, for example, the death threats faced by the latter's most prominent advocate, Leo Melamed. The chapter also tells the story of how the CME achieved its central role in the trading of financial futures, which included crucial interventions in the 1970s in congressional politics and a reworking of the legal boundary between gambling and legitimate futures trading. The chapter ends with a discussion of why price changes in the Chicago share-index futures market tend to lead those in the underlying shares.

Chapter 3 explores the huge HFT-induced transformation of US share trading, viewing that transformation initially through the lens of the early HFT firm Automated Trading Desk. The chapter describes the difficulties faced by the firm in its efforts to trade on pre-HFT share-trading venues. It then shifts to Island, the first "HFT-friendly" share trading venue, and its emergence from what were in the 1990s the disreputable margins of the US financial system. The chapter explores the mutually reinforcing relationship in the US between automated trading and new trading venues such as Island, a relationship that was strengthened, largely inadvertently, by actions taken by the stock-market regulator, the Securities and Exchange Commission. The chapter ends with brief discussions of the way in which a similar relationship transformed European share trading, and of the "signals" employed by HFT algorithms trading shares in both the US and Europe.

Chapter 4 turns to the trading of sovereign bonds and foreign exchange, where a market structure very different from those that have come to prevail in futures and shares still largely survives. That market structure is organized above all around a distinction in socioeconomic roles, between "dealers" (nowadays, mainly large banks) and "clients," where the latter are not usually private individuals but smaller banks, nonfinancial corporations, and especially institutional investors. Even the world's largest such investors are still usually treated simply as clients in the trading of bonds and currencies. In sovereign bonds, for example, this dealer–client market structure is anchored in the system of government-designated "primary dealers": banks (or sometimes also other securities firms) that commit always to bid in the initial auctions of government bonds and to act continuously as market-makers in their subsequent trading, receiving privileges in return.

Chapter 5 focuses directly on the material technical systems within which HFT takes place. The chapter discusses the cables and wireless links that convey the crucial signals for HFT from one datacenter to another, emphasizing, for example, the huge importance of how closely a link follows the geodesic between datacenters. The chapter then moves to how trading firms' computer systems materially interact, within datacenters, with exchanges' computer systems. Among the phenomena described is how the macro-scale importance of spatial location in fiber-optic and wireless transmission is mirrored in miniature: the designers and programmers of the specialized computer chips (field-programmable gate arrays, or FPGAs) that are now involved in all of the fastest forms of HFT must also pay close attention to where exactly on these chips computations take place.

Chapter 6 focuses on the two main species of HFT algorithm: market-making algorithms that systematically place in exchanges' electronic order books both bids to buy the financial instrument being traded and offers to sell it (at a slightly higher price); and liquidity-taking algorithms that seek to identify opportunities to profit by executing against existing bids or offers. The chapter then turns to the "material politics" efforts by exchanges and other trading venues to alter the interaction of HFT algorithms by deliberately modifying—sometimes overtly, sometimes in lower-profile ways—the material features of the technical systems within which trading takes place. Chapter 7, the conclusion, reviews what the previous chapters have revealed about HFT and its material political economy. It ends by discussing the extent to which that latter perspective might productively be applied to other spheres of economic life, taking the examples of cryptocurrencies and of the online advertising that is the economic foundation of much of the everyday digital world. An appendix briefly discusses the existing literature on HFT. Social-scientist readers may wish to turn to that appendix before moving to the chapters that follow.

2

To the Towers

A path in Chicago's outer suburbs, more than thirty miles from the Loop and downtown's skyscrapers. The path passes suburban housing and logistics depots, and crosses little-used railroad tracks. It runs through a flat landscape dominated by power lines. On a wet, unseasonably cold weekday morning in October, no one else is walking or running.

In the distance, towers appear. At first, they look like yet more electricity pylons, but closer up it's clear that they are far taller. They are microwave towers. The antennas on them link the trading going on in the datacenter of the CME, the Chicago Mercantile Exchange, to that taking place in other, similar datacenters elsewhere. In the first instance, these are the New Jersey datacenters in which shares, sovereign bonds, and currencies are bought and sold, but signals radiating from the towers also cross the oceans, by submarine cable or shortwave radio, to datacenters in Greater London, Frankfurt, Mumbai, Singapore, Hong Kong, Tokyo, and beyond—to everywhere that automated trading takes place.

The microwave towers are the clearest material manifestation of a feature of the financial system that was long in the making: the central role of futures trading—in particular, of trading on the CME—as a driver of what happens on many other exchanges. Fifty years ago, it would have been hard to imagine that either Chicago (already experiencing postindustrial decline) or futures could become central to global finance. Futures, as noted in chapter 1, are standardized, exchange-traded contracts that are nearly equivalent

FIGURE 2.1. Electricity infrastructure in the Chicago suburbs. Author's fieldwork photograph.

economically to one party undertaking to buy, and the other to sell, a set amount of a given commodity on a set future date, at a price agreed today. At the start of the 1970s, the commodities involved were almost all agricultural. The 1930 Art Deco skyscraper of the Chicago Board of Trade, founded in 1848, was and is a city landmark (see figure 2.3). Its "pits," stepped, usually octagonal amphitheaters designed so that hundreds of traders could crowd onto the steps and see—and, at quieter times, hear—each other, dominated the trading of, for example, grain futures (see figures 2.4 and 2.5). The Chicago Mercantile Exchange is younger, established in 1919, and its pits began by trading futures on butter and eggs. By 1970, the CME's signature product, first traded in 1961, was a futures contract each instance of which was equivalent to committing to buy or to sell 30,000 pounds (13.6 metric tonnes) of pork bellies, the slabs of frozen, uncured pork that are the raw material of rashers of bacon (Tamarkin 1993: 128–29).

To shift from futures on wheat or pork bellies to futures on financial products might seem radical, but the skills of many futures traders were rooted more firmly in their grasp of the socioeconomic and bodily dynamics of Chicago's trading pits than in their understanding of the supply of and demand for the underlying commodities. They were traders, not agricultural economists. Thus they had no reason fundamentally to object to the expansion

FIGURE 2.2. A tower of the kind employed in ultrafast communication in finance. Author's field-work photograph.

of their market to futures on financial commodities. During the decades immediately following the Second World War, that expansion would, however, not have been an enticing prospect, since much of the financial system globally was under at least a degree of formal or informal government control, and the US government would most likely have opposed a market that, by trading in financial products, might undermine that control. But by the early 1970s, government control was eroding. Its centerpiece was the

FIGURE 2.3. The Chicago Board of Trade building, designed by Holabird & Root. Photograph by Joe Ravi, 2011. Creative Commons license CC-BY-SA 3.0.

FIGURE 2.4. Pits in the trading room of the Chicago Board of Trade in 1908. *Source:* Baker (1908: 111).

FIGURE 2.5. "Open-outcry" trading in the wheat pit of the Chicago Board of Trade in 1920. *Source:* Library of Congress, Reproduction Number LC-USZ62–41292.

system of fixed exchange rates among currencies established by the 1944 Bretton Woods agreement. That system had involved the US's undertaking to sell gold to other governments at a fixed dollar price. However, at a time when the US economy was seen as performing badly, in particular relative to Germany and Japan, it was becoming clear that the exchange rates for the dollar, especially against the Deutschmark and the Japanese yen, would be hard to sustain. On August 15, 1971, President Nixon closed the "gold window," as the commitment to sell gold was called, and over the next five years efforts by the US and many other governments to shore up fixed exchange rates gradually petered out.

As the leash tethering financial markets to governments loosened, the Chicago Board of Trade and the CME seized the opportunity to expand their product ranges. In the early 1970s, the CME began to trade futures contracts on currencies, and the Board of Trade launched futures on mortgage-backed securities and Treasurys (US sovereign-debt securities). Although these efforts were successful, further development of financial futures was constrained by what had become the established way that a crucial, sensitive, cultural divide—between legitimate futures trading and simply placing a bet on the outcome of some coming event—was turned into a legal distinction.[1] The question of how to draw that distinction arose in many jurisdictions (including, e.g., the UK and Germany), but the issue was particularly sharp in the US, whose futures exchanges had had to fight legal and political battles in the late nineteenth and early twentieth centuries against two different threats. One was against "bucket shops," in which members of the public could wager on movements in the price of grain or other commodities, and which were viewed by futures exchanges as simply gambling dens. The other battle was against agrarian populists, who saw the activity of these very exchanges as itself no better than gambling, and in particular often blamed speculative futures trading for drops in the price of farm products.

These sharp conflicts in the US gradually gave birth to a stable way of drawing a legal boundary around legitimate futures trading: the doctrine of "contemplating delivery" (Levy 2006). The parties to a futures trade had to envisage the physical delivery of the grain or other commodity in question. If they did not, if a trade could be settled only in cash (as was the case in a bucket shop), it was a wager—and so illegal in Illinois and most other states in the US. Drawing the distinction between gambling and legitimate trading in this way protected futures exchanges from legal challenges while in effect outlawing bucket shops. Furthermore, since what was required was merely envisaging, not actually making, delivery, futures exchanges were allowed to continue their practice of settling contracts with cash transfers; physical delivery was in actuality rare.

The doctrine of contemplating delivery nevertheless required that delivery of the commodity underlying a futures contract be *possible*; if it was not, how could the parties to a trade be said to contemplate it? As the Chicago Board of Trade and the CME moved in the 1970s into the trading of financial futures, the need for delivery limited the futures contracts that the exchanges could legally trade. Futures on foreign currency or Treasury securities, for example, definitely could be traded, because that currency or those securities could be delivered, even though devising a satisfactory delivery mechanism for Treasurys turned out to be complicated. What, though, of a future on an index of share prices such as the Dow Jones or Standard & Poor's 500, or a future on interest rates? It might be conceivable, if somewhat clumsy, to settle a share-index futures contract by delivering an appropriate bundle of share certificates or their electronic equivalents, but a Eurodollar interest rate (so called because the main interbank dollar-lending market was based in Europe, especially London, not New York) is intangible. As Leo Melamed, who became chair of the CME in 1969 and led its move into financial futures (see figure 2.6), put it: "You can't deliver a rate of interest; instead, you can pay *in cash* the value of the differential in interest rates between the time of purchase and time of sale, or vice versa" (Melamed and Tamarkin 1996: 291, emphasis in original). A futures contract of that kind, for which delivery was impossible, was, however, still blatantly illegal.

"Every constituent eats"

It took something of a crisis to end the legal requirement that delivery of the underlying commodity be possible. It was, ironically, a crisis not of financial but of agricultural futures. The early 1970s saw rapid increases in the cost of food and a concomitant boom in the prices of agricultural futures. The prices of Chicago's grain futures—fueled in part by the US's starting large-scale grain sales to the Soviet Union—hit was then an all-time peak, notes the CME's historian, Bob Tamarkin (1993: 207). "The prospect of cashing in on fast changing commodity prices," continues Tamarkin, attracted the interest even of some laypeople, "from the Des Moines dentist to the New York psychoanalyst."

However, while only a small minority of the public speculated on futures prices, "[e]very constituent eats" (Tamarkin 1993: 218). Food-price inflation created an opportunity—rare, as noted in Chapter 1—for potential political

FIGURE 2.6. Leo Melamed in the Chicago Mercantile Exchange's datacenter, 2012. Photograph courtesy of Melamed & Associates, Inc.

rewards from intervening in the regulation of trading. Since 1936, when Congress passed the Commodity Exchange Act, futures exchanges had been regulated, not always energetically, by the Commodity Exchange Authority, a small subunit of the Department of Agriculture. The surge of inflation in the early 1970s sparked the suspicion that speculation, futures trading, and weak regulation were at least partially to blame for rising food prices. Three well-known, ambitious senators—Gary Hart, Hubert Humphrey, and George McGovern—separately had their staffs prepare bills calling for the replacement of the Commodity Exchange Authority by a full-fledged federal futures regulator (Tamarkin 1993: 218).

"You never want a serious crisis to go to waste," as Rahm Emanuel, a Chicago politician of a later generation, famously said at a *Wall Street Journal* conference during 2008's global banking crisis. "What I mean by that is an opportunity to do things that you think that you could not do before."[2] It would have been easy for the Chicago futures exchanges to see the eruption of interest on Capitol Hill in the early 1970s in regulating them simply as a threat, but the CME's Leo Melamed seems to have glimpsed "an opportunity to do things." As he told me in an interview in November 2000 for an earlier project (MacKenzie 2006), the creation of a new federal futures regulator could increase the standing of markets that had been damaged by periodic scandals. It would "legitimatize what we were doing. Anyone that has a federal agency over it is a legitimate thing. You don't have a federal agency over gambling."

Melamed told me that he also had a second reason for supporting the creation of a new federal regulatory body: such a body could potentially end the restriction of futures trading to contracts on assets that the seller could actually deliver to the buyer. Around 1969, Melamed had asked the CME's lawyers about the legality of a futures contract that could be settled only by a cash transfer, and had received the standard answer: trading such a contract would be classed as gambling because it did not "contemplate delivery." Melamed had himself trained as a lawyer, and he realized that a head-on challenge in the courts to the decades-old doctrine could fail. "I knew that [the doctrine] might hold strong," he says.

The specific opportunity seized by Melamed and his allies—in particular, the commodities lawyer Philip McBride Johnson (who was general counsel of the Chicago Board of Trade)—arose in the House of Representatives. The long-serving Texas Democrat W. R. Poage had risen through the seniority system to hold the powerful role of chair of the House Agriculture Committee, and was concerned by the hearings on agricultural-futures trading being held by the chair of the House Subcommittee on General Small Business Problems, Iowa Democrat Neal Smith. As Melamed put it in his memoirs, Poage's committee (along with the Senate Agriculture Committee) "by tradition should have had jurisdiction over our markets. [Poage] knew nothing about futures and couldn't care less, but we [the Chicago exchanges] gained his ear, if for no other reason than to stop Smith from poaching on his jurisdiction" (Melamed and Tamarkin 1996: 215). Poage turned the matter over to the House Agriculture Committee's associate counsel, John Rainbolt, and as part of what Melamed calls "a normal defensive tactic in D.C.," the committee began hearings of its own, calling spokespeople from the futures industry such as Melamed to testify (Melamed and Tamarkin 1996: 215).

There was broad support in both the House and the Senate for the creation of a new futures regulator (Neal Smith was among those in favor;

see Smith 1996: 262–64). Rainbolt persuaded Poage to set up a subcommittee to draft the necessary legislation, and, notes Melamed, "some of us became immersed as special advisors" to that subcommittee, ensuring for example that the new regulator, the Commodity Futures Trading Commission (CFTC), "should have exclusive jurisdiction" over futures trading and "barring the SEC [the Securities and Exchange Commission, which regulates share trading] or regulators from the separate states" from intruding on that jurisdiction (Melamed and Tamarkin 1996: 216–17).

The plan to create a new federal regulator of futures trading was nearly derailed when the Ford administration, which had set out to reduce government regulation and so was reluctant to be seen to be creating an additional regulatory body, offered jurisdiction over the futures markets to the already-established SEC. In a decision that does not seem to have felt important to those who made it, but has had major consequences for the shaping of automated trading in the US and beyond, the five commissioners who headed the SEC turned down the offer of jurisdiction. Two of my interviewees who were SEC officials at that time had the same recollection of the decision.

> We [the SEC] were asked whether we wanted that jurisdiction and I have a pretty clear memory of some of the commissioners saying, "what do we know about pork bellies!" . . . They have since come to regret that, but . . . I don't think there was any debate about it really. They all concluded they didn't want to deal with that. (Interviewee RG)

Interviewee RF recalls almost exactly the same words: "Why would we mess around with pork bellies?" The way the commissioners reacted, he says, was "[v]ery snooty, very East Coast."

There was, however, still a risk that President Ford might veto the legislation establishing the CFTC. Melamed decided to speak to him directly.

> When I talked with President Ford, I wanted to dissuade him from vetoing the proposed CFTC bill. I explained that the idea for financial futures is a big idea and will change the universe of futures. In such case, Congress would create [an] oversight agency anyway. If we passed the present bill, it will give us a chance for a much better agency as well as the personnel that understand futures. The President agreed.

In turning down the supervision of futures trading, the SEC's commissioners seem to have underestimated—or simply failed to notice—the potential breadth of the CFTC's jurisdiction. In helping draft the amendments to the Commodity Exchange Act that created the new regulator, Melamed's ally

Johnson had added 20 carefully chosen words to the long list of commodities ("wheat, cotton, . . .") whose futures trading was governed by the Act: "and all services, rights, and interests in which contracts for future delivery are presently or in the future dealt in."[3] Rather than simply reallocating jurisdiction over existing regulatory tasks, the creation of the new regulator, the CFTC, was simultaneously the creation of new tasks: new markets, previously illegal, that the CFTC would regulate, and thereby make legally permissible.[4] Without mentioning futures on share indexes explicitly—that overt intrusion into its domain would certainly have sparked SEC opposition—Johnson's words implicitly cleared the way for them, as well as for Melamed's hoped-for futures on Eurodollar interest rates.

The CFTC did not, however, immediately permit cash-settled futures on "intangible" commodities such as indexes or interest rates. James Stone, appointed its chair by President Jimmy Carter, seems not to have been an enthusiast for ending the traditional way of distinguishing a futures contract from a wager. In 1980, however, President Reagan appointed Philip Johnson (the drafter of the crucial 20 words) CFTC chair, and Melamed and his allies began a final, successful push to end the requirement for delivery. Melamed, who says he had lobbied energetically for Johnson's appointment, had "one-on-one meetings with every CFTC commissioner" (Melamed and Tamarkin 1996: 292). On December 19, 1981, the CME began to trade Eurodollar interest-rate futures.

Gaining permission to trade share-index futures was more complicated, because potential opposition from the SEC had to be defused, but the once-heretical idea of cash settlement ("an idea I had from the very creation of the CFTC in 1974," says Melamed) helped John Shad, Reagan's appointee as SEC chair, reconcile himself to index futures. "In negotiations with the SEC relative to our contract of stock index futures the concept of cash settlement came up again," Melamed reports. Shad feared the disruption to stock markets that might be caused by temporary surges in demand if actual shares were needed to settle futures contracts (Millo 2007). Cash settlement was less of a worry for Shad, and, as Melamed reports, "was included under the Shad-Johnson Agreement," a deal between the SEC and CFTC that temporarily resolved the fierce jurisdictional dispute between the two government agencies and cleared the way for the CME to launch Standard & Poor's 500 futures on April 21, 1982.

The new share-index futures, regulated by the CFTC, not the SEC, followed the procedures of futures trading, not those of share trading, which gave them systematic advantages over the latter. It was simpler, faster, and cheaper to trade a single futures contract than to buy or sell the 500 stocks that made up the S&P index, and creating a "short" position—one that would benefit from a drop in price—was a matter merely of selling futures. Shorting shares, in contrast, was cumbersome (it required one to borrow shares, sell them, and then buy them and return them) and hemmed in by regulation, because shorting was often blamed for drops in share price. Furthermore, as with other futures contracts, one could trade S&P 500 futures with only a modest sum of money as a margin deposit with one's broker or the CME's clearinghouse, a deposit that one had to add to only if prices moved against one. The regulations governing share trading, in contrast, made it difficult or impossible to achieve the equivalent high level of leverage (the size of a trading position relative to the required level of capital).

Simplicity, cheapness, ease of shorting, and high leverage therefore made the new S&P 500 futures an attractive way of profiting quickly from (or hedging against the arrival of) new information relevant to the overall value of US shares. Although the CME had had no previous involvement with shares, it soon became clear that, as a result of these advantages, the prices of the CME's S&P 500 futures tended to move before—in 1984–5, as much as 20–45 minutes before—the prices of the underlying shares (Kawaller, Koch, and Koch 1987: 1309). "Futures lead," which (as we will see in chapter 3) is historically the most important of all the "signals" used by HFT algorithms to inform their trading of shares—and is still an important signal today—had come into being.

Pit Trading

The high-frequency trading of shares based on movements in Chicago's share-index futures prices was of course automated. Paradoxically, though, the source of the signal, Chicago futures exchanges, remained dominated by face-to-face interaction between embodied human beings. Anthropologist Caitlin Zaloom has provided a superb ethnographic portrayal of the vitality of Chicago's trading pits in the late 1990s (Zaloom 2006), and I too found them packed and lively when I visited in 1999 and 2000 for the research that led to MacKenzie (2006). Deals were struck by voice, if a trading pit was quiet enough to allow that, or by eye contact and hand signals, using a specific code—sometimes called "arb," short for arbitrage[5]—that all traders and their clerks had to learn. Palms facing out conveyed an offer to sell, palms facing the trader's body, a bid to buy; vertical fingers encoded the digits one to five, horizontal fingers, six to nine; a clenched fist meant zero.[6] Pit reporters employed by the Chicago Board of Trade or CME listened to the hubbub and scanned the gesticulating bodies, trying as best they could to identify transactions and record their prices. They recorded those prices on computer terminals, and it was that stream of numbers—electronic, yes, but at root embodied—that formed the crucial input to the early HFT algorithms that traded shares.

For a decade or more—from the first experiments in HFT in shares at the end of the 1980s, to the growth in momentum in electronic futures trading in the late 1990s and early 2000s—a connection thus remained between the "digital" materiality of automated trading and the "analog" materiality of trading pits, and the connection survived even longer in the options markets, in which some face-to-face, on-exchange trading continues (although, at the time of writing, it was resuming only cautiously as the coronavirus crisis abated). Trading pits had come to Chicago in the 1870s (Falloon 1998: 72–77), and by the 1990s the pits in which the most important financial futures were traded had become very large. When I toured the trading floors of the CME in November 2000, I was told that on some days two thousand brokers and traders would crowd into the Eurodollar pit, the CME's largest. The pits firmly connected the Board of Trade, the CME, and the Chicago Board Options Exchange (set up by the Board of Trade in 1973) to the surrounding city. By the late 1990s, some fifty thousand people had jobs immediately involved with the exchanges, with perhaps a further hundred thousand indirectly dependent on them (anon. 1999).

"Look at my glasses," said a trader I interviewed in 2000 after the close of trading in the CME pit that traded Standard & Poor's 500 index futures. "They're all dirty," he said, the result of spittle from the shouting mouths that had surrounded him all day. Another trader (interviewee MC) recalled in 2012: "It was so cramped in our pit that I was able to pick my feet up and was suspended between people." The crush of bodies meant that he had to have his glasses repaired almost every week, so he switched to contact lenses. In busy pits, there was constant jostling, in part simply because of crowding, in part because of competition for the best places to stand. For a trader, lines of sight to the brokers who brought big client orders to the pit were vital. Often the jostling became verbal aggression; sometimes, verbal aggression became a fistfight. Even in the absence of fights, physical size mattered: taller traders were easier to see. Interviewee MC reported that it was common for traders in the CME's giant Eurodollar pit to be very tall: "basketball players, football players." The trader who showed me his dirty glasses also said that in the late 1990s the CME had to impose a rule on the maximum size of platform heels that could be worn. "What happened when you wear shoes like this, you really have no balance. So there were some injuries there. So they outlawed those shoes. Now [November 2000] you can wear two-inch [heels], that's it." It was an overwhelmingly male environment, but not exclusively so. As several interviewees reported, in the early 2000s the individual trader who took on the largest positions in the Eurodollar pit was a woman, Margery Teller.

Even in the most mathematicized form of Chicago trading, options trading, the open-outcry method demanded bodily skills. As an options trader told me in 2000, those skills included "presence in a crowd so your voice can be heard . . . when . . . people [are] yelling and screaming," plus the street-smart instinct of knowing "who's going to panic and who *needs* to have something." Even the biggest pits were far from anonymous places. The same people turned up to trade in the same pit day after day, year after year, often standing in exactly the same spot. It was like forever being in high school, says interviewee MC. Fellow traders were not necessarily friends, and indeed were sometimes bitter enemies, but if they traded at all frequently they were people you knew, often by high-school-like nicknames. (MC, for example, is known even today among those who traded with him by a nickname based on the three-letter identifier on the badge that he, and all the other traders, wore on the trading floors.) In a situation in which deals involving large sums of money were struck by voice or hand signal, brokers and traders had to trust that their counterparts would not later deny that they had entered into a deal if prices had subsequently moved against them. "Your reputation was everything," noted another trader (interviewee AB). Reciprocity was important, especially between traders and brokers. A broker would normally bring traders profitable business, but could sometimes also, as MC reported, call on them "to kind of help the broker out," for example by shouting, "Ten at five, *I need these*."[7]

Interpersonal interaction did not take place only in the pits. Until November 2000, when the CME became a publicly traded corporation, the Chicago exchanges were all membership organizations, in which all important decisions (and, as interviewee ER said, some unimportant ones: "what went in the refrigerator, what kind of mustard . . . in the break room") could be the subject of votes. "[W]e had two-hundred-and-something committees," Leo Melamed told me in a March 2012 interview, and to achieve change required classically political skills, which Melamed in particular spent much time and energy deploying. For example, in the crucial 1997 battle over the E-Mini, discussed below, Melamed and his supporters "held meetings with members individually as well as in groups . . . arguing, cajoling, and imploring. I called in all the chits accumulated over the years" (Melamed 2009: 40).

Endlessly fascinating as open-outcry pits were as places in which economic life involved intense embodiment, intricate politics, and deep sociality, they should not be romanticized. They took their toll on the human bodies that crowded into them. One of my interviewees, for example, who had been in his own words "a screamer," had needed several operations on his vocal cords. The subtle webs of reciprocity and trust on which open-outcry trading depended could turn into informal cartels that operated to the disadvantage of other pit traders or of external clients, orders from whom were called "paper," a term that referred to the medium on which they most commonly arrived in a pit, but also drew an implicit contrast with the animated human bodies that crowded it. Broker groups—consortiums of brokers who pooled their fee income—were particularly prone to become cartels. The rules of the CME and Board of Trade permitted dual trading, that is, a broker could both act for external customers and trade on his or her own account. There were strong suspicions that members of broker groups steered profitable "paper" to fellow members who were acting at that moment as own-account traders, and that brokers who owned clearing firms favored traders who cleared through their firm, because of the clearing fees that would be generated (interviewee ES; see below for the process of clearing). In the late 1980s, two FBI agents worked undercover at the CME and two at the Board of Trade, secretly tape-recording conversations and seeking to document breaches of the law, an operation that led to the August 1989 indictment of 45 traders and a clerk.[8]

Although he was not alone in objecting to cartel-like behavior within broker groups (many independent brokers and traders did so), the CME's Leo Melamed, who had led its move into financial futures, was a particularly prominent opponent of cartels. As the immigrant son of two members of the Jewish radical-socialist *Bund* party in Eastern Europe, Melamed was—as he told me in my first interview with him in November 2000—also strongly committed to the free-market economics of his personal hero, the University of Chicago economist Milton Friedman. Broker groups behaving as cartels offended both the Bundist and the free-marketeer in Melamed. When he and other members of the Equity Owners Association, founded in January 1996 to contest the power of broker groups, sought to have the CME adopt regulations limiting the amount of trading that a member of a broker group could do with fellow members, Melamed began to receive death threats, which the CME took seriously: it "provided me with an off-duty Chicago policeman to act as a bodyguard and protect the entrance to my office" (Melamed 2009: 30).

The dispute over broker groups was interwoven with controversy over shifting from face-to-face to electronic trading. From the viewpoint of a broker or trader in Chicago's pits, that was a far more radical change than the expansion from agricultural to financial futures had been. A broker's "income, for practical purposes, was totally dependent on the open-outcry architecture" (Melamed 2009: 26). With electronic trading, a bank or even an institutional investor might no longer have to pay a broker simply to bring its orders to market but could itself enter its orders at a computer terminal; the resultant prospect of reduced costs meant many such financial institutions favored automation. In contrast to brokers, traders might hope to continue to flourish in electronic markets. However, they too were often ambivalent or hostile. Open-outcry trading was a demanding but familiar business, and much of its embodied skill—"you traded off of visceral reaction, noise, smell, [a] look on someone's face," says interviewee MC—could not be transferred to the computer screen. Particular objects and physical locations became emblematic of trading success. Traders had lucky ties— "We had somebody whose tie just became a matter of five or six threads but he wasn't going to change that tie," reports ES—and lucky pencils. The decision by the CME, demanded by the Commodity Futures Trading Commission, to stop traders from using pencils to fill in the trading tickets on which deals were recorded in the pit and insist on the use of pens took eight months of negotiation. Enlarging a pit even a little could prove hugely contentious. Traders and brokers won the right to stand in a particular place by seniority and by fending off challengers (sometimes by jostling or pushing them), and could be fiercely hostile if a change impacted "sightlines and locals' [traders'] ability to have access to orders," says ES. "So that became a . . . very long and difficult thing."

Given that strength of attachment to even the physical details of face-to-face pit trading, it was unsurprising that electronic trading, which threatened to sweep it away altogether, should be opposed implacably. It was a "mortal conflict," a "life-or-death battle," Melamed wrote in the second volume of his autobiography (2009: 5 and 12). Interviewee ES, who was also a prominent supporter of electronic trading, "had people spit in my face. I've had people pour drinks all over me." The CME did eventually automate futures trading, but it took nearly two decades.

Globex

Leo Melamed had not always been an enthusiast of electronic trading. He joined the CME as a runner in 1953, already entranced by its trading pits. As he put it in the first volume of his memoirs:

> The shouting among the traders, the movement of their bodies and hands, captivated me like nothing before. . . . [T]here was a life force on that floor that was magical and exciting, and . . . I wanted to be a part of it. (Melamed and Tamarkin 1996: 87)

Two decades on, in 1977, with the CME's new financial-futures pits beginning to flourish, Melamed—by then chair of the CME—still believed firmly that open outcry played an irreplaceable role in futures trading (Melamed 1977). His moment of conversion came only in the 1980s. He had just finished writing *The Tenth Planet* (Melamed 1987), a science-fiction novel centering around a hugely powerful computer, and, as he said in March 2012, in my second interview with him:

> [I] was standing at my desk . . . watching the S&P pit [which traded futures based on the Standard & Poor's 500 index of shares] . . . and seeing these runners running back and forth with the orders to the pit . . . a maze of them back and forth and some of the orders being dropped on the floor and whatnot . . . and said to myself, in *The Tenth Planet*, Leo, you created a computer that ran five different planets . . . you don't need to tell me you can't figure out how to create one computer to run the orders between pits.

Melamed had no desire to kill his beloved pits, but "[c]onvinced that technology, whether we liked it or not, would force fundamental changes to our way of life," he chose to embrace it rather than "be left in the historical trash bin of status quo obstinacy. The idea grew into an obsession," the central project of the remainder of his working life (Melamed 2009: 10).

An impetus broader than Melamed's private change of heart was provided by the rise of financial markets in Japan, Hong Kong, and Singapore. It was difficult for those who traded on them also to buy or sell Chicago futures; when the pits were open it was evening or night in East Asia. Traders there might therefore choose instead to send their orders to LIFFE, the London International Financial Futures Exchange, set up in 1982 in response to the success of the Chicago exchanges in trading financial futures, and originally closely modeled on those exchanges. London's time zone meant that LIFFE's pits started trading before the end of the business day in East Asia. "LIFFE's time zone advantage made me very concerned," recalled Melamed (Melamed and Tamarkin 1996: 316–717).[9]

An electronic trading system could counter the threat from London by permitting trading to continue when Chicago's pits were closed. Melamed approached the global-news and foreign-exchange giant Reuters and proposed that it lead the construction of such a system. The Reuter Monitor, launched in 1973, had been an early success in the on-screen dissemination of prices, and, as will be described in chapter 4, Reuters had developed the first system for electronically mediated foreign-exchange trading. In 1987, Reuters agreed to join the CME in the development of a system for the electronic trading of futures, which was christened Globex because Melamed wanted it to be "the international standard for electronic trading" (Melamed 2009: 16). France's futures market, the Marché à Terme International de France (MATIF), was persuaded to join, and approaches were also made to the New York Mercantile Exchange, LIFFE, and, crucially—because without its support no system could truly claim to encompass the globe's futures markets—the Chicago Board of Trade, still the world's most prominent futures exchange. A year of weekly meetings secured the Board's participation, but only temporarily; in April 1994, the Board withdrew (Crawford 1994). LIFFE's directors agonized, fearing Globex as a competitive threat and uncertain whether the CME and Reuters were genuine in their expressed intention "to open up GLOBEX to other exchanges" (Kynaston 1997: 182). Eventually, LIFFE too withdrew, putting its main efforts into its own system, Automated Pit Trading.

Gaining the support of the Chicago Mercantile Exchange's own members for Globex was almost as hard. Globex's proponents knew that most members would tolerate its development only if they could be convinced it would not become a rival to the pits, and that indeed was signaled by its initial name, Post Market Trade. Melamed and his supporters won an October 1987 referendum of the CME's membership approving Globex, but only on the basis that the electronic system would never be used to trade the same products as the pits when the latter were open. Originally, Globex did not operate at all during the Chicago working day. The system opened for trading at 6:00 p.m. and ran until 6:00 a.m.[10]

The demanding task of constructing a potentially global trading network against the background of intricate, unstable exchange politics, some of it local, some transnational, made the technical development of Globex difficult. It began operation only in 1992, five years after the initial agreement with Reuters. Trading volumes were modest: fewer, usually many fewer, than twenty-five thousand contracts per night, and initially mostly in MATIF's products, not the CME's. By the mid-1990s, it was clear that Globex was limping, Melamed told me in 2012. Another interviewee, EF, who worked during this time for a Japanese bank, remembers installing Globex terminals in its dealing rooms, but all that the terminals "accomplished was gathering a great deal of dust." Reuters, which had spent some $100 million developing the system in return for a fee of $1 per trade, was not receiving an attractive return.[11] Not only had Globex failed to become truly global, but the entire project of introducing electronic trading to the CME was faltering.

Before we turn to the product that saved it, we need to consider the road not taken: a radically different form of automation. Before its temporary participation in Globex, the Chicago Board of Trade had an automation project of its own, known as Aurora. Also intended for trading when the pits were closed, and also designed to have a global reach (especially to East Asia), the Aurora project, announced in March 1989, involved the Board of Trade and three information-technology companies: Apple, Texas Instruments, and Tandem. The involvement of Apple indicated what was distinctive: Aurora sought to visually simulate a trading pit. "We chose to attempt to replicate the trading floor," said Burt Gutterman, who served on the executive committee of the Board of Trade at the time of the Aurora project, in an interview in 2012. Each trader using Aurora would be represented on the screen of an Apple Macintosh by an icon with the same identifier that was on his or her trading-floor badge, and the system would display the number of contracts each was bidding for and/or offering (provided they were quoting at the highest bid or lowest offer price).[12] A user of the system could then choose which trader to deal with by clicking his or her computer mouse on the icon of the chosen trader. Even the most basic limitation of the trader's human body was to be reproduced electronically in Aurora, says Gutterman: one's icon could not be present in more than one simulated pit at any given time.

In Globex, no attempt was made to replicate a trading pit, and its representation of the market for a given product was a window on the terminal's screen with a simple, anonymous list of the prices at which the contract was being bid and the prices at which it was being offered for sale, together with the quantities being bid for and offered; see figure 2.7. Figure 2.8 shows the window a trader would use to place an offer on Globex and figure 2.9 an example of a full Globex screen. Don Serpico, then the CME's chief of management information systems, told me in a 2012 interview that members of his team "were able to give them [Reuters] the rules for how to do trading in our world," but did not pressure Reuters to try to simulate the

```
 ▬|    mSPH7  79410S  17:05       |+|-|
 Bid Px      Qty|Offer Px    Qty
 79410         1|79415          1
 79405         1|79425          1
 79400         1|79430          1
 79395         1|79435          1
 79390         1|79445          1
 79385         1|79450          1
 79380         1|79455          2
 79375         1|79465          1
 79370         1|79470          1
 79325         1|79510          1
```

FIGURE 2.7. Globex's representation of the market for the E-Mini, ca. 1997. The left-hand box lists the prices at which the E-Mini (discussed in the next section of the text) is being bid for and the quantities bid for; the right-hand box lists offers. This is a test screen; in actual use, the quantities of bids and offers were much larger. Screenshot courtesy of Miles Szczurek and Michael J. Kane.

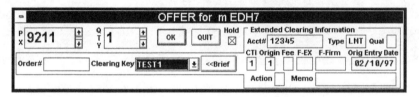

FIGURE 2.8. The window on the screen of a Globex terminal used to submit an offer, ca. 1997. The product here ("m EDH7") is a Eurodollar future with a March 1997 maturity. Screenshot courtesy of Miles Szczurek and Michael J. Kane.

trading floor. In part, that was a matter of technical limitations, but it was also because Melamed and his supporters did not want the floor replicated, at least in any full way:

> [T]hey [the Board of Trade] actually replicated the fact that you could pick a trader in [the] pit . . . we wanted to give the fairest: first come, first served. They wanted to pick their brother-in-law . . . for us it was the natural thing: how do you avoid all of that? First come, first served. (Melamed interview, 2012)

If one was fighting broker groups' hold on trading on the actual trading floor, as Melamed increasingly was, there was no reason to design a virtual trading floor that would allow them to reproduce their practices electronically. Thus not only were the bids and offers on the screen of a Globex terminal anonymous, but when there was more than one bid or offer at a given price, Globex's matching algorithm gave priority simply to the one received first.[13]

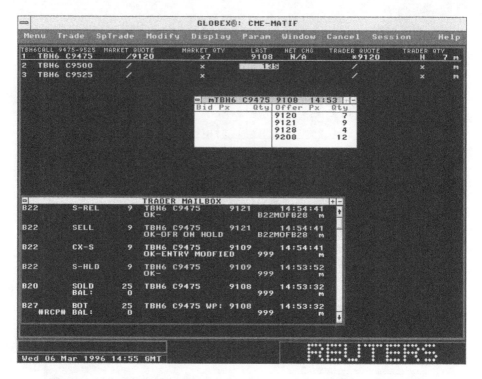

FIGURE 2.9. A full Globex screen, 1996. Screenshot courtesy of Miles Szczurek and Michael J. Kane. The products being traded are US Treasury Bill call options with a March 1996 expiration and a "strike price" of 9475. Such an option is roughly the economic equivalent of the right to buy Treasury Bills at a price corresponding to a yield on the bills of 5.25%. The messages in the trader mailbox record his/her interactions with Globex. For example, the earliest, bottommost message is a confirmation of the trader's purchase of 25 options each at a price of $91.08.

Aurora and Globex thus embodied two different visions of what it was to automate a market. Aurora was canceled by the Chicago Board of Trade not because its vision was unattractive—most pit traders and brokers on most exchanges might well have preferred an Aurora-style system.[14] It was canceled because of a mundane technological consideration: it became clear that its visual representation of trading pits would overburden the then-available bandwidth of global digital communication. The Aurora project "reached a point where we started describing . . . what bandwidth was going to be required to transmit the data of where the icon was globally, and at the time the only really global bandwidth that was available was 19.2 [kilobits per second]," says Gutterman. "[A]ll of a sudden, I saw, wait a minute, this isn't going to work," and he went back to the Board of Trade's executive committee to report that Aurora was not feasible.

In consequence, when the automation of futures trading finally began to gather momentum in Chicago in the late 1990s, it did so not via Aurora or a system like it, but via Globex. The "market" built into Globex's software was not the embodied "social" market of Aurora, but a more abstract, anonymous market (the one portrayed, for example, in Souleles 2019), in which offers and bids, supply and demand, were almost completely disconnected from their human initiators. One could not, for example, choose with whom to trade: the first bid or offer to be executed was simply the first to have been entered at the appropriate price. Time priority—"first come, first served"— thus structured how traders' orders encountered each other in Globex in the late 1990s, when use of the system first became important. It was a contingent outcome, not an inevitability (since the bandwidth constraints that doomed Aurora turned out to be historically transient), but it was a consequential one.

The Bigs and the Littles

The process by which electronic trading shifted from being an unimportant adjunct to the pits to becoming their replacement began with an external threat to one of the CME's most vital products, Standard & Poor's (S&P) 500 index futures, second in importance only to the CME's Eurodollar futures. Although the S&P 500 was the main performance benchmark for institutional investors, it was less well known to the wider public than the Dow Jones Industrial Average. Dow Jones & Co., however, had never licensed its index to the futures markets—"they refused to let some gamblers in Chicago use their instrument," Melamed told me—and had won a protracted legal battle against the Chicago Board of Trade's view that index levels were not private property but public facts on which it could legitimately base a futures contract. In 1997, however, Dow Jones finally relented, and there was intense competition between the Board of Trade and the CME for the license. In February 1997, the Board had opened a giant new open-outcry trading floor, the largest in the world, and badly wanted—and was prepared to pay heavily for—a Dow Jones future to trade on it (Falloon 1998: 263–75).

Sensing that the CME would lose, Melamed and those around him—Fred Arditti, Barry Lind, Bill Shepard, and Rick Kilcollin—began to plan their response (Melamed 2009: 37–39). They feared that a Dow future would be especially attractive to the general public, and knew that the CME's S&P 500 future contract was too large for most lay investors, since a one-point move in the S&P 500 index changed the contract's value by $500, making a single contract equivalent to stocks worth around $500,000. In October 1997, the CME reduced the multiplier from $500 to $250, but even with that change an S&P 500 future remained dauntingly large. Perhaps, though, a contract with a multiplier of only $50 (thus the equivalent of stocks worth around $50,000) might be attractive to well-to-do retail investors, such as those who were clients of Lind's firm? Perhaps, too, this new "mini" contract could be traded electronically, not just after hours, but also when the pits were open? Perhaps it could be an *E-Mini*?

The proposal for the E-Mini was bitterly controversial, Melamed told me. "There was a big community on the [trading] floor [who] said that that was a violation of the [October 1987] referendum . . . that you could not list anything that was being traded [in a pit] on an electronic screen during the day." Melamed argued, however, that the E-Mini was *not* the same contract as the pit-traded S&P 500 future, and the CME's counsel, Gerry Salzman, backed Melamed's interpretation. The threats to Melamed's life resumed—"You got little notes," he says, "and there were rumors, always a rumor"—but when on June 5, 1997, Dow Jones announced that it was indeed licensing its index to the Chicago Board of Trade, Melamed and those around him launched an all-out push to get the E-Mini up and running. An extraordinary technical effort, led by Jim Krause of the CME's information systems department, made it possible for the E-Mini to begin trading on September 9, 1997, a month before the launch of the Board of Trade's new Dow Jones future.[15]

The E-Mini would not, of course, have been an effective response to the Dow Jones future if trading in it were as sporadic as in most existing products on Globex. The crucial innovation in this respect was thought up by Melamed's ally Bill Shepard. It exploited the mathematical fact that while the E-Mini was different from the pit-traded S&P 500 future, it was also economically the same: five E-Minis were economically identical to one pit-traded contract. If the relative prices of the two diverged, therefore, there would be an attractive opportunity for arbitrage, for riskless (or at least low risk) profit, by buying the cheaper instrument and selling the dearer. Shepard's idea was to place Globex terminals in close vicinity to the S&P 500 trading pit, so that traders using them could see—and to some extent hear—what was going on in the pit, and exploit any temporary price discrepancies. A large, semicircular structure was built overlooking the pit, with more than a hundred Globex terminals arranged on it in tiers, and a CME program made radio headsets available to help traders using terminals on the platform communicate with their colleagues in the pit below.[16]

Thus was born "the bigs and the littles," the arbitrage between the pit-traded S&P 500 future and the E-Mini. Pairs of traders would collaborate, one in the pit and one sitting above it at a Globex terminal, communicating by hand signals or radio headsets. A trader in the S&P 500 pit whom I interviewed in November 2000 drew my attention to the new structure, which when viewed from the bottom of the pit seemed to loom over it:

> [W]hen you went to the floor, did you see the almost towers, kind of towering by the S&P pit? Almost gets to the ceiling, and you get a bunch of guys sitting there with terminals? That's the guys that trade the E-Minis . . . some of these guys are doing very, very, very well, extremely well.

Among the newly created firms that traded the bigs and the littles were two that were to become crucial to HFT: Jump Trading, launched in 1999 by CME pit traders Paul Gurinas and Bill DiSomma, who were among the early users of headsets,[17] and Getco (Global Electronic Trading Co.), established, also in 1999, by Daniel Tierney, formerly a trader on the Chicago Board Options Exchange, and CME broker Stephen Schuler.

"The bigs and the littles," the platform, and the headsets turned the S&P pit and Globex into what was in effect a single market. Trading volumes grew rapidly, with the electronic contract soon beginning to outstrip its pit-traded counterpart, and in the process the S&P E-Mini's ticker symbol, ES, became familiar not just to futures traders but also to all professional share traders. Not only did the ES succeed in warding off the threat to the CME from the Chicago Board of Trade, but, as already noted, it became in a sense the primary overall price-discovery market for US shares. The ES market typically responded most quickly to new information relevant to the overall value of shares, rather than just that of the shares of particular corporations.

"The bigs and the littles" also began to change the logic of what it was to trade futures electronically. Recall that in Globex the first order to be executed was simply the first to arrive at the matching engines (the parts of the Globex computer system that maintain the CME's electronic order books and find bids and offers that match). "First in, first out," together with the fact that the price discrepancies being arbitraged were fleeting, meant that those seeking to exploit discrepancies between the prices of the "big" and the "little" had to place a huge priority on speed: delay for even an instant, and either one's Globex order for the "little" would not be filled, or the discrepancy would have vanished by the time it was filled. At least two firms took computer-gaming joysticks and reprogrammed them to simulate the keystrokes on a Globex terminal that placed orders for E-Minis, so as to allow their traders to outpace those using a keyboard.

Even a human being with a joystick was, however, slower than a computer. Originally, as noted in chapter 1, the universal assumption had been that automated trading would involve a human being inputting orders on a computer terminal—all the early efforts to automate exchanges of which I am aware assumed this—but the growing liquidity of E-Minis and the need for speed when trading them undermined this assumption. Perhaps profits could be made purely within the market for E-Minis, without having to trade in the pit as well, and perhaps human beings could then be removed altogether from electronic trading and replaced by entirely automatic systems? Designed, as almost all electronic trading systems of the 1980s and 1990s were, on the assumption of input from human beings at terminals, Globex did not originally have what would now be called an application programming interface, or API, a direct means by which trading algorithms could interact with the Globex system. However, firms like those that had cut their teeth on "the bigs and the littles" began to develop what interviewees call a "screen-scrape" process, in which incoming data intended to drive the visual display on a Globex or other trading terminal was diverted directly into the firm's computers, and the requisite response to it was formulated and dispatched as the computer-generated equivalent of the effects of a human being hitting the keys of the terminal (interviewee AB).

The ES (the original S&P 500 E-Mini), and especially the NQ, a similar electronically traded futures contract launched in 1999 and based on the Nasdaq-100 index, formed the crucial link between the increasingly automated trading of futures and the nascent high-frequency trading of shares, especially on the new electronic share-trading venue Island, described in chapter 1. (Recall that this was the period of the dot-com and telecommunications share-price boom and bust, and most such shares were listed on Nasdaq.) Among the shares traded on Island were those of the exchange-traded fund known to traders by its ticker symbol, QQQ. A share in the QQQs (sometimes known informally as the "triple-Qs" or "cubes") is in effect a fractional holding of a portfolio of Nasdaq-100 shares. Once again, the careful political work of Leo Melamed, Phil Johnson, and their allies in the 1970s continued to pay off, more than two decades later. Futures still led: changes in the price of the NQ, the futures contract, would often give early indications of likely moves in the share, the QQQ, and the risk of positions accumulated in the QQQs could be offset by buying or selling the NQ, according to interviewee AB. From trading the QQQs algorithmically on Island, using the movements of the NQ as the crucial "signal," it was a short step to automated trading of the underlying Nasdaq shares, not just on Island but on other venues as well. Not all the HFT firms active on Island had their roots in futures trading—for example, Automated Trading Desk, the focus of chapter 3, did not—but those that did were an important part of the HFT business as it began to take shape in the early 2000s.

The Threat from Europe and the Death of the Pits

In Chicago, however, the E-Minis (the ES and NQ) remained initially an island of automation: most members of the CME and the Board of Trade remained strongly committed to face-to-face open outcry, and—as I have already said—such trading remained fully vibrant when I visited the Chicago exchanges in 1999 and 2000. Nevertheless, developments in Europe in the late 1990s showed that even well-entrenched open-outcry futures exchanges were potentially at risk from electronic competition and that pit trading itself might be in danger. As noted above, Chicago's success in launching the trading of financial futures—and also the organized trading of options—sparked imitators internationally. (These too had to overcome legal difficulties, similar to those in the US, concerning gambling. In Germany, for example, existing law "said that trading options and futures is . . . gambling," as interviewee GB reports, and although gambling was not illegal in Germany, gambling contracts were not enforceable in law. "[W]e had to . . . convince the parliament to change" the law that classed options and futures as wagers before an exchange that traded them, the Deutsche Terminbörse, could be launched, and that legal change happened, reports GB, only in November 1989, "six weeks before we started with the trading.")

Some of the new European futures and options exchanges (such as the initially most successful of them, LIFFE, the London International Financial Futures Exchange) were based, like the CME and Chicago Board of Trade, on open-outcry trading pits. Others, though, notably the Swiss Options and Financial Futures Exchange and Germany's Terminbörse, opted from the start for electronic trading. Both Switzerland and Germany had decentralized, federal political systems, making it difficult to reach agreement as to which city should host a face-to-face exchange and benefit from all the employment and income such an exchange would bring. "[W]hat should the other places do if we start[ed] [an] options market in Frankfurt?" said interviewee GB. "[T]hey most probably would like to install an option trading market in Dusseldorf or Hamburg or in Berlin or in Munich. It makes no sense at all to have a little plant [financial futures and options trading] coming out of [a] green field and now we should divide this plant . . . I don't know, in six, seven, eight parts." An electronic exchange would not require a large staff to run it, and that seemed to make the question of which city should host it much less contentious. (Because, as already noted, it was assumed that orders would be entered by human traders with their slow reaction times, not ultrafast machines, no one seems to have anticipated that the spatial location of the exchange's computer datacenter would matter greatly.)

When the Deutsche Terminbörse launched in 1990, LIFFE's trading pits had been in operation for eight years, and had successfully developed a futures contract on *Bund*s, German sovereign bonds. In US share trading, as will be discussed in chapter 3, competition among exchanges was facilitated by the existence of a single national clearinghouse. (Clearing is the process of registering, guaranteeing, and processing trades. In a market with a clearinghouse, a deal between a buyer and seller is turned, nearly immediately, into two deals, one between the seller and the clearinghouse, the other between it and the buyer. That not only protects the buyer and seller from the other defaulting on the deal, but also makes it possible to preserve anonymity.)[18] No national clearing system existed—or exists even today—in futures trading in the US (or, indeed, Europe), which makes it notoriously hard for a new futures exchange to compete with an incumbent by launching replicas of its products. The incumbent's clearinghouse can simply refuse to clear its rival's contracts, thus making it impossible to buy a futures contract on a new exchange and sell it on the incumbent exchange, or vice versa.

Despite the absence of a common clearing system, the Deutsche Terminbörse nevertheless successfully overturned LIFFE's dominance of *Bund* futures in 1997. Its electronic equivalent to LIFFE's open-outcry *Bund* future seized nearly all of the market that LIFFE's trading pits seemingly had captured permanently. The shockwaves reverberated throughout the world of futures. In 1998, MATIF in Paris switched entirely from open outcry to electronic trading, and LIFFE followed suit in 1999–2000 (Scott and Barrett 2005). Chicago still clung to the pits, but—together with the development of handheld devices (such as the CME's Galax-C) that permitted traders to quote prices, buy, and sell electronically while standing in the pits—the clear threat to pit traders' way of life prompted what a few years earlier would have been unthinkable concessions. In August 1998, the members of the Chicago Board of Trade voted to allow electronic trading of its Treasury futures contracts while the pits were open, and in January 1999 a referendum of the CME's membership produced an even clearer majority removing the constraint the 1987 vote had placed on Globex. From then on, all of the CME's futures could be traded electronically, whether the pits were open or not (Melamed 2009: 56–57).

Commitment to open outcry nevertheless remained strong in the pits of the Chicago Board of Trade and in the CME's largest and most important pit, the Eurodollar pit. "With few exceptions," Melamed wrote, "the Eurodollar community—traders, independent brokers, members of broker groups—continued to trade in the pit as if nothing happened" (Melamed 2009: 57). The Chicago pit traders' defense of their way of life finally broke down when the potential threat from Europe became actual—indeed, physically visible. In 2003, the all-electronic Eurex futures exchange, formed in 1998 by a merger of the Deutsche Terminbörse and the Swiss Options and Financial Futures Exchange, declared its intention to begin trading in the US. In February 2004, LIFFE too announced it was planning electronically traded Eurodollar futures directly competing with the CME's pit-traded contracts. Eurex leased space in the Sears Tower, the tallest building in the Americas (and a short walk from both the Board of Trade and CME). It "handed out free coffee to traders on LaSalle Street and lighted the top of the Sears Tower in the Eurex colors of green and blue" (Roeder 2004), even taunting the Board of Trade by playing a searchlight on its building (Melamed 2009: 102).

Of the CME and the Chicago Board of Trade, the latter was the more vulnerable. The CME owned its own clearinghouse, but the Board did not. Its clearinghouse was a separate company, which, as interviewee DI pointed out, was owned largely by banks, and many of the latter welcomed the prospect of the emergence of a new US competitor for the Board of Trade, because competition might reduce the exchange fees and brokerage charges they had to pay. Eurex bought a stake in the Board of Trade Clearing Corporation and gained its agreement to clear Eurex's equivalents of the Board's futures. The barrier that normally protects futures exchanges against competition thus crumbled. The threat in 2003–4 from Eurex to the Board of Trade (and, less directly, from LIFFE to the CME) provoked months of tumultuous change in Chicago. The Board had been leasing Eurex's A/C/E electronic trading system. At the end of December 2003, it stopped using it and in great haste switched to LIFFE's LiffeConnect trading system. It began pursuing electronic trading with unprecedented vigor, and opened negotiations to shift its clearing to the CME's clearinghouse, despite the decades of rivalry between the two exchanges. An agreement was struck in April 2003, and a huge, concerted technical effort achieved the transition by

January 2004, beginning the process that led to the Board of Trade's merger with the CME in 2007, a merger that was, in effect, a takeover by the CME.

LIFFE's threat to the CME's Eurodollar contract did not take the immediately palpable form of Eurex's threat to the Board of Trade, but prominent figures in the CME—its chair, Terry Duffy, chief executive Craig Donohue, Leo Melamed, and others, including Bill Shepard and John Newhouse—were deeply concerned by it, and resolved to bring matters to a head. Although the thousands of Eurodollar traders were "the most successful and hard-bitten open-outcry constituency in existence anywhere" (Melamed 2009: 108), the CME's leadership threatened to close the Eurodollar pit unless at least a quarter of the trading of the most liquid Eurodollar contracts took place electronically on Globex. They held a succession of huge meetings with Eurodollar traders and brokers. Melamed remembers one with "1,000 angry faces in the room. . . . The fear, frustration, and distrust was palpable. The emotionally charged atmosphere had many characteristics of a lynch mob" (Melamed 2009: 108).

As trader Ryan Carlson has emphasized to me, however, the Eurodollar pit had already begun quietly changing of its own accord. There was a row of Globex terminals above the brokers' booths on its west side. When the pit opened, the terminals' users normally shut them down, got up, and started to trade in the pit. Carlson remembers a day in 2003 or 2004—in retrospect a pivotal moment—when two of the Globex users remained seated at their terminals, "making markets" (i.e., continuously posting both bids to buy and offers to sell), at first cautiously, but soon in competition with the traders in the pit. He had an instinct that this "signified the beginning of the end for the Eurodollar pit." The shift from the latter to the Globex screen had begun, and it turned out to be faster and more complete than the partial transition that the CME's leadership had demanded. "Within a year," says Carlson, "I stopped going into the trading pit anymore."[19]

From 2005 onward, Chicago's pits rapidly emptied out. The end of a way of life more than a century old affected some traders very deeply. One interviewee, for example, recalls his trading partner continuing to spend his days on the steps of a near-silent, virtually deserted pit, despite his efforts to persuade him to come to terms with what had happened. By the time I next visited Chicago's pits, in October 2011, they were quiet and sparsely populated. Occupy Wall Street had begun its takeover of Zuccotti Park in Lower Manhattan's financial district the previous month, and its Chicago supporters often gathered on LaSalle Street, directly opposite the Board of Trade Building, which now housed both what had been the Board's pits and the CME's. When I asked one of the remaining pit traders how business was, he replied, "It's bad," and added, "I'll be joining the protesters." I wasn't certain that he was joking.

Futures Lead

The demise of face-to-face trading was a huge shift, and change continued apace even after electronic trading's triumph. The Globex computer system that underpins it has been reengineered several times, with a particularly important redesign in 2014 (see below). One pattern, however, remained largely intact throughout all these changes: moves in the market for the CME's share-index futures typically occurred before—in the 1980s, tens of minutes before; by 2005, around a tenth of a second before; by 2011, less than a hundredth of a second before—corresponding moves in the markets for the underlying shares.[20] Why? The reasons for the persistence of the pattern I call "futures lead" are of interest because of that pattern's importance to HFT, but discussion of them inherently involves a deeper level of financial technicality than this chapter's earlier sections provide, so general readers may, if they wish, skip at this point to the start of chapter 3.

Three possible reasons for the longevity of "futures lead" can be ruled out. The first *does* help explain futures lead, but only in the first decade or so of the pattern's existence, in the 1980s and early 1990s: the lack of any way of constructing a trading position to benefit from or hedge against changes in the overall level of prices that was as quick and straightforward as buying or selling the CME's S&P 500 index futures. That lack ended with the creation from 1993 onward of exchange-traded funds (ETFs), sophisticated, algorithmically constructed shares that track the level of an index or other underlying set of assets, just as futures do (albeit by a different mechanism), and which can readily be used to profit from or hedge against overall share-price changes.[21] The most widely traded of all the ETFs—indeed, the world's most widely traded share—is State Street's Standard & Poor's 500 Depository Receipt (SPDR, better known to traders as "the Spider," or by its ticker symbol, SPY), an ETF created in 1993 that tracks the same index as the ES, the CME's electronically traded S&P 500 future. The SPY and the ES differ economically in only minor ways, yet for more than two decades starting in 1993 the future (the ES) continued typically to lead the share (the SPY), as is confirmed by both interviewees and econometric evidence.[22] Indeed, the ES still often seems to do so even today, although, as interviewees report, less consistently than in the past.[23]

A second possible explanation of the way that share-index futures tend to lead shares is that the systems on which futures are electronically traded are more sophisticated than the systems on which shares are traded. But if anything, the opposite has been the case. At least until 2014, HFT interviewees reported that the CME's system was slower and more subject to unintended, unpredictable delays than its counterparts in share trading, and also that the datafeed from the CME's system was less helpful to them.[24] (In 2014, the CME launched a new trading system—in which FPGAs, the field-programmable gate arrays discussed in Chapter 5, play crucial roles—whose speed and predictability are more comparable to the systems on which shares are traded.) So, paradoxically, the CME, until recently the technologically less advanced market, has led the more advanced share-trading market.[25]

"Nasdaq [which trades shares and options] does way more messaging throughput than the CME," said interviewee AJ in March 2012, "and they're doing it in micros [microseconds] and the CME is in milliseconds." "Equities [shares] was the premier low-latency [i.e., fast-trading] space," says interviewee CN, "and so by comparison what CME had in futures didn't seem that good." As we will see in chapter 3, there was intense competition among the venues on which US shares were traded electronically, and this sharply focused attention on speeding up those venues' systems. In contrast, the 2003–4 crisis of Chicago's futures trading faded—Eurex never established a firm foothold in the US, and LIFFE ultimately did not succeed in threatening the CME's Eurodollar futures—with the result that the CME has not faced continuous competition, at least in financial futures, and has thus experienced less pressure to make its system as fast as possible. The CME's main continuing rival has been an Atlanta-based electronic futures exchange, the Intercontinental Exchange or ICE, established in 2000. ICE has a strong position in futures on physical commodities, especially oil and gas, but has never posed a real threat to the CME's hold on financial futures. Nevertheless, AJ, in my 2012 interview with him, credited competition with ICE (which "got really fast," he says) for sparking increased focus by the CME on the speed of its system.

A third conceivable, but also incorrect, way of explaining "futures lead" would be that it is somehow intrinsic to futures. As discussed in chapter 4, however, "futures lead" is far from universal across different types of financial asset. Interviewees reported, for example, that Treasury futures do not consistently lead the market in the underlying Treasury securities, and that the pattern in foreign exchange tends if anything to be the reverse of that in shares, with the markets in which currencies are traded directly usually leading the foreign-exchange futures market.[26]

So why did "futures lead" with respect to shares, with the pattern's idiosyncratic origins in the 1970s and 1980s, persist, even if it has weakened somewhat? Two factors, not mutually exclusive, are particularly relevant to this book.[27] The first is simply that, as discussed in chapter 1, liquidity is "sticky," or path dependent—once it becomes concentrated in a particular trading venue, it tends to stay there—and (other things being equal) price changes tend to manifest themselves in the most liquid venues before they do so in less liquid venues. If an institutional investor wants to execute a very large trade (for example, the sale of 75,000 ES contracts, the equivalent of selling shares worth $4.1 billion, which triggered the May 2010 "flash crash" in US share prices, discussed in chapter 7), he or she will turn to the market best able to handle the largest trades, which, participants report, has—at least until quite recently—been the CME's index futures.[28] In so doing, that investor helps maintain that market's capacity to do so, and thus helps its prices continue to lead those in markets in which shares are traded.

The second factor in entrenching futures lead seems to have been leverage. While ETFs such as the SPY have many of futures' other advantages, and regulatory limits on leverage in professional share trading have gradually weakened, interviewees reported that it was still easier to achieve high leverage in futures than in shares (including even ETFs). "[F]utures is first, right, because of the leverage it provides . . . you're going to hit the [ES] first," said interviewee AP. Leverage is built into the very design of futures contracts, while, as a former high-frequency trader told me in conversation, for a small or medium-sized firm trading shares, achieving high leverage requires that it find a dealer prepared to grant that leverage, which may not be easy since it exposes the dealer to the risk that the firm could fail. (Note too that futures trading does not have a systematic leverage advantage over the trading of Treasurys or foreign exchange, which most likely explains why futures do not lead those assets in the relatively consistent way in which they have led shares.)

The continuing difference in leverage between the ways that US futures and US shares have been traded—even ETF shares, some of which, as noted, are nearly identical economically to share-index futures—rested at least to some degree on the continuing split in jurisdiction between the CFTC and SEC. From the 1987 stock-market crash (which sparked influential demands to end the split and to harmonize leverage requirements) to the 2012 Frank-Capuano Bill, which proposed a merger of the CFTC and SEC, all efforts to create a single regulator have failed. The futures industry has fought, and would most likely again fight, such a move vigorously. The Chicago

Mercantile Exchange, which became the world's leading exchange by market value—and often one of the most profitable companies in the US (see, e.g., Stafford 2017)—continued Melamed's emphasis on having a strong voice in Washington.[29] Such a fight has, however, mostly been unnecessary, because those who favor a CFTC-SEC merger are often dissuaded by an immediate barrier, whose roots stretch back to the 1970s. Divides in the financial system (between futures trading and share trading; between futures exchanges such as the CME and stock exchanges; between the CFTC and SEC) are echoed in a divide between congressional committees, especially Senate committees. Because of futures' agricultural roots, the CFTC reports to the Senate Agriculture Committee, the SEC to the Senate Banking Committee.

"I've been in many conversations about the merger of the SEC and CFTC," former regulator RF told me. "The conversation quickly stops because people say, 'but the [Senate] Ag[riculture] Committee: this [merger] is never going to happen.'" Asked why the SEC and CFTC have never merged, another former regulator agrees: "You can probably begin and end your discussion with the Ag Committee. . . . It's powerful" (interviewee RG). If the SEC and CFTC merged, the Agriculture Committee would lose its jurisdiction over the latter and the regulation of financial futures. "That would then move [to] the jurisdiction of the Senate Banking Committee," says interviewee RF, to which, as just noted, the SEC reports. Both interviewees cited the importance of campaign contributions from the finance sector (see figure 2.10):

> The Senate Ag. Committee gets all of this money [contributions]. They're not going to give up jurisdiction, so you can't put it [the regulation of US financial markets, currently split between the CFTC and SEC] together. (Interviewee RF)

Interviewee RX, who says that he "spent a couple of years of my life" on an unsuccessful proposal to merge the CFTC and SEC, tells me that the point at which a shift in jurisdiction was most likely was in 1989–90, a year or so after President Reagan appointed the New York investment banker Nicholas Brady as Secretary of the Treasury. Brady had headed the presidential task force investigating the 1987 crash (Brady Commission 1988), and another sharp fall in US stock prices on October 13, 1989, seems to have prompted renewed attention in the Department of the Treasury to the split regulation of US capital markets. According to interviewee RX, the Treasury

> tried to push through a jurisdictional change that would've moved financial futures or some portion of financial futures to the SEC. That failed

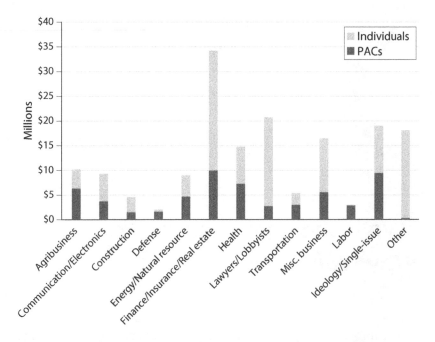

FIGURE 2.10. Sectors contributing to members of the Senate Agriculture, Nutrition and Forestry Committee, 2016 election cycle. Data from www.opensecrets.org, accessed March 1, 2017.

because the Merc [Chicago Mercantile Exchange] and the Board of Trade were damn good lobbyists and the Agriculture [Committee] had no interest in losing their control.

It is, of course, difficult to be certain just how important the SEC/CFTC split has been to the longevity of "futures lead" in shares. As already noted, a full explanation is likely to involve a combination of factors.[30] To the extent, though, that split regulation is important, it is an example of one of this book's central arguments. The signals, such as "futures lead," that inform HFT are not determined simply by the nature of technological systems or by the inherent economic characteristics of the financial instruments being traded. They also reflect political processes—Melamed's grasping of the opportunity provided by Poage's wish to protect his committee's jurisdiction; Johnson's crucial 20-word addition to the relevant law; and so on—and the outcomes of the conflicts that those processes involve. Although those conflicts may now be long past, some of their outcomes continue to structure today's world of automated trading in profound ways. That is true too of the conflictual history of US share trading, to which we now turn.

3

"We'll show you our book.
Why won't they?"

Charleston, South Carolina, is not where I would have expected to find a part of the origins of today's ultrafast trading. The past can seem ever present here: in the beauty of the cobbled streets and antebellum houses; in the shaded paths of the College of Charleston, Spanish moss swathing the paths' live oaks; in the inescapable reminders that this was once North America's busiest slave port. Nor, if I had happened upon it in the early 1990s, would I likely have been impressed by a makeshift, computer-packed office in a 1950s cinder-block motel building on Charleston's Wappoo Road, occupied by (as one of them put it) "kids, barefoot, T-shirts, shorts." Before a decade was out, though, those kids' computers were trading shares worth over a billion dollars every day (Collier 2002); at its peak, almost one in every ten shares traded in the United States was bought or sold by their firm, Automated Trading Desk, or ATD (Philips 2013).

Because ATD was founded in 1989—a full decade before HFT started to become large-scale—its history straddles two quite different phases of the evolution of US share trading. In the first phase, which lasted until the mid-1990s, ATD found electronic trading often difficult and always expensive. Its algorithms were frequently successful in predicting share-price changes, but the resultant trading profits were often swallowed up by the fees ATD had to pay to trading venues and traditional intermediaries. Then, with the creation in 1996 of Island (the new trading venue mentioned in chapter 1 and discussed in greater depth later in this chapter), that all began to change.

ATD was initially at the heart of the changes, but—as described at the end of this chapter—from 2001 onward it began to lose its central position. By the early 2000s, however, the transformation of US share trading was well under way. HFT firms had boosted trading volumes on exchanges and other trading venues with HFT-friendly features, while other venues were, first, forced by competition to adopt those features, and then chose to embrace them as ways of earning revenue.

ATD's chief inspiration was cofounder David Whitcomb, an academic economist. He taught finance at Rutgers University until his retirement in 1999, and was one of the pioneers of market microstructure theory. While much of economics "abstracts from the mechanics of trading" (O'Hara 1997: 1), researchers in this new field modeled and investigated empirically how particular ways of organizing trading can influence outcomes, and how intermediaries such as market-makers set their prices.[1] A crucial step in Whitcomb's path from this academic specialism to the practice of high-frequency trading was a consultancy contract. In the 1980s, electronic share trading was already available in the US, mainly via the Instinet system (described below), but usage of Instinet by its intended institutional-investor clientele was disappointing. Instinet hired Whitcomb to investigate how to attract more users. He proposed that it supply institutional investors with what would now be called execution algorithms. As described in chapter 1, these are computer programs that investors can use to break up big orders into small parts and execute them automatically (Whitcomb interview 2).

Instinet did not adopt Whitcomb's suggestion. However, one of his former students, James Hawkes, who taught statistics at the College of Charleston, ran a small firm, Quant Systems, which sold software for statistical analysis. Whitcomb and Hawkes had earlier collaborated on a statistical model to predict the outcomes of horse races. Their equation displayed some predictive power, but because of bookmakers' large "vigs," or "takes" (the profits they earn by setting odds unfavorable to the gambler), it did not earn Hawkes and Whitcomb money (Whitcomb interviews 1 and 2). Hawkes, though, also traded stock options, and had installed a satellite dish on the roof of his garage to receive a share-price datafeed. He mentioned this to Whitcomb, and the latter began to investigate whether a predictive model, similar to the one the pair had used for horse racing, could be developed for share prices.

Whitcomb raised most of the initial capital of $100,000 (see, e.g., Whitcomb, 1989a) for a joint venture with Hawkes, which they christened Automated Trading Desk. (The name reflected their initial plan to develop and sell execution algorithms to institutional investors, but Whitcomb found it difficult to persuade investors to experiment with an entirely new, automated way of trading.) Hawkes provided the programmers, two College of Charleston students—both of whom later became leaders of ATD—who wrote statistical software for him. Whitcomb, who continued to teach at Rutgers and live in New York, designed the relatively simple mathematical model described in the next four paragraphs, faxing instructions and formulas to Charleston to be turned into code by Hawkes's programmers. Around the equation that was the core of the model, Whitcomb designed and the programmers coded the components of what was eventually to become a full automated-trading system. It consisted of a module to process incoming market data; a pricing module that implemented Whitcomb's equation; a module that tracked the system's accumulated trading position in each stock and adjusted its trading strategy accordingly; a decision module that calculated how best to trade based on the existing trading position and the pricing module's predictions; a module that dispatched the resultant orders and if necessary canceled existing orders; a module that calculated in real time the profits or losses being made; and so on—eventually requiring in total some 80,000 lines of code (interviewee BT).

Both Whitcomb's and Hawkes's horse-race predictions and ATD's efforts to predict stock prices had the same mathematical form: a linear-regression equation, in which the values of a number of independent, or predictor, variables are employed to predict the value of a dependent variable.[2] In the case of horse racing, Whitcomb explained, the variable to be predicted was "the horse's speed at that distance," and the predictor variables included "the weight the horse was carrying today relative to the other horses, the jockey's previous winning percentage, the horse's speed in the past relative to other horses, [and] some dummy variables for the kind of race," all of which were publicly available information (Whitcomb interview 2). In the case of share trading, the dependent variable to be predicted was what Automated Trading Desk called the ATV, or adjusted theoretical value, of the stock in question, a prediction of its price 30 seconds in the future. (ATD experimented with different time horizons, but found the exact choice not to be critical.)

What were the predictor variables that could be used in the automated trading of shares? They too had to be public, and knowable in Charleston without undue delay. (In its later years, ATD, like other HFT firms, placed computer servers in the same buildings as exchanges' systems, but early on all its computing was done in the firm's offices, first in Charleston and later in Mount Pleasant, across the Cooper River from Charleston.) By the late 1980s, a number of companies had rented capacity on communications satellites to transmit financial data to places, such as Charleston, far from major financial centers. (The satellites were in orbits high above the earth's surface, making data transmission slower than the fastest terrestrial links, but in the 1980s and 1990s small delays of that kind did not seem crucial.) ATD subscribed to one such satellite-based service, Standard & Poor's ComStock, a manual for which is still in interviewee BT's files (S&P ComStock, 1990). ATD received the signals first via the satellite dish on top of Hawkes's garage, where the ATD programmers worked in a cubicle, and then via a dish on the roof of the old motel on Wappoo Road.

In the late 1980s and early 1990s, there was much that ComStock could not report because it was not public knowledge. For example, as discussed in chapter 1, the full "book" of unexecuted bids for and offers of a stock on the New York Stock Exchange was still largely private to the stock's NYSE "specialist." Initially, therefore, ATD's regression model simply used the size of the highest-priced bid relative to the size of the lowest-priced offer, along with a short-term trend variable in the transaction prices of the stock (Whitcomb interview 3). Later, the firm constructed another proxy for the still incompletely known balance of supply and demand. ATD's system calculated two variables, "down volume" and "up volume," which indicated whether transactions were on average taking place at the highest price at which there were bids to buy or at the higher price at which there were offers to sell. If the latter, for example (if, in other words, up volume exceeded down volume), "that's indicating, well, gosh, everybody seems to be paying up" (interviewee BT), and thus a price rise was likely.

More important, however, for the predictive capacity of ATD's algorithms than any other factor was the variable whose history was explored in chapter 2: share-index futures prices, especially the prices of futures contracts based on the Standard & Poor's 500 index, contracts that in principle track (but, as discussed in chapter 2, in practice tend to lead) the changing aggregate prices of the US's most important stocks. As described in chapter 2, pit reporters employed by the Chicago Mercantile Exchange turned traders' shouted or hand-signaled deals into an electronic stream of futures prices. That stream flowed to data services such as ComStock, and from there into ATD's computers. Futures prices were "the prime market indicator that we were using," as Whitcomb puts it; they were "definitely the key variable" (interviewee BT). Indeed, so important were they that ATD's trading system had a futures-only mode, in which all other predictors were switched off.

Share Trading Before HFT

In the summer of 1989, a computer simulation convinced David Whitcomb that ATD could indeed make money by using his predictive model in the automated trading of shares. Simulated trading, though, was one thing; actually conducting automated trading was quite another. In the late 1980s and early 1990s, there were three main ways of trading US shares: via the New York Stock Exchange (NYSE), via Nasdaq, or on Instinet's electronic trading system. It is worth sketching all three, because they (especially the NYSE and Nasdaq) constituted the main parts of a world of share trading that would eventually be transformed utterly by its collision with HFT.

THE NEW YORK STOCK EXCHANGE

The New York Stock Exchange was the oldest and most prestigious of the three trading venues, but it was not well suited to the kind of trading ATD wanted to do. Although orders could be sent electronically to the busy trading rooms in the NYSE's buildings at the junction of Broad Street and Wall Street, once there the execution of those orders was still a predominantly manual process, often involving ad hoc trading-floor auctions conducted by the specialist, the officially designated trader who coordinated the buying and selling of the stock for which he (it was an almost exclusively male role) was responsible.[3] A firm that was not a member of the NYSE—and Whitcomb's ATD was not—could not itself trade on the NYSE or even directly send orders there; it had to employ a broker or dealer firm that was an NYSE member, paying fees that would considerably reduce any prospective trading profits.

The NYSE's dominance had faced a serious threat in the 1970s. By the end of the 1960s, the manual settlement processes that underpinned share trading (the transfer of money and especially of shares, which were then still paper certificates) had become clogged. Piles of unprocessed documents, delays, omissions, errors—and even theft of share certificates—accumulated (SEC 1971). This "paperwork crisis," as it became known, was exacerbated by a sharp downturn in US share prices at the end of the 1960s. Stockbrokers began to fail in increasing numbers, threatening to leave hundreds of thousands of members of the public who had invested via those firms with large losses. Just as food-price inflation focused attention on the trading of agricultural futures (as discussed in chapter 2), Wall Street's very public debacle motivated sharply increased congressional interest in reforming the way shares were traded. Led by Maine Senator Ed Muskie—who "was looking for big issues" on which to build his run for the 1972 Democratic presidential nomination (Lemov 2011: 120)—Congress rapidly passed the 1970 Securities Investor Protection Act, which set up an insurance scheme, funded in part by the federal government, to compensate the customers of failed brokerages. Other members of Congress, especially California Democrat John Moss, who was a consumer-protection advocate, continued to press for further reforms, pressure that led to the passage of the Securities Acts Amendments of 1975 (Rowen n.d.).

The 1975 amendments increased the legal powers of the stock-market regulator, the Securities and Exchange Commission (SEC), which had longstanding concerns about the extent of the structural advantages enjoyed by some traders and some exchanges (especially the NYSE). The SEC had, however, done little to act on these concerns. It "really was a disclosure and enforcement agency" that engaged in a "limited amount of market regulation" and made few efforts to change market structure, says former SEC official RX. The 1975 amendments, though, gave the SEC the authority to intervene in and alter how the trading of US shares was organized: "by rule or order, as it deems necessary in the public interest and for the protection of investors . . . to remove impediments to and foster the development of a national market system and national system for the clearance and settlement of securities transactions" (Securities Acts Amendments 1975: 139). It was these new SEC powers that formed the core of the threat to the NYSE's dominance of share trading. To some at the NYSE, its very existence seemed in danger in the 1970s. As interviewee XZ put it, "Congress in the mid-70s said they wanted to shut down the New York Stock Exchange in favor of a national market."

Law, though, "has life only to the degree that those in power are willing to enliven it" (Danner 2017: 4). The political rewards for intervening in the way shares were traded diminished as memories of the late-1960s crisis faded. Moss, for example, returned to more general consumer-protection matters (Lemov 2011). The SEC was left in the second half of the 1970s facing, largely on its own, an issue on which it had received no clear congressional guidance: the material design of the national market system that the 1975 legislation had mandated it to create.

One proposed design of that system was indeed a direct threat to the NYSE. The proponents of that design sought to remove barriers to competition and cut costs by creating a single, centralized, nationwide electronic order book—a consolidated limit order book, or CLOB—into which all orders to buy or sell shares would have to be entered.[4] The CLOB's most prominent supporters were Junius Peake, a financial thinker who in the 1960s had led an early Wall Street computerization drive at the brokerage Shields & Co., and Donald Weeden, whose family firm, Weeden & Co., was prominent in the "third market," a controversial penumbra of broker-ages that—often in the face of hostility from the NYSE—traded NYSE-listed shares without going through the exchange, undercutting NYSE's fixed com-missions (Weeden 2002).

Had the CLOB been constructed, it could have been the perfect way for Automated Trading Desk to buy and sell shares. There was interest in and enthusiasm for the CLOB among the staff of the SEC in the 1970s. As several of them told me, it was common on Friday afternoons for a group of them to go to one of the bars (The Dubliner or Kelly's Irish Times) close to what was then its Washington, DC, headquarters building. There, they sometimes "went through a variety of designs of CLOBs on paper napkins for a number of years" (interviewee RX). The more experienced of them, however, knew that the exercise was hypothetical. "It was clear to us . . . that [the CLOB] just wasn't going to happen in the political realm that we were in," says former SEC official RE. Even with the SEC's new legal powers, it was not prepared to try to force through a proposal for a centralized national market system that would undermine the position of both the NYSE—which, as RE puts it, was "a very powerful institution back then"—and of the regional exchanges in cities such as Boston, Philadelphia, and San Francisco. Although those exchanges operated in the shadow of the NYSE, they too still had political clout via the congressional delegations from their states.

The NYSE itself took the lead in developing the alternative design of the national market system that was adopted in place of the CLOB: the Intermarket Trading System, or ITS. This much less tightly integrated net-work design was based on an existing NYSE system—the Common Message Switch, which connected brokers' offices to the specialists' trading-room booths—and thus could quickly be put into operation (Pardo-Guerra 2019: 284–285; see also Kennedy 2017: 905–907). The ITS enabled a specialist on the floor of one exchange (e.g., the Boston Stock Exchange) to send a specialist on another (e.g., the NYSE) a request for a trade. As a political compromise, the ITS was well crafted and acceptable to all but the CLOB's most fervent supporters. In particular, it offered members of the regional exchanges something they craved: direct access to the NYSE trading floor, and thus the capacity to strike deals with the NYSE's specialists without having to pay a fee to an NYSE broker. This capacity was attractive to the regional exchanges' specialists because it could enable them to unwind whatever trading position they had accumulated during a day's trading, rather than having to hold it overnight (interviewee MG). The leaders of the regional exchanges therefore backed the ITS, despite pleas from CLOB advocate Donald Weeden for them not to do so (Weeden 2002: 106).

The ITS was launched in 1978 and remained in operation until the early 2000s. The recipient of a request-to-trade message via the ITS had two minutes (eventually reduced to 30 seconds) to respond. The system thus operated at a human pace, and was often frustrating to use. If, for example, a specialist received an ITS message seeking to execute against one of his quotes, he could simply decline to honor the quote, saying if challenged that he was in the process of changing it (interviewee RG). It thus remained simpler and quicker for most institutional investors to send large orders, via brokers or dealers, to the exchange with most liquidity, the NYSE (or to its similarly structured, albeit less prestigious, New York rival, the American Stock Exchange, if the stock in question was listed there) rather than to use regional exchanges and the Intermarket Trading System. The ITS thus helped preserve the central role in US share trading of the NYSE's trading rooms.

Unlike the CLOB's proposed order books, which would most likely have been visible to all participants, the NYSE's order books (which, as described in chapter 1, were until the 1980s handwritten on preprinted forms—see figure 3.1—then became electronic) remained largely private to the specialist for the stock in question even in the 1990s. "[H]is book at any given price might have hundreds of orders or nothing. He was the only one who knew that," says former NYSE trading-floor broker XZ. In the epoch in which the "book" was handwritten, a trading-floor broker could perhaps glance at it when a specialist or his clerk had to open it to write down the order (or, in later years, maybe glimpse the order book's contents on the display screen in the specialist's booth), even though doing that was against the NYSE's rules:

> [W]hen he [the specialist or his clerk] would open the book there would be [the] left hand page that would be buy orders and the right page would be sell orders [see figure 3.1]. . . . If you were caught looking at it, it was disaster. He would just read you the riot act; it was a nightmare. You did not want to get caught looking at the book. But if you could read upside down and backwards very quickly, it was an advantage. (XZ) [5]

As noted in chapter 1, a 1991 NYSE rule change gave floor brokers the right to ask specialists about the general balance of bids and offers in their order

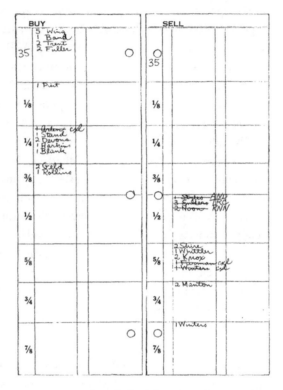

FIGURE 3.1. An NYSE order book from the early 1960s. The
prices are in the traditional eighths of a dollar, and the sizes
are in "round lots" of 100 shares. The names are of the NYSE
member placing the order, most likely on behalf of an external
customer. Orders that are struck through have either been
canceled ("cxl") or executed against. For example, three
orders to sell at $35½ have been matched with orders to buy
at that price; the member firms responsible for the buy orders
are identified by a three-letter acronym. *Source:* SEC (1963:
part 2,491).

books. To those (such as Automated Trading Desk) not physically present
in the NYSE's trading rooms, though, the full books for the stocks traded on
the NYSE remained invisible until the early 2000s; before then, the NYSE
distributed externally, via the SEC-mandated Consolidated Quotation System, only the price and aggregate size of the best bid and offer. As noted
earlier in this chapter, potentially powerful predictor variables (the balance
of bids and offers for a stock, and the ways in which that balance was changing) were therefore simply not available to ATD's algorithms.

NASDAQ

With the threat from the CLOB neutralized, the main challenger to the NYSE in the 1980s and early 1990s was Nasdaq, the Automated Quotation System of the National Association of Securities Dealers (NASD). The SEC had encouraged the creation of the NASD in 1939, and granted it powers to regulate its members' conduct, in the hope of curbing widespread malpractice and fraud in over-the-counter—that is, not exchange-based—share trading. (The NYSE and the other exchanges imposed requirements on companies seeking to list their shares, and shares that traded over the counter were originally usually those whose issuers could not meet those requirements.) Launched in February 1971, again in part in response to pressure from the SEC for greater price transparency, Nasdaq was an electronic system for the on-screen dissemination of price quotations (bids to buy shares and offers to sell them) from the NASD's authorized market-making firms. By the 1980s, the stigma that earlier had surrounded over-the-counter share dealing had largely dissipated, and technology companies such as Apple, Microsoft, Intel, and Cisco, which could, as they grew, have listed on the NYSE, often chose instead to remain on Nasdaq, making the latter an increasingly important share-trading venue.

Unlike the NYSE and the regional exchanges, Nasdaq never had a face-to-face trading floor. In order to be allowed to trade directly on Nasdaq, a securities firm had to first become a member of the National Association of Securities Dealers, which—as ATD discovered when it sought to do this, having identified the opportunity described below—involved "enormous bureaucratic hurdles," as Whitcomb told ATD's shareholders (Whitcomb 1995). Once accepted into membership, a sufficiently well capitalized firm could then register with the NASD as a market-maker for one or more stocks. Only then did a firm get the Level III access, via a Nasdaq terminal, needed to post bids and offers on Nasdaq's screens. To trade without that access, even a firm that was a member of the NASD generally had to either strike a deal by telephone with a market-maker or use Nasdaq's Small Order Execution System (SOES, set up in 1982), via which a member firm could send an order for a thousand shares or fewer from a retail customer—that is, a member of the general public—to a market-making firm to be executed automatically at the price the market-maker was quoting on-screen.

In a period in which the minimum unit of price for US shares (and thus the minimum spread between the prices at which a market-maker would buy a stock and sell it) was still an eighth of a dollar, being a Nasdaq market-maker was a profitable business. The role brought with it both formal obligations to make markets (i.e., to continuously post both bids and offers) and an informal norm—vigorously policed by the harassment of those who violated it by their fellow market-makers—not to display "odd-eighth" price quotes such as $20⅛, $20⅜, and so on (Christie and Schultz 1994). To post a bid or offer with an odd-eighth price would "break the spread" (reduce it from its normal minimum of 25 cents to 12.5 cents) and—unless the bid or offer was very fleeting—could trigger abusive telephone calls from other market-makers. (The spread between the highest bid to buy a stock and the lowest offer to sell it is the main source of market-makers' revenues.) One dealer who experimented with using odd-eighths price quotations told the journalist Gretchen Morgenson:

> My phone lights up like a Christmas tree [indicating multiple incoming calls]. "Whaddya doing in the stock? You're closing the spread. We don't play ball that way. Go back where you belong." (Morgenson 1993: 76)

INSTINET

In contrast to Nasdaq, Instinet offered a way to trade that was more fully electronic; it was in fact among the earliest electronic trading systems.[6] Instinet was founded in 1969 by stock analyst Jerome Pustilnik, his colleague Herbert Behrens, and computer scientist and entrepreneur Charles Adams, to "enable institutional investors [to] deal directly with each other without going through an intermediary," such as an NYSE member firm.[7] At first, Instinet communicated with its subscribers via the teletype machines often used in the 1970s and 1980s to send messages between large organizations. A teletype machine could print incoming messages and had a keyboard for inputting messages for dispatch.

> You would type in what you wanted to buy and how much, and it [Instinet's central system] would link up all the different teletype machines and you would just see [printed out on those machines] that somebody wanted to buy 5,000 shares of IBM. We [Instinet] knew who it was but the other parties didn't. (Interviewee GN)

These teletype machines were later replaced by computer terminals equipped with visual-display screens and linked by a modem and telephone lines to Instinet's central system. On the terminals' green screens, "supply" and "demand" were displayed—much as they were on the screens of the

Chicago Mercantile Exchange's Globex terminals, discussed in chapter 2—in the form of an anonymous list of bids to buy and offers to sell each stock.[8]

As already noted, though, investment-management firms were much less keen to use Instinet than its founders had hoped, and, according to interviewee GN, the firm "barely survived." Trading shares via a big dealer such as a major investment bank was indeed more expensive than using Instinet, but (as discussed in MacKenzie 2019d) it often brought an investment-management firm other benefits: face-to-face meetings with senior managers of corporations in which they were considering investing; potentially highly profitable priority access to shares in the initial public offerings, or IPOs, of those shares; and, especially, "soft dollars." In return for an investment-management firm paying trading commissions to a dealer, it received—and receives—"free" research reports, along with, in the past, other rewards such as subsidized travel and sometimes outright cash payments. The economic rationale for these soft-dollar arrangements is that trading commissions are expenses that investment-management firms can pass on in full to the pension funds, mutual funds, and other savings that the firms manage. They are therefore not "hard dollars"—actual expenditure—from the viewpoint of investment-management firms. However, cash rewards and other benefits—getting "free" research from an investment bank or other dealer saves hard dollars—went directly to those firms. In consequence, says interviewee GN, while Instinet "wanted [institutional investors] to be part of it," these investors, with only limited exceptions, "didn't want to be part of it. They didn't want to trade away from Wall Street [the big dealers]."

Automated Trading on Instinet and the New York Stock Exchange

Given that Instinet was computerized, that there was no major barrier to joining it, and that David Whitcomb was already familiar with it because of his consultancy work, it is not surprising that it was the system chosen for Automated Trading Desk's first efforts at automated trading. ATD's modest capital was insufficient to support any substantial amount of trading, but Whitcomb's accountant introduced him to a man (whom he does not wish to name) who ran what has subsequently become a well-known hedge fund. It provided the requisite capital.

In Charleston, ATD's young programmers enjoyed the challenge of rigging up a system capable of real, not just simulated, automated trading. They worked out, for example, how to "screen scrape" (interviewee BW)—that is, to divert the incoming stream of binary digits that drove an Instinet terminal's screen directly to an ATD computer that decoded and processed it. These programmers did not simply write code. "There were days," says a former ATD programmer, "when I was on a ladder running cable through the ceiling. There were days where I was splicing cables." The buildings in Charleston in which they had offices were, he told me, often rundown.

> The parking lot was sloped into the front door of the office space and so when it would rain the water would run underneath the door and so we had all of our tables, we would have to put the computers up on top of the tables because the water . . . We had . . . cockroaches.

In September 1989, just as ATD was beginning live trading, it was shut down for two weeks by Hurricane Hugo, a giant storm that made landfall just north of Charleston (Whitcomb 1989b). Yet, despite all these difficulties, and the unavoidable moments of stress, automated trading "was fun . . . unlike today":

> INTERVIEWEE: Now it's very much ultra-low latency [extreme speed] and math. Back then, it was more just the act of doing the trade was so difficult. . . . It was . . . figuring out how to not have rooms full of traders and automate as much as possible, and that involved . . . I don't want to use the word "hacking" because that's negative but just . . .
>
> AUTHOR: The original meaning of "hacking" wasn't negative [see below].
>
> INTERVIEWEE: Yes, it was us hacking around, not breaking into things but just trying to reverse engineer a lot of things that were going on and figuring out how to take advantage of it.

In ATD's first live trading test, in September 1989, Whitcomb's model, incorporating futures prices and the other variables discussed above, displayed predictive capacity. As Whitcomb reported to ATD's shareholders, the model "was not perfect," and ATD "did some fine tuning while we were trading," but in ATD's experiment its system still earned gross trading revenues of around 2.5 cents per share traded (Whitcomb 1989b). To use Instinet, however, ATD had to pay it commissions of around 4.5 cents per share. A portion of those commissions was then returned to ATD as a soft-dollar reimbursement. (Although Instinet was designed to allow investment-management firms to trade cheaply with each other, it seems to have found that it too had to offer those firms soft-dollar incentives to do so.) However, the hedge fund sponsoring the trading experiment required ATD to pass Instinet's soft-dollar payments to it (Whitcomb 1989b), so ATD was trading at a net loss.

ATD had, of course, been aware of Instinet's commission rates. A problem it had underestimated, though, resulted from Instinet's decision in the early 1980s, in the face of only modest amounts of trading by investment-management firms, to grant access to its system to dealers as well as to institutional investors.[9] That decision allowed Instinet to finally become a commercial success, because it solved a practical problem for Nasdaq's dealers. With spreads of 25 cents between the prices at which dealers would sell shares to clients and buy shares from them, they could readily make money, but often at the cost of taking on potentially risky trading positions. Instinet offered dealers a way to reduce or eliminate those positions by trading electronically with each other, and Nasdaq's dealers embraced the system as a convenient mechanism for doing so.

The problem for ATD seems to have been that Nasdaq dealers' central role in the trading of Nasdaq-listed shares meant that they possessed information (about large deals they had just done with clients, for example, or perhaps about their clients' intended trading) that could not be deduced from an Instinet screen. As Whitcomb told ATD's shareholders, "broker-dealers are always active in the market and possess the most current 'fundamental' information and orderflow information for the stocks they trade." Instinet's own traders (who acted for firms not prepared to use its system directly) told ATD that it was getting "bagged": dealers would buy from ATD when they had information that meant prices were likely to rise, and sell to it when they expected prices to fall (Whitcomb 1989b). In effect, dealers' central role in trading gave their human traders predictive capacities that, at crucial moments, were greater than those of ATD's algorithms.

For its next trading experiment, conducted in April and May of 1990, ATD shifted to what was then still the core of US share trading, the New York Stock Exchange. As already mentioned, ATD could trade on the NYSE only via a member firm, and these firms' usual commissions—which in the late 1980s averaged nearly 7 cents per share traded (Berkowitz, Logue, and Noser 1988: 104)—would have rendered it impossible for ATD to trade profitably. However, Whitcomb found an NYSE member, a major investment bank (which, again, he prefers not to name), that had an internal trading group that also used predictive models in share trading—albeit with a much longer time horizon than ATD's—and therefore understood immediately that because ATD's trading was automated, the bank would not have to provide it with many of the services that most clients needed. In light of this difference, ATD was able to negotiate specially reduced commissions of only 3 cents per share. The investment bank also provided high-speed modems, set up two dedicated telephone lines between ATD's Charleston office and the bank's Manhattan headquarters, and allowed ATD's electronic orders to flow from there through its high-speed connection to the specialists' booths in the NYSE's trading rooms. During the test, ATD traded 3.2 million shares, and its model again showed predictive power: the firm's gross trading profit averaged 1.9 cents per share (Whitcomb 1990). That, however, was less than the commissions it was paying the bank. Again, ATD was trading at a loss.

The investment bank, though, knew that it could itself trade at a cost much lower than even the reduced commissions it charged ATD. It therefore proposed to ATD an arrangement in which ATD would pay only an estimate of the bank's actual costs of trading (around 1.4 cents per share), while the bank would keep the bulk of ATD's profits, on a sliding scale that equated to a roughly 75:25 split between it and ATD (Whitcomb 1990). This arrangement allowed ATD finally to begin trading profitably, and it secured—at least temporarily—the firm's survival.

What is in retrospect most striking about the arrangement with the investment bank is that Whitcomb viewed it as equitable. It "was a very fair and honorable deal," he says. "I have only praise for [the investment bank]" (interview 2). That there were set socioeconomic roles in financial markets—that not everyone could trade as they wished, and that they might have to pay what, if they traded on any large scale, would be substantial sums to the occupants of the relevant role (an NYSE member, an official Nasdaq dealer, and so on) in order to trade—was simply the taken-for-granted reality of everyday life in those markets. That reality, however, was about to be challenged. A tiny breach had opened up in this fixed-role system.[10]

"Among the despised"

The breach was in Nasdaq, and it was created, quite inadvertently, by the stock-market regulator, the SEC. During the October 1987 stock-market crash, many Nasdaq dealers, fearing continuing precipitous price drops, stopped processing sell orders (mostly originating from individual investors) sent to them via SOES, Nasdaq's automated Small Order Execution System. The dealers thus in effect refused to honor their on-screen bids to buy shares. After the crash, the SEC successfully pressured the National Association of Securities Dealers to make it obligatory for its members to fill SOES orders at the prices they were displaying on Nasdaq's screens (Ingebretsen 2002: 99–100).

That ruling opened the breach. If a dealer's employees were not monitoring Nasdaq's screens attentively enough, they might not alter their price quotations fast enough as market conditions changed. Traders who were paying closer attention could then use SOES to send orders (which a dealer now *had* to fill) that "picked off" these stale quotes, for example by buying shares at a price that the market-maker had not yet increased as prices rose.[11] Growing numbers of semiprofessional traders (whom Nasdaq dealers called "SOES bandits") seized these opportunities, in effect renting Nasdaq screens and SOES access from day-trading firms that had succeeded in becoming NASD members. (Day trading referred to the short time horizons involved: the goal of trading was to close a position quickly and profitably, not to hold shares for any length of time and certainly not overnight.)[12]

By the mid-1990s, there were more than two thousand such "bandit" traders (Harris and Schultz 1998: 41), many of them based in crowded, frequently improvised trading rooms, often in rundown buildings in lower Manhattan. At least stereotypically—no demographic data are available—they were often "city college kids from the backwaters of Staten Island, Queens, and the Bronx, the ones who didn't stand a chance at a big bank like Goldman or Morgan" (Patterson 2012: 100). Visiting the offices of the new electronic trading venue Island, on the sixth floor of 50 Broad Street, with its "cramped halls and stained ceiling tiles" (Brekke 1999), two *Forbes* journalists were also taken into second-floor rooms occupied by a day-trading brokerage. They walked "through a sparsely furnished office suite" into "a dimly lit, makeshift trading room."

> There, from 9:30 a.m. to 4 p.m. each weekday, sit 50 people all males eyes firmly attached to monitors. The players are mostly under 30, wearing T shirts, blue jeans and baseball caps. They talk to one another even as they pound on the keyboards. More often they just stare intently or blurt insults at the screens (Schifrin and McCormack 1998).

One leading figure in SOES banditry reportedly patrolled his firm's trading room, sometimes bellowing, "FUCK 'EM. FUCK DA BASTAHDS" (Patterson 2012: 101), the "bastahds" being Nasdaq's dealers. Although SOES banditry could be very profitable, bandits could also incur gut-wrenching losses: "No one blinked when a chalk-faced guy doubled over a garbage pail and puked violently, never leaving his seat and trading right through the puke" (Patterson 2012: 113).

SOES gave these bandit outsiders a direct route into the heart of a major fixed-role market. The occupants of its privileged roles—Nasdaq's dealers, especially the registered Nasdaq market-makers—tried everything they could to seal the breach. They tried to bar access to SOES by "professional" traders; they tried to get the SEC's permission to replace SOES with a new system without compulsory execution of trades; death threats were even made to individual bandits. "They hated us," says interviewee BW.[13] Nothing worked. For example, the SEC was persuaded to adopt a rule denying access to SOES by traders deemed to be professionals, but a number of such traders contested the ban, and in 1993 it was overturned by the US Court of Appeals for the District of Columbia Circuit, on the grounds that the rule's definition of professional trader was too vague.[14]

The initial profitability of Automated Trading Desk's successful early 1990s NYSE trading had shrunk rapidly. In 1994, "we . . . made practically no money," Whitcomb told ATD's shareholders (Whitcomb 1995). He realized that "we needed a completely different act" (interview 2). An acquaintance of his, a professor of accounting, had a former student who had become a SOES bandit. ATD formed a joint venture with the professor and the trader, seeking to develop what Whitcomb calls "an automated SOES bandit system" (Whitcomb interview 2; in his letters to ATD's shareholders, Whitcomb used the more neutral term "SOES activist"). ATD's traders "just sat down" with bandits, watching what they did and asking them why they did it (interviewee BW).

It quickly became clear to ATD's traders that the bandits predicted price changes by carefully monitoring changes in the array of dealers' bids and offers (which were not anonymous) on Nasdaq's screens. If, for example, even a small number of dealers lowered their bids (and especially if they were dealers whose actions were regarded by bandits as likely to presage price movements in the stock in question), then the bandits would use SOES to sell as quickly as they could while the remaining dealers were still quoting unaltered bid prices. (Although Nasdaq had no equivalent of the NYSE's officially designated "specialist," it was common for a Nasdaq-listed stock to have what was informally acknowledged to be a leading dealer, known variously as "the name," "the ax," or "the ball"; see Morgenson 1993.) As interviewee BW tells it, "[T]hey'd [the bandits] be like, 'two . . . people [dealers] left [lowered their bids]' or 'Goldman [Sachs] leads in this stock, and when Goldman leaves, everybody leaves, so I saw Goldman leave [lower its bid], so I hit it [i.e., sold the stock]'."[15]

ATD automated the bandits' predictive reasoning. "Our computer scans the NASDAQ digital data feed for several hundred stocks," Whitcomb told ATD's shareholders in January 1995, "watching for indications that the [dealers] in a stock are about to 'fade their quotes' on one side [i.e., either bids or offers]." Despite the distance between ATD's offices (which had by then moved to Mount Pleasant, South Carolina) and Nasdaq's computer center in Trumbull, Connecticut, ATD's automated SOES bandit proved faster than the human beings whose predictive reasoning it mimicked. "What we were competing against [was] the . . . SOES guys," says BW. "Goldman leaves the offer, there would quickly be a thousand people trying to hit the offer [i.e. buy shares] . . . most of them . . . 'point and click' [manual traders]." HFT was still nascent in the mid-1990s, and in my interviewing I have found only one other firm which at that time operated an automated SOES system akin to ATD's (I was told about it by interviewee AG), so ATD did not face much in the way of computerized competition.

The pocket of predictive structure in the fluctuations of share prices that the human and automated SOES bandits seem to have exploited successfully was created by the sociotechnical organization of Nasdaq. As noted, only an authorized NASD member firm that had registered as a market-maker in the stock in question could post bids and offers on Nasdaq's screens. Those bids and offers were therefore limited in number and, because of the need to telephone the market-making firm in order to trade on any large scale, not anonymous. The most likely reason that monitoring these on-screen bids and offers enabled the bandits to predict price movements was the issue that ATD had already discovered in its trading on Instinet. At least the bigger dealers—and certainly the "name" or "ax"—did not simply make markets (post bids and offers) but also handled large orders from institutional investors (Smith, Selway, and McCormick 1998: 34). If, for example, a dealer was in the process of executing a large sell order, or had learned that such an order was either being executed or was about to be executed, then it would lower its bid prices to avoid buying shares at a price that was likely to fall. In effect, Nasdaq's arrays of nonanonymous on-screen bids and offers thus broadcast, to anyone prepared to monitor them attentively, dealers' private information. This is the same information that had been the undoing of ATD's trading on Instinet, on which, unlike trading on Nasdaq itself, the bids and offers that ATD's systems could see were both anonymous and much sparser, and therefore less rich in information.

Being "among the despised" SOES bandits, as Whitcomb puts it (interview 2), was sometimes uncomfortable for ATD: "We knew—or we felt—that

TABLE 3.1. Staff roles at Automated Trading Desk, early 2000s

Senior management	6	9%
Administration/compliance/marketing	17	25%
Technical	29	43%
Quantitative analysis	2	3%
Trading	5	7%
Mixed roles including trading	9	13%
	68	

Source: Staff list in interviewee BT's files, exact date unknown. Mixed roles include,
e.g., trading/research and trader & modeler.

NASD would like nothing better than to shut down a SOES bandit firm for a violation." Whitcomb helped set up an Electronic Traders Association to make the case to the SEC and Congress that "SOES bandits were not doing anything evil or dishonest, and might even be performing a service by putting some pressure on spreads," in other words reducing the extent to which the price of the lowest offer to sell shares exceeded that of the highest bid to buy them (Whitcomb interview 3). But making SOES banditry respectable was not easy. On one occasion, Whitcomb watched, horrified, as a leading bandit "in effect threatened . . . physically" a top NASD official. "He made moves toward him while using exceedingly profane language" (interview 2).

Automated "SOES banditry" was, however, crucial to ATD's survival in the mid-1990s: "It saved us," says Whitcomb (interview 3), permitting the firm to grow eventually to around 70 employees (see table 3.1). It was perfectly possible sometimes to make a profit of 25 cents per share traded. "You just made, whatever, $250 off of them [a dealer]," on the maximum size of a SOES order, for 1,000 shares, interviewee BW told me. But the mere survival of an HFT firm, in the stigmatized periphery of the US financial markets, could not transform those markets. That transformation began with a quite different development, albeit one that also had its roots in SOES banditry.

"Island is here!"

While bandits used SOES to create their trading positions, they could not, unless they were very lucky, use it to profitably close those positions (Harris and Schultz 1998). To do so, they typically had to use, via their brokerages, either Instinet, which was not cheap (and which, says interviewee AF, "was very particular about not giving access to pure day-trading firms") or

SelectNet, a screen-based system set up by Nasdaq for its dealers to trade with each other without paying fees to Instinet. SelectNet was not anonymous, so a SOES-bandit brokerage that was trying to trade on it was identifiable. "They knew it was you," says interviewee BW. Nor was it compulsory for dealers to honor the prices they had posted on SelectNet.

There was, therefore, an opportunity to create trading venues specifically to cater to the needs of bandits and other day traders, especially to facilitate the unwinding of the trading positions that those traders had created by using SOES. The first and most influential such venue was the one with which this book begins: Island, a start-up based in the Broad Street offices of Datek, a Nasdaq brokerage that had many SOES-bandit traders and clients. As Josh Levine, Island's original software architect and programmer, told me, the first version of Island, launched in February 1996, "was, like most code [computer programs] in the world, more evolved than designed" (email to author, May 21, 2012).[16]

Island's two founders were Levine (who, after having "[d]ropped out and/or failed out" of an electrical-engineering degree program at Carnegie Mellon University, was earning his living writing software for the finance sector in New York) and Jeffrey Citron, originally hired by Datek as a clerk.[17] Once there, Citron began to trade, eventually striking out on his own and recruiting Levine to a number of joint ventures, several of which involved the development of software to aid traders such as those working for or trading via firms like Datek. Both Citron and Levine retained close links to Datek, with Levine remaining based in the firm's 50 Broad Street office.

Levine built a series of systems that helped Datek's clients and similar traders make money buying and selling Nasdaq stocks. Watcher, the system from which Island was born, began "as just a program to watch for incoming executions and keep track of a trader's position," but Levine gradually added further features that turned it into a full-blown trading system that gave traders market news and up-to-date information on Nasdaq dealers' changing bids and offers, permitted traders to enter orders, and allowed them to send messages either to other individual users or to all the traders using Watcher (email from Levine, January 27, 2012; anon. n.d.; anon. 1995–97: June 15, 1995). As Patterson (2012: 90) notes, Levine's Watcher, designed as it was by a programmer who knew traders' practices and priorities intimately, far outperformed Nasdaq's clunky proprietary terminals, helping Datek become preeminent among lower Manhattan's bandits.

Thoroughly immersed as they were in the world of the traders who used Watcher, Citron and Levine knew that it was common for one Watcher user to want to sell shares at a given price and another to want to buy them at that price, but to be unable to do so via Nasdaq. So they added a facility to Watcher (Customer to Customer Jump trades) that allowed users to entirely circumvent Nasdaq and trade directly with each other. "It worked like this," says Levine:

1) You and me are sitting next to each other. I hear you mutter that you are upset that you can[not] sell the 100 shares of INTC [Intel Corporation] that you are currently long.
2) I am actually trying to buy INTC right now, so I say to you "Hey, I'll buy those 100 INTC from you [for] $125/share."
3) You want to sell your INTC, so you agree to do the trade.
4) I enter a Jump Trade into my Watcher and we both instantly see our positions and P&L [profit and loss] updated—yours to reflect selling 100 INTC and mine to reflect buying 100 INTC. (email to author from Levine, May 21, 2012)

That way of proceeding, however, depended on random, one-to-one interactions. Island broadened the scope of trading of this kind, although initially just to Watcher users at large. "The idea . . . was just simply an 'island' where investors could meet directly," as Island's former chief executive Matt Andresen told me, instead of having to go through the intermediation of Nasdaq's dealers (Andresen interview). "Island is here!" Levine told users of Watcher on February 16, 1996. "If you put up 1000 shares ZXYZ at 22 3/8 [$22.375] and someone else enters an Island order to buy 500 at 22 3/8," then that buy order would be executed automatically. Correspondingly, he continued,

if you see 4000 shares for ZXYZ for sale at 22 ½ on Island and you want to buy stock at 22 ½. . . . You would press <Shift 2> to enter an order to buy 1000 shares (2 lots of 500). . . . Want to buy 2000 shares? Just press <Shift 2> twice. Fun. (anon. 1995–97: February 16, 1996)

As was typical in the world of SOES banditry, the physical setting of Island was unprepossessing. To interviewee RH, a regulator who visited 50 Broad Street, Island's offices resembled "a frat house. . . . guys in T-shirts and no shoes." The offices were untidy, with "wires hanging down from the ceiling" (interviewee RH), "piles of garbage" (interviewee AQ), a "pile of trash, pizza boxes, and things like that" (interviewee RH), a computer-controlled milling machine (no help in trading, but Levine wanted to use it to make a jewelry box for his wife, said interviewee AN), and—vivid in the memory of several interviewees—an improvised turtle tank constructed from a toddler's paddling pool. "[T]hey stunk" (interviewee BW), at least "if you didn't clean the filter with . . . appropriate regularity. That was one of your jobs . . . if you worked there" (interviewee AF).

Island's computer room, in the basement of 50 Broad Street, had a similarly makeshift appearance, with "big temporary fans" used to try to cool all the machines packed into it, and what interviewee AX described as thousands of "very inexpensive Dell . . . very thin desktop PCs that we bought and turned them on their sides and put them on bakers' racks" (In Island's computer room, these PCs of course did not have their normal screens and keyboards). When two newly recruited Island programmers first saw its system—"so radically different from anything I'd seen before," says one of them—"we didn't think it would work, except that it was up and running, so clearly it worked" (interviewee AN).

The improvised look of Island's computer system belied its systematic, innovative design. "[T]hey knew what they were doing technically," concedes RH, the regulator who had thought Island's offices resembled a frat house. Writing software for earlier systems to support electronic trading had usually involved a division of labor. Says interviewee AN, "You'd write a spec [a specification of what the system was supposed to do] and you'd hand it to your consultant," typically a software-development team at a business consultancy firm, where the software would be written by programmers without firsthand experience of what the business domain was. That was a time-consuming and expensive process, and though the resultant system usually worked, it was typically neither elegant nor efficient.

Island's system, in contrast, had both been conceived and most of its original core software written by just one person, Josh Levine. His approach was captured by Steven Levy's description in *Hackers* (Levy 1984), even though the programmers Levy discusses were from an earlier generation. Hackers, as the term was originally used, were not necessarily people who broke into computer systems, but rather programmers who saw themselves as part of an informal but identifiable subculture, with a loosely related set of beliefs and preferences: distrust of authority, bureaucracy, and centralization; disdain for organizational rank; support for freedom of information and for ready, widely available, hands-on access to computer systems; and, perhaps above all, a distinctive programmer's aesthetic. Hackers prized efficiency, in the form of succinct, elegant programs that ran fast and minimized their demands on computer hardware, and they prized it not simply for practical reasons but because, as Levy puts it, "[t]he code of a program held a beauty of its own." What mattered to hackers was the respect of their programming peers, which came not from extraneous matters such as formal credentials or wealth, but from being known for having written programs of that kind, programs with "the fewest lines [of code]," put together "so artfully that the author's peers would look at it and almost melt with awe" (Levy 1984: 30–31).

Money-making commercial enterprise that it was, Island (and especially Josh Levine) nevertheless exemplified, at least to a degree, what Matt Andresen referred to in an interview with me as the "hacker ethos" (the term used in Levy 1984 is the "hacker ethic")—including the aesthetic preference for thoughtfully succinct, efficient code.[18] What is most striking about the system that Levine designed for Island is that its efficiency and speed were far greater than required for the immediate practical purpose of allowing "bandit" traders to trade directly with each other. As noted in chapter 1, the core of Island's system, its matching engine, could execute a trade in a couple of milliseconds (thousandths of a second). Given that the lower threshold of the human perception of time is at least 100 milliseconds (Canales 2009), Island's matching engine could have been many times slower than it was and still satisfied traders' needs.

The speed of Island's system did not come from expensive, specialized, ultrafast hardware. "Josh was like, 'No, no, no, I don't want any piece of hardware that costs more than four grand'" says Andresen. Rather, what made Island's system fast was the way its software ran on the inexpensive, standard hardware from which the system was built. Levine, and the other programmers who joined Island (and, for example, rewrote its matching engine) were sharply aware of computing's materiality, especially the materiality of computer memory. They were aware, for example, of the huge differences in speed of access to cache (in the sense of memory that's physically part of the silicon of a processor chip), main memory (implemented in silicon, but separate from the processor chip), and long-term storage, typically implemented on a hard disk. Depositing data on or retrieving it from a hard disk took—and still takes—milliseconds; even with the technology of the mid-1990s, use of cache was many orders of magnitude faster than that.[19]

The programmer AX, who described to me the thousands of "cheap . . . simple" PCs packed into the basement of 50 Broad Street, told me that "[n]one of those machines ever touched their hard drive," meaning that the way Island's system was programmed, its component machines would seldom if ever have to access their slow hard disks. What, above all, made this possible was a radical departure from previous practice in matching-engine design. Matching engines up till then had been designed to ensure what interviewee AF calls "transactional integrity," by not executing or even acknowledging an incoming order until an exchange's computer system had recorded it, usually in a relational database on a hard disk or some other form of permanent memory. This approach, perhaps natural for software designers working for large, bureaucratic organizations, meant that matching engines were constantly having to pause for "two-phase commits"[20] to check that changes in the order book were being correctly recorded in permanent memory. Island's matching engine did not do this. As interviewee AN puts it, "The [Island] matching engine . . . broadcasts out its messages in a stream that everyone [all other relevant system components] reads." Order-book changes were thus stored "simultaneously (or in-parallel) in memory on multiple machines [with] geographic diversity" (interviewee AF).

The heart of Island's matching engine was an algorithm called the "enter-2order" procedure, which Levine wrote in FoxPro, a programming language for database management developed by Fox Software. Levine found a simple way of speeding up the matching process, an artful, efficient piece of code that possessed Levy's "beauty of its own." In Levine's later paraphrase, what the "enter2order" procedure did when the Island system received a new order was to

> see if there was a record from a recently canceled order that we can reuse for this new order. This is hugely important because that record will likely still be in the cache and using it will be *much* faster than making a new one. (Levine n.d.)

After generating a sequence number and time stamp for the new order, the algorithm then checked whether the order could potentially be filled by matching it with orders already in the book. If so:

> Start matching! Starting at the top of the book [if the new order was, e.g., an order to sell, the "top of the book" is the existing buy orders with the highest price] until we either run out of shares or orders to match against. (Levine n.d.)

Levine also developed two succinct, efficient computer protocols that are now widely used in the fastest forms of automated trading: Ouch, via which bids, offers, and cancellations of orders are encoded for fast, automatic processing by a matching engine; and Itch, which disseminates anonymized versions of these bids, offers, and cancellations in a continuous stream that allows computers to continuously synthesize their own mirrors of the order book, rather than having to wait for periodic updates to that book.

"Money started to fall from the sky"

For all of Island's speed and sophistication, its origins in the world of SOES bandits caused it to be viewed initially as disreputable. Island employees, for example, were told "never, ever [to] mention . . . who was a client of Island . . . people did not want it to be known that they were trading on Island," says interviewee BW. Automated Trading Desk had no such preju-dice, and quickly saw how well suited the new venue was to algorithmic trading. It became the first outside firm to trade on Island, and soon became a heavy user, boosting Island's trading volumes and thus its attractiveness as a trading venue. Island initially had a daily limit of 999,999 orders per connection. The scale of ATD's activity on Island was brought home to interviewee BT one day when he realized that ATD was about to overrun that limit—"I was like, oh crap"—but fortunately had another connection available to him.

Island's speed and computer-friendly design helped attract not just ATD but, before long, other nascent HFT firms as well. Culturally, the fit was close. The young, tech-savvy people—again, mostly men—who ran Island (and the other electronic-communication networks, or ECNs, that were cre-ated to trade shares in the late 1990s) looked like those who staffed the new HFT firms; indeed, employees circulated between Island and those firms. Another crucial reason why Island was an ideal venue for high-frequency trading was that, being fully automated and requiring only a handful of employees to run it, it was able to charge unprecedentedly low fees: a quar-ter of a cent per share traded (Biais, Bisière, and Spatt 2003: 6), less than a tenth of the level of fees that had made the profitability of ATD's Instinet and NYSE trading so precarious. In addition, Island was among the first trading venues to make payments called rebates—in Island's case, a tenth of a cent per share—to firms or traders that "provided liquidity," that is, that entered into their order books bids or offers that were subsequently executed against. Rebates (which later became pervasive in US share trad-ing) encouraged ATD and other HFT firms to act as automated market-makers (see chapter 6); in other words, ATD and other HFT firms could continuously keep both attractively priced offers and slightly lower-priced bids in Island's order book, constantly changing their prices (by cancel-ing existing orders and submitting new ones) as market conditions shifted. Island's speed reduced the risks inherent in doing this. "[Every] millisecond I don't know something, is a millisecond of risk," says interviewee AJ, and a fast matching engine, fast dissemination of data on order-book changes, and fast processing of orders and, especially, cancellations of orders all helped make market-making less risky.

There was a sharp contrast between Island and the New York Stock Exchange in terms of the feasibility of automated market-making by a firm such as ATD. Attempting that activity on the NYSE in the 1990s was very difficult, reports interviewee BT. Accessing the NYSE involved paying high fees and receiving no rebates, and (as already noted) traders other than its "specialists" could obtain only partial information about the contents of its order books. Although the execution of trades on the NYSE became more automatic over time (Hendershott and Moulton 2011), it was still common in the 1990s for a specialist to have to authorize them, for example by pressing "Enter" on his computer terminal (interviewees XM and GG). Acknowl-edgment of cancellations of orders—crucial in preventing a market-making algorithm's price quotes from going stale—was often delayed on the NYSE for several potentially vital seconds, says BT. When trading was intense, data from the NYSE reflecting changes in the best bid and offer prices, which were input manually by the specialists' clerks, could lag behind trading by as much as 30 seconds.[21]

Island, though, was not in direct competition with the NYSE. It, like most of the other new electronic share-trading venues that followed it (as noted above, these became collectively known as electronic communica-tions networks, or ECNs), was wary of trading NYSE-listed shares, fear-ing being forced by the SEC to use the slow Intermarket Trading System. (The Chicago-based ECN Archipelago did trade NYSE stocks, and used the Intermarket Trading System, but found it hard and frustrating. Archi-pelago frequently lodged complaints that specialists on the NYSE and other exchanges were breaking that system's rules, and, reports interviewee EZ, even developed a computer program, "The Whiner," that automated these complaints.)

Instead, Island and the other ECNs at first traded mainly Nasdaq-listed shares. The late 1990s and early 2000s were the years of boom, crash, and plentiful trading of dot-com stocks, and Nasdaq was where most dot-com companies were listed. An apparent small technicality helped Island and the other ECNs seize an ever-increasing share of the high volumes of trad-ing of these dot-com and other Nasdaq stocks. While Nasdaq's prices were denominated in eighths of a dollar (reduced, in the late 1990s, to sixteenths of a dollar), the ECNs operated with a finer price grid. Island's minimum price increment, for example, was 1/256th of a dollar, meaning that it was possible for HFT firms to post bids and offers on Island at prices marginally better than those of Nasdaq's dealers, thus undercutting them, while still earning healthy profits. By March 2000, ECNs had captured 26 percent of the dollar volume of the trading of Nasdaq-listed shares; just over a year later (June 2001), that had risen to 37 percent (Biais et al. 2003: 6).

ECNs, especially Island, prospered in good part because, for the reasons discussed above, they attracted HFT. In its turn, HFT gained shape and gathered momentum in trading on Island and other ECNs. As sketched in chapter 1, among the HFT practices introduced on Island was co-location, with Island encouraging trading firms to place their servers in its Broad Street building, even in the basement alongside Island's computer system. When Island began operations in 1996, only one of the main classes of HFT signal listed in table 3.2 below ("futures lead") was fully available to HFT algorithms; Island's order book was visible to them, but it initially formed only a small portion of the market for Nasdaq shares; and there was as yet only limited fragmentation of trading across different trading venues.

"Futures lead," however, was enough to make HFT on Island highly profitable. An example of one among the wave of HFT firms launched at the end of the 1990s was a firm mentioned in chapter 1, Tradebot, created in October 1999 by Dave Cummings, a computer-science and electrical-engineering graduate who had traded in the open-outcry pits of the Kansas City Board of Trade. As Cummings writes in his autobiography, when Tradebot began to trade shares, "Our initial stock trading models were primitive. We tried lots of new ideas. Many of them did not work. It was hit or miss" (Cummings 2016: 42). What transformed Tradebot's fortunes was discovering—independently, says Cummings; no one told the firm this—that price changes in the ES (the Chicago Mercantile Exchange's electronically traded S&P 500 share-index future) normally preceded similar changes in the SPY, the corresponding exchange-traded fund, which was among the shares traded on Island:

> We noticed that a move in the ES would usually cause a similar move in the SPY a fraction of a second later. While it was only a fraction of a second, the lead-lag relationship was visible to the naked eye on our charts. . . . We placed bids and offers on Island in SPY based on prices in ES. When ES went up, we raised our bid. When ES dropped, we lowered our offer. . . . At first, our new SPY trade was like shooting fish in a barrel. Money started to fall from the sky. It was amazing. Our trading volume started to climb quickly. (Cummings 2016: 43)

The Chicago Mercantile Exchange had also begun to trade a new share-index future, the NQ, which tracks the Nasdaq-100 index of shares. Just as

Tradebot had discovered with the ES and the SPY, changes in the market for the NQ were, as described in chapter 2, a hugely useful signal for trading Nasdaq shares, and especially for market-making on Island in the QQQ, an exchange-traded fund, very popular in the dot-com years, that also tracks the Nasdaq-100.

The "Hinge"

A "hinge," as described in chapter 1, is the sociologist Andrew Abbott's term for a process that creates rewards in more than one sphere of activity. The mutually reinforcing relationship between HFT and new share-trading venues such as Island was the precursor of a broader hinge that linked—and still links—the development of exchanges and the growth of HFT. The original core process was this: profits earned on Island helped the new HFT firms grow, providing capital that enabled them to expand into other markets. Simultaneously, the liquidity (plentiful trading, along with plentiful, attractively priced bids and offers in order books) that HFT firms provided helped Island, and soon the other ECNs as well, command an ever-larger proportion of the trading of Nasdaq-listed shares and of exchange-traded funds such as the SPY and QQQ. HFT firms could boost volumes of trading on venues with HFT-friendly features because, as interviewee AF puts it, they "could operate on very, very, very slim margins" compared to "banks and others whose costs were higher. There were trades that were profitable for the HFT firms to do [that] would've been unprofitable for banks to do." As interviewee DB, who moved from an ECN to an HFT firm, says:

> [I]t was the same [HFT] firms who were the big customers of Island and [other ECNs], and they all had the same wants and desires out of an electronic trading system . . . that's why . . . you start to see market structure coalesce around . . . low latency [i.e., fast speed], pricing tiers [lower fees for firms trading large volumes of shares], very similar [technical] functionality, because the same principal actors [HFT firms] who were feeding the same list of desires to exchanges globally and they all say, "If you do A, B, C to X, Y, Z, I will be able to do more business on your platform."

By the early 2000s, this process began to affect even long-established exchanges such as the New York Stock Exchange, and, as we will see below, it became manifest in Europe too, albeit a few years later than in the US. There is a sense, too, in which the "hinge" extended even into the domain of government regulation. Although in the 1970s the Securities and Exchange Commission had backed away from a decisive challenge to established exchanges such as the NYSE, the SEC's appetite for reform, especially for measures to enhance competition among trading venues, never evaporated completely. It was revived in the 1990s by accusations that it was common for Nasdaq dealers to engage in malpractice that hurt both individual and institutional investors. In 1993, Gretchen Morgenson, then a young reporter for *Forbes* magazine—she was later to become one of America's leading financial journalists—published a scathing exposé suggesting, among other things, that Nasdaq dealers sometimes "front ran" clients' orders (for example, buying on their own account before executing a client's buy order), and sometimes disguised this by deliberately delaying confirmation reports to their clients (Morgenson 1993).

A year later, economists William Christie and Paul Schultz (1994) confirmed what was perhaps Morgenson's most easily testable accusation: that Nasdaq dealers systematically avoided odd-eighths price quotations. That finding, smacking as it did of insiders boosting their profits by cartel-like behavior, was widely reported in the press, with catastrophic results for Nasdaq dealers' reputations. The dealers' use of odd-eighth quotes increased sharply—literally overnight, following the first press reports of Christie and Schultz's findings on May 26, 1994 (Christie, Harris, and Schultz 1994)—but it was too late. The result was class-action litigation against the dealers—settled (without admission of wrongdoing) in December 1997 for a reported $910 million, at that point the largest civil antitrust settlement in history (Ingebretsen 2002: 153)—and sharply focused SEC attention on Nasdaq.

Facilitating, at least de facto, the rise of the ECNs was a straightforward way for the SEC to reduce Nasdaq dealers' structural advantages in trading. The SEC's 1996 order-handling rules—along with, according to interviewee RZ, the efforts of a former SEC official who had moved to a senior role in the National Association of Securities Dealers—opened up Nasdaq's screens to the new electronic trading venues, allowing them to post their best bid and offer prices alongside those of Nasdaq's dealers. The SEC's 1998 Regulation ATS [Alternative Trading Systems] made it easier to set up new trading venues (Castelle, Millo, Beunza, and Lubin 2016). The SEC also moved US share trading as a whole some of the way toward Island's fine price grid, in 2000–1, reducing the minimum price increment in US share trading from a sixteenth of a dollar to one cent, a process that market participants called "decimalization."

At least equally important, however, to the rise of new HFT-friendly electronic trading venues were the long-term effects of much earlier events:

the 1960s' "paperwork crisis" and the resultant pressure from Congress for reform of the processes of clearing and settlement. These processes were, and remain, crucial material underpinnings of share trading, in that they involve the registration and guaranteeing of trades, the transfer of the ownership of shares, and the corresponding cash payments (for which see Millo, Muniesa, Panourgias, and Scott 2005). As noted above, the 1975 Securities Acts Amendments mandated not just a "national market system" of integrated trading—which came about, as discussed earlier in this chapter, in only an attenuated form—but also a "national system for the clearance and settlement of securities transactions" (Securities Acts Amendments 1975: 139). The latter *was* created, with the exchanges' (and Nasdaq's) separate systems integrated into what was to become a single, centralized system, run by a single organization, the Depository Trust & Clearing Corporation.

Compared to the staunchly resisted centralization of the glamorous and profitable world of trading, the centralization of clearing and settlement—of "the dreary task of administering back offices" (Seligman 1982: 455)—provoked much less resistance. Back offices, after all, were where taken-for-granted clerical work, increasingly done by women, went on, and were perhaps also viewed as places in which money was spent rather than profits made. It most likely helped, too, that the most powerful exchange, the NYSE, was at the heart of the centralization of settlement, via its Central Certificate Service, created in 1968 to minimize the need to physically move stock certificates.[22] However, like the SEC's failure to see the value of having jurisdiction over pork bellies (see chapter 2), the exchanges' failure to resist the creation of a single, nationwide, readily accessible clearing and settlement system was consequential. Unlike, for example, in the sovereign bond market, discussed in chapter 4, clearing and settlement were not a fundamental barrier to the emergence of new share-trading venues such as Island, since with a single, centralized clearing and settlement system it was relatively straightforward to buy shares on an incumbent venue and sell them on a new venue, or vice versa.[23]

One final regulatory action decisively broadened the scope of the hinge linking HFT and trading venues. As already noted, during the rise of ECNs like Island in the late 1990s, the NYSE—and thus the trading of the shares of the blue-chip corporations that were listed on the NYSE—remained protected from competition from the new electronic venues by the requirement that if they wanted to trade NYSE-listed stock, those venues would have to keep pausing trading to wait for the result of a request-to-trade message sent via the slow Intermarket Trading System. In 2005, the SEC's Regulation

National Market System ("Reg NMS"), the current framework governing US share trading (SEC 2005), stripped the NYSE trading floor of the protection of the Intermarket Trading System. If a price quotation was available only from a human being on a trading floor, it was no longer in effect protected, and electronic trading need no longer pause while an order was routed to that human being.

Just as the ECNs ate into Nasdaq's share of the trading of Nasdaq-listed stocks, so the SEC's adoption of Reg NMS triggered an even more dramatic collapse of the NYSE's share of trading in NYSE-listed stocks. From 2005 to 2010 that share fell from 80 percent to just over 20 percent (Angel, Harris, and Spatt 2013: 20, figure 2.17). Nasdaq and the NYSE both reacted to the new danger they faced by buying the most threatening ECNs. Island's owner, Datek, had sold it to Mitt Romney's Bain Capital in 2000, which then in 2002 sold it on to Instinet, ending Island's independent existence but not the influence of the hinge it embodied or its ultrafast technology. By buying Instinet's US business in 2005, Nasdaq acquired that technology and in many ways reshaped itself to resemble its erstwhile most dangerous rival. Also in 2005, the NYSE bought Archipelago (the ECN that had taken the lead in trading NYSE-listed stocks). That acquisition brought trading volume that made up for some of the NYSE's loss of market share, and also technology that could be drawn on to reshape NYSE's systems, a process described to me by interviewee FB. The attitudes of established venues like Nasdaq and the NYSE toward HFT changed radically. In Automated Trading Desk's early years, recalls interviewee BT, "we were begging to get on systems," and meeting resistance. "New York: 'Oh, don't even come here.'" By the early 2000s, the established venues discovered that this stance was no longer tenable. They *needed* HFT firms to sustain and build their trading volumes in the face of competition from new venues such as Island. Again, BT: "[T]here came a point where they were begging to have us bring our volume to their systems. . . . New York: 'Oh, please come here.'"

Nasdaq's 2005 acquisition of Island, and the NYSE's of Archipelago, removed two formidable rivals to the incumbent trading venues, but other ECNs remained, keeping competition for market share alive. Most important in this respect was a new ECN launched in 2005, called BATS (Better Alternative Trading System). It represented a particularly close form of the hinge between HFT and trading venues. BATS was created by a team from Dave Cummings's Kansas City HFT firm, Tradebot, with capital supplied in part by another leading HFT firm and two brokerages that specialized in catering to HFT. Cummings says that he feared that the acquisitions of

TABLE 3.2. The main classes of signal used in HFT in US shares

1. Futures lead: changes in the market for share-index futures usually slightly precede changes in the market for the underlying shares.

2. Order-book dynamics: transactions in the shares being traded and other changes in the order book for those shares on the venue on which an algorithm is trading, e.g., changes in the balance of bids to buy and offers to sell.

3. Fragmentation: transactions in or changes in the order books for the same shares on different trading venues.

4. Related shares and other instruments: changes in the market for, e.g., shares whose price is correlated with that of the shares being traded.

Note: A signal is a data pattern that informs an algorithm's trading. A number of other classes of signal are in more specialized use, such as machine-readable corporate or macroeconomic news releases. There are many other sources of information used in trading, including automated analysis of social media "sentiment," satellite data on, e.g., oil-tanker movements, etc. (although such data are often more useful to trading firms with longer time horizons than those of HFT).

Island and Archipelago meant that what he calls the NYSE/Nasdaq "duopoly" was being rebuilt: "Competition was what had lowered our trading costs by over 90%. Were prices going back up?" (Cummings 2016: 90). Like Island a decade earlier, BATS offered low fees and fast technology (the latter rivaling even Nasdaq's Island-inspired new system). In April 2013, interviewee EZ told me of constant pressure within BATS to speed up its matching engines: "It's . . . Board presentations, quarterly, in terms of how fast the matching engine [is]. Have we cracked the 200-microsecond [barrier]?"

The transformation of US share trading brought about by processes of this kind involved an expansion of the range of "signals" available to HFT algorithms (summarized in table 3.2). In particular, two of those classes of signal (fragmentation and order-book dynamics) can be seen as the outcomes of the conflicts discussed in this chapter, just as the first class of signal ("futures lead") was the outcome of the struggles discussed in chapter 2. The successful challenge mounted by Island and the other ECNs to the preexisting world of share trading meant that the same shares were now traded in meaningful amounts on multiple trading venues, making what happens on one of these venues a crucial signal for algorithms trading on other venues. There was nothing inevitable, though, about this outcome. If, for example, the CLOB (Consolidated Limited Order Book) had been successful, all US share trading would have taken place within a single order book, and "fragmentation" as a class of signal would simply not exist. That its existence in US share trading is contingent (and not, for example, a simple consequence of technological change) is also shown by the contrast between US share trading and US financial-futures trading. There is little fragmentation of the latter; it remains dominated by the Chicago Mercantile Exchange.

Simultaneously, the success of Island and of other venues organized around anonymous order books that were electronically visible to all participants created pressure on the incumbent share-trading venues to move toward that market structure. Island, for example, mounted a publicity campaign focused on the slogan "We'll show you our book. Why won't they?" (interviewee BW). From 2002 onward, the NYSE began to make its order books fully visible to those not on the trading floor, albeit at first only in aggregate form, rather than at the level of individual orders, and initially with updates only every 10 seconds, rather than in Island's continuous stream (Harris and Panchapagesan 2005: 26, 28, and 65). Also in 2002, Nasdaq (which traditionally did not have a fully centralized order book) introduced an electronic order book called "SuperMontage," and its old structure as a market organized around officially designated dealers disintegrated fast, to be replaced by a structure much more like that of Island and the other ECNs.

Visible, continuously updated, anonymous order books (with the generic format shown schematically in figure 1.5) gradually became standard across exchanges and ECNs, and the changes in their contents became a crucial signal for HFT algorithms.[24] If, for example, one side of the order book for a particular stock starts to "crumble" (if, e.g., bids at the best bid price are either executed against or canceled, and are not replaced at that price), that is an indication that prices are about to change. Similarly, if there is a bid or an offer that seems always to be replaced immediately whenever it is executed against, that might indicate that an execution algorithm is in the process of buying or selling on a large scale.

Indeed, exchanges (which, as mentioned in chapter 1, in the early 2000s nearly all demutualized—that is, abandoned their traditional status as member-owned organizations to become profit-seeking corporations, often publicly listed) soon came to see the datafeeds that enable trading firms' servers to mirror an exchange's order book as more than a necessary concession to HFT firms. In fact, those feeds became an increasingly important way of earning money from the HFTs and other traders. Exchanges can charge substantial amounts for both the feeds themselves and for cross-connects, the fiber-optic cables within an exchange's datacenter that link its systems to its users' systems and carry the data necessary to mirror the exchange's order book. (For an insightful economic model of aspects of the "hinge" such as this, see Budish, Lee, and Shim 2019.)

The "Hinge" in Europe

As in the United States, share trading in much of the rest of the world (the Far East, Australia, India, and Brazil, for example) has also been transformed by high-frequency trading, although not always as thoroughly as in the US. However, this book focuses on the US and to a lesser extent on Europe, where the transformation has been nearly as complete. The processes involved were also analogous, with a similar "hinge" at work in Europe too, and similar classes of signal becoming available to HFT algorithms.

High-frequency trading in European shares was initially unsuccessful. In the early 2000s, most European share trading took place either in a dealer-client market of the kind to be discussed in chapter 4 (in the case of European shares, the dealers were mainly London-based investment banks), or on so-called national champion exchanges such as the Paris Bourse and London Stock Exchange. Paris and London, despite their long histories of face-to-face trading, had already switched to electronic trading and had successfully warded off sporadic challenges from rival pre-HFT electronic trading venues (Muniesa 2003; Pardo-Guerra 2010 and 2019). The American HFT firm for which interviewees AF and BF both worked "had all the [exchange] memberships lined up," but—just as Automated Trading Desk had discovered in the US in the late 1980s—the firm found that "[o]ur exchange costs, our clearing costs . . . all these costs" were "way too high" for HFT market-making to be viable. Simply put, "It was too expensive for us to trade" [BF].

By the early 2000s, though, the early profitability of HFT in the US meant that the firms involved, while still limited in size, had more money and more personnel than ATD had had a decade earlier. AF and BF's firm devoted some of these resources to changing the aspects of the economic environment in Europe that were inhibiting HFT. BF proposed to Instinet, which had bought Island, that it create a new, pan-European ECN. That was much more difficult in Europe, which, unlike the US, with its one share-trading clearinghouse, had, and still has, multiple clearinghouses that process and guarantee share transactions. The established European clearinghouses, which often had close links to the existing exchanges, seem not to have been enthusiastic about a new ECN. Thus Instinet's new European ECN, Chi-X, which launched in April 2007, ended up having to persuade the Belgo-Dutch bank Fortis to set up an entirely new clearinghouse, called the European Multilateral Clearing Facility (EMCF), with much lower fees than the existing clearinghouses. Chi-X promised share trading that was, like Island's, "ten times faster, ten times cheaper" than on the established exchanges (interviewee EA). Chi-X's speed came mainly from its ultrafast matching engine, whose code was written by a former Island program-mer. In addition, the new trading venue had close links to Europe's emerging HFT sector: in January 2008, two HFT firms became shareholders in Chi-X (Instinet 2008). In October 2008, the American ECN BATS (which had, as noted above, been set up by the HFT firm Tradebot) launched a European arm similar to Chi-X, also initially with the EMCF as its clearer.

As in the US, these new European share-trading venues were facilitated—in Europe, largely inadvertently—by changes in regulation. Although there was widespread agreement among European Union (EU) policy makers and politicians that the capital-markets union project—the integration of national markets into a single EU-wide market—was, in the words of one of those politicians, "a flagship piece of work," there was persistent disagree-ment on how best to achieve it (described, e.g., by interviewees SC and II). The UK, "[s]upported by a bloc [including] the Netherlands . . . Ireland and . . . the Scandinavian countries" (SC), wanted to open share trading up to competition, while another bloc (usually headed by France, and including Spain, Italy, and sometimes Germany) wished to protect national-champion exchanges (see Quaglia 2010). The influence of the latter bloc can be seen, for example, in the EU's 1993 Investment Services Directive, which permitted member states to impose "concentration rules" that de facto required market participants to route orders only to national stock exchanges.

After "bitter and complex" negotiations and "fierce clashes between the incumbent stock exchange sector and the emergent brokerage/OTC [i.e., dealer-client] sector" (Moloney 2014: 438), the European Union's Markets in Financial Instruments Directive (MiFID I, as it is now known) was approved in 2004.[25] The clashes had not been over new ECN-like trading venues, none of which yet existed in Europe in 2004, but the new venues nevertheless ben-efitted from MiFID I. Just as Reg ATS had done in the US, MiFID I created a clear procedure for setting up an ECN-like "multilateral trading facility" or MTF, and the "best execution" requirement that MiFID I imposed on deal-ers made it more difficult for the latter to ignore the new venues when their prices were better than those on incumbent exchanges. Pressure—some commercial, some from Brussels policy makers—was brought to bear on Europe's other share-trading clearinghouses to "interoperate" electronically with the EMCF (interviewees EA and BF), and, just as in the US, a more integrated clearing system facilitated competition among trading venues. Above all, in the words of a senior figure in one of the new venues, "MiFID I broke the concentration rules. . . . BATS and Chi-X wouldn't be here prob-ably" if those rules had remained in place (interviewee GX).

The process, centered on Chi-X and BATS, that transformed European share trading did indeed closely resemble what had happened in the US five to ten years earlier. New, fast, cheap trading venues, with minimum increments of price usually smaller than those of the established venues, facilitated HFT, while HFT helped those venues grow. Initially, for example, Chi-X's share of European stock trading was a mere 1–2 percent. Then, data given by Chi-X to economist Albert Menkveld show, an HFT market-making firm began to trade on Chi-X; my interviews suggest that this was the US firm that previously had been forced to abandon trading European shares because it was too expensive and that had encouraged the establishment of Chi-X. Menkveld's data reveal that the prices of the bids and offers in Chi-X's order book improved quickly and dramatically—there was "a 50% drop in the bid-ask spread"—and Chi-X "jumped to a double-digit share" of the European market. By 2011, Chi-X had surpassed all the incumbent exchanges to become Europe's largest-volume share-trading venue (Menkveld 2013: 713–714).

Epilogue: ATD and the New World of HFT

Despite the huge changes in share trading in the US and elsewhere, money did not keep on falling from the sky on HFT firms in the way that it had when the "hinge" first clicked into place on Island. Automated Trading Desk's algorithmic "SOES bandit," and then its trading on Island and the other ECNs, earned healthy profits between 1995 and 2001. In the first quarter of 2001, for example, ATD traded around 55 million shares a day, and made an average profit of almost 0.9 cents per share (calculated from the figures reported to ATD's shareholders in Whitcomb 2001), around twenty times what my HFT interviewees regard as a welcome profit rate nowadays. ATD built a $35 million, hurricane-resistant headquarters (designed in modernist, campus-like style, with a reflecting pool and landscaping) in Mount Pleasant, South Carolina, choosing a postal address, 11 eWall Street, that ambitiously echoed that of the then still partially manual New York Stock Exchange. South Carolina's governor attended the new building's groundbreaking ceremony. When *The State* sent reporter Joe Collier to Mount Pleasant in 2002 to report on ATD, he was struck by the incongruously expensive cars parked in the strip mall in which ATD still had its base (it had not yet moved into its new offices). He met a 21-year-old College of Charleston student who, in two years working for ATD, had earned enough to buy "a home and a Porsche Boxster" (Collier 2002).

Even as Collier wrote his story, however, all was once again not well with ATD. In 2003, the firm "recognized a loss of $16.0 million" (Swanson and Whitcomb 2004), a huge sum for what was still only a medium-sized enterprise. Paradoxically, one of the reasons for the change in its fortunes was a measure central to the transformation of US share trading: decimalization. As noted earlier, this was the SEC-imposed transition from pricing shares in eighths or sixteenths of a dollar to a minimum increment of price of a single cent, a transition that was completed by April 2001.

Whitcomb, who had energetically advocated the reform, had expected the typical spread (the normal difference between the price of the highest bid for a stock and the lowest offer) to drop from a sixteenth of a dollar (6.25 cents) to around 2.5 or 3 cents. Almost immediately, however, the spread collapsed for most heavily traded stocks to a single cent (Whitcomb interviews 2 and 3). It was a decisive moment in the shift from human to algorithmic trading. With spreads of a single cent between the highest bid and lowest offer, market-making by human beings was normally no longer economically viable. Yet the shift hurt ATD. It was, after all, itself largely a market-maker, even if unofficial, and a smaller spread reduces market-makers' revenues. Furthermore, there had previously been profit opportunities in the difference between the coarse pricing grids of mainstream venues such as Nasdaq and the finer grids of new venues such as Island. Decimalization involved the regulatory imposition of a uniform price grid across all trading venues, which eliminated these opportunities.

But the more profound cause of ATD's difficulties was that HFT's speed race had begun. ATD soon realized that its systems, though faster than the fastest human being, were most likely slower than those of many of the new firms that had begun high-frequency trading. ATD responded by cutting costs and raising capital, for example by selling and leasing back its new headquarters. It stepped up efforts to improve its predictive modeling, and set up "a taskforce to attack latency" (Whitcomb interview 2), in other words to eliminate delays in its systems. Considerable speeding up was achieved, but ATD's war on latency also caused collateral damage. Updating an algorithm, a young trader-programmer accidentally interchanged a plus sign and a minus sign. "Unfortunately, the . . . error was in the interpretation of inventory [the program's holdings of shares]," says Whitcomb. Rather than keeping inventory safely close to zero—as was the intention—the program increased it in "geometric progression . . . [it] doubled and redoubled and redoubled and redoubled." It took only 52 seconds for the trader to "realize . . . something was terribly wrong and he pressed the red button [to stop trading]. By then we had lost $3 million" (Whitcomb interview 2). ATD's systems formerly had risk controls that would have stopped the geometric progression before it caused serious losses, but those controls had been removed in the effort to reduce delays.

ATD survived not by winning the speed race but by finding a new niche. It deployed the modeling and technological expertise built up in its HFT to become one of the first of a new generation of high-technology "wholesalers." As noted in chapter 1, these are firms that execute orders from members of the general public, which are sent to the wholesaler by the brokers that enable the public to trade. Since members of the public rarely possess information that is not already widely known to financial practitioners, a wholesaler whose costs are low enough (because its market-making, like ATD's, is automated) can afford to pay retail brokerages to send it their customers' orders, and even with one-cent spreads still make a steady profit executing those orders. Although these retail orders have to be processed quickly by ordinary human standards, and automated price prediction is still needed in order for algorithms to decide whether to fulfill an order internally or send it on to the public markets, the demand for speed is much less than in HFT in those markets. "You literally have hundreds of milliseconds or maybe up to a second to respond," says interviewee BD.

On July 2, 2007, the banking giant Citigroup announced it was paying $680 million to buy ATD, not as an HFT firm but as a wholesaler. ATD's "wholesale market-making arm . . . is what Citi acquired," says BD. The date of the purchase is significant. Banks such as Citigroup had become hubristic during the years of what some commentators had started to call "the great moderation" (Bernanke 2004), and that seemingly benign period was soon to end in the most dramatic fashion imaginable. In the weeks after Citigroup paid that huge sum to buy ATD, it started to become clear that the banking system, Citigroup included, was in deep difficulty.

The stricken bank did not make a success of its expensive purchase. One afternoon in October 2014, an interviewee took me to see the new, attractive offices that Automated Trading Desk had built a dozen years earlier, which remained the base of the wholesaling operation bought by Citigroup. All was quiet, the parking lot nearly empty. True, the trading day had ended, but it was not yet late. In the 1990s and early 2000s, ATD's premises would still have been buzzing with life, its young trader-programmers "tak[ing] . . . out frustration and stress" at the close of trading by using their powerful, interconnected computers to play "shooter games, Counterstrike, and Doom, and Quake" before "head[ing] back to their office[s] [to] . . . crunch numbers and work on code" (interviewee BT).

The empty parking lot was a harbinger. By May 2016, ATD was no more: Citigroup sold the company's wholesaling business to the Chicago hedge fund and HFT firm Citadel, which closed it, merging it into its own wholesaling activities. But while the story of ATD had come to an end, the world it had helped create had not. The next chapter shows the specificity of that world, by examining markets, in sovereign bonds and foreign exchange, in which trading's established order has resisted the challenge from HFT more successfully than it did in share trading.

4

Dealers, Clients, and the Politics of Market Structure

October 2017. I'm sitting beside a dealer in US Treasurys in a crowded midtown Manhattan office. He has bought and sold Treasurys (the sovereign debt securities of the United States) for more than thirty years, and vividly describes to me the teeming, raucous bond-trading room of the investment bank Salomon Brothers in its heyday at the end of the 1980s. It was the world of *The Bonfire of the Vanities* (Wolfe 1988) and *Liar's Poker* (Lewis 1990).

The dealer, interviewee YA, had work to do that afternoon as well as stories to tell. The role of the dealer is an old one: selling securities to clients such as institutional investors, buying them from clients, and unwinding the trading positions thus taken on by trading with other dealers. (A dealer can also act simply as an agent, buying and selling on a client's behalf.) The tools available to a Treasurys dealer have, however, changed during interviewee YA's career. Thirty years ago, nearly all trading would have involved the human voice: shouting across the trading room, clients and dealers speaking on the telephone, dealers and interdealer brokers (whose role is to coordinate trading among dealers) talking over permanently open telephone lines.

Now, my interviewee mainly trades electronically. As I arrive, he places a bid to buy $50 million of US Treasury two-year notes. The action is as casual as answering a routine email. He opens up his interface to an electronic trading system called BrokerTec, and with his keyboard and mouse selects the Treasury security he wants to buy, the quantity, and his bid price. A window opens up on his screen, asking him to confirm the order. A slight move of his

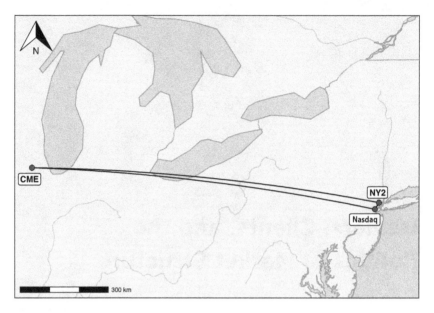

FIGURE 4.1. The "Treasurys triangle." *Source:* author's interviews.

mouse and a click on "yes" submits the bid. Almost instantaneously, it appears on-screen among the other bids—all of them anonymous—in BrokerTec's electronic order book.

Most likely, his bid is in a small minority in being the result of a direct human action. Most buying and selling on BrokerTec is done by algorithms, especially HFT algorithms. They run on computer servers or are implemented in specialized silicon chips (the field-programmable gate arrays, or FPGAs, described in chapter 5) in a New Jersey computer datacenter, NY2, in which BrokerTec's computer systems are located. The dealer's bid will have traveled under the Hudson River to NY2 along a fiber-optic cable. Once there, it has entered what market participants sometimes call the Treasurys triangle: the three datacenters—interconnected by the cable, microwave, and millimeter-wave links discussed in chapter 5, and each packed with computer servers—in which Treasurys and Treasury futures are traded (see figure 4.1).

My interviewee, though, has an alternative to entering the ultrafast, automated Treasurys triangle. He shows me how he also uses another trading system, Bloomberg FIT (Fixed-Income Trading). Buying on FIT is different from bidding on BrokerTec. His on-screen FIT window has buttons containing the names of a dozen of the 23 primary dealers in Treasurys. These firms, all but one of them large banks, have been granted that official status by the Federal Reserve Bank of New York, which is the market agent of the Department of the Treasury. (The one primary dealer that is not a bank is the interdealer broker Cantor Fitzgerald, discussed below.) My interviewee clicks a sequence of these buttons to send the corresponding primary dealers a message containing an RFQ, or request for quotation, asking for the prices at which they will sell him $50 million of two-year Treasury notes. Their offers appear almost instantaneously, generated by the primary dealers' automated systems. With another couple of clicks, he could accept one of these offers, but he does not; this is only a demonstration. Because of that, he has chosen a standard-sized small trade—small, that is, in a market in which it is routine for Treasurys worth around $500 billion to be bought and sold daily (and as much as $1 trillion daily in the coronavirus-induced tumult of March 2020).[1] If his request had been for a price quotation for a much larger quantity, it would have gone to a human being, and he does not want to make a nuisance of himself by wasting a trader's time—unlike BrokerTec, FIT is not anonymous. Indeed, if he had a big enough trade to do, he would not need to use a system such as FIT. He could send a Bloomberg instant message to negotiate a person-to-person deal with a primary dealer. He could even do what would have been done thirty years ago: pick up his telephone and make the deal verbally.

Dealers and Clients

That it is straightforward and routine for my interviewee to trade with a primary dealer nonanonymously via a request for quotation, an instant message, or a telephone call indicates that the Treasurys market is still to a large extent a dealer-client market (see figure 4.2). As noted in chapter 1, a market of this kind is structured by a distinction between socioeconomic roles. Those organizations that are classed as clients or customers—which can include even the largest hedge funds, investment-management firms, or nonfinancial corporations, as well as, for example, smaller banks—do not trade directly among themselves, but only via dealers. In contrast, dealers (the biggest of which in the trading of Treasurys are nowadays almost always big banks) trade both with clients and with each other, in the latter case often via interdealer brokers. In a dealer-client market, in other words, dealers are "price-makers" (disseminating, either continuously or on request, the prices at which they will trade), while clients are essentially "price-takers."[2] The dealer-client distinction is not utterly rigid—a small dealer like the firm for

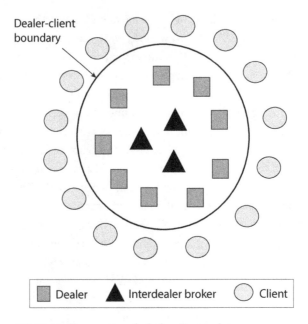

Dealer-client boundary

| ■ Dealer | ▲ Interdealer broker | ◯ Client |

FIGURE 4.2. The structure of a dealer-client market.

which my interviewee works can have its own clients and also be in a client relationship with bigger dealers—but nevertheless structures how trading takes place. We have, in fact, encountered dealer-client markets already in this book: that was how Nasdaq was organized until, as described in chapter 3, the challenge from SOES bandits, Island, and the other ECNs rendered that market structure no longer sustainable; and there was also a dealer-client market in European shares that competed with exchange-based trading of the latter.

As in those two cases, dealer-client market structures in some of the world's major financial markets have eroded considerably, and have largely been replaced by the combination of algorithms and anonymous electronic order books. It is true that the erosion is nowhere complete. For example, neither individuals nor institutional investors can gain entirely unmediated access to the main mechanisms of US share trading; they must do so via a "broker-dealer" registered as such with the SEC. In practice, though, a big investment-management firm can, if it wishes, readily get a broker-dealer to grant it what market participants call direct market access so that its human traders and algorithms can trade directly with only limited electronic oversight by the broker-dealer's system.[3] In other words, share trading has

TABLE 4.1. Differences in market structure among the main classes of highly liquid financial instrument

	US	Europe
Futures	Dominated by anonymous order books and HFT	Dominated by anonymous order books and HFT
Shares	Largely dominated by anonymous order books and HFT	Largely dominated by anonymous order books and HFT
Sovereign bonds	Dealer-client market, but with anonymous order books and HFT in inter-dealer trading	Much electronic trading, but almost intact dealer-client market, with virtually no HFT
Foreign exchange	Dealer-client market; partially colonized by anonymous order books and HFT	Dealer-client market; partially colonized by anonymous order books and HFT
Listed options	Anonymous order books but only limited amounts of "classic" HFT; some face-to-face trading (suspended in coronavirus crisis)	Some anonymous order-book trading but much dealer intermediation
Interest-rate swaps	Much electronic trading, but largely intact dealer-client market; only limited HFT	Almost intact dealer-client market; little HFT

Source: Author's interviews.

in effect become what market participants call an all-to-all market: one in which any major participant, if it wants to, can trade directly, and in which the distinction between a dealer and a client has only limited significance. Most big all-to-all markets in finance have at their center an anonymous electronic order book, and, as we saw in chapter 3, this is precisely the kind of market in which HFT algorithms flourish.

As indicated by tables 4.1 and 4.2, however, the anonymous order book/ HFT market structure is far from universal, and in some markets dealers still play central roles. This chapter examines the markets for sovereign bonds and foreign exchange, in which HFT algorithms have made inroads but have not displaced the traditional dealer-client structure completely. What is at issue in those two markets is not blanket resistance to technological change; electronic trading has been adopted widely, but the way it is structured still

---

TABLE 4.2. Proportion of trading that is dealer-intermediated in selected markets (2015 unless otherwise indicated)

US shares	17%
European shares (2018)	19%
US Treasurys	65%
UK Gilts	90%
German Bunds	>95%
Foreign exchange	60%
Interest-rate derivatives (e.g., swaps)	90%

Sources: Anderson et al. (2015), Cave (2018).

largely respects the distinction between dealers and clients. To a substantial extent, especially in the case of sovereign bonds, markets are bifurcated, with separate electronic systems for interdealer trading (of which BrokerTec is a leading example) and for trading between dealers and clients (such as Bloomberg FIT).

Trading Treasurys

It is striking that the trading of shares and of sovereign bonds has become so different, because it was traditionally quite similar. Shares and bonds were bought and sold on the trading floors of exchanges such as the New York Stock Exchange, its London equivalent, and the Paris Bourse. In the 1920s, US bond trading began to shift from the NYSE to a telephone-mediated, dealer-client market: first, the trading of Treasurys and municipal bonds, then, in the 1940s, the trading of bonds issued by corporations (Meeker 1930: 260; Biais and Green 2019). Institutional investors with a large purchase or sale to complete seem to have preferred trading in private with a dealer to the more public arena of the NYSE, and dealers imposed only relatively modest price markups on these valuable clients. (In contrast, Biais and Green [2019] demonstrate that what retail investors—that is, private individuals—paid to trade bonds via dealers in the first decade of the twenty-first century was higher than the equivalent costs on the NYSE in the 1920s. As discussed in chapter 2, and as Biais and Green also point out, there is an element of self-fulfilling prophecy to the perception of a market as the most liquid: investors keep it that way by sending their trades there, with the result that "liquidity may not gravitate to the most efficient trading venue" [2019: 270].)

The Second World War, which involved huge increases in US government borrowing, led the Department of the Treasury and its market agent, the Federal Reserve Bank of New York (FRBNY), to begin working closely with Treasurys dealers (e.g., via the Treasury Borrowing Advisory Committee, established in the immediate aftermath of the war; McCormick 2019). In 1960, the FRBNY began to designate selected banks and securities firms as primary dealers.[4] These firms took on obligations to bid in the initial auctions of Treasurys, and coordinated the subsequent trading of them.

Salomon Brothers was perhaps the most high-profile of these primary dealers, and interviewee YA described a typical dealer-client interaction there: "A customer [i.e., a client] would phone up, and either they would know exactly what they wanted to do, or you would engage in a conversation," with the client asking, for example, "What are you seeing? . . . What is your desk trying to do?" If, for instance, the client decided to buy $50 million of 10-year Treasury notes, the Salomon salesperson who had taken the phone call

> would then more than likely stand up [to] shout . . . towards the trading desk . . . "Tom, offer $50 million ten-years for so-and-so [naming the client]." . . . The trader would then shout over to you a price. . . . You would then tell your customer the price and your customer then had the opportunity to either say yes or no. (Interviewee YA)

As already noted, dealers used—and still use—the interdealer market to unwind the positions they took on in trading with clients. In the 1980s, interdealer trading took place mainly through interdealer brokers such as Cantor Fitzgerald, over permanently open telephone lines connecting each individual trader at each dealer with the half dozen or so interdealer brokers who serviced him (again, it was an almost exclusively male occupation). Originally, interdealer brokers would repeatedly quote "runs"—lists of prevailing prices—verbally to dealers, but by the 1980s all the main interdealer broker firms provided dealers with visual display screens on which prices could be seen (interviewee XV); see figure 4.3. Providing these price screens to clients was, however, taboo. When the interdealer broker RMJ Securities started to do this in the late 1980s, it "blew up on them, right?" (interviewee XV). RMJ "lost almost all of their [interdealer] business overnight" (interviewee XP). Within a week, the firm reversed course, retreating to its traditional role as an intermediary among dealers.

As the biggest of the interdealer brokers, Cantor Fitzgerald was not as easily disciplined as RMJ. Its screens were widely regarded by dealers as

FIGURE 4.3. Traders' desks at a Treasurys dealer, late 1980s. Photograph courtesy of interviewee XU.

an indispensable guide to the interdealer market, and it was able, without retaliation, to give at least some nondealers (Chicago pit traders, such as interviewees CY and MG, who traded Treasury futures) access to those screens. Originally neither dealers nor the Chicago firms could directly place bids and offers on the screens that Cantor Fitzgerald or other interdealer brokers provided; they had to ask a broker to do so. In 1999, however, Cantor made its internal electronic system (rechristened "eSpeed") "accessible through your own keyboard and through your own ability to input trades" (interviewee YD), giving dealers direct access to Cantor's electronic inter-dealer Treasurys order book.

Dealers' clients, though, were still not given access to eSpeed. Dealers nevertheless feared that sooner or later Cantor "was going to disintermedi-ate banks" (interviewee XO) by granting clients access, thus turning Trea-surys into an all-to-all market. "[W]e [major dealers] got together," says XO, "and said let's put this consortium [of dealers] together so that [clients] can directly access our bids and offers and not go through Cantor." The result was Tradeweb, launched in 1998, an electronic trading system (similar in structure to the later Bloomberg FIT system described at the beginning of this chapter) that was not an anonymous order book, but rather a means of automating the process whereby an institutional-investor client telephoned a small number of dealers to ask them to quote prices, in an interaction in which each party knew the other's identity. As an innovation that respected the dealer-client distinction, and required only modest changes to existing work processes (a structured electronic query rather than telephone calls or ad hoc Bloomberg instant messages), Tradeweb was strikingly successful.

Nor were the major dealers content to allow Cantor's eSpeed to dominate electronic interdealer trading. As one dealer puts it, "You couldn't deal with one guy. You just couldn't deal with one guy. . . . You couldn't let Howard [Cantor Fitzgerald's well-known chief executive, Howard Lutnick] have every bit of the information" (interviewee XO). Another consortium of major dealers, BrokerTec, was formed, and in 2000 it launched a rival anonymous electronic interdealer trading platform. Cantor was then struck by horrific human tragedy. Its main offices were on floors 101 to 105 of the North Tower of the World Trade Center, above the point at which the hijacked airliner hit the tower on September 11, 2001, and 658 of its brokers and other employees died, more than two-thirds of Cantor's total workforce. Lutnick's brother died, and he himself survived only because his son had started kindergarten that morning and he had wanted to accompany him. ESpeed's computer systems, however, were across the Hudson River in Rochelle Park, New Jersey. The trading platform was quickly made operational again, and eSpeed and BrokerTec remained locked in a struggle for market share in interdealer Treasurys trading.

A process akin to the "hinge" (discussed in chapter 3) between share-trading venues and HFT firms began in the trading of Treasurys. HFT firms had gained expertise and capital trading shares, and started to put out feelers to BrokerTec and eSpeed. The trading platforms anticipated some dealers being "pretty upset that the market was now being diluted" (interviewee CA), but also knew that giving HFT firms access could increase trading volumes markedly. Once one platform allowed HFT firms in (my interviews contain tentative evidence that BrokerTec, which initially had a smaller market share than eSpeed, was the first to do so), the other had to do so too. As interviewee AB, whose HFT firm became heavily involved in the interdealer Treasurys market, says, "It was very important for us to be operating on both [BrokerTec and eSpeed] . . . because then one wouldn't kick us off, out of fear that we would help the other take more market share." By the time dealers realized that they now had formidable competitors—HFT firms are "way faster, they're picking off the dealers [executing against dealers' price quotations that had not been updated quickly enough]"—"it was too late" to resist. "The advantages [for BrokerTec and eSpeed] were so much for having the HFTs on" (interviewee CC).

As in share trading, the hinge between BrokerTec, eSpeed, and HFT firms utterly transformed the Treasurys interdealer market. For example, both BrokerTec and eSpeed had a feature known as the workup protocol, deeply irritating to high-frequency traders such as interviewee AC, which paused trading when a deal was struck to give the two parties to it (assumed to be human beings) a chance to negotiate a larger transaction at the same price. This pause, a practice inherited from the way human brokers orchestrated interdealer trading, was gradually made shorter and shorter, leaving eSpeed and especially BrokerTec structurally very similar to the HFT-friendly share-trading venues. In 2012, for example, BrokerTec began leasing Nasdaq's ultrafast Genium Inet share-trading maching-engine technology, which is a descendant of the Island matching engine discussed in chapter 3, and was thirty times faster than BrokerTec's previous system (interviewee CC). In 2013, Nasdaq itself bought eSpeed from Cantor. (That is why, along with NY2 [BrokerTec] and the Chicago Mercantile Exchange, the third vertex of the Treasurys triangle in figure 4.1 is Nasdaq's datacenter.) By 2015, only two of the ten largest-volume trading firms on BrokerTec, which has become the dominant interdealer platform, were dealers (JP Morgan and Barclays); see table 4.3. The other eight were all HFT firms, and—as noted in chapter 1—in little more than two months of 2015 those firms had traded Treasurys worth around $7 trillion.

An All-to-All Treasurys Market: Direct Match

Despite some unhappiness among dealers, neither BrokerTec nor eSpeed faced a revolt against allowing HFT algorithms into the interdealer Treasurys market. What dealers "really cared about more," says interviewee CA, "was not having client flow on screen"—in other words, ensuring that clients continued to trade only via dealers, not directly. While I was interviewing in New York in 2016, however, a new anonymous electronic order-book trading platform, Direct Match, designed to allow clients to trade Treasurys not just with dealers but with each other, was being readied for launch. It was a controversial initiative. After I had switched off my tape recorder, interviewee GN, a former dealer, told me that "it can be a career-threatening thing" simply to invite a representative of an all-to-all trading platform of that kind to give a presentation at a major dealer. Nevertheless it was attracting a lot

TABLE 4.3. Most-active participants in Treasurys trading on BrokerTec in May and June 2015, by trading volume

	Trading volume (billions of US dollars)	Share of "top-ten" trading volume
Jump	2,291	28.5%
Citadel	1,004	12.5%
Teza	905	11.2%
KCG (Knight Capital Getco)	798	9.9%
JP Morgan	649	8.1%
Spire-X (Tower)	564	7.0%
XR Trading	554	6.9%
Barclays	483	6.0%
DRW	400	5.0%
Rigel Cove	400	5.0%
Overall top-ten trading volume	8,049	

Source: BrokerTec unpublished list, as reproduced by Smith (2015). As Smith notes, the top-ten volume seems to exceed the total volume that can be inferred from BrokerTec's reports of average daily volumes in May and June 2015; thus top-ten volume is most likely being measured over a slightly longer period. The dominant role of HFT firms, particularly Jump, is, however, consistent with what interviewees report.

of attention and the timing seemed promising. As noted, the largest dealers are almost all banks, and the more stringent capital requirements imposed by regulators since the 2008 financial crisis (especially the limits on permissible leverage ratios, which constrain the size of trading positions a bank can take on without having to raise more capital from investors) have considerably reduced banks' willingness and/or capacity to hold large inventories of bonds.

Direct Match was, in effect, an effort to create for the Treasurys market an equivalent of Island, the electronic share-trading venue discussed in chapter 3. Treasurys have "got to look more like equities [shares]," said an interviewee (CC) who was heavily involved in Direct Match. Direct Match's matching engine was built to the same basic design as Island's, and—just as Island had—it planned to offer a smaller "tick size" (minimum increment of price) than BrokerTec's and eSpeed's. If Direct Match had succeeded as Island had, the combination of high-frequency trading and anonymous order books might have transformed the entire Treasurys market, not just its interdealer segment.

The chief obstacle to Direct Match turned out to be clearing. As noted earlier, in the trading of shares and of futures a central clearinghouse stands between the two parties to a trade (buying from the seller, and selling to the buyer), preserving anonymity and protecting each party from a default by the anonymous other. In the Treasurys market, that role is played by the Fixed Income Clearing Corporation (FICC), making it essential for a trading platform to have access to FICC. The qualifications for FICC membership, though, were and are daunting—"a net worth of at least $25 million and cash on hand of $10 million or more" (Smith 2016: 44)—and Direct Match, as a small start-up, could not meet them. It had, however, secured the apparent agreement of a major bank that was an FICC member (but neither a primary dealer nor a major trader of Treasurys, and so did not seem to have a conflict of interest) to handle the clearing of trades on Direct Match. Nevertheless, around a week before Direct Match was due to launch, the bank "stopped answering calls. Finally get them on the phone and they bail out of it, citing conflicts [of interest]. Never really got explained," said interviewee CC. Without access to FICC, and unable to raise the $25 million for FICC membership, Direct Match never launched.

HFT Firms and Bilateral Trading

Direct Match had sought to emulate in Treasurys the "all-to-all" trading of shares via an open, anonymous, electronic order book. Share trading had also seen the emergence of dark pools, electronic trading venues in which the order book is not visible to participants. Interviewee CC's HFT firm, for example, had successfully set up its own share-trading dark pool, and it would have been straightforward to transfer the idea and software to the trading of Treasurys. "[T]he technology force[d] us," however, to take a different route in Treasurys, he reports. The single most important technical system by which participants in the Treasurys market make trading decisions is the Ion Group's aggregator, which collects bids and offers on display across the market. A dark pool with a hidden order book would have been invisible to the Ion system and thus to the majority of market participants.

CC's firm, and other HFT market-making firms active on BrokerTec and eSpeed, therefore did not try to create dark pools for Treasurys trading. Nor, in general, have they sought to trade directly with dealers' clients, because cultivating these clients would mean spending money ("we would need a sales force going out and talking to everyone," says interviewee AG) with no certainty of success. Instead, HFT firms have sought to supplement their activity on BrokerTec and eSpeed with direct bilateral trading arrangements with individual dealers: at first, midsize Treasurys dealers (banks such as

Jefferies and the Royal Bank of Canada), then more recently even the largest dealers. In an arrangement of this kind, the HFT firm streams electronically executable Treasurys prices to the dealer—prices that can, for example, be incorporated into the dealer's Ion system—while (in some cases) the dealer's systems also stream executable prices to the HFT firm. For the latter, this private bilateral arrangement is attractive because its algorithms are not at risk of being "picked off" by other, faster HFT algorithms, as they are in anonymous order-book markets such as BrokerTec and eSpeed. Thus the HFT firm can offer better prices than in those markets, which in turn makes bilateral trading with an HFT firm attractive to dealers.

What is fascinating about these private, nonanonymous, bilateral arrangements is that HFT firms are careful not to exploit the greater speed of their systems:

> [I]f Goldman is leaving a stale price on their book . . . and I then lift that price . . . I'm going to get a phone call from Goldman saying, "Hey . . . that was a bit painful, cut it out," or we can amend [the transaction]. And we do. . . . There are times where our own strategies will lock down [shut off automatically] if we've made too much [profit]. In other words, we'll stop trading with Goldman because we've made too much (interviewee CA).

Private bilateral arrangements have the disadvantage that they are costly to set up. They take time and effort (both technical and in meeting regulatory requirements, especially "know your customer" rules). However, a new platform, Liquidity Edge, launched in 2015, drew on the software employed by one of the new foreign-exchange trading venues discussed below, Currenex, to systematize the bilateral trading of Treasurys and thus reduce its costs. Unlike Direct Match, Liquidity Edge is not an overtly all-to-all trading platform, although, as its equivalents in foreign-exchange trading do, it allows not just bank dealers but also HFT firms to electronically stream executable Treasurys prices to clients. Trading is on a disclosed, not fully anonymous, basis (participants' identifier numbers and the type of trading they engage in are made known to their counterparties), and firms can choose "who they want to price [stream executable prices to] and how ['aggressively or conservatively']" (interviewee GL). This means, in effect, that banks need not fear being picked off repeatedly by participants with faster algorithms. Banks, interviewee GL reports, are nevertheless not of one mind about the virtues of the new platform ("Depends on who you talk to in the bank," says GL, with dealing desks in particular not always happy), but enough of the banks' more profitable business seems to be preserved to stop outright opposition to Liquidity Edge from emerging.

"Remember, today is a Thursday"

High-frequency trading has thus come to play an important, even a dominant, role in the interdealer Treasurys market, but a much less important role in trading with clients. No full-fledged, anonymous, all-to-all Treasurys market has emerged, and the dealer-client structure of Treasurys trading is at worst eroding only slowly. The other sharp contrast with share trading is the absence in the Treasurys market of any equivalent of the interventions by the Securities and Exchange Commission in how shares are traded, interventions that (as we saw in chapter 3) helped reshape market structure and indirectly facilitated the growth of HFT. The SEC is a much weaker presence in Treasurys than in shares, and it has simply not sought to enact for Treasurys measures similar to those that have transformed US share trading. Treasurys are exempt from much of the legal framework (e.g., the 1934 Securities Exchange Act and 1975 Securities Acts Amendments) that governs securities trading and gives the SEC its authority. The SEC has to share its limited jurisdiction over the trading of Treasurys with the Department of the Treasury and its agent, and the Federal Reserve Bank of New York, both of which have seemed content with the status quo (at least until quite recently, as concerns about liquidity have emerged). "[I]t's very hard," says a former SEC official (interviewee RF), for the SEC to act "with Treasury Department opposition."

The Department of the Treasury is ever present in the market for Treasurys as the borrower, and the Federal Reserve Bank of New York created and supervises the primary-dealer system, but with only two real exceptions government agencies have not intervened in recent decades to influence the structure of the Treasurys market, and neither exception was dramatic. The first was in 1991–2, when it was discovered that a senior trader at Salomon Brothers had been circumventing an "anti-cornering" rule (that no single firm could receive more than 35 percent of the Treasury securities in any auction) by making bids in Salomon's clients' names without their knowledge (Gabor 2016: 975). In response, the Department of the Treasury, the SEC, and the Federal Reserve broadened access to Treasury auctions and tightened surveillance of them, but left the primary-dealer system intact (Department of the Treasury et al. 1992). The second intervention followed price gyrations in Treasurys—a huge, quickly reversed, upward price spike—on October 15, 2014. Again, no major regulatory change to market structure followed, although a diluted form of the TRACE (Trade Reporting and Compliance Engine) deal-reporting system for bonds issued by corporations (mandatory since 2002) was introduced for Treasurys in 2017.[5] While, as discussed in chapter 3, nearly all US share trading flows through a unified nationwide clearing and settlement system (mandated, ultimately, by Congress), much trading of Treasurys takes place outside the ambit of the Fixed Income Clearing Corporation, and HFT firms, although major participants in the interdealer Treasurys market, are not usually members of FICC, typically accessing it indirectly through a bank that is an FICC member.

Why the lack of intervention in the trading and clearing of Treasurys by government regulatory agencies of the kind that has been so influential in shaping the way shares are traded? "[R]emember, today is a Thursday," a former Department of the Treasury official (interviewee VS) said to me in October 2016. On most Thursdays—indeed, most working days—Treasurys need to be sold. "Usually Monday through Thursday, there is one or more auctions that take place, and a primary dealer, whether you like it or not, you have to submit your bids," said VS. For the Department of the Treasury, that obligation is "reassuring," he continues, and the primary-dealer system gives the Federal Reserve Bank of New York the capacity to "use moral persuasion." The Treasurys market "is not like the equity [i.e., share] market. . . . This market is special. . . . It's the market that finances the sovereign."

The United States likely could maintain its almost continuous sales of Treasurys without the aid of primary dealers (even the very large volumes of sales necessitated by what are, at the time of writing, greatly increased government deficits), but policy makers cannot be certain of that in advance. Primary dealers thus seem to enjoy what Braun (2018) calls "infrastructural power"—the power that private actors accrue by being part of the mechanisms by which states act financially. This greatly limits the appetite of policy makers for interventions that might, for example, enhance competition (as analogous interventions in share trading have done) but might weaken the primary-dealer system and perhaps even cause banks no longer to be prepared to take on the obligations involved in being a primary dealer. Little government regulatory intervention in the trading of Treasurys has meant that the dealer-client structure of that market has remained far more intact than its equivalents in share trading. High-frequency trading in Treasurys has largely had to compromise with this existing market structure, rather than (as in share trading) helping to overthrow it.

HFT Blocked: Sovereign Bonds in Europe

The inroads made by HFT in the trading of European sovereign bonds have been much more limited than its partial successes in the trading of US Treasurys. As in the US, European sovereign-bond trading is bifurcated, with separate interdealer and dealer-client markets. Although telephone trading remains important, especially in the UK, there are mature systems for electronic trading in both markets. Just as they do in the US, clients use Tradeweb's and Bloomberg's systems (or the dealer-client system of MTS, for which see below) to electronically request price quotations from primary dealers.

The hugely salient difference from the US is that, as far as I can discover, no HFT firm has gained access to any European sovereign-bond interdealer market. The UK interdealer market remains dominated by voice brokers (as interviewee FZ reports). The Eurozone interdealer market is more comparable to that in the US, because there is a long-established, heavily used interdealer electronic platform, MTS. Founded in 1988 as the Mercato dei Titoli di Stato by Italy's Treasury and central bank, MTS was privatized in 1997 and gave birth in 1998 to a pan-European interdealer platform, EuroMTS. BrokerTec and eSpeed also launched European sovereign-bond trading platforms, but by 2006 their joint market share was only 0.1 percent (Persaud, 2006, table 1), and my interview data make clear that they remain entirely overshadowed by MTS. In the words of interviewee EK, MTS became

> almost part of the European *acquis* [the obligations and rights of EU member states]: if you became part of the Euro, in particular, you had to have your MTS market, because that gave you not only bond trading but . . . also . . . repos [the capacity to buy bonds with loans collateralized with those bonds: see Gabor 2016] which were critical for the money markets.

Governments, primary dealers, and MTS became part of what the MTS Group (2003: 3) described as a "liquidity pact." This involves primary dealers, which, as in the US, are nearly always large banks (see the lists in AFME 2017). The primary dealers take on commitments to bid in the auctions in which a government's debt-management office sells that government's sovereign bonds, and to facilitate subsequent trading of those bonds by "adhering to specified criteria" for the continuous posting of executable price quotations (MTS Group 2003: 3). These obligations to bid and continuously make markets can easily be loss making (interviewee YB; see Lemoine

2013), but banks continue to act as primary dealers in part for fear of being "put on a . . . list" (interviewee YB) and informally excluded from more profitable government business such as debt syndications and privatizations.

In 2006, US-based HFT firms, by then successfully trading US Treasurys on BrokerTec and eSpeed, began approaching MTS for access to European interdealer sovereign-bond trading. In Europe, MTS was sufficiently dominant that there was no equivalent of the fierce battle for market share between BrokerTec and eSpeed that had facilitated the entry of HFT in the US. There had, however, been criticism—for example, in a report (Persaud 2006) commissioned by the London-based interdealer broker ICAP, which had bought BrokerTec—of rules that (in Italy, for example) designated MTS as the platform on which primary dealers had to fulfill their market-making obligations. When requests for access from HFT firms started to arrive, MTS's leadership, which had ambitions for growth and international expansion (Chung and Tett 2006) that HFT might have facilitated, "felt the need to listen [and] started a conversation" (interviewee YB).

In the US, the competing interdealer platforms had given access to HFT firms without publicity and without (as far as I can tell) seeking permission from the Department of the Treasury or the Federal Reserve Bank of New York. In Europe, in contrast, most likely because of MTS's semiofficial role in the Eurozone, MTS decided to speak publicly about the "conversation" with HFT, and its chief executive talked to the *Financial Times* about it (Chung and Tett 2006). The reaction from dealers was hostile. While the tone of the European Primary Dealers Association was measured—"Allowing third party access . . . may upset the delicate balance in the euro government bond market" (quoted in Chung and Tett 2007)—behind the scenes some in "the dealer community . . . just went berserk. They literally went berserk" (interviewee YB). One banker warned the *Financial Times* that "[p]eople are furious. You could end up with a full-scale rebellion . . . that could rip the system apart" (Chung and Tett 2007).

The controversy, says interviewee YB, cost several of MTS's senior executives their jobs, and any suggestion of allowing HFT firms access to European interdealer sovereign-bond trading seems to have been shelved indefinitely. HFT interviewees describe UK, Eurozone, and other European interdealer markets as impossible to access. "They wouldn't let us in" (interviewee BU); it's "a club that we can't get into" (AG).[6] This is not arbitrary exclusion but a matter of explicit rules and taken-for-granted understandings. Rules include, for example, minimum capital requirements for participants in interdealer markets that considerably exceed the sums available to most HFT firms (for a sample of requirements, see AFME, 2017). The taken-for-granted understanding is that "membership is limited to institutional intermediaries (essentially banks)" (Ministero dell'Economia e delle Finanze 2017: 11).

Rules can of course be changed, and tacit understandings challenged, but European governments, however pro-competition and "neoliberal" their overall ideologies, have not done so. The energetic European Union reforms of the market structure of share trading from the early 2000s onward (for example, the elimination of concentration rules; see chapter 3) have not been echoed in the trading of sovereign bonds. As interviewee SC, a politician heavily involved in regulatory reform, told me:

> Dealers . . . have to be authorized by [government debt management offices] to participate. . . . [P]roprietary trading houses [such as HFT firms] would not meet the criteria . . . in most cases.
> AUTHOR: [Do] you get a sense that people in the regulatory/political sphere are perfectly content with that?
> INTERVIEWEE SC: They can control a small number of dealers, so they can control their primary issuance [the initial auctioning of sovereign bonds] in a way they wouldn't be able to if they actually took it totally and utterly to a much broader audience.

Interviewee CR, for instance, reports the Italian Ministry of Finance as being "a bit uncomfortable with non-banks" such as HFT firms, because their entry would further reduce "the profitability of being a primary dealer" and potentially threaten banks' willingness to take on the role. A primary dealer, similarly, spells out the reasons for governments' reluctance to be swayed by HFT firms' argument that "algo trading makes the market more efficient":

> [Y]ou can shout and scream as much as you want and you call about clubbing [barriers to entry] but . . . if I'm an Italian [government] debt manager and I have [€] 2 trillion debts to service of which [€] 300 billion a year to issue, I don't care if you're a hedge fund in America and you talk to me about price efficiency. Go and take a hike. . . . [I]f you want to come, guarantee to me that you're going to buy 3 percent of my debt and get a banking license, come on board. If not, go to hell . . . if I'm a sensible regulator, I'm a sensible politician, do I really want to cater for my people in difficult times or do I want to cater for the profitability of these [algorithmic-trading] geniuses? (Interviewee YB)

In 2019, I took part in a conference on sovereign debt attended by members of the debt-management offices of many European governments.

Although some worries were expressed about the capacity of banks to keep making markets in government debt on the requisite scale (especially in Italy, with its particularly large national debt and therefore huge sovereign-bond market), the commitment of government debt-management offices to the primary-dealer system (and thus to a dealer-client market structure) still seemed to be strong. Thus there appear to be few near-term prospects for HFT firms to become major traders of European sovereign bonds.

Foreign Exchange: "You're asking me to undress in public"

Along with shares, futures, and sovereign bonds, foreign exchange was also potentially an attractive market for the nascent high-frequency trading firms of the early 2000s. There was already a considerable volume of electronic foreign-exchange trading, and the major currency pairs (such as euro-dollar, dollar-yen, dollar-sterling, etc.) were heavily traded. In foreign exchange, though, just as in sovereign bonds, HFT collided with a largely intact dealer-client market. As in the case of Treasurys (but unlike the case of European sovereign bonds), HFT has managed to establish itself in foreign-exchange trading, but only—as we shall see below and in chapter 6—after protracted conflict with incumbents and by making substantial compromises with the established order of the foreign-exchange market. Even more than is the case in sovereign bonds, the organizations central to the politics of market structure in foreign exchange have always been private-sector bodies. The trading of foreign exchange is an intrinsically transnational activity, and most aspects of its market structure are therefore outside the jurisdiction of regulatory bodies set up by national governments.[7]

The biggest foreign-exchange dealers have traditionally been major commercial banks. (As late as the early 1990s, even the most prestigious investment bank was still simply a "client" or a "customer" of these commercial banks. For example, as interviewee FU recalls, even "Goldman [Sachs] was a customer. It was not a dealer player.") In the 1970s and much of the 1980s, the foreign-exchange market operated similarly to the Treasurys market. A client seeking a currency transaction would telephone a salesperson at one of the dealer banks and ask for a price quotation. If a deal was then agreed to, and it was large, the dealer would proceed to unwind the risk he had taken on (again, it was an almost exclusively male occupation, sometimes luridly so, as Salzinger 2016 documents) by trading in the interdealer market, also by voice, either by telephoning and verbally agreeing to a trade with a dealer in another bank, or by transacting via an interdealer broker or brokers, in this case by talking to the brokers on permanently open telephone lines of the same kind as in the Treasurys market. These uses of voice in foreign-exchange trading were supplemented by Telex messages, employed for example to confirm verbally agreed-upon deals. (The Telex system used teletype machines—of the kind employed by Instinet, as described in chapter 3—to allow messages, which operators usually prepared in advance on punched tape, to be exchanged among large organizations.)

The leading role in introducing the display of prices on computer screens and eventually electronic trading to the predominantly telephone-mediated foreign-exchange market was played by the British-based news service and financial data provider Reuters. It had to proceed cautiously so as not to spark too much resistance from dealers. (One of the pioneers of the effort, interviewee FV, remembers trying to persuade a continental European foreign-exchange dealer of the virtues of having its indicative price quotations displayed on Reuters screens in other banks' trading rooms, only to receive a memorable explanation of why this was unattractive: "But Mr. [FV], you're asking me to undress in public.") Several Reuters employees, perhaps especially those based in the United States, where early experiments in electronic trading such as at Instinet were already under way, were attracted by the idea of introducing full-fledged interdealer electronic trading of foreign exchange. Others, though, realized that for Reuters to move directly to that would be unacceptable to dealers.

The stepping-stone that Reuters introduced was what it called Reuter Monitor Dealing, later renamed Conversational Dealing. The electronic "conversations" involved were brief, Telex-like text messages sent directly by dealers themselves (rather than by the clerical staff who normally operated the Telex system), thus replacing or supplementing dealers' use of the telephone to negotiate trades with their counterparts in other banks. The messages were distributed via Reuters' own network, which was fast enough to permit a dealer in one bank to have a conversation-like exchange of messages with a dealer in another, asking for price quotations and (if one of those was acceptable) agreeing to a deal. In 1975, Reuters demonstrated a prototype of this system to European banks, being careful to emphasize that it did not involve electronic trading in the sense of the automated matching of bids to buy and offers to sell. As a Reuters internal report, quoted in Donald Read's history of the firm, put it:

Our presentation stressed that the objective involved no change in current market practice. Personal contact, a sensitive subject among dealers, would not be undermined by the proposals. Dealers would continue to use the telephone. There was no attempt to create a matching system. (Read 1999: 366)

Although the most prominent organization of foreign-exchange dealers, the Association Cambiste Internationale, "said 'what we are not going to have is automated dealing,'" it "endorsed" the less threatening conversational system, with its preservation of dealing's "person-to-person" aspect (interviewee FS). Developing the system was, however, far from straightforward. There were tensions between Reuters' own technological staff, who were trade-union members, and the nonunionized consultants brought in for the project, and it proved challenging to persuade Europe's still state-owned telecommunications monopolies to lease the necessary lines to Reuters.[8]

Despite these difficulties, Reuter Monitor Dealing was successfully launched in Europe and North America in 1981, and then in 1982 in the Middle East and Far East (Read 1999: 369). It proved popular among dealers; the capacity to send near-instant electronic messages to their counterparts in other banks speeded up the most routine aspects of their work, while still providing enough flexibility to add pleasantries or snippets of useful information to messages negotiating trades, thus preserving valuable friendships and personal relationships among dealers. Indeed, these messages provided an important source of data for classic research by Karin Knorr Cetina and Urs Bruegger in the academic field of this book, the "social studies of finance."[9] By 1993, the *Financial Times* reported that conversational dealing was available on 19,000 Reuters terminals worldwide, and that "some 50 per cent of global foreign exchange transactions take place on them" (Blitz 1993).

That this early Reuters system was so heavily used caused renewed alarm among dealers when, in the late 1980s, the company began development of the full-fledged interdealer matching system that it had originally disavowed in order to defuse opposition to "conversational" electronic dealing. By then, the idea of electronic matching was much less controversial than it had been in the 1970s, but the threat that the role of Reuters might expand even further caused deep concern in the banks that dominated foreign-exchange dealing. Interviewee FT recalls discussing this with fellow bankers: "Somebody . . . asked, 'What kind of market share do you think Reuters has in the foreign-exchange business?'" Someone else replied, "Oh, 50 percent. . . . [B]y the

way, what's this 2000–2 [electronic matching] thing that they're doing?"
Interviewee FT answered:

> "Oh," I says, "it looks like they're trying to automate what the brokers do."
> "What market share do the brokers have?" "30–35 percent." You could
> see, the light bulb went on over everybody's head right at the moment.
> They're [Reuters is] going from 50 percent to 85 percent and it's our
> [dealers'] business. Now, there is a real threat to [dealers'] franchise . . .
> we've got to do something now.

Just as Treasurys dealers feared that Cantor Fitzgerald would grant dealers'
clients access to electronic trading, their equivalents in foreign exchange
worried that Reuters would do just that:

> Some bank dealers . . . argue that Reuters could change the structure
> of the currency market, if it so wished, by selling more systems to non-
> banking customers who are becoming important movers of international
> capital. (Blitz 1993)

Exactly as was to happen in Treasurys trading, a consortium of a dozen
of the world's leading foreign-exchange dealing banks was formed to set up
an electronic interdealer trading system (Electronic Broking Services, or
EBS) to compete with Reuters; a further consortium, Minex, which focused
on bringing electronic trading to East Asian banks, was also set up. In 1992,
for example, Reuters, EBS, and Minex faced off against each other at the
annual congress of the Association Cambiste Internationale in Sydney, with
the Reuters stand (which was reported to have cost $1 million) combining
what was advertised as "The Best Bar in Town" with an 80-seat theater for
demonstrations of its new electronic trading system (anon. 1992).

The construction of EBS was a hugely demanding technological endeavor.
Much of the physical infrastructure already existed—Citibank, a consortium
member, had an electronic network that spanned much of the globe, and
made it available to EBS—but two distinctive aspects of foreign-exchange
trading had to be taken into account. The first is that there is a sense in which
each participant in foreign-exchange trading "sees" a different market. That
is because in foreign exchange there is no equivalent of the clearinghouses in
shares, futures, and (to a more limited extent) Treasurys, which, as already
discussed, remove the risk to market participants that a counterparty will
default on a deal by turning it, nearly immediately, into two deals: one
between the seller and the clearinghouse, and one between the clearinghouse
and the buyer. Since 2002, there has been a bank-owned foreign-exchange

settlement system (Continuous Linked Settlement), but it is not a clearing-house; it safeguards only the final currency transfers between the parties to a deal. Thus each participant in foreign-exchange trading is exposed to the risk of default by its trading partner until the point at which the deal is processed by Continuous Linked Settlement. Each bank therefore continuously calculates and limits the extent of its exposure to every other bank:

> If I don't have credit [with another bank] or my credit ran out, I will not see their price . . . which means that you cannot broadcast the price like an exchange like Nasdaq can . . . You have to compute and send a specific price for everybody. Everybody sees a different price. (Interviewee FL)

The second distinctive feature of foreign-exchange trading is that, to a greater extent than in any other class of financial asset, it "moves with the sun" (interviewee FL; see also Knorr Cetina and Bruegger 2002a), with a daily cycle that begins in East Asia, then moves to Europe, and eventually to the Americas. There were two main competing designs for EBS: one was to have a single central system, maintaining the matrix of interbank credit limits and matching all trades globally; the second involved three communicating but separate matching engines, in Tokyo, London, and New York. In testing, the first design's single matching engine could not cope with the demands on it. "With fifty banks connected to the [central] matching engine [it] was not able to run" (interviewee FL). So when EBS launched, in 1993, it was with the three matching engines and the world's foreign-exchange dealer banks connected to them, in some cases via intermediary nodes in cities that did not house one of the three matching engines.

The ambitions and complications of EBS's global system created teething troubles, but with the world's major dealer banks behind it and their traders incentivized to post bids and offers on it (so reports interviewee FL), EBS largely won its competition with Reuters for market share of electronically matched foreign-exchange trading. (The East Asian system, Minex, eventually merged into EBS.) As interviewees reported, the Reuters system became dominant in "cable"—the trading of the pound sterling against the US dollar, called cable because of the traditional role in that market of transatlantic telegraphy—along with British Commonwealth currencies, but EBS became the main platform for interdealer electronic trading of the world's other leading currency pairs, such as the Deutschmark (and, later, euro) versus the US dollar and the yen versus the dollar.

It is, however, worth noting what did *not* happen. First, there was only limited automation in the beginning. Nearly all trading on EBS in its early years was directly initiated by human beings, using specially designed keypads. Directly connecting a computer to EBS "was forbidden by EBS's contract; you were not supposed to attach any automated, nonhuman things to this" (interviewee FL). That was why traders at Lehman Brothers developed the Clackatron shown in figure 1.2. It struck the keys of an EBS keypad, but was not directly connected to it.[10] Second, "conversational dealing" continued in parallel with electronic trading using EBS (or sometimes the Reuters matching system).[11] Third, and perhaps most important, the dealer-client structure of foreign-exchange trading did not change in any fundamental way. "You couldn't just come in and say, 'I want to trade on EBS,'" says interviewee FL. "[I]f you didn't have credit relationships with banks you wouldn't see their prices. It would be pointless." EBS (and in the markets in which it was salient, also the Reuters matching system) became part of dealers' routine work practices, without changing the way in which those practices were structured by the dealer-client divide. As a former dealer (interviewee XI) told me:

> A typical trade would be a hedge fund would call a salesperson, say "Can we ask for a price at a hundred million dollars against the yen?" The salesperson would shout across to me, I'd look at EBS, make the judgment whether [exchange rates] were going to go higher or lower, [and] would shout back. They would trade and then I'd have the [trading] position. Pretty standard.

"Well, that's how it works in FX"

In the early 2000s, though, the dealer-client structure of the foreign-exchange market was challenged by new electronic trading platforms that were often inspired by the success of Island and similar share-trading venues. "[J]ust to put our mindsets back into the era," says interviewee FX, the end of the 1990s "was the era of internet 1.0 and it was a very, very exciting time," with large numbers of dot-com businesses being launched. Setting up an electronic system for trading foreign exchange, for a wider clientele than the big dealer banks that dominated EBS and Reuters, was an attractive project around which to build companies that could present themselves as dot-com start-ups and benefit from the favorable capital-raising environment of the late 1990s.

Most of the new electronic trading venues that were launched in this period did not contest the division of the foreign-exchange market into "dealers" that made prices and "clients" that were price-takers. Some were simply systems set up by a bank to allow its clients to access its price quotations electronically rather than by a telephone call. Citibank and Chase Manhattan Bank launched such systems in the late 1990s (anon. 2000), and eventually all the major foreign-exchange dealer banks did so. Other systems (FX Connect, Atriax, and Currenex) were platforms on which multiple dealers could electronically stream prices to clients, or via which clients could request price quotations from a number of different dealers. Again, platforms of this kind ran with the grain of the existing market structure in foreign exchange, not against it.

Two new electronic foreign-exchange trading venues did, however, offer clients the capacity not just to transact against dealers' price quotations but to post prices themselves in the venue's electronic order book. One was Matchbook, launched in 1999 and oriented to individual traders (along with smaller hedge-fund-like trading groups). Matchbook was based on a reengineered version of the matching engine that had been developed by one of the electronic share-trading venues, NexTrade, and it saw itself as "set[ting] out to democratize the foreign-exchange market in much the same way that Island" had aimed to do in shares (interviewee FX). Matchbook found, though, that without the participation of banks it needed its own dealers to populate its order books. When the dot-com boom turned to bust in 2000, Matchbook found raising further capital very difficult, and eventually it closed down. However, another of the new venues, Hotspot, had an electronic order book in which corporations, institutional investors, and other traditional large clients could themselves bid and offer rather than simply execute against dealers' prices. "[W]e wanted banks to participate too, so . . . I wouldn't say quickly, but certain banks adapted . . . and started to decide, all right, we can still make money off this process and, plus, we can make money off of . . . clients that aren't necessarily our clients" (interviewee FW).

HFT firms were slower to begin foreign-exchange trading than they had been to enter the Treasurys interdealer market. "That was a particularly difficult market . . . to crack into, really," says interviewee AB. "It was a bank-dealer network. The platforms that existed were mainly to facilitate the bank-dealer network. . . . And, yes, banks certainly wanted it to stay that way. They made a lot of money at that time off of those markets." To achieve any substantial participation in foreign-exchange trading, an HFT firm had to find a bank that would sponsor it and underwrite the credit risk involved in trading with it. "[W]hen someone calls" to request access to a trading platform, says interviewee EN, "we ask them if they have existing bank relationships."

By 2005–2006, though, HFT firms were beginning to seek and gain access. Banks are large organizations, different parts of which can have different priorities. While a typical bank's foreign-exchange traders were unlikely to welcome competition from high-frequency trading, its prime-brokerage unit could and did earn fees from HFT firms by sponsoring their trading and extending credit to them. There is some evidence in my interviews that the first foreign-exchange trading venue to open up to HFT firms was Hotspot. "They would take anyone," says interviewee FU. The process that had played out in share trading, in which HFT helped build the market share of trading venues that allowed HFT participation, began in foreign-exchange as well. Hotspot's market share rose. That then put pressure on other venues, especially EBS, also to open up to HFT. Interviewee FU recalls talking to the banks that owned EBS, telling them that they had to choose between opening up, including to HFT, and still having "some control" over the process of trading, "or you can have it [trading] go to Hotspot [and] you have none [no control]." Even on Hotspot, though, the entry of HFT firms sparked considerable unhappiness on the part of dealer banks. The systems that banks used to post prices on Hotspot were slow ("When the markets moved, it could take them 100 milliseconds [a tenth of a second] to move their price," says interviewee FW), and periodically a bank's system would hiccup and its prices would freeze. HFT firms, therefore, "had a lot of free money for a while" at the expense of banks (interviewee FW).

Foreign-exchange trading was, however, structurally different from the trading of shares and futures, in which clearinghouses make it possible to buy or sell without ever discovering the identity of the other party to the trade. There is, as noted above, a sense in which foreign exchange was, and is, not a single market but an aggregate of a large number of bilateral trading relationships, which seldom remain entirely anonymous throughout. Even on one of the new trading venues, a bank might be able to discover at least the identifier number of a market participant that was costing it money. As an interviewee put it, "there were . . . sometimes, depending on who you were, client identifiers . . . 'It's 40657.' Then that way the banks could just say, 'I'm sick of 40657. I just lose $50,000 a month on this guy, and he's not my client.'"

Sometimes, a platform will expel an HFT firm that has been the subject of too many complaints of this kind. Interviewee BK reports that his firm had started to trade on a new platform, "but I got turned off in two days' time because they said we were too predatory." Expulsion, though, seems to be unusual, "because they're [the platform is] making money out of you" (interviewee FI). More common is a bank asking a trading platform to stop making its prices available for a specific participant to execute against (perhaps by setting the bank's maximum credit exposure to the participant to zero), and the platform agreeing to do this. Interviewee FW recalls the process and the anger involved in both banks and HFT firms:

> [W]hat happened is the banks got really mad. So the ECNs [electronic trading venues] basically had filters that we could shut off high-frequency players to certain people that were market-makers, so that's what you could employ, and then the high-frequency guys would get mad: "Why am I not getting more access?"
>
> "You've made every bank on the platform mad . . . and they're not willing to stream [quote executable prices] to you."
>
> "Well, that's not fair."
>
> "Well, that's how it works in FX [foreign exchange]."

For a bank to refuse to have its prices displayed to HFT firms because trading with them was costing it money was, however, only a partial solution. It did not, for example, stop HFT firms from undercutting the bank's price quotations on EBS and other trading venues, especially when these venues (following in a sense in the footsteps of Island) "decimalized"—that is, reduced the minimum increment of price by a factor of 10.[12] In a market in which there were multiple competing electronic trading platforms, it was not feasible simply to exclude HFT firms en masse. Nor did foreign-exchange dealers have any functional equivalent of the primary-dealer roles that have helped protect the established arrangements for the trading of European sovereign bonds. Conflict over market structure in foreign exchange has, therefore, largely taken different, more directly material forms, to which I will turn in chapter 6.

Different Histories, Different Signals

The very different histories of the markets for the four types of financial instrument discussed in this and the previous two chapters—futures, shares, sovereign bonds (especially Treasurys), and foreign exchange—have left material traces, including differences among the "signals" available for HFT in the four markets. These are summarized in table 4.4. Since widely used signals in the trading of US shares have already been discussed in chapter 3,

TABLE 4.4. Availability of three classes of signal in the main markets in which HFT firms are active

Signal	Futures lead	Order-book dynamics	Fragmentation
Shares	Yes	Yes, with partial exception of "dark pools"	Yes
Futures	Not applicable	Yes	No
Benchmark Treasurys	Varies over time	Yes, but many venues have no order books	Yes, but HFT firms not present in most dealer-client venues, so limited exploitability
"Spot" foreign exchange	Only sporadically	Yes, but many venues have no order books	Yes, but "last look" and other measures often prevent its exploitation by HFTs

Source: Interviewees. A dark pool is a trading venue in which the order book is not visible to participants (although its contents can sometimes be inferred by "pinging," i.e., repeatedly entering small orders). The benchmark US Treasurys are the most recently issued 2-, 3-, 5-, 7-, and 10-year notes and 30-year bonds. Spot foreign exchange refers to transactions for near-immediate delivery. Last look is an automated procedure whereby before a venue's computer system executes a trade against a market-maker's price quote, the venue's system sends the market-maker's system a message alerting it to the impending transaction and giving it a short period of time in which to reject the trade.

let me compare those with the signals available in the trading of futures, Treasurys, and foreign exchange.

FUTURES: NO FRAGMENTATION

By far the sharpest contrast between US share trading and futures trading is that, by means of the process described in chapter 3, share trading has become fragmented across multiple trading venues (and that fragmentation is the source of a crucial class of signal), while, as noted in chapter 3, almost all financial-futures trading takes place on a single venue, the Chicago Mercantile Exchange. In 2015, the CME's market share of all US futures trading (including trading of futures on physical commodities) was 89 percent, and its share specifically of financial futures is even higher: as an example, the CME hosts 99.97 percent of the trading in the US of interest-rate futures and options on those futures (Meyer 2015).

Since futures usually "lead" their underlying assets (with the important exceptions mentioned below), that leaves available to algorithms trading futures essentially only one of the three classes of HFT signals on which I have focused, order-book dynamics. "Futures in general . . . in the most actively traded products, it's all order-book dynamics, regardless of what it is you're trading," says interviewee AC. Certainly, HFT interviewees from the futures market seemed focused far more exclusively on the order book than their colleagues in shares were. "Spoofing"—entering bids or offers into the order book with the goal of fooling algorithms that make predictions based on its contents, which is now banned as a form of market manipulation (see chapters 6 and 7)—also seemed a far greater concern to them. In addition, the absence of fragmentation, and the resultant single pools of liquidity, in share-index futures trading—the most important such futures, in particular those based on the Standard & Poor's 500 and Nasdaq-100 indexes, are traded only on the CME—may help explain the remarkable longevity of "futures lead" in share trading, examined in chapter 2.

As described in chapters 2 and 3, the conditions that led to fragmentation in shares have been absent in futures trading. With no equivalent congressional push for structural reform behind the 1974 Amendments to the Commodity Exchange Act, and with those allied to existing futures exchanges influencing their drafting, the amendments did not mandate a unified clearing and settlement system for futures (which the 1975 Securities Acts Amendments mandated for shares), making it much harder for new futures venues to challenge incumbents. Nor did the 1974 amendments grant the new futures regulator, the Commodities Futures Trading Commission, the explicit powers to intervene in market structure that the 1975 legislation gave the SEC. In addition, while the SEC is a permanent federal body, the CFTC is dependent on periodic congressional reauthorization, without which (as at the time of writing) it is reliant on year-to-year funding. Although the SEC's funding is also dependent on Congress, the fact that the CFTC has no absolute guarantee of permanence, interviewee RE suggested, may leave it less able than the SEC to pursue policies that might generate strong finance-industry opposition.

TREASURYS AND FOREIGN EXCHANGE

Signals in the two markets discussed in this chapter, sovereign bonds (especially Treasurys) and foreign exchange, also differ from those in share trading. As described above, the market for Treasury securities—even for the benchmark (most actively traded) Treasurys, which are among the world's most liquid securities—is split into two largely separate segments: the interdealer market, to which HFT firms have had access since the early 2000s, and the dealer-client market, to which they are still marginal. Fragmentation in the trading of Treasurys is therefore not fully exploitable by high-frequency traders, because of their limited participation in trading venues other than the main platforms on which dealers trade with each other. Furthermore, much dealer-client trading does not involve a central order book with firm bids and offers, limiting the extent to which order-book dynamics is relevant to that trading. Nor is there a straightforward pattern of "futures lead." There are periods, interviewees reported, in which the underlying Treasury securities lead Treasury futures, rather than vice versa. The most plausible explanation is that very high levels of leverage are possible in the trading of Treasury securities, because of the longstanding institution of "repo" (repurchase), in which those securities are pledged as collateral to guarantee loans to buy them.[13]

In foreign exchange, there is considerable fragmentation of trading across multiple venues, but again the capacity of high-frequency trading algorithms to exploit it is limited, in this case by a combination of the exclusions from trading described earlier in this chapter and the "material politics" measures discussed in chapter 6. Nor is there any unequivocal "futures lead" pattern in foreign-exchange trading. Interviewees report that, at least much of time, the spot markets in foreign exchange (markets such as EBS, Reuters, and their newer rivals, in which currencies are traded for near-immediate delivery, and in which high levels of leverage have traditionally been available) tend to lead the futures market, with the effect that signals from Chicago are less crucial to foreign-exchange trading than to, say, share trading. For example, when (as described in the next chapter) a new, ultrafast fiber-optic cable was laid to connect the Chicago futures markets to the East Coast datacenters in which shares, Treasurys, and foreign exchange are traded, interviewee BB's HFT firm, which traded both futures and foreign exchange, decided not to pay for an ultra-expensive, highest-speed "tier one" fiber, but only for the cheaper service in which the strand of cable it leased was coiled to slow transmission by around a millisecond. In contrast, HFT firms that traded futures and shares, or futures and Treasurys, had little choice but to pay, if they possibly could, for the fastest forms of the material transmission of prices.

Differences in the signals available to HFT algorithms in different markets thus have their counterparts in HFT firms' different material priorities. More broadly, the politics of market structure is often a material politics, a question of how the material world of trading should be arranged. It is time, therefore, to turn in greater depth to HFT's materiality.

5

"Not only would I lose my job, I might lose my legs too!"

Let's begin in a datacenter. Chicago's Cermak, shown in figure 5.1, has played an important role in the short history of automated trading. For example, that history's most dramatic episode—the "flash crash" of May 6, 2010, described in chapter 7—began there. Completed in 1929, Cermak was originally a printing plant, the largest in the US, and most likely in the world. Its giant presses printed *Time*, *Life*, the Sears catalog, telephone directories. Those presses are long gone, but the specially reinforced floors on which they stood now house row upon row of computers. Some belong to telecommunications companies. "The backbone of the Internet" goes through Cermak, the host of my visit told me. Cermak's "meet-me room" is one of the places where the separate, private networks owned by carriers such as Comcast, Verizon, and BT (formerly British Telecom) fuse to form the seemingly unitary, seamless online world. The computer system of the Chicago Mercantile Exchange was in Cermak until 2012, when it moved to the purpose-built suburban datacenter mentioned in earlier chapters, making Cermak less salient than it once was. It continues, however, to host automated trading, and many HFT firms maintain a presence there.

To tour Cermak is to walk through endless, windowless corridors, with white walls and anonymous blue doors. Even someone like my host who knows the building well can easily lose his bearings. The rooms behind the doors are still noisy, but the clanking of printing presses has been replaced by the steady roar of multitudes of fans and hard disks. Cermak is unusual

FIGURE 5.1. Cermak. Author's fieldwork photograph.

among datacenters in having multiple floors, but the fact that the building was originally a printing plant helps connect those floors. They are pierced by 21 big vertical shafts, through which giant rolls of paper were once raised and lowered, and running a cable through one of those shafts can shorten it handily.

My host's job is to sell firms space in Cermak in which to install their computer systems. Reflecting on that, he said, "I sell electricity." By 2012, Cermak had become the second-biggest electricity consumer in Illinois, after Chicago's O'Hare Airport (Equinix 2012: 5). Cermak is connected to two different grids, which can deliver 100 megawatts of electricity, and large tanks of diesel stand ready to fuel the big standby generators—of the type, my host explained, that power cruise liners—that would kick in if both grids failed. Nearly all the electricity that flows into Cermak is transformed eventually into heat. The crucial parameter in any datacenter, interviewee CZ told me, is power density, often measured by the maximum level of electrical-power input per rack that a datacenter can support. (A rack is a standard-sized metal framework into which computers and other equipment are installed.) [1] The constraint on a datacenter's power density is not usually electricity supply; rather, it is the need to extract heat from the building so that the temperature will be low enough for the computers it contains to run reliably. In the case of Cermak, that requires a high-capacity cooling system containing a brinelike refrigerant: 8.5 million gallons (32 million liters) of it are needed. As you walk around Cermak you often see the pipes that carry refrigerant through the building, and every now and then you encounter a blast of very cold air.

Even my guide couldn't enter most of Cermak's rooms, which are protected by doors with biometric locks. Once you're inside a room, you get only tiny clues as to what's going on. At least in the rooms housing trading firms' servers, the computers are generally in tightly packed, locked cages. What I have learned about what goes on in the datacenters crucial to HFT thus comes more from talking to people than from walking around. Although the configuration of different exchanges' systems varies, there is enough structural similarity to generalize somewhat, as in figure 5.2. Consider an order (a bid or an offer) dispatched by a component in a trading firm's system in the datacenter that houses the computers of the exchange on which that firm—let's call it firm A—is trading. (Physically, this component might be a full-blown computer server, but it could also be a field-programmable gate array, or FPGA, a specialized silicon chip of the kind described at the end of this chapter.) Inside the datacenter, the electronic message that encodes the order flows through cables, usually in the form of laser-generated pulses of light in optical fiber; the wireless technologies described later in the chapter are used to communicate between datacenters, not inside them. Typically, a trading firm leases from the exchange at least two cables to connect its system to the exchange's system. Messages can flow through these cables in both directions, but it's wise to have a second connection available in case an equipment failure interrupts the first.

Having most likely passed through at least one digital switch, the electronic message that constitutes trading firm A's order will arrive at a component of the exchange's system often called an order gateway. (A gateway can be a computer server, but need not be a separate machine, and the Chicago Mercantile Exchange, for example, now uses FPGAs as order gateways.) The gateway acts as a check that the message is properly formatted, perhaps also time-stamps it (i.e., records the precise time at which it was received), and routes it to the correct matching engine. Most major exchanges have

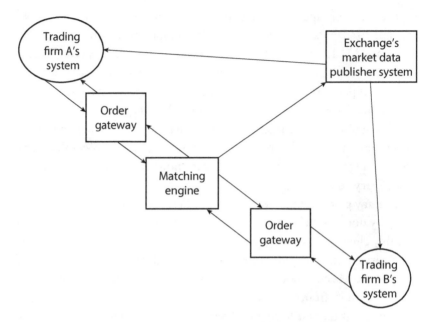

FIGURE 5.2. Inside a datacenter: highly schematic. Arrows indicate the direction in which electronic messages flow. For example, a trading firm's system sends orders (and cancellations of orders) to an order gateway, which in turn sends that system a "confirm" message when, e.g., one of the firm's orders has been added to the order book, and a "fill" message when one of its orders has been executed. For the trading firm's system to learn as quickly as possible about transactions (and other order-book changes) not involving the firm, the latter must pay the exchange for the datafeed from, and an ultrafast connection to, its market-data publisher system. *Source:* author's interviews.

multiple such engines, each of which maintains the order books for a particular subset of the financial instruments it trades.

If the relevant order book contains an existing order that the matching engine can match with the incoming order from firm A's system—if the incoming order is, for example, a bid to buy at or below a specific price, a match would be an existing order to sell at or above that price—the matching engine executes the trade and the exchange's computer system sends each of the two trading firms' systems a "fill" message, notifying it that its order has been executed. (If one of the orders is larger than the other, then the fill may only be partial.) If, on the other hand, there is no existing bid or offer in the order book that can be matched with the incoming order, then the latter is simply added to the book, and a "confirm" message to that effect is dispatched to the trading firm's system.[2] Similarly, if a trading firm's system sends in a message canceling or modifying one of its existing orders, a confirm message is sent to it when the exchange's system has done that.

The matching engine also sends the messages encoding new orders, executions of orders, and cancellations or modifications of orders to the exchange's market-data publisher system, or feed server.[3] Nowadays, these messages are almost always anonymized before being disseminated (i.e., the identifier numbers of the firms, trading groups, or individual traders submitting orders are removed), and the market-data publisher system dispatches this anonymous stream of order-book update messages—again, normally in the form of pulses of light in fiber-optic cables—to the computer systems of those firms that have purchased this fast, "raw" datafeed. Those systems sometimes react directly to individual messages (for example, to a message that reports a big trade), but mainly use the datafeed to maintain an up-to-date "mirror" of the exchange's order book.[4] The raw datafeed will normally travel from the exchange's systems to each firm's system through the same cable as the exchange uses to send fill and confirm messages, but the paths taken within the exchange's system by the datafeed and by direct messages will not be the same, so one path can be faster than the other. We shall return to this point later in the chapter, because issues that we might refer to as "the materiality of the small" (having to do with configurations and material procedures inside datacenters and even inside individual computer systems) can be highly consequential.

The Gold Line

Let us first consider, though, "the materiality of the large"—how signals are transmitted over the kilometers, tens of kilometers, or even thousands of kilometers between datacenters. Signals from outside are often at least as important to an HFT algorithm as what is going on inside the datacenter in which it is running. The most crucial path among the world's financial datacenters is the route from Chicago to the datacenters in New Jersey in which shares, Treasurys, foreign exchange, and options are traded (see figures 1.4 and 4.1). For the reasons explored in chapter 2, signals from Cermak and, since 2012, especially from the Chicago Mercantile Exchange's suburban datacenter are crucial to algorithms trading in New Jersey.

When high-frequency trading began to develop momentum in the late 1990s and early 2000s, the technology of choice for transmitting signals over substantial distances was fiber-optic cable, and telecommunications companies had already laid extensive networks of such cables. For nearly all human purposes, those existing networks were and are amply fast, so that telecoms had not needed to focus on speed of signal transmission. Rather, they chose paths (such as alongside railroad lines) along which it was easy to negotiate permission to dig trenches to lay their cables; they shaped their networks so that they served the maximum number of large population centers; and they often used hub-and-spoke configurations, sending signals not via the most direct path between two points but via their own switches or a meet-me-room in a centrally located datacenter such as Cermak or Halsey, a datacenter in Newark that is the main telecom hub in New Jersey. As will be discussed below, telecom companies also prioritized ease of repair over minimum cable length.

In HFT's early years, when pioneers like Automated Trading Desk were competing primarily with slow human beings, existing fiber-optic networks were fast enough for HFT as well. By the early 2000s, however, HFT firms increasingly found themselves competing with each other, and HFT's speed races began. The huge importance of the signals from Chicago meant that HFT firms started to focus on the time it took to transmit those signals to East Coast datacenters. But they found it frustratingly difficult to get telecommunications providers even to understand this concern. Simply asking a telecom company to provide the fastest route did not work:

> [Y]ou could go to your Verizon salesperson, and they had no such product in their catalog. They just sold circuits. The Verizon provisioning systems . . . didn't have the capacity to actually understand shortest path. They just knew you wanted a T-1 or a T-3 [or] whatever between point A and B, and they would provision on whatever [cables] happened to be available.[5] And by the way, they would reprovision it [shift to different cables] if they needed to do some load balancing . . . they never actually thought that anybody cared [about the exact physical route]. (Interviewee TO)

This attitude was even common when HFT firms tried to recruit telecom specialists:

> I was looking for a new head of the operations team and interviewed a whole bunch of people. Anytime somebody said, "I have all this experience [and] I know how to save you money," it was like, it's not the right fit. (Interviewee CF)

CF's priority, of course, was the speed of transmission, not its cost. Eventually, though, he found and began working closely with a particular salesperson for a telecom company who grasped that objective. That salesperson then "pitched the idea of him coming to [the HFT firm] and bringing one of his guys, and setting up basically a dark-fiber connection" between Chicago and the East

Coast that would follow "the most direct route" (CF). Dark fiber is a strand of a fiber-optic cable that is permanently available for the exclusive use of a particular firm, rather than in the shared use normal in telecommunications.

Chicago traders came to call that carefully planned dark-fiber connection the "gold line." Its speed gave the HFT firm in question a considerable advantage in the critical years in the first decade of the twenty-first century in which the HFT business was taking shape. The firm was predominantly a market-maker, systematically posting attractively priced bids and offers in order books that others could execute against, and, as described in chapter 3, electronic market-making of this kind helped foster the growth of trading venues with HFT-friendly economic and material features. As will be discussed in chapter 6, a major risk faced by market-making algorithms is that their bids or offers become stale (they are not updated fast enough when the market moves) and are then picked off by a faster algorithm. Having the gold line—the fastest connection between Chicago and the East Coast—gave the market-making firm in question a considerable degree of protection against this risk. (In contrast, if market-making algorithms are at high risk of being picked off, they have to increase the spread—the typical difference in price between their bids and its offers—to compensate for the resultant losses, so making prices on the trading venue in question less attractive.) Although it is impossible to be certain, it was therefore perhaps consequential that in those crucial years it was a market-maker, and not, in the terminology of chapter 6, a "taker," that had the gold line. The scale at which the firm was able to make markets strengthened the crucial "hinge" (discussed in chapter 3) between HFT market-making and HFT-friendly trading venues.

The gold line was not a new cable; rather, it was "pars[ed]" or "knit[ted]" together (interviewee CC) by leasing existing segments of fiber-optic cable close to the geodesic from Chicago to northern New Jersey and Manhattan. (As noted in chapter 1, the geodesic, or great circle, is the shortest path on the earth's surface between two given points.) Even a decade later, interviewees typically either did not know or were reluctant to tell me the gold line's exact route. Interviewee CC, however, says, plausibly, that it roughly followed Interstate 80 across northern Ohio, Pennsylvania, and northern New Jersey.[6]

"Just laying fiber"

Given that the gold line was constructed from segments of existing cables, it could not follow the geodesic exactly. It is not surprising, therefore, that at least one trader realized that if one owned a cable closer to the geodesic, any firm whose algorithms depended on the fast transmission of prices between Chicago and the East Coast would *have* to use it, and could therefore be charged high fees. Options trader Dan Spivey raised the money to construct an entirely new cable of this kind; the main investor was James Barksdale, former chief executive of Netscape Communications, a pioneering firm in web browsing.

Spivey and Barksdale's new firm, Spread Networks, negotiated with dozens of local governments and landowners for the rights to lay the new, more direct cable. The first chapter of Michael Lewis's *Flash Boys* (discussed in the appendix of this book on the literature on HFT), contains a wonderful description of the difficulties the firm faced as it negotiated the right to lay cable beside and beneath "small paved roads and dirt roads and bridges and railroads, along with the occasional private parking lot or front yard or cornfield" (Lewis 2014: 11), and then coordinated the work of 250 separate teams, of 8 people each, as they dug, drilled, and laid cable. Spread Networks kept the project secret for as long as possible. Since each team worked on only a small portion of the route, it would have been difficult for the workers to guess its purpose, and they were told that if anyone asked what was going on they should blandly reply, "Just laying fiber" (Lewis 2014: 8). Spread Networks spent at least $300 million (one interviewee suggested it may have been as much as $500 million) laying the new cable, but its bet that trading firms would have no alternative but to pay large sums to lease strands of fiber in the cable turned out to be correct. Former high-frequency trader Peter Kovac (2014: 3) reports that the fee was $176,000 per month, with a requirement to enter into leases several years long.

Proximity to the geodesic brought physical difficulties: for one thing, the Allegheny Mountains lay in the way, although interviewee TO tells me that the extent of drilling through rock is exaggerated in existing accounts, including one by this author and colleagues (MacKenzie, Beunza, Millo, and Pardo-Guerra 2012). Most telling, however, were two apparently minor episodes, described without comment by Lewis (2014: 20–22). The site of the first was in Chicago's once heavily industrialized southern outskirts, at the point where Spread's planned route met the Calumet River. Six efforts to drill under the river failed; Spread overcame the barrier only when it discovered a long-disused tunnel under the river through which it could run the cable. The second episode occurred in a small town in rural Pennsylvania, just east of a bridge over a formidable obstacle, the broad Susquehanna River. Spread had managed to get permission to drill through the bridge's concrete supports and run its cable under the roadway. At the eastern end of the bridge, though, the road ran along the riverbank, rather than continuing directly east. For Spread's cable to do that, the firm needed to obtain permission to lay it under one or the other of two parking lots. Their owners were each offered over $100,000, but initially neither budged. One operated an ice cream plant, and feared that the cable might be an obstacle if he wanted to expand it; the other had previously fallen out with the contractor whom Speed was employing at that point in the route. Only when the second owner finally relented were the new cable's eastern and western sections joined up.

The two episodes were the first clear manifestation of what we might call the tyranny of location in HFT. Einsteinian materiality—the way in which the speed of light becomes a binding constraint when nanoseconds become important—makes HFT, as noted in chapter 1, hugely sensitive to precise spatial locations. There were other places at which Spread's cable could have crossed the Calumet River, and the cable could simply have bypassed the Pennsylvania parking lots. But doing either of those would have introduced a small but potentially important time delay. As far as I can tell, the owners of neither the tunnel nor the parking lots realized that they controlled what had suddenly become a "pinch point," in interviewee DE's apposite phrase, quoted in chapter 1: a literal, not simply metaphorical, "obligatory passage point," to use the terminology of actor-network theory (Callon 1986: 204 and 205–6). Soon, though, those who owned or controlled crucial locations *did* start to realize that they could charge heavily for access to, or passage through, those pinch points. As discussed in chapter 1, in economists' terminology those owners can exact "rent": payments (much) higher than the minimum that would ordinarily persuade them to grant access or passage. (Most people who own parking lots in small towns in the US countryside would, I imagine, be delighted to accept considerably less than $100,000 for the minor inconvenience of having part of the lot cordoned off for a few days while a trench is dug, cable laid, and the trench filled in and resurfaced.)[7]

The western end of Spread's new cable, which began to operate in August 2010, was initially Cermak; it was later extended further west to the Chicago Mercantile Exchange's new suburban datacenter. From Cermak, the cable runs south and east close to the shore of Lake Michigan, then across rural Indiana and Ohio, along the south shore of Lake Erie, and then across rural Pennsylvania to New Jersey and Nasdaq's datacenter, before turning north to the Halsey datacenter in Newark (which is, as already noted, New Jersey's main telecom hub), then other New Jersey financial datacenters, and finally Manhattan. This close-to-geodesic routing was the cable's rationale, but the prioritization of speed had other effects that are not discussed even in Lewis's fine chapter. When laying a normal telecommunications cable, a construction crew's standard practice is to add considerable slack (typically 5–10 percent of a cable's total length):

> [W]hen you run fiber you put slack in . . . you take the cable and you just coil it up at each of [the amplifier] centers or . . . in manholes, and the reason you do that is because every once in a while the fiber gets cut. Someone is doing construction, a train derails, a bridge abutment erodes, whatever, and the cable breaks . . . What you want is a cable that's a little loose and you can pull the two ends together, splice them together, and you're good to go. (Interviewee TO)

It was difficult for Spread Networks to get the workers laying the cable (who, as noted, were not told its purpose) to depart from this standard practice:

> [A]t Spread there was a constant fight with the construction crews because they wanted to do what they've always done: "Why wouldn't you want slack in the network?" They didn't understand latency considerations: "Why do you care about a few microseconds [millionths of a second]?" (Interviewee TO)

The prioritization of speed also affected how trading firms used the new cable. Modern fiber-optic transmission employs an approach called dense wave division multiplexing, in which multiple channels of communication on a single fiber are kept from interfering optically with each other by using a different wavelength of light for each. A telecommunications firm will want to maximize the transmission capacity of each fiber, and so might use as many as a hundred different channels with different wavelengths. The firm will accept that this dense packing causes a small amount of optical interference, and, to take account of that, will employ software that processes the messages being transmitted, adding extra binary digits to them that enable errors in transmission to be detected and corrected. This "forward error correction," as it is called, adds a tiny delay, so HFT firms generally do not employ it. Instead, reports interviewee TO, they packed many fewer communications channels (perhaps as few as ten) into a single fiber of the Spread cable.

Speed, though, was not the only imperative that imposed itself on the Spread cable. The other, perhaps surprisingly, was perceived fairness. It would have been hard to recruit subscribers if they had feared that other subscribers would still be able to have a speed advantage. So Spread devoted considerable effort to ensuring that this would not happen to a subscriber who paid for premium access.[8] The distance between Chicago and New Jersey is sufficiently great that optical or electro-optical amplifiers are needed along the route, and Spread built 11 concrete bunkers to house this equipment. The bunkers are only about 15 meters long (50 feet), but as interviewee TO put it, "the reality is you're going up, down, and across, and so on. And if you do that 11 times it starts to add up." Different paths through the bunkers can aggregate to a consequential time difference, even when light pulses are traveling at 200,000 kilometers per second (about 125,000 miles per second). Spread therefore took great care to ensure that the paths in each bunker of each subscriber's fibers were equal in length. Even the slight physical inhomogeneity of the glass in the different strands of fiber was compensated for, an interviewee told me (although I haven't had this independently confirmed). The strands that had marginally lower refractive indexes were made ever so slightly longer—by a small amount of coiling—to ensure transmission times that were as equal as possible.

The new, direct cable laid by Spread Networks had immediate effects on trading. Automated trading firms that had been unable to, or had chosen not to, pay the high costs of using it suddenly found themselves at what in some cases was a serious disadvantage. Interviewee CV's firm, for example, had been an influential Chicago pioneer of the trading not just of Treasury futures but also of the underlying Treasury securities. "I couldn't pay Spread Network's prices," says CV, "I wasn't big enough for that." Other firms, with their faster New Jersey to Chicago link, "were beating us," he says:

> You couldn't get to the connection quick enough. You couldn't get to the other side [of the trade]. You'd get one side, and you'd put the order in for [Treasury securities in] New Jersey, and by that time it was gone. . . . It was a mess and the company was losing a lot of money.

"Cheap and quiet and fast"

For all of Spread Networks' focus on speed, the firm could do nothing about the physical phenomenon referred to in chapter 1: the slowing down of light by the glass from which optical fibers are made. Spread used Lucent's True-Wave® RS fiber, the fiber with the lowest refractive index, and thus the highest transmission speed, that could be used without requiring more frequent amplification and thus more delay-inducing bunkers. The refractive index of the glass in TrueWave is around 1.47 (Lucent Technologies 1998; the exact value depends on the wavelength being used), and that means that

TABLE 5.1. State-of-the-art one-way transmission times from the Chicago Mercantile Exchange's datacenter to Nasdaq's datacenter in New Jersey, in milliseconds (ms)

Prior to Spread Networks	around 8 ms
Spread Networks (August 2010)	6.65 ms
Limit in glass fiber (refractive index 1.47)	5.79 ms
AB Services/Alex Pilosov microwave link (September 2010)	5.7 ms
Fastest microwave links (May 2016)	3.98 ms
Einsteinian limit	3.94 ms

Sources: Laughlin et al. (2014), Alex Pilosov, McKay Brothers/Quincy Data, and miscellaneous. The Einsteinian limit is the time of transmission along the geodesic if it took place at the speed of light in a vacuum. Microwave links have been improved since 2016, but more recent transmission times are not fully public. Comparisons are not all like-for-like, for example, because of the 2012 relocation of the CME datacenter.

light travels in it at only just over two-thirds of the Einsteinian limit, the speed of light in a vacuum (see table 5.1).[9] Those who planned the Spread Networks cable were perfectly well aware that a potential alternative was radio transmission through the atmosphere, which has a refractive index that varies with air pressure, temperature, and concentration of water vapor, but is only marginally larger than 1.0, meaning that wireless signals travel at almost the speed of light in a vacuum. In previous decades, microwave wireless transmission had indeed been in widespread use for long-distance telephony. In particular, in the 1950s, AT&T had built an extensive US microwave network, the Long Lines system. That network, though, was decommissioned when fiber-optic cables entered widespread use.

Microwave wireless transmission, thus easily dismissed as yesterday's technology, initially seemed to pose little threat to the ultrafast Spread cable. Microwave is a "line-of-sight" technology: it requires a nearly direct, straight line through the atmosphere from source to receiver. Because of the curvature of the Earth, therefore, on any long path, such as that between Chicago and New Jersey, intermediate repeaters (typically on tall towers such as that shown in figure 2.2) are needed to receive, amplify, sometimes electronically filter, and retransmit signals. This equipment introduces delays that, although imperceptible to human senses and of no consequence in the use of microwaves in everyday telecommunications, seemed as if they would more than use up any speed advantage that microwave might have over the Spread Networks cable.

Perhaps, though, delays in microwave-repeater equipment might simply be the result of its designers having had no reason to focus on speed, and so perhaps microwave could still be faster even than Spread Networks' geodesic-hugging cable? The first person to build a Chicago–New Jersey microwave link for HFT was a Soviet-educated computer scientist, Alex Pilosov, who had emigrated to the United States, done consultancy work for various Wall Street banks, and set up a business as a provider of high-speed internet connections. "I sold my house," he told me, and "I borrowed as much money as I could," but he still had no more than around $500,000 to work with, very little for a major engineering project. The latter, he says, had to be "cheap and quiet and fast." He could not afford big expenses, to alert potential better-resourced competitors, or to have a lengthy delay before his link was operational and earning money.

In 2009, Pilosov began visiting HFT firms in the hope of recruiting a customer. He cut an unconventional figure. Alexandre Laumonier, in a wonderful account of HFT's microwave links (see the appendix on the literature), reports that Pilosov's Manhattan apartment was often a refuge for "geeks, artists, writers, and activists," including some involved in Occupy Wall Street (Laumonier 2019: 48), and Pilosov told me that at one HFT firm his nickname is "Kittens," because of the image on the T-shirt he wore at his first meeting. On his visits to firms, Pilosov did not disclose the transmission technology he intended to use, saying only that his link would be "faster than fiber." One HFT firm promised to pay Pilosov if he did indeed provide them with such a link, with Pilosov making an escrow deposit "just to show that I'm not a crackpot."

Pilosov found a small Czech company whose microwave-repeater equipment was fast by the standards of the day. Its speed was an accidental by-product of the simplicity of its design, and Pilosov paid the company to make improvements that further increased the speed. He and his main collaborator, engineer and computer scientist Anton Kapela (for whom see Laumonier 2019: 49–51), kept their microwave link low profile. Pilosov did not install what would have been telltale antennas on the roofs of either Cermak or the datacenter that was the link's New Jersey endpoint, but placed them some distance away. (At one point, his link ran via antennas on a van that he had persuaded the owner of a bowling alley close to the New Jersey datacenter to allow him to station in the bowling alley's parking lot.)

Pilosov himself researched in detail the best route for his microwave link, for example figuring out that the way to achieve a line-of-sight wireless connection over Lake Michigan—which from Chicago is around 80 kilometers (50 miles) across—was to install antennas on top of a lakeside skyscraper (he chose the Aon Center, which is 347 meters—more than 1,100 feet—tall).

He wrote his own computer code to ensure that interference with other signals would not be a barrier to approval by the Federal Communications Commission of the antennas making up his link (he delayed submitting the necessary "path-coordination notices" because they "would alert others that I'm building something"); did the structural calculations himself to show that his chosen towers were strong enough to support the antennas he wanted to install; and submitted the necessary paperwork to get the permission of tower owners, municipalities, and so forth to do so. It was hands-on work. Laumonier (2019: 53) describes Pilosov offering a couple of bottles of Scotch to the superintendent of a building in New Jersey, on the roof of which Pilosov had installed antennas, to turn a blind eye while he ran a cable down from the roof to the sidewalk. Pilosov saved money wherever he could. For example, he told me that one of the towers he used had been part of AT&T's Long Lines, and it still had an old antenna that Pilosov brought back into service rather than buy a replacement.

The tyranny of location temporarily softened. To fulfill Pilosov's contract with the HFT firm that was his customer, his microwave link simply had to be faster than Spread Network's cable, and the physical speed advantage of microwave over optical fiber gave him considerable latitude to depart from the geodesic and choose towers that would not cost too much and on which antennas could be installed without undue delay. He was even able to find a route on which he could use a radio frequency of 6 GHz (gigahertz) throughout its length; that is the most reliable of all the microwave frequencies available for commercial use in the US, but its popularity means that on some towers the risk of interference with existing links can make it impossible to install new 6-GHz radios. Pilosov's route ran as far south as the southern outskirts of Pittsburgh (some 100 kilometers, or 60 miles, from the geodesic), but even so Pilosov and Kapela succeeded in their goal of being faster than Spread's cable; see table 5.1.[10]

No microwave link, though, can escape the contingencies of the material world, either in its construction or its use. The antennas that transmit and receive microwave signals are awkwardly shaped, and often large and heavy—a big one can be 2.4 meters (nearly 8 feet) in diameter, and can weigh 500 pounds, or nearly a quarter of a metric tonne[11]—and antennas need to be hoisted up a tower that can be over 100 meters (more than 300 feet) tall, positioned exactly, and kept watertight, with both antennas and wiring attached to the tower securely enough to withstand gales (see figure 5.3). The tower climbers who do all of this require both the physical courage and strength to climb to and work at the top of a tower such as that shown in figure 2.2,

FIGURE 5.3. Microwave antennas. Courtesy of McKay Brothers.

and also meticulous attention to detail in that work. Pilosov found that the climbers to whom he contracted the installation of the antennas had the first of these characteristics, but not always the second; he discovered that his antennas had sometimes not been aligned properly, cables had not been tightly secured to the tower, and so on. His firm (and at least two others with which I have conducted interviews) ended up hiring its own climbers rather than simply using contractors. Pilosov tells me that he employed a small team "on full-time payroll," based at roughly the midpoint of the route in western Pennsylvania, "to respond to emergencies and do maintenance." Although put together quickly, his network proved impressively reliable. "I think the longest outage was 24 hours," he says, the result of a lightning strike. That should not have damaged his equipment, but when he investigated he discovered that the copper earthing wire that should have protected it had been stolen.

"Better be first 99 percent of the time than second 100 percent of the time"

Despite Pilosov's efforts not to reveal exactly what he was doing, HFT firms quickly realized that microwave links could be applied in trading. Once it was known that someone was offering to build a link faster than Spread's, it was not difficult to guess the likely technology. Around 15 to 17 Chicago–New Jersey microwave links were constructed from 2011 onward (interviewees do not agree on the exact number). Competition in speed among the links revived the rent-generating tyranny of location. Around a year after he completed his link, Pilosov told me, one of the tower companies came to me, and was like, "What the hell is going on? We have now six other people who all want to build this New York to Chicago route, basically almost the same tower[s]. They all [say they] have the business purpose of some disaster recovery" or some other bullshit. I was like "Well, I'll tell you what's going on but you have to promise me that you have to charge them three times what you're charging me. And I promise you that they will pay." And that's what happened. That happened.

Several of those new links were directly commissioned and owned by HFT firms, but those directly owned links have now been winnowed down by competition to two main ultrafast, geodesic-hugging links: one belongs to Vigilant (which is owned by the HFT firm DRW), the other to New Line, which is jointly owned by the HFT firms Getco (and now Virtu, following its takeover of the latter) and Jump. Vigilant's and New Line's longest-established competitor is McKay Brothers, founded by Robert Meade and Stéphane Tyč, both physicists who had done extensive work in finance. McKay Brothers does not itself trade (although Meade and Tyč have both done so in the past); it sells trading firms either private bandwidth—microwave's equivalent of dark fiber—or, via an affiliate company, fast data. Vigilant, New Line, and McKay are locked in an intense competition to be fastest. The older, slower links owned by trading firms other than those that own Vigilant and New Line seem generally to have been sold, or simply abandoned, because there is little point in spending money operating a link that is slower than the speed that can be obtained by leasing bandwidth on McKay's link.[12]

Meade and Tyč had met as physics PhD students at Harvard University, and McKay Brothers is named after Harvard's Gordon McKay Applied Science Laboratory. Although they too had "sunk most of [their] personal money" into the project, says Tyč, they had more capital than Pilosov, and worked more slowly. They were well aware that their new link would face eventual competition, and focused on designing it in such a way that it would be very hard for a competitor to be as fast or faster. To do so, they had to break with the existing cautious tradition of microwave-network design for telecommunications, which had placed great emphasis on reliability and virtually none on speed. As Tyč puts it:

> [W]e realized . . . that networks did not have to be designed in the "old and conservative way." Microwave engineers had applied recipes which worked perfectly but which imposed constraints that we relaxed. This

relaxing of engineering constraints allowed [us] to focus on the most important constraint for us, which was the total path length. We ruthlessly optimized this parameter to create a long-lasting network.

Meade and Tyč placed some of their repeaters much farther apart than had been previous practice, in part because they too had to cross Lake Michigan, but also because long "hops"—gaps between towers—minimize the number of repeaters and thus the delays they cause. Their longest hop was around 110 kilometers (about 70 miles). "Most microwave engineers will tell you that this is crazy stupid," says Tyč, because those engineers believed that transmission would become unreliable or even infeasible over that distance. Tyč remembers one engineer even "saying that microwave links over 50 kilometers were not possible."

The pursuit of speed required more than simply long hops. As already noted, of the wavelengths available for commercial microwave transmission in the US—6, 11, 18, and 23 gigahertz—6 GHz is the most reliable. As frequency increases, links become more vulnerable to what those involved call "rain fade": attenuation or loss of signal when it rains. (As Tyč explains, rain droplets "are conductive, so they interact with the [electromagnetic] field . . . and the field expends energy moving electrons inside the droplets. So [it] weakens itself.") If, however, McKay Brothers had restricted themselves to 6 GHz they would have had to depart from the geodesic, because by the time they built their link there were simply too many existing 6-GHz links close to the geodesic for them to be able to use only that frequency. So Meade and Tyč's firm used not just 6 GHz but also frequencies of 11, 18, and even 23 GHz to keep their route as close as possible to the geodesic, even though they knew it increased the likelihood of disruption by rain. As Tyč said to me, "We had a little motif: better be first 99 percent of the time than second 100 percent of the time."

The new McKay Brothers link entered service in July 2012. By then, the microwave speed race was well under way, and, as noted above, it has remained fierce ever since. All aspects of microwave transmission have been subjected to relentless scrutiny. Previous practice had been to place repeater equipment in a rack in a shelter at the base of each tower, but that means that the signal has to travel down the tower and back up again, so repeater equipment for microwave links for HFT is now weatherproofed and placed high up on towers, right beside antennas. To Pilosov's horror, digital systems (with their capacity to employ advanced filtering techniques to reduce the risk of interference with and from other signals) were discarded in favor of the speed obtainable using simpler, purely analog repeaters. Technological sophistication and speed do not always march hand in hand.

The early microwave links for HFT had used towers that were already in place, or sometimes buildings such as the Aon Center, which McKay Brothers also employed at first as the western end of the crucial hop over Lake Michigan. Existing towers, though, were often less than optimally sited with respect to the geodesic, or already crowded with antennas, or prohibitively expensive; their owners had grasped the potential to exact rent. When, for example, I asked Tyč about a surprising kink in McKay's initial route, he told me it was to circumvent a tower whose operator had seemed to agree to a lease but then suddenly telephoned McKay. "They were essentially trying to strong-arm us into getting something for themselves because they knew we needed that last asset to open [McKay's link]."

To keep competitive in speed it soon became necessary to build new towers. For example, a microwave route that follows the relevant geodesics from Chicago to northern New Jersey exactly will have to cross Lake Erie, but even though the crossing may be long it is likely to be at no great distance from the lake's southern shore (see figure 1.4). As late as January 2018, Tyč told me that as a result it was not necessary to actually cross the lake. "It suffices to be close to Lake Erie," he said. However, by November of that year, he reported that McKay was moving their route even closer to the geodesic, and that it would indeed now cross Lake Erie. The small community on Kelleys Island, about five kilometers (three miles) from the southern shore, had agreed to the building of a tall tower. Laumonier (2019: 57) reports that it is 137 meters, or 450 feet, high. The tower "will improve cell coverage," says Tyč, because it carries cellphone antennas as well as microwave dishes, and "also brings money to the island," while from McKay's viewpoint it allows Lake Erie to be crossed, not in one excessively long hop, but two more modest hops.

Just how competitive the Chicago–New Jersey microwave speed race is can be seen in how small the differences in speed are on a route for which the Einsteinian limit is just below four milliseconds (see table 5.1; a millisecond is a thousandth of a second). In May 2020, Tyč told me that the three fastest microwave links from the CME datacenter to the NY4/5 cluster of datacenters are now within a microsecond (a millionth of a second) of each other, and he expects that soon also to be the case for the other New Jersey endpoints (the Nasdaq and NYSE datacenters). That closeness in speed has meant a sharp focus on even the most minor sources of delay. Among these is "fiber tail," the short distance, which has to be traversed in "slow" fiber-optic cable, between a firm's equipment in a datacenter and its nearest microwave antenna. Originally, the antennas of the main competing microwave networks that were closest to the Chicago Mercantile Exchange's suburban datacenter were all on towers some distance away. Then, in 2016, an affiliate of the HFT firm Jump Trading paid nearly $14 million for a field on the far side of a road that runs near the datacenter, and placed a generator and two microwave antennas in a corner of the field (Louis 2017). Quite likely, Jump's expensive purchase was sparked by Webline Holdings, an affiliate of Jump's competitor DRW, having received a license from the Federal Communications Commission to place microwave antennas on a pole that is also closer to the CME's datacenter than the towers are. McKay Brothers, in its turn, obtained the permission of the relevant municipality to build a small new tower on the other side of the road from Jump's antennas.

In competition of this kind, the goal is no longer just to place antennas as close as possible to a datacenter, considered simply as an entire building; rather, what needs to be considered is exactly where cable from the nearest antennas can enter that building. The CME has never permitted firms to place their antennas in what would be the optimum location, on the roof of the datacenter. Only a small set of entry points can be used (interviewees disagree on the exact number), and the CME does not allow firms to site their equipment closer than 100 feet (just over 30 meters) to any of those entry points. "[W]e're at 101 feet from the [entry point]," Tyč told me in November 2018. "Literally, we taped it. We're slightly over 100 feet just to make sure that we're within CME regulations."

All of these painstaking, expensive efforts—each of which will have saved the microwave link in question a tiny but economically crucial amount of transmission time—were then trumped by the datacenter's owner erecting a tower of its own that is even closer to the building. At the time of writing, that new tower is the closest one can get to the datacenter. It is at most only a few tens of meters closer than the antennas that Jump, DRW, and McKay had installed near the datacenter's entry points, but the further small reduction in fiber tail that the new tower permits is sufficiently consequential that the speed-race competitors have no option but to pay to have their microwave antennas on it. I have, unfortunately, not been able to discover how much that costs.

The microwave speed race is thus very much characterized by sensitivity to—and therefore the tyranny of—exact location. It also manifests other entanglements with the everyday material world. Perhaps most important is the way in which rain may cause microwave signals in the higher frequency bands (especially 18 and 23 gigahertz) to fade, perhaps to such an extent that a link fails. As already noted, these higher bands may have to be used because of crowding at lower frequencies along the geodesic. Strikingly, as will be described in the next chapter, patterns of prices even in today's high-tech automated markets therefore seem sometimes to be influenced by whether or not it is raining between Chicago and New Jersey. Snow, especially wet snow, can also be disruptive, and severe gales can blow antennas out of alignment, while making it unsafe for tower climbers to realign them. More surprising, because it can be triggered by something as benign as a summer sunrise, is the fading of a microwave link that results from "ducting," a phenomenon in which local atmospheric conditions (similar to those that can lead to increased concentrations of pollutants) cause the paths of microwave signals to bend in such a way that they are attenuated or even not received at all.[13] "Ducting," Tyč reports,

> often occur[s] . . . around sunrise or . . . when there's a source of heat at a constant temperature, such as a lake which gets heated up in the summer and at night the surrounding ground goes cold but the lake stays warm.

Pilosov, similarly, says that on his link, "basically every summer morning you would experience attenuation."

Millimeter Wave and Lasers in New Jersey

What gave and still gives the Chicago–New Jersey fiber-optic and microwave links their huge importance to HFT is the signal that I call "futures lead" (whose history was explored in chapter 2) and, more generally, the connections between the trading of futures and the buying and selling of shares and other underlying financial instruments. Another class of signal, which I call fragmentation (by which I mean signals that are generated by the trading of the same shares in different places; see table 3.2), grew in significance as the number of exchanges and other venues trading US shares increased. Those exchanges and trading venues, and their matching engines, are almost all based in the triangle of New Jersey datacenters shown in figure 1.3. (A fourth datacenter, NJ2, close to the Hudson River, was important in the recent past but no longer plays a large role in HFT.[14]) With all the leading shares being traded in all the New Jersey share-trading datacenters, the transmission of data among those datacenters—New Jersey "metro," as those involved call it—has become an activity nearly as salient as the microwave links to

Chicago. There is a similar cluster of metro links around Greater London, and also in Chicago between Cermak and the Chicago Mercantile Exchange's suburban datacenter. For simplicity, however, I concentrate here mainly on New Jersey, the most important of these clusters. (For the same reason, I'm also not going to discuss the financial world's long-distance microwave routes other than Chicago–New Jersey. The most important of these other links are those between Washington, DC, where the release of US macroeconomic data takes place, and the trading datacenters in Chicago and New Jersey; and the link that connects London's financial markets to Frankfurt. The latter route is examined in detail in Laumonier [2019].)

The importance of speed of transmission among the various New Jersey datacenters in which shares are traded—now axiomatic—took time to be recognized fully. As Mike Persico, founder of Anova Financial Networks, puts it, when he first got involved in New Jersey metro in 2009, "low latency [fast speed] was [often] just a marketing term." Those who used the term often "didn't believe it. They didn't live it." It seems, for example, to have been quite common for the big banks that acted as brokers for institutional investors simply to lease fiber-optic links from telecom companies without inquiring in detail into the routes taken by those links. Thus it could easily happen, as interviewee TO told me, that the cables leased by banks did not run directly between the New Jersey share-trading datacenters but indirectly via the telecom hub, Halsey, in Newark. (It is, for example, quite possible that some of the complaints about HFT algorithms exploiting institutional investors' orders reported in Lewis's *Flash Boys* [2014] were the result of issues of this kind, with banks not paying enough attention to the material means by which those orders were distributed among datacenters.)

Even a specialist in financial communications networks such as interviewee UD did not initially prioritize speed. "The criteria [were] much more ensuring that it [his network] worked and that it worked consistently, rather than optimizing for low latency," he says. He did indeed end up creating a low-latency fiber-optic London metro network, but almost by accident. "[I]n 2007 . . . fiber optics were sold by the kilometer. . . . And because we didn't have a lot of money, I looked at buying the shortest [routes], which meant the cheapest fiber-optic network." In other words, trying to save money indirectly led him to save transmission time.

The low priority of speed did not last, either around London or in New Jersey. A number of specialist firms started to create fast, direct fiber-optic routes among the New Jersey datacenters. Those companies knew they could not hope to create an attractively fast New Jersey metro network just by leasing existing cables, but nor did they wish to incur the heavy expense involved in digging completely new routes. As Mike Persico says:

> [Simply by leasing] you're not going to end up with a path that's differentiated. So what you end up doing is . . . searching for what's called the "private right-of-way." Many times that could be a university. It could be a business. You petition them for use of their land, and they would grant you an easement to . . . dig up their property . . . pull the glass [fiber], and then you connect that to the public right-of-way. The proper parlance for that is . . . "microbuild." So you would microbuild in certain strategic segments to improve an undifferentiated path.

As Persico's company, Anova, was doing microbuilds in New Jersey, he also became aware of the long-distance microwave link that Alex Pilosov had constructed, and learned that it was even faster than Spread Network's geodesic-hugging cable. So he started to think about doing something similar in New Jersey. But using microwave there was not attractive. Its transmission capacity is limited, interviewees report, to around 90–150 megabits per second. That is not a major constraint on the transmission of data from Chicago to New Jersey, because only a small number of Chicago futures contracts—the major share-index futures, especially the ES (discussed in chapter 2), along with the most heavily traded Treasury and interest-rate futures, and perhaps the leading energy futures, foreign-exchange futures, gold futures, silver futures, and so on—are crucial to the trading in New Jersey of shares and other underlying cash instruments such as Treasurys. As Persico says:

> Not many people put the grains [grain futures] or the eggs on a microwave line. It's just not important because they're more insular [markets]. The reason to export things [market data] out of the CME [the datacenter of the Chicago Mercantile Exchange] is because [of the] effect . . . they have on a corresponding product [traded elsewhere].

The situation is different when the signals used in share trading are generated by the trading of the same shares on other exchanges. An HFT firm will often trade hundreds or even thousands of different stocks, so its algorithms in one datacenter need information on what is happening in the order books for all those stocks in the other New Jersey datacenters. That can mean that in effect the entire stream of order-book update messages being generated in one datacenter needs to be transmitted to the others (although, as noted below, it is still possible to "edit down" the stream strategically). It would be difficult, at times even impossible, to transmit these large volumes of data in any timely way by microwave.

Persico and others began to cast around for alternative transmission technologies, and identified millimeter-wave wireless as a candidate. Because millimeter-wave transmission is often used to connect mobile phone masts to the parent mobile-telephony company's computer systems, suitable millimeter-wave radios, operating in the E-band frequency range (70–80 gigahertz), were readily available. Crucially, millimeter-wave links have substantially higher transmission capacity—around 1 Gb (gigabit), or a billion binary digits, per second—than that of microwave links. Operating two millimeter-wave radios in tandem, with their waves cross-polarized (one at 180 degrees from the other) could increase bandwidth to 2 Gb/second. That, says Persico, was often enough to transmit almost complete streams of share-trading data in 2010.

Millimeter wave's transmission capacity, though, came with a major drawback: even greater vulnerability to rain than that of microwave transmission. Persico took the issue to the engineers in his company:

> I was looking for high-capacity, low-latency radios, and what I found was millimeter wave, but the downside was that in order to get [almost 100 percent] availability . . . which is a telco [telecommunications] standard, you needed to only go one or two miles [i.e., the chain of antennas could have only very short hops]. I looked at my engineers at the time, and I said, "OK, let's say it's not raining, how far can they go?" "They could go 12 to 15 kilometers." I said, "Yes, that's what I'm gathering." They said, "Your availability will be in the dumps." I said, "95 percent in the dumps?" They said, "Yes, horrible." I said, "Build it." They looked at me and . . . they said, "This is insane."

Having large numbers of antennas and repeaters in a millimeter-wave link would slow it down too much, which is why Persico was prepared to accept quite a high level of interruption by rain in order to achieve higher speed. Potential contractors, though, shared his engineers' skepticism:

> They would laugh and say, "I'm going to tell you something: 1) you're an idiot, and 2) we're not going to do it, and you should say 'thank you' because I'm doing you a favor because it'll never work."

Persico nevertheless persisted, and in late 2010 opened the first millimeter-wave link for the financial industry. It connected the New York Stock Exchange to NY4, the New Jersey datacenter that housed the matching engines for one of the new electronic share-trading venues, Direct Edge. The connection was, however, indirect. Even though the New York Stock Exchange had opened its new datacenter in New Jersey in August 2010, it did not at first allow direct external access to it. Trading firms could connect to it only via a number of NYSE POPs ("points of presence"), one of which was in 111 Eighth Avenue, a Manhattan datacenter with a central role in the Internet (see Blum 2012: 163–64). Persico's new millimeter-wave link ran from there to NY4, a distance of 11 kilometers (about 7 miles), in two hops of modest length, one from 111 Eighth Avenue to just across the Hudson River, the second from there to NY4. The new link was an immediate commercial success. "We had a tranche of capacity and it sold out in six hours," says Persico.

Intense efforts then followed to build fast millimeter-wave networks among the New Jersey datacenters shown in figure 1.3, with at least seven such networks being created (see the list in Tyč 2018). Keeping the paths of those links as close as possible to the geodesics among the New Jersey datacenters is just as crucial as on the Chicago–New Jersey route, so quite specific locations—either towers or suitable tall buildings, often in unprepossessing industrial areas—are greatly sought after. As Persico says:

> Sometimes these landlords end up with the equivalent of a Willy Wonka golden ticket, because when they purchase[d] these properties, this was the furthest thing from their mind, and all of a sudden . . . it becomes very lucrative.[15]

Fiber tail, too, is just as much an issue in New Jersey as in Chicago. The ideal location for a route's final antennas is directly on the roofs of the two datacenters it links, but access to the roofs of the Nasdaq and New York Stock Exchange datacenters is restricted (SEC 2013b and 2015). Antennas can be placed on the roof of NY4, but exactly where on the roof is important. In one of my interviews with him, Tyč used McKay Brothers' remarkable system that shows both the precise routes of the firm's wireless links and the layout of datacenters:

> If you look at NY4, for instance, if you overlay the actual map of the datacenter, on the roof there are rails . . . Here [pointing] there's a rail . . . and here [again pointing] they can . . . go down [run cable into the building] here. Our cabinet [in NY4] is not too far from that rail. The cable goes down here [pointing] and goes to our cabinet and clients next to us would connect efficiently. That's the type of thing that we try to optimize.

The New York Stock Exchange datacenter is "one of the largest technical challenges" for millimeter-wave transmission in New Jersey, says Persico:

> It sits in a bowl [a shallow dip in the landscape]. Then on the rim of that bowl are old-growth forests. So there are very few ways in and out of [the New York Stock Exchange datacenter] to [NY4&5 and the Nasdaq datacenter]. There are [angles which] may be the best on a piece of paper or on Google Earth to get to your final destination, they [local communities] may let you put up a tower but you're not touching a tree. . . . So . . . some of the very first networks were circuitous.

Building a very tall tower at the New York Stock Exchange datacenter would have solved the problem of the dip in the landscape, but such a tower would have been highly visible and, says Tyč, unlikely to be permitted by the prosperous community that surrounds the datacenter. The solution, reports Persico, turned out to be to build a tall tower some distance south of the datacenter, in an area in which it was easier to negotiate permission, and then be able to "shoot down"—that is, to transmit millimeter waves to and from an antenna high on that tower to a lower antenna close to the datacenter, at an angle sufficient to clear the rim of the bowl and the trees on it.

Millimeter wave's vulnerability to rain, however, remained a persistent obstacle, not just in its financial uses but also in its use to connect mobile-phone masts to their parent systems. Focusing on the latter use of millimeter waves, a firm called AOptics had seized on laser transmission through the atmosphere as a possible complementary technology. Rain has little effect on laser transmission, though fog is a major problem; millimeter wave is heavily disrupted by rain but not by fog. Drawing on technology developed for laser communication among fighter jets, AOptics developed a dual-mode transmission technology that employs both millimeter wave and laser.

Anova Financial Networks, which was active in providing millimeter-wave links in New Jersey metro, formed a joint venture with AOptics to apply the latter's laser technology in finance. Persico was alerted to that technology by a magazine article "about how the Department of Defense was using [it on] fighter jets. They would take a laser and they would mount it on the belly of a plane. It would be on a 360-degree gimbal, and it would swivel and allow the jets to talk to each other." If AOptics's adaptive (i.e., self-aligning) laser technology worked in that hugely demanding environment, reasoned Persico, "wouldn't it work if a tower twists and sways [in the wind]?" Anova licensed the technology from AOptics (finally buying the full rights to it when AOptics, which had not found the major mobile-telephone

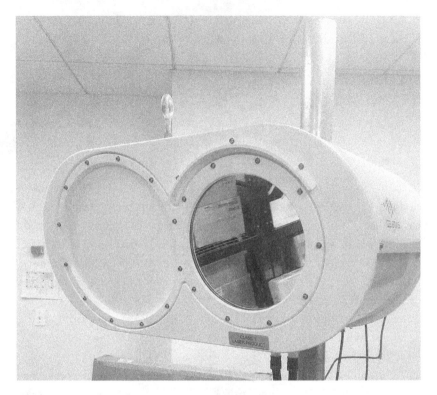

FIGURE 5.4. Anova Financial Networks' integrated millimeter-wave/atmospheric laser unit. The millimeter-wave system is on the left, the laser system on the right. Author's fieldwork photograph.

customer it sought, went out of business), and built a weather-resistant network of integrated laser/millimeter-wave links among the New Jersey share-trading datacenters, using computer-controlled hybrid devices (one of which is shown in figure 5.4) to seamlessly switch between laser and millimeter-wave transmission as weather conditions change.[16]

High tech as that is, an utterly mundane material phenomenon threatened to cause a substantial difficulty: with the equipment needing to be in the open air, on towers or on top of tall buildings, it was inevitable that bird droppings would fall on the glass of the laser units, potentially blocking signals. As Persico told me:

There were literally seven figures [a sum in excess of $1,000,000] spent on creating a [coating] that was resistant to bird droppings, and the way that [bird droppings were] simulated [in testing coatings] is that honey has the same viscosity [and it was poured] on the units to develop a [coating] where that would slough off.

Material Constraint and Structural Advantage

A deeper difficulty than bird droppings was that, as share trading in the New Jersey datacenters ramped up, rates of order-book update messages began to exceed the typical 1-gigabit-per-second transmission capacity of millimeter-wave links. Bursts of data from venues such as Nasdaq and the New York Stock Exchange can rise to, and indeed briefly beyond, the full 10-gigabit-per-second capacity of the fiber-optic cables that typically carry that data. Such bursts are reasonably short-lived—"at least 10 microseconds," says Tyč, but "never . . . 10 milliseconds"—but the data transmitted during a burst of activity are crucial to trading.

Firms trading shares in other New Jersey datacenters can pay Nasdaq and NYSE to receive their full raw datafeeds transmitted over millimeter wave by companies that are affiliates of those exchanges. When, however, a burst of 10-gigabit-per-second data has to be transmitted through a wireless "pipe" with a much more limited capacity, it will encounter what network specialists call "buffering delay": it cannot be transmitted as fast as it is received (see the example in Tyč 2018). That constraint, though, can be circumvented by an HFT firm that possesses its own millimeter-wave link (as at least one such firm does) or leases private bandwidth on such a link. It can "edit down" the raw datafeed to 1 gigabit per second or less, keeping only signals useful to its algorithms' trading, which can then be transmitted without buffering delay. Such a firm might, for example, transmit by millimeter wave only actual transactions, and not other order-book updates (or even perhaps only transactions in the leading stocks, and not all stocks), while relying on fiber-optic cables or the more "public" millimeter-wave services to fully update its systems' mirrors of order books in other datacenters.

A capacity of this kind to receive signals useful in trading before others do is of course a source of structural advantage. It is therefore of some interest that it has been suggested by communications supplier McKay Brothers that this specific structural advantage could be nullified by use of a different form of wireless transmission: LMDS (Local Multipoint Distribution Service). This employs a segment of the frequency spectrum—26–31.3 gigahertz—that is intermediate between microwave and conventional E-band millimeter wave. Access to LMDS frequencies was auctioned by the Federal Communications Commission in the late 1990s, at which point it was believed that LMDS would be used for local-area television broadcasting. This never happened, so the bidder that had won the right to use LMDS throughout New Jersey did not exercise that right. In 2013–14, says Tyč, McKay

Brothers "went to the owner and said, 'Can we lease that from you?'" in the areas needed to connect the New Jersey datacenters. Having struck a deal with the owner, McKay then set about working with radio specialists to develop radios for transmitting and receiving signals in this frequency band; because the band had never been used, LMDS radios were not available commercially.

In its digital aspects, says Tyč, an LMDS radio is not very different from a conventional E-band millimeter-wave radio, but the analog components of an LMDS radio are easier to improve, in particular to make more "linear." So the transmission capacity of LMDS can be closer to what information theory posits as the maximum possible, given the physical characteristics of the channel (closer, in other words, to the "Shannon Limit").[17] This gives LMDS greater capacity than E-band. McKay Brothers reports a capacity of five to seven gigabits per second being achievable with LMDS, closer to the maximum data rate of full raw datafeeds. On McKay's calculations, this greater capacity (together with an LMDS link being slightly faster than E-band, because LMDS needs fewer hops and it is possible for an LMDS link to hug the geodesic particularly closely) is sufficient to remove any structural advantage of private links over quasi-public data transmitted via LMDS.[18] McKay's LMDS network (which became fully operational in the summer of 2019) is, however, not the final act in the material political economy of data transmission in New Jersey, as we shall see in chapter 7.

The Materiality of the Small

HFT's "materiality of the large" (the mechanisms of data transmission among datacenters) has an even larger-scale transoceanic aspect: the submarine fiber-optic cables, shortwave radio links (Van Valzah 2018), and—perhaps eventually—swarms of low-earth-orbit satellites that carry financial data from continent to continent. Let me, though, set these aside here (for discussion of them, see MacKenzie 2019c), and end this chapter on HFT's physicality by returning to "the materiality of the small": to what goes on inside datacenters.

My introduction to its more controversial aspects came early in the research, in my first meeting, in October 2011, with a young Chicago trader. "Everyone's colocated," he said. HFT firms all have their computer systems in the same building as the exchange's system. "[B]ut how are you obtaining the information of what's trading?" he went on. "Are you waiting for the exchange to give you that information?" In saying that, he was referring to the pathway, shown in figure 5.2, via which information flows to trading firms' systems from the exchange's market-data publisher system in the form of the datafeed that the exchange sells to trading firms. "Some companies do [wait]," he continued, but "some companies don't wait for the exchange to tell them what's trading." Intrigued, I tried to pursue the issue:

> AUTHOR: Oh, so how do you manage to . . .?
> INTERVIEWEE AC: That I can't . . . I mean not only would I lose my job, I might lose my legs too!

It wasn't just a vivid turn of phrase, AC told me in one of our subsequent meetings. He had received this warning from a senior employee of his company. "The look on his face was stone seriousness. He was not joking at all." A year and a half after my first meeting with AC, an article in the *Wall Street Journal* (Patterson, Strasburg, and Pleven 2013) revealed the mechanism that he had been referring to, and so enabled him to talk to me about it explicitly. If a trading firm had a bid or an offer in one of the order books of the Chicago Mercantile Exchange, and that bid or offer was executed against, the "fill" message reporting that transaction typically reached the firm's system before the trade appeared in the CME's datafeed. (One Chicago trading firm reported average time differences, in two weeks of December 2012 and January 2013, of one to four milliseconds, or thousandths of a second; Patterson et al. 2013: 2.) As a result of the time difference, said AC, it was worth placing small "scout orders" in the order book simply to obtain early information that prices were changing.

In 2018, the HFT firm Quantlab Financial, based in Houston, told the *Wall Street Journal* that in December 2017, the median time difference between a fill message from the CME's system arriving at Quantlab's system and news of the corresponding execution appearing in the CME's datafeed was about 100 microseconds (Osipovich 2018). John Michael Huth, Quantlab's Chief Operating Officer, called the time difference a "loophole" that could be exploited by "canary orders" equivalent to AC's scout orders:

> [It] not only provides a material advantage . . . but it also incentivizes weird behavior that distorts . . . true supply and demand . . . Because the largest . . . fill advantage is obtained by the orders nearest to the top of the queue [for execution], firms have an incentive to race to carefully position detector orders to capture the largest time advantage. Participants might line a price level with small, 1-lot, passive buy orders that they fully expect to take losses on so that even larger profits can be obtained

by aggressively selling based on the early fill information gleaned—these detector orders are sometimes referred to as sacrificial "canary orders." (Huth 2018)

A spokesperson for the Chicago Mercantile Exchange pointed out to the *Wall Street Journal* that it had "dramatically decreased the latency between public market data and private trade confirmations" (Osipovich 2018); the Quantlab figure was indeed only around a twentieth of the average time difference reported in 2013. Nor is the fact that a fill message can arrive faster than the report of the corresponding execution in an exchange's datafeed necessarily the result of the exchange's having consciously decided that this should happen. Additional computer processing is involved in assembling order-book updates into a datafeed, and it can be difficult technologically to ensure that a simple fill message is not faster (interviewee BM). At the same time, it is not necessary that fills should be first. Europe's leading future exchange, Frankfurt-based Eurex, also used to send fills first, but in 2012 Eurex reconfigured its systems so that the report on its datafeed of an execution now almost always arrives before the private fill message (Osipovich 2018).

Whether a fill message reporting execution of an order *should* be sent before the execution is reported on an exchange's datafeed is an issue of material political economy on which the world of HFT is divided, with strong opinions on both sides. Several Chicago traders defended the sending of fills first. You are "getting a fill" because you are "taking risk," said one, and in any case "it's a known thing"; interviewee AC's manager had been wrong if he imagined that other trading firms had not also noticed the time difference. I was in Chicago in May 2013, a week after the publication of the original *Wall Street Journal* article on the phenomenon (Patterson et al. 2013), and another trader (interviewee AJ) told me that that the time difference, originally "seconds," had shrunk to "one or two milliseconds," and he particularly objected to the issue being portrayed as a "loophole" beneficial to HFT firms such as his:

> I am not getting 50 percent of the fills, so it's hurting me more than it's benefitting me. . . . [It] benefits everyone who gets the fill. That's just how it is.

AJ had even complained to the lead journalist's editor, telling the latter that he was no longer going to work with the *Journal*'s other reporters.

Six years later, in October 2019, interviewee DI told me that he viewed the early arrival of at least some fill messages as a welcome, perhaps even necessary, incentive for firms whose systems are not the fastest to make markets (post bids and offers in order books) in futures contracts. It is "a way to generate an edge," he said. If his firm's system received notification of a fill on a futures contract (such as a Treasury future or share-index future) that tends to move in price before the underlying asset or assets, it could take advantage of that. As DI says, "You can 'get out of the way' on BrokerTec or Nasdaq . . . or you can 'aggress.'" In other words, if your algorithms are market-making in Treasurys on BrokerTec or in shares on Nasdaq, they can cancel bids or offers that are about to become stale; or they can profitably execute against other firms' stale bids or offers. Eurex, he continued, was "losing control of their market" as a result of the system change that results in fill messages now arriving after the corresponding information in Eurex's datafeed. The reason, in his view, is the reduced incentive for any other than the fastest HFT firms to make markets on Eurex. He attributed the news that Eurex is experimenting with a "speed bump" of the kind discussed in chapter 6 as an unwelcome, belated effort by the exchange to extend material protection to slower market-making algorithms.

Cables, Getting Close to the Metal, and the Materiality of Messages

The impassioned dispute about whether fill messages should be quicker than an exchange's datafeed is an example of the political economy of HFT's "materiality of the small." It is an issue in which alternative ways of configuring a technological system are economically consequential and in a broad sense political (because the alternatives favor some participants and disadvantage others). Another economically consequential issue is the cabling of datacenters, in particular the cables that connect a trading firm's colocated servers to an exchange's systems. (Colocation, as already noted, is the placement of trading firms' servers in the same building as an exchange's computer system.) Since it takes around a nanosecond (a billionth of a second) for a pulse of light in a fiber-optic cable to travel 20 centimeters, having a cable that is shorter by as little as a meter thus saves five nanoseconds. Ten years ago that would have given only a very small advantage; now, on many exchanges, a five-nanosecond advantage could well be the difference between success and failure in trading.

In the early days of colocation, it seems that exchanges often did not have fixed procedures governing where in a datacenter trading firms' servers should be placed. In a situation such as that, says interviewee BZ, "you have to find out where things are," including where exactly the exchange's matching engines are located. "You have to understand physically the layout," not just the spatial layout but also any digital switches through which signals pass. Gaining that understanding could involve what BZ calls "a bit of social engineering"—"taking people out for beers"—as could acting on the knowledge thus gained. "You have to know people," he says. "You have to be able to get your equipment into that [optimal] location in the datacenter."

In my interviews, especially at the start of the research (2011–13), I would often hear rumors of HFT firms secretly drilling through walls (or, in the case of Cermak, through the building's floors) to shorten the cables that connect them to exchanges' matching engines and market-data publisher systems. Most major exchanges now have a policy that dictates a set, equal length for "cross connects," the cables that link each colocated trading firm's servers to the exchange's system, a policy that is implemented by lengthening (by coiling) the cables that connect those servers that are located closer to its system. (Cable coiling of this kind is also what enables NY4 and NY5, though they are separate buildings, to be run in effect as a single datacenter. Cross-connect cables to the exchanges in those datacenters are of equal length, wherever in the buildings a trading firm's systems are located.)

It can, nevertheless, still be possible for firms to get a speed advantage by paying for a higher-capacity cable to connect its system to the exchange in question.[19] As with the millimeter-wave links in New Jersey, a higher transmission capacity means lower buffering delays. In at least some cases, too, the more expensive connection bypasses digital switches that introduce small but significant delays to signals traveling through less expensive connections. In January 2017, an interviewee told me that his firm had measured an average time difference—potentially hugely consequential—of three microseconds (three-millionths of a second) between the slowest and fastest fiber-optic connections offered by one exchange.

The need within HFT for close attention to the material world is not restricted to cables and switches. I had learned this at the first HFT conference I ever attended, in November 2011, when a technology firm's sales staff fanned out across the lunchtime tables, trying to sell trading firms liquid cooling systems to enclose their computer servers and a specially designed server that came already fully submerged in coolant fluid. Their pitch was that HFT firms could then safely "overclock" their computers, or run them faster than the speed at which they were designed to operate, which normally makes them heat up dangerously and begin to fail.

Above all, the programming of HFT algorithms must take into account the materiality of the machines on which those programs will run. There is widespread use in HFT of the programming language C++, which many of my interviewees regard as the most suitable for HFT because it allows a degree of "close-to-the-metal" control over the physical implementation of a computer program that can be hard to achieve with other programming languages. With C++, says interviewee CZ, "you can build a level of abstraction, and then, when you need to, you can just blow right through it and get down to the hardware." (Not all my HFT interviewees, I should note, are enthusiasts of C++. Proponents of Java argue that its skillful use can achieve similar speeds. Indeed, the easiest way to spark heated debate among practitioners of HFT is often simply to ask which programming language best suits the activity's demands.)

Another aspect of HFT's materiality is the physicality of bids, offers, order-book updates, and other messages. These travel through the cables connecting a trading firm's system to the exchange's system in the form of what a computer specialist would call packets: structured sets of binary digits (each consisting of perhaps a few thousand such digits). In the cables of a datacenter, a packet is physically a collection of laser-generated pulses of light. As such, it takes time for a packet to be transmitted and to be received. The light pulses that encode thousands of binary digits can't be transmitted all at once. On a standard 10-gigabit connection (in other words one via which around ten billion binary digits can be transmitted per second), each binary digit takes on average a tenth of a nanosecond to be transmitted or received, so a typically sized packet of, for example, 5,000 binary digits takes around 500 nanoseconds to be fully received or fully transmitted. A trading firm's system may, therefore, be able to save time by processing an incoming packet "bit-by-bit" (binary digit by binary digit) rather than, as would be normal in nearly all other forms of computing, waiting for the full packet to be received and checked for errors in transmission before beginning processing. (Packets have a standard format, and binary digits early in a packet may contain crucial information for trading.)

The most intriguing aspects of the materiality of messages are techniques of HFT based on the physicality of orders, of bids and offers. (These techniques are important, but inevitably rather technical, so readers, if they wish, can skip the remainder of this section and move to the chapter's final section. With two exceptions [Mavroudis and Melton 2019: 158; Mavroudis 2019: 8], the techniques have not been discussed to my knowledge in the academic literature on HFT, only in a blog by trader Matt Hurd.)[20] What come into play here are what interviewee DH calls "weird tricks you can play when you're at the level of the hardware, where you can do strange things on the network to make things go just a tiny bit faster." In particular, the placement and cancellation of orders can be speeded by what interviewee DD calls "speculation," which GR calls "speculative triggering." If, for example, a firm's system anticipates a price movement, it can start to send to the exchange's system a packet or series of packets encoding an order that responds to that movement. If, as it does so, no data containing evidence of the movement are received, the system can then kill the order, for example by simply ceasing to transmit, or, as DD puts it, by "scrambl[ing] the checksum."[21] In either case, the exchange's system will treat the incoming packets as malformed or erroneous and discard them, meaning that no order is actually placed.

Sometimes, indeed, says DD, "packet-sending preemption . . . may be more systematic . . . you may always be sending [packets] . . . regardless [in] the hope you may get a trigger at a time [at which it is possible] to add [appropriate binary digits] to the packet" to turn it into a valid order. When I first learned of the preemptive dispatch of incomplete order messages, I could not determine whether it was common. Gradually, I have come to realize that most likely it is quite widespread. The ultrafast response time of 42 nanoseconds quoted by interviewee CS (see chapter 1) seems as if it must involve it. A response that fast would be impossible to achieve with a conventional computer system; it requires a specialized FPGA chip of the kind described in the next section. As far as I am aware, both the incoming signal and outgoing order would have to pass through the portion of the FPGA known as the SerDes (serializer/deserializer), and DD estimates that this takes around 20 nanoseconds in each direction, so speculative triggering seems necessary to achieve a response time as fast as 42 nanoseconds.

Speculative triggering seems sufficiently widespread that the world's two leading futures exchanges, the Chicago Mercantile Exchange and Eurex, have felt the need to mitigate its effects. Their fear seems to be that their systems will be overloaded with order messages that trading firms' systems start to send speculatively and then kill by ad hoc techniques such as scrambling checksums. The Chicago Mercantile Exchange has applied for a patent on a set of mechanisms for detecting speculative triggering (Lariviere et al. 2018), while in February 2020 Eurex told its market participants that it was taking "steps to disincentiv[ize] behaviour that may be detrimental for market and system structure" and that could lead to "excessive system usage" (Eurex 2020). Eurex is not trying to prohibit speculative triggering, but intends to provide a mechanism by which a participant's system that has started to send fragments of an order message can divert it by sending a fragment that includes a "discard IP [Internet Protocol] address." This will have the effect that the fragments of a speculative order need not be processed by an order gateway and so do not overload Eurex's core systems.[22]

Hardwired HFT

HFT's need for speed has led it to become ever more deeply embedded in the material world. "Now," said interviewee AG, as long ago as October 2016, the computation needed for at least the fastest forms of HFT is "all in FPGAs and hardware." An FPGA, or field-programmable gate array (see figure 5.5), is a silicon chip into which have been imprinted large—indeed often enormous—numbers of "gates" (tiny circuits that implement simple logical functions) that are programmable in the sense that they can be configured electronically, by someone using the FPGA, to perform a specific computational task. Typical such tasks include processing and/or editing the datafeed from an exchange, detecting the presence of a simple signal (such as a price move in a relevant futures contract, an order-book imbalance, or a big trade), and dispatching in response an appropriate order or cancellation of an order to that exchange. An FPGA can be electronically reconfigured by a trading firm's conventional computer server even in the midst of trading. The FPGA, however, "reacts [to incoming signals] without the CPU involved" (interviewee CS; the CPU is a computer's central processing unit), and that is what gives an FPGA its speed advantage.[23]

Configuring the layers of an FPGA chip is an inherently material process. "I'm a software guy by training," says CN, whose trading firm, at the time of my interview with him in 2017, had begun implementing its HFT in FPGAs. "In software now everything is kind of virtual. I can have as much memory as I want." Not so with FPGAs, whose materiality could never be ignored. "The [FPGA] chip is only so big, so you have this real-estate issue," CN continues. If the computation you are trying to do, or its demands on memory, "doesn't fit on the chip, you're done"—that is, the implementation of the algorithm in the FPGA is not feasible. Just as spatial location is crucial in HFT's "materiality of the large," so it also matters on the layers of an FPGA chip. Computation in an FPGA, as in most computer devices, is coordinated by a "clock": an oscillator that sends out electrical pulses separated by tiny, regular time intervals. "[I]f the elements in your design"—in other words, the physical circuits in different locations in the FPGA chip that implement

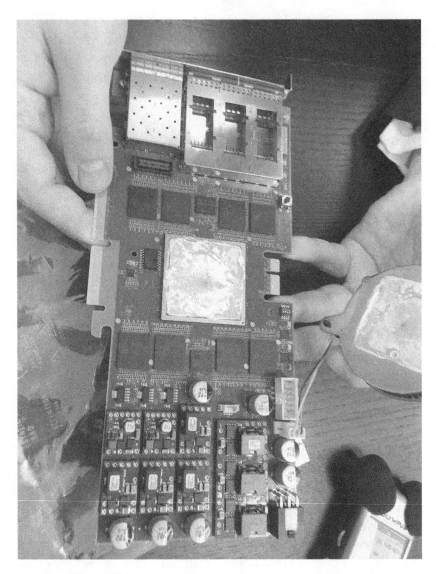

FIGURE 5.5. A field-programmable gate array (FPGA) in a "development kit" for programming and testing. The FPGA is the large central chip with white paste on it. Author's fieldwork photograph.

the computation you are seeking to hardwire into the FPGA—"are separated too much by . . . physical distance, where the signals can't get to where they have to be before the next clock cycle, you don't have a stable design," says CN. Physical location in the FPGA is "very important," agrees interviewee UC. Although the tools used by FPGA designers automate the necessary "placing and routing" (as it is called), "people lean on the tools" indirectly to influence physical location. "It's kind of a tough thing to get right" (CN). "That's the hardest [skill]: understanding the physical constraints of it," concurs UC.

The material configuration of FPGA chips may seem a long way away from questions of political economy, but it is worth noting that what is being hardwired into these chips often seems to be the capacity to detect and respond ultrafast to simple classes of signal such as "futures lead"—signals whose political economy was explored in chapters 2 and 3. I also find it intriguing that at least some of those whose business is the design of FPGAs (and ultrafast digital switches based on FPGAs) seem uncomfortable with the activity. I never directly ask those to whom I speak for their views on HFT's speed races, because it is more revealing if they themselves raise the topic, and if so how. Mostly they do not bring it up; they seem to take for granted that those races are an aspect of how things are and have to be. I was therefore struck when, during fieldwork at an industry event, I talked with one vendor of FPGA-based technology for HFT, who—within five minutes of starting to talk to me—told me that he was part of what he believed to be an arms race. Pointing at the ultrafast digital switches laid out on the table in front of him, he said, "You'd see similar stuff at an arms fair." He was by background an academic and said he would prefer to be researching and writing, but he had found that an academic salary was insufficient to live on in the kind of city in which he wished to live.

Another FPGA expert, interviewee UC, told me how specialist vendors of FPGAs "every so [often] release an update that's going to shave 5–10 nanoseconds" off an FPGA's processing time. Shaving off nanoseconds may eventually, he suggested, have advantages in other domains such as network security, but, for now, he said:

> I don't think . . . there is any other industry than the finance industry that can pay for it. . . . [I]t's . . . mind-numbing to look at this whole industry where you have a lot of people with extended training that spend night and day shaving nanoseconds. Where, if you could put that brainpower to something else, maybe something different, but that's what it is. . . .

Why, though, is today's world of trading "what it is"? Why is an expensive arms race in speed embedded so deeply in HFT's materiality? To answer that question, we must examine how HFT algorithms interact with each other. That is the topic of the next chapter.

6

How HFT Algorithms Interact, and How Exchanges Seek to Influence It

An HFT algorithm acts by bidding to buy the shares or other financial instruments being traded, by offering to sell them, or by canceling or modifying one of its existing bids or offers.[1] As we shall see, a cancellation can be just as crucial as a bid or an offer, but let's start with those. Market participants classify a bid or an offer into two broad categories. The categorization sounds at first like a small technicality, and I'm embarrassed by how long it took me to grasp that we're dealing here with what is in many ways the central divide in HFT. It is at the heart of the field's speed races, sometimes providing a defining characteristic of participants' skill sets and occasionally even of their self-identities.

I'll call the two categories of order "making" and "taking," although participants' terms for them vary. What makes an order one rather than the other can indeed at first seem minor: its price relative to that of the existing orders in the order book. Let's refer once again to the book used as an illustration in chapter 1, shown again here for convenience (figure 6.1). Consider a bid to buy shares at $29.49. That would be called a "liquidity-providing," "adding," or "passive" order. In what follows I'll call it a "making" order, because the most systematic use of orders of this kind is in "market-making." The matching engine cannot execute a bid at $29.49 immediately, because there are no offers to sell at that price to match it with. Instead,

BIDS TO BUY

$29.49	100	100	200
$29.48	50	30	
$29.47	100		
$29.46	50	100	100	100
$29.45	200		

OFFERS TO SELL

$29.54	100	200	
$29.53	50		
$29.52	40	50	
$29.51	50	50	200
$29.50	100	100	100

FIGURE 6.1. An order book. In most exchanges, the bids and offers at each price are in a time-order queue, with the earliest received (on the left in this diagram) executed first.

the matching engine would simply add it to the order book's list of bids at $29.49. It remains there—available for other market participants to execute against (hence the terms "market-making," "liquidity-providing," "adding," or "passive")—until it is executed or canceled. In most exchanges, the list of bids (and also the list of offers) at each price is a queue, a time-priority list. A new bid to buy at $29.49 will be executed only when all earlier bids at that price have been executed or canceled. Now consider a bid to buy shares at a price that is only a single cent higher: $29.50. That would be a "taking" order. (Other terms for it would be "aggressive" or "removal.") The matching engine can execute a bid at $29.50 immediately (although perhaps only partially if it is large), because there are offers to sell at that price. Doing so removes these existing orders from the book; hence the terminology of "taking" or "removal."

In an exchange of the sort in which HFT is prevalent, most "making" and most "taking" orders are placed by algorithms. The core mechanism of direct interaction among trading algorithms (including, e.g., execution algorithms used by institutional investors, although my focus in this chapter is how HFT algorithms interact with each other)[2] is the straightforward process of matching these orders one with the other. "Taking" orders are matched with—that is, executed against—"making" orders at the same price. That mechanism is so simple that it is hard to imagine that much pivots on it, and the difference between the prices of a making and a taking order on a modern electronic exchange is indeed normally very small. The one-cent difference in figure 6.1 between a bid that "makes" and a bid that "takes" is 0.03 percent of the market price, and differences of roughly that size are typical. Yet this simple mechanism and tiny difference resonate strongly, generating the elaborate material arrangements discussed in chapter 5, and—at least for some participants, to some extent, some of the time—possessing a moral, affective weight.

That moral weight is worth exploring briefly before turning in more detail to the material practices of algorithmic making and taking. The words chosen by interviewee BQ are unusually strong, but the underlying sentiment is not unique: "I tend to want to work at [HFT] companies that are 'makers' because I see the inherent evil in the 'takers.'" This moral preference for making rests on the legitimacy of its most systematic form, market-making. As described in previous chapters, this involves an algorithm continually keeping *both* bids to buy *and* offers to sell in the order book, at or close to the highest bid price and lowest offer price. In the order book in figure 6.1, for example, the first-in-the-queue bid to buy 100 shares at $29.49 and the first-in-the-queue offer to sell 100 shares at $29.50 might both have been entered by the same market-making algorithm. Although the goal is economic (to earn the one-cent difference between those two prices, along with any "rebates" or other payments the exchange may make to incentivize market-making), algorithmic making inherits the legitimacy of a traditional human role: that of the market-maker, who stood constantly ready both to buy the financial instrument being traded and to sell it (at a higher price, the difference in the past usually being proportionally much larger than the one-cent difference in table 6.1).[3]

Because the bids and offers of other market participants arrive only sporadically, market-makers, whether human or algorithmic, provide a service to market participants who want to transact immediately. Interviewee OH highlights the potency of that source of legitimacy when she recounts an episode—at the height of the global financial crisis of 2007–8—in the algorithmic market-making firm for which she then worked (a firm I have visited several times to speak to others in it). A software developer had left the firm, saying, "I couldn't look my grandmother in the face anymore and say I worked in finance." The firm's chief executive called a meeting of all its employees in the large, open-plan trading room at the center of its offices, and (as my interviewee recollects) told them, "I'm going to explain to you why you should be able to look your grandmother in the face: because we're market-makers and we provide liquidity." Another interviewee (OG, who managed to shift another algorithmic market-making firm toward "taking" strategies) describes the resistance he faced from the firm's traders: "Ask them, do we market-take? 'No, no, no,' as if you asked them if they would stab their sister, really strongly against that. But we had to change."

Specialists in taking reject this moralization of making (as indeed do some specialists in the latter). For example, interviewees BY and CV, both from the same taking firm, cite taking's central role in what economists call price discovery; its role (via arbitrage; see below) in keeping prices in different markets aligned; the "service" (interviewee CV) it provides to those who wish to trade using making orders (which, other things being equal, is cheaper than taking); and the plain fact that without taking an exchange would have no trading. Furthermore, invocations of market-making's legitimacy can sometimes smooth over what one might call rough edges in the actual practice of automated trading. At a trader's conference in Amsterdam in 2019, I listened to a spirited defense of Dutch HFT firms by a senior member of the country's financial-regulatory body. He praised "market-makers formerly known as prop[rietary] traders or high-frequency traders," arguing that "trading on a trading venue is only possible because of market-makers," and launching a thinly veiled attack on his French counterparts, who, coming from a country whose big banks are still active in trading but which does not have HFT firms like those in the Netherlands, were seeking to impose bank-style capital requirements on proprietary trading firms. Just the previous day, however, I had sat in a café with an experienced Amsterdam trader, interviewee CS, who had told me how arbitrage (which involves exploiting fleeting price discrepancies by buying and selling as close as possible to simultaneously, and thus typically involves "taking") was interwoven with market-making, both in what he individually did and in the wider trading of the city's HFT firms. "[B]asically any money you can see lying around you will pick up," he said.

Legitimacy—being able to "look your grandmother in the face"—is, furthermore, seldom a day-to-day concern of market-makers. More pressing is the often precarious economics of the activity. As AG puts it, "You make a little bit of money" when your algorithm repeatedly sells at a price higher than that at which it buys, but "you periodically get run over"—that is, your market-making algorithm buys when prices are about to fall, or sells when prices are about to rise. No market-maker reported being able to entirely avoid being run over, but all try as hard as they can, often successfully, to ensure that the resultant losses do not fully cancel out the repeated small gains. To avoid this, a market-making algorithm has to keep its "inventory" (its aggregate trading position) reasonably small. "[Y]ou have to actively control your inventory," says AE. If inventory starts to rise, a market-making algorithm will "shade" its bids or offers so as to reduce it. If, for example, too many of its bids have been executed, it will reduce the price of its offers so as to make those more attractive. If that fails, it may begin to take, reducing its inventory by executing against existing bids in the order book. (That occasional need for a market-making algorithm to take is one of the ways in which the divide between making and taking is almost never absolute.)

In addition, almost all market-making algorithms employ the signals, such as "futures lead," discussed in previous chapters, to make predictions of near-term price movements, and use those predictions to minimize the risk of being "run over." As BL says, "Markets move and you need to know when they're going to move because [otherwise] you'll be inventorying at a terrible price." These signals need to be "squashed," as BM puts it, meaning that to inform the way an algorithm trades, the signals need to be reduced to a single indicator. Although a variety of mathematical forms of "squashing" are in use, HFT interviewees consistently report that by far the most common is still one that was employed by Automated Trading Desk in the early days of HFT. In essence, algorithms combine signals by means of a linear-regression equation, in which (as described in chapter 3) a set of predictor variables (here, signals) are each weighted so that in combination they best predict the value of a single dependent variable. Interviewees used a variety of expressions to refer to this dependent variable—"fair value" (AF and AQ), "fair price" (AE), "microprice" (AN), and even "perfect price" (AM)—but it was most commonly called a "theoretical value."[4] Neither of those two words should, however, be overinterpreted; what the term refers to in HFT is simply a near-term prediction of the price of the financial instrument being traded, "the price you can reasonably expect to transact at in the near future" (AF). One market-making HFT firm, London-based XTX Markets, even advertises the salience of regression as a way of making that prediction. I had assumed its name was one of the quasi-acronyms common in business, but when I read it etched in glass I realized that it was X^TX, a pervasive operation in regression analysis (the multiplication of a data matrix by its "transpose").

"Getting good places in the queue"

(Note to the reader: This section is a little technical. As the main analytically important issue in it will be discussed in Chapter 7, it can be skipped if desired.) Market-making's goal of repeated small gains requires, of course, that others execute against a "making" algorithm's bids and offers. The obvious way of boosting the chances of that is to compete on price: to post bids at higher prices and offers at lower prices than others do. But the possibility of competition on price is affected strongly by a market's "tick size," the minimum allowable increment of price. Tick size is set either by government regulation (as in the trading of US shares, in which the tick size for shares costing a dollar or more is one cent) or by the exchange or other trading venue in question. If the tick size is small (as it was on Island, or on foreign-exchange trading venues after the equivalent of share-price decimalization took place in that market), market-making algorithms can indeed often compete on price. Many markets (for example, many futures contracts, Treasurys, and many US stocks) are, however, "tick-constrained": in other words, the price of the lowest offer is nearly always one tick above that of the highest bid, as it is in the example in figure 6.1. Because a trading venue's computer system will reject a bid or an offer at an intermediate price, a market-making algorithm cannot then directly compete on price. An increased bid (in the order book in figure 6.1, a bid to buy the shares at, for example, $29.50) would be a "taking" order—it would be executed against the lowest-priced offer—not a "making" order.

What then happens in a tick-constrained market when prices move? Suppose, for example, that in the order book in figure 6.1 all the offers to sell at $29.50 are executed against, so that this price "level" (as market participants would call it) is exhausted and the lowest-priced offer is now $29.51. Market-making algorithms will most likely then want to place bids to buy the shares in question at $29.50. What therefore becomes crucial is, in the words of a former market-maker, "getting good places in the queue," as this new level—bids at $29.50—forms (interviewee DB). As already noted, in most of the markets in which HFT is active, the bids or offers at a given price form a time-priority queue. The first bid, for example, to be executed at the new best bid price of $29.50 will be the one that arrives at the matching engine first.[5] It is therefore critical that a market-making algorithm's bids and offers be as close as possible to the front of the queue. Not only is an order at the head of the queue more likely to be executed, but interviewees report that an order at or near the back of the queue is at greater risk of being executed in adverse circumstances. In the terminology used later in this chapter, it can easily become stale and be picked off. That can happen, for instance, when a price level is "crumbling": when bids, for example, are being executed or canceled and not replaced, which often indicates that prices are about to fall and it is therefore a disadvantageous moment at which to buy.

The crucial role of queue position in successful HFT market-making means speed in the placement of orders is critical. As interviewee AX put it, "Queue position matters so much . . . you've got to get in quickly." In US share trading, though, a further complex of factors is also vital to the race to be at the head of the queue.[6] Those factors arise from the centerpiece of the current regulation of US share trading, 2005's Reg NMS (referred to in chapter 3 and also discussed in chapter 7). In Reg NMS, the stock-market regulator, the SEC, tried simultaneously to achieve two goals: to ensure competition among exchanges and other trading venues, while also keeping what goes on in those different venues consistent. The chief way in which Reg NMS seeks to achieve this is, in the words of a regulator (interviewee RV) heavily involved in it, by "connecting markets virtually," rather than via the fiercely controversial Consolidated Limit Order Book, or CLOB. (Even more than a quarter of a century after the 1970s conflict over the CLOB discussed in chapter 3, "the dreaded CLOB . . . still just made blood boil," says RV.)

To connect markets virtually, Reg NMS imposed—and today still imposes—"order protection." The orders that are protected are the highest-priced bid or bids for a particular stock at any given point in time, and the lowest-priced offer or offers, across all the share-trading exchanges in the US. Other exchanges are forbidden from executing trades at prices inferior to those of these protected bids or offers; doing so would be a prohibited "trade through." They must instead send on orders for execution on the exchange or exchanges whose order books contain the protected bids or offers.[7] An exchange also must not display in its order book an offer to sell shares at a price equal to the national best bid, or a bid to buy shares at a price equal to the national best offer. To do that would be to "lock the market," which is also forbidden.

The difficulty with these Reg NMS order-protection rules is that they implicitly assume a Newtonian world, in which it is in principle possible for an observer such as a trading firm's or exchange's computer system to become aware instantaneously of events at a distant location, so making it conceivable that the system could compare the prices on all exchanges at exactly the present moment. (As Budish [2016: 2] puts it, "Reg NMS . . . implicitly assumes that there is literally zero latency between exchanges.") The world of HFT is, however, not Newtonian. As described in chapter 1, it is "Einsteinian": it is a world in which the tiniest time differences are salient, and therefore a world sharply constrained by Einstein's postulate that no signal can travel faster than the speed of light in a vacuum. What an observer can "see" is therefore inherently dependent on where that observer is, and on the timescales of HFT (rather than those implicit in Reg NMS) that is important.

Interviewee BD talked me through the implications of HFT's Einsteinian materiality for algorithmic market-making that is constrained by Reg NMS's ban on "locking" a market (in what follows I have altered the prices in his example to match those in figure 6.1). Imagine that an algorithm is trading shares in Nasdaq's datacenter in New Jersey and what I have described above happens: that all the offers at $29.50 in Nasdaq's order book for the shares in question are executed against, without being replaced, and a market-making algorithm therefore seeks to place a bid at $29.50. The difficulty it faces is that the same shares will almost certainly also be in the process of trading in the datacenter of the New York Stock Exchange, around fifty kilometers (about thirty miles) from Nasdaq, and in the cluster of exchanges (now owned by the Chicago Board Options Exchange) that were set up by the ECNs BATS and Direct Edge, and which are now located in the NY4 and NY5 datacenters, around twenty-five kilometers from Nasdaq's. Because share trading in this equities triangle (shown in figure 1.4) is so tightly integrated, it is very likely that all the offers at $29.50 on those exchanges will also already have been executed against, or are about to be executed against. However, even setting aside the additional sources of delay (such as fiber tail) discussed in chapter 5, the fastest that news of those executions can travel is the speed of light in a vacuum, and so it will take a minimum of at least 80 microseconds (millionths of a second) for the news to reach Nasdaq's matching engines, which is a very long time by HFT standards.

If a market-making algorithm seeks to enter into Nasdaq's order book an ordinary bid to buy at $29.50 during those 80 or more microseconds, it will be rejected by Nasdaq's computer systems because—given what those systems can electronically "see"—there will still appear to be offers at $29.50 on other exchanges (offers that are at the lowest price available nationally, and are therefore protected). The bid at $29.50 would therefore appear to "lock the market" and thus violate Reg NMS. Some market-making algorithms have no choice but to wait for the news of the disappearance of these offers from other exchanges' order books to reach Nasdaq—perhaps the algorithms will have to send in the same bid over and over again, in the hope that eventually it will be accepted and get close to the head of the queue— but they would be at a serious disadvantage.

"[W]here the competition [to get to the front of queues in US share trading] lies today [2019]," says DB, "is the Post-Only Day Intermarket Sweep

Order." An Intermarket Sweep Order or ISO, is an order bearing a computerized flag indicating that the firm submitting it has also sent orders that will execute against and thus remove from the order books of all the other exchanges any protected orders that would otherwise be traded through or locked by the exchange receiving the ISO if its matching engine were to add the order in question to its order book. (The "day" in the name of the order simply indicates that it remains valid throughout a trading session until canceled—that is, it is not an "immediate-or-cancel" order, one that is canceled immediately if it cannot be executed. "Post-only" orders are orders that the exchange's matching engine will automatically cancel if the effect of adding them to the order book would be that they would "take," in other words execute against an already-present order. Post-only orders are used by market-making algorithms to remove the risk of accidentally "taking" in a situation in which an order book's contents are changing fast.)[8]

Using a post-only day ISO to try to get to the head of the queue, under circumstances like those described, inherently involves prediction. Let me continue with the example of the market-making algorithm in Nasdaq's datacenter. To make its use of the ISO valid, the algorithm needs to send orders to execute against the offers at $29.50 in the other datacenters *before* it can know with certainty that those offers have disappeared. (Although, as discussed in chapter 5, a trading firm may use private millimeter-wave links to receive the news of their disappearance faster than Nasdaq's system does, the same fundamental Einsteinian constraint still applies.) Whether those offers *have* disappeared can therefore only be a probabilistic matter. If they have not, then the market-making algorithm can easily incur a nontrivial loss: it will inadvertently have "crossed the spread," as a market-maker would put it, and will have paid fees rather than receiving a rebate.[9] The decision by a market-making algorithm to employ an ISO in the way just described is a routine one (ISOs are heavily used in the sophisticated trading of US shares), but such algorithms always need to weigh the possible loss against the benefit to be gained by achieving a position at or near the head of the time-priority queue.[10]

The use of post-only ISOs is utterly crucial, DB reports, to success in HFT market-making in US shares. (Earlier HFT interviewees such as AE had also told me about the importance of ISOs, but at that point my understanding of HFT market-making was too primitive for me to fully grasp the issue's ramifications.) The reason why only some HFT firms can use them is that to be able to employ the ISO flag a firm must either itself be registered with the SEC as a broker-dealer (which, as far as I can tell, all the bigger

HFT firms are) or must be entering its bids and offers via a broker-dealer that will allow it to use the flag. That, in its turn, creates the need for the HFT firm or broker-dealer to have what DB calls a "compliance infrastructure." Given the pace of trading, it is impossible for an unaided human being to show that the requirements of the proper use of an ISO flag have been met. What is needed is quite a sophisticated technical system, capable of capturing in real time the market data needed to document compliance. It is an issue on which even major HFT firms can find themselves tripped up, and can be particularly demanding for smaller broker-dealers.[11] As one of the latter told me:

> We have a client . . . that would like to do ISO orders . . . They're getting their own market data so if they were to get a market snapshot [capturing the market data necessary to demonstrate compliance], that's not good enough because we need to have control over the elements of getting that snapshot. . . . We would need to both review the code and make sure that the client could not change the code without us being there. (Interviewee YF)

Not to be able to use ISOs can be a serious disadvantage for HFT firms trading US shares. "A large amount of wealth transfer happens here," via the favorable queue positions achievable by those able to use ISOs, says interviewee AE.[12]

Taking I: "Taking in the world's information"

Let me now move from "making" to "taking." The latter is more heterogeneous than "making." (The most salient difference in styles of making concerns one particular firm whose currently very successful approach is quite different from that of the majority of market-makers whom I interviewed. It is, however, impossible to discuss that approach in any detail without causing that firm to be identifiable to others within HFT.) All HFT "taking" strategies involve identifying situations in which it is likely that executing against existing bids or offers in the order book will be profitable, but how that is done varies in important ways, explored in this and the next two sections.

One approach is for taking algorithms to process larger amounts of information than is processed by making algorithms, or to process it in ways that are mathematically more sophisticated. If, by doing this, a taking algorithm can improve on making algorithms' price predictions, then there will be profit opportunities. These do not happen continuously, but interviewees (e.g., BY) report that when they arise, taking algorithms typically buy or sell substantially larger quantities of the financial instrument being traded than making algorithms do. (In the trading of US shares, taking of this kind is another use of the intermarket sweep orders, or ISOs, discussed in the previous section.) Among high-frequency traders, quantitatively sophisticated taking is highly regarded. It is an "aspiration," says interviewee BW, who had worked for a firm whose taking was mainly of the simpler kind described in the next section, but a demanding aspiration. "It's harder to get into," he says. "[I]t's harder to do, it requires more capital, hold times are longer, you think about risk slightly differently; stuff like that."

Interviewee CV gave, as an example of this highly demanding form of trading—"taking in the world's information and being able to translate that to predict the next tick [price movement]"—an algorithm trading 10-year US Treasury futures in the Chicago Mercantile Exchange's datacenter. The algorithm will take into account the pattern of bids, offers, and trades in those futures, as well as patterns in the trading of the other Treasury and interest-rate futures also traded in that datacenter. The algorithm will receive, via microwave links, data on the buying and selling of the underlying Treasurys, which are traded in the two datacenters in New Jersey shown in the map in figure 4.1. Via Hibernia Atlantic's ultrafast transatlantic cable, it will receive data on the trading of futures on UK sovereign bonds (these futures are traded in a datacenter just outside of London) and the equivalent German futures, traded in a datacenter in Frankfurt called FR2. Data on Japanese government bonds will come from a transpacific cable and yet more microwave links. The algorithm will continuously fuse all this information into a prediction of the price of the futures it is trading, taking when it looks profitable to do so.

All of this information is also available to market-making algorithms, at least those deployed by the larger HFT firms. Market-making algorithms, though, often have to be ultrafast (and therefore not too complex), because of their need to be at or close to the head of the time-priority queue for execution and the danger of their quotes becoming stale and being picked off (which is discussed in the next section). As CB, from a very sophisticated market-making firm, puts it, "We add, subtract, multiply, and divide really, really well"; in other words, very fast indeed. "[W]e're not doing high math and high quant." There is, in contrast, seldom a queue to "take." Taking algorithms, which "aren't fighting for queue position," therefore "maybe have just a little more time to quantitatively evaluate what the market is really saying," says BY. One interviewee, with a background predominantly in market-making, was struck to discover when he began work at a firm heavily involved in taking that "their machines are pretty slow." At his previous market-making firm, he says, "we'd laugh at this kind of machines, but they make money" in algorithmic taking.

That speed can therefore be a less extreme priority in some forms of taking than in making was, to me, a counterintuitive finding from the interviews, but one consistent with the financial-economics literature (Brogaard et al. 2015). Interviewee CV, however, warns that the lower priority of speed lasts only until another taking firm "begins competing with you"—that is, discovers and starts to exploit the same predictive pattern. Put more generally, the computationally complex, quantitatively sophisticated taking discussed in this section is at one end of a spectrum; at the other end is the taking discussed in the next section.

Taking II: Picking Off Stale Quotes

As discussed in chapter 2, large transactions in the Chicago Mercantile Exchange's datacenter, or significant changes in the contents of its most crucial order books, typically presage changes, both locally in that datacenter and worldwide, that immediately render many market-making algorithms' bids or offers out-of-date ("stale"). If that happens, a "taking" algorithm has no need for complex modeling; it can simply "pick off"—profit by trading against—clearly stale bids or offers. The archetype of this simple, ultrafast form of taking (described by many interviewees and by Budish et al. 2015) is when the price of the ES, the share-index future that corresponds to the Standard & Poor's 500 share index, suddenly rises or falls. This is typically followed—nowadays, less than a hundredth of a second later—by moves in the same direction in the price of the SPY (the corresponding exchange-traded fund [ETF], which as noted in chapter 2 is a composite share that tracks the same index) and in the prices of the underlying shares. In particular, if the algorithms making markets in the SPY do not cancel their existing bids or offers quickly enough, a taking algorithm will pick them off. Substantial changes in the other simple signals universally understood within HFT to have predictive value (see tables 3.2 and 4.4) give rise to similar picking-off opportunities. As noted in chapter 1, Aquilina, Budish, and O'Neill have used electronic-message data from the London Stock Exchange to measure the prevalence of these speed races, which are normally invisible in the data available to financial economists.[13] Strikingly, they find an average of 537 speed races a day in each of the 100 leading stocks traded on that exchange.

Essentially, each of those stocks experiences an average of one race every minute of the trading day (Aquilina et al. 2020: 3–4).

Picking off creates a speed race within HFT that is at least as important as—and perhaps more important than—the race among market-making algorithms to be at the head of the queue.[14] The picking-off race is between making algorithms, seeking to cancel stale bids or offers (in other words, bids or offers that are mispriced in light of the arrival of a signal such as a move in the ES), and taking algorithms trying to pick off—to execute against—those stale quotes. The exigencies of this race force the HFT algorithms involved in it to operate at nanosecond speeds, and those exigencies are central to the mundane economics of HFT. They create, for example, the incentive—and in many cases the need—to pay to build or use the microwave, millimeter-wave, or atmospheric-laser links described in chapter 5. In addition, the race makes cancellations of orders not a minor administrative matter but absolutely critical to the economics of market-making.

The use in this race of wireless links also makes evident the material nature of the interaction between making and taking algorithms. Remarkably, rain, that most mundane of material phenomena, seems sometimes to influence the interaction of algorithms. In particular, the microwave links that carry futures prices from the Chicago Mercantile Exchange's datacenter to the share-trading datacenters in New Jersey can fail when it rains, and it is a noteworthy event for trading when this happens. (Interviewee CC, for example, told me that a siren would go off in his HFT firm's offices to alert its traders "whenever the microwave link would go down.") Consequent effects of rain on the interaction of HFT algorithms have had two distinct phases. Traces in price data of the first phase, in 2011–12, were found by economists Shkilko and Sokolov (2016). In that phase, as described in chapter 5, a number of HFT firms had created microwave links between Chicago and New Jersey, and seem to have used them above all for picking off the stale prices of market-making algorithms still dependent on fiber-optic cables. When rain interrupted the microwave links, those making algorithms were able to resume market-making without being picked off, and, as Shkilko and Sokolov demonstrate, standard measures of liquidity temporarily improved.

The second phase began after the communications supplier McKay Brothers opened the new Chicago–New Jersey microwave link described in chapter 5. McKay has subsequently kept refining the link in its fierce speed race against the privately owned links. The McKay link is widely used by market-making firms, and has given their algorithms a degree of protection from being picked off. In this second phase, the effect of rain on the interaction of algorithms seems to have reversed. Now, if it rains heavily enough to interrupt the McKay link, market-making firms cannot know for certain that the private links used by taking algorithms have also failed. So, reports McKay's Stéphane Tyč (and also another interviewee, OW), market-making algorithms have to "widen spreads," as market participants put it: reduce the prices of their bids and increase the prices of their offers, thus lowering the risk of being picked off (but also reducing one of the standard measures of liquidity).

As discussed in chapter 5, the vulnerability of microwave transmission to rain is not a fixed physical effect; it increases as higher frequencies are used. As noted in that chapter, of the frequencies commercially available in the US, the most reliable is 6 GHz, but that band is crowded near the Chicago–New Jersey geodesic (microwave signals at the same frequency can interfere with each other). Thus keeping close to the geodesic requires use of higher frequencies more vulnerable to rain, such as 18 GHz and 23 GHz. However, the influence of rain on the interaction of algorithms seems to be absent in Europe. The European analog of the Chicago–New Jersey geodesic is the microwave route from Greater London to Frankfurt's FR2 datacenter, which hosts both Eurex's futures trading and the Deutsche Börse's share trading. McKay Brothers was able to build its London–Frankfurt link using mostly frequencies below 10 GHz, and so, reports Tyč, rain has little effect and market-making algorithms in Europe therefore do not need to widen spreads when it rains heavily, as their US counterparts may need to.

Taking III: Cat and Mouse

"Taking" algorithms can profit not just from a "making" algorithm being unable to cancel stale quotes quickly enough but also by anticipating predictable behavior by that algorithm. Predictability can, for example, arise from the way in which many making algorithms employ linear-regression equations to combine widely used signals (of the kind listed in tables 3.2 and 4.4) into a price prediction. As interviewee AJ says, identifying an opportunity to profitably "take" can involve an algorithm predicting other algorithms' predictions: "What do you think the [price prediction] will be in a minute, in 30 seconds, in a millisecond, in ten minutes?" If a taking algorithm can anticipate the typical prediction, it can anticipate how other algorithms will react. If, for example, market-making algorithms are trading the ES (the index future that corresponds to the S&P 500 share index), they will likely be receiving signals from the market for the NQ (the index future, also traded in the Chicago Mercantile Exchange's datacenter, corresponding to the Nasdaq-100 share index). If a taking algorithm can predict movements in the market for the NQ (for example, by analysis of the balance of bids and offers in the order book for the NQ), and then anticipate how the price predictions of the algorithms making markets in the ES will change in response to those movements, it can thus sometimes identify a "coming [order] book imbalance" in the ES, and therefore a predictable shift in price quotations from which it can profit (interviewee CG).

Even more subtle is for a taking algorithm to "predict what this guy [this specific market-making algorithm] is going to do," and thus profitably play a "game of cat and mouse" (CG). If, for example, a specific market-making algorithm can be identified, and observed repeatedly, it can be possible to infer when it is approaching an inventory limit (the maximum trading position it can hold in a particular stock or other financial instrument) and will begin to "shade" its prices to reduce its inventory. A sophisticated taking algorithm can then take on a trading position in anticipation of being able to liquidate it at a profit against those shaded prices. The shading, and thus the profitability of the trade, will typically be small (on the order of the minimum price increment: for example, one cent per share, as in figure 6.1). If, however, the algorithmic behavior that has been identified is repetitive and frequent, such small profits can accumulate.

A taking algorithm successfully playing a game of cat and mouse with a specific making algorithm is perhaps the most demanding computationally of all the forms of taking. The volumes of data generated by financial markets are huge (and, in markets of the kind focused on in this book, usually anonymous), and established statistical techniques such as linear regression are not well suited for identifying the signatures of specific algorithms in these masses of data; more recent machine-learning techniques are needed. Also required is a powerful grid of multiple computers—sometimes a thousand or more—on which to implement these techniques. This grid can run offline (with programs running overnight or on weekends if necessary) when signatures are being searched for; the taking algorithms that are the result of this research have to be simpler to run—as they have to—on a single computer, and fast. They are, however, not very simple. Here, the state-of-the-art technologies that are a result of the speed race are used not to achieve nanosecond reaction times but to permit more complex computation. As CG puts puts it, "Speed allows you to do complicated things in the same time" in which "others do simple things."

The game of algorithmic cat and mouse traditionally relied on human intelligence—"One of our traders has a friend who works on that [HFT firm's trading] desk," says BM—and the human capacity to spot "hints of [order] size, timing, what price levels, how they hedge" that are characteristic of a firm's algorithms (BM). However, just as in the case described in the previous paragraph, machine-learning techniques can also implicitly detect predictable behavior by other algorithms. Interviewee DD described using a "random forest" (a widely used form of machine learning), again "trained" offline on a grid of interconnected computers, to improve how his firm's trading system made its inferences, from changes in the order book, that a future's price was about to change.[15] The problem inherently involves behavior by other algorithms, says DD:

> It [the random forest] just learns when it's appropriate to do that [trade on the assumption that prices are about to change]. Most people do similar things. That's an interesting game because you're trying to work out, well if this is your threshold [for deciding when to trade], other people are looking at the same data, they're going to come with the same threshold, do you want it [your system's threshold to be] before or after that threshold? How do you want to adjust it, given other people are going to be doing similar things? And that's a game in itself.

The use of the random forest substantially increased the firm's trading profits, says DD. His judgment is that it did so by implicitly learning about other algorithms' thresholds and behavior, at least in aggregate. "That's exactly what it does," he says.

Cat-and-mouse trading, using machine-learning techniques to identify behavior by specific algorithms, is facilitated, reports CG, by technological changes in exchange systems. "Most people's [computer] systems are very deterministic," he says. For example, the time taken by an HFT firm's system to respond to an incoming signal (e.g., by sending the exchange a new order) varies between firms, but for each particular firm it tends to be reasonably constant. This creates a potentially identifiable signature, but one previously masked by inconsistencies among exchanges in how time is measured and by "jitter" in exchange systems (quasi-random fluctuation in the time taken to process orders, which is discussed in chapter 7). Precise atomic-clock synchronization to the global time standard, UTC (Coordinated Universal Time), and greater determinism in exchange systems (systems that are increasingly being programmed in C++, which allows fuller control of the material implementation of computational processes, and sometimes also employ the FPGAs discussed in chapter 5) have, however, removed much of that masking.

Illegitimate Algorithms? Market-Impact Trading, Quote Matching, and Spoofing

As far as I can tell, cat-and-mouse taking of the kind just described remains fairly unusual. The first two forms of taking—quantitatively sophisticated price-prediction taking, and the picking off of stale quotes—most likely account for the bulk of the interaction between making and taking HFT algorithms. Sophisticated prediction is, as noted, highly regarded. Picking off, in contrast, is often seen as far from praiseworthy; one interviewee said that if an HFT firm focused on it, it was "morally hard to defend your business model." At a traders conference in Chicago, a member of an HFT firm that has a reputation in the industry for successful picking off, but which was developing bilateral trading relationships with banks, talked of the need to counter "the stigma attached to an HFT."[16]

Other forms of algorithmic action are also sometimes controversial. One is market-impact trading, in which an algorithm reflexively exploits the likely influence of its own actions on other algorithms. That can be an extension of cat-and-mouse taking. If, for example, another firm's algorithm is well enough understood by the taker's system, then the latter can trade in such a way as to create specific, exploitable effects on the algorithm's behavior. Again, getting understanding of that kind can involve intensive, sophisticated research, or else human intelligence, perhaps in the form of traders who have moved between firms. As a trader put it to me, "You know how their systems work and you know the decisions they're making." However, rather than exploiting in easily detectable ways the knowledge of how another firm's algorithms react to specific signals—by "shooting at [i.e., trading in such a way as to influence] the signals that seem obvious"—he believed it better to "shoot in ways that they're not going to detect for longer." Market-makers, perhaps especially the smaller firms, can certainly be "worried that people will dig and find what we're doing and understand how we exit"—that is, learn how the firm's algorithms reduce inventory and liquidate a trading position. "So if they understand how far they have to push us to puke, then it could be used against us," says interviewee BM. (What is meant by "push" here is to trade in such a way that prices move against a firm. To puke is to be forced to liquidate a position at unfavorable prices.)

One—unsubtle—form of market-impact trading, described by interviewees AC and CS, involves identifying situations in which many of the bids or offers in the order book are from small firms that will "cut their losses" (CS) or "puke" (AC) if prices move against them by more than a certain amount.

If a well-capitalized firm's algorithm can detect a "weak-hand moment" of this kind, it can "sweep" or "swipe" (CS) the order book, for example by executing against all the bids at multiple price levels, so driving the market down, forcing "weak-hand" algorithms to liquidate inventories at temporarily low prices, and profiting from the difference between those prices and the average price in the "swipe" sales. Some interviewees doubted that this tactic would work. CJ argued that few participants in mainstream financial markets are so capital constrained that they can be forced out of trading positions in this way. However, one interviewee admitted to having "profile[d]" other users and swept the book at these weak-hand moments, and a group of regulators I spoke to told me that they had observed, in market data, episodes consistent with use of the tactic. Interviewee CS, likewise, had witnessed them, although he commented that the profits to be made from the tactic were often surprisingly limited:

> It's amazing, you see those swipes and they're huge swipes, millions and millions and millions of dollars [of] underlying value, and if you look at it, the actual profit of one of these trades is $2,000 or something like that. (CS)

Sweeps or swipes of this kind would be considered by many market participants to be illegitimate behavior, and the regulators I spoke to seem to view them as potentially illegal market manipulation, if their goal is to force others to puke. (Regulators have, however, seldom taken action against sweepers; they have given much more attention to the "spoofing" discussed below.)

Issues of legitimacy do not concern only algorithmic taking. In the past at least, one controversial use of "making" orders seems to have been to "quote match" when there was a large order at, for instance, the best bid price that had been in the order book for some time. In a market with a small tick size (such as, for example, foreign-exchange trading venues after decimalization), a quote-matching algorithm would enter a making bid at a price one tick higher than that of the big bid. If the algorithm's bid was executed against, then the algorithm had a free option, so to speak. If prices went up, it would profit; if they went down, it could limit its loss to a single tick by executing against the original bid, at least if that was still present.[17] The heyday of quote matching seems to have been when relatively slow human traders still entered large orders into electronic order books manually, on specialist terminals, or with keyboard and mouse.

Much of dealers' anger about HFT algorithms in foreign-exchange markets concerned alleged quote matching by those algorithms, and this anger contributed to the reversal of at least some of the changes in market structure discussed in chapter 4 (in particular, as described below, the partial reversal of decimalization). Similar anger was created among Instinet's users when their bids or offers were quote matched on Island. Instinet's and Island's clientele were largely separate. Island's SOES-bandit roots meant that many established large firms would not trade on it, while Instinet's client base was mainly institutional investors, dealers, and brokers. So it was even possible, an interviewee told me, to successfully quote match Instinet bids and offers on Island at a marginally worse price. These quotes on Island would be executed against often enough that his quote-matching algorithm could make "$5-10-20,000 a day just consistently with zero risk." Controversy over quote matching was decidedly one-sided; I know of no efforts to publicly defend its legitimacy. Indeed, one of my interviewees who had co-developed a quote-matching algorithm ("The markets were closed early one day . . . [X] and I went to a bar . . . and we came up with this") gave it the distinctly illegitimate-sounding (although, of course, purely internal) name of Stalker, because of the way it would change its price whenever the price of the order it was mirroring changed.

Stalker, however, was indisputably legal. The widespread practice of spoofing is where illegitimacy begins most prominently to blur into illegality. (Originally, most spoofing, even in electronic markets, was not conducted algorithmically, but by human traders with keyboard and mouse. Even today, when algorithms are often used, they seem usually to be slow and simple by HFT standards.) At one level, spoofing resembles legitimate market-making, in that it involves entering both bids and offers into order books. A spoofer—human or algorithmic—places one or more large orders on one side of the order book (such as the offers to sell 3,000 and 1,800 shares in figure 6.2) and another order or orders, typically much smaller, on the other side (perhaps one of the bids to buy 100 shares). The big orders alter the level of what is perhaps the most pervasive HFT signal, the balance of bids and offers in the order book. While in figure 6.1 the bids and offers are roughly in balance and there is no clear reason to predict either a rise or fall in prices, in figure 6.2 the spoofer's offers "tilt" the order book. The preponderance of offers that the spoofer has created could be read by HFT algorithms as signaling an imminent fall in prices. That might then cause those algorithms to sell, probably by "taking," in other words executing against bids already in the order book, such as the spoofer's bid at $29.49. The spoofer would then cancel the big offers, and perhaps reverse the exercise, fooling HFT algorithms into predicting a price rise, and so be able to sell, at an advantageous price, the shares that have just been bought.[18]

BIDS TO BUY

$29.49	100	100*	200
$29.48	50	30	
$29.47	100		
$29.46	50	100	100	100
$29.45	200		

OFFERS TO SELL

$29.54	100	200	100	3000*
$29.53	50			
$29.52	40	50	1800*	
$29.51	50	50	200	
$29.50	100	100	100	

FIGURE 6.2. An order book with "spoofing," with the spoofer's orders marked with an asterisk. The human or algorithmic spoofer has added two large offers (to sell 1,800 and 3,000 shares) to the order book, but will cancel them before they are executed. The effect of those orders is to create an imbalance in the order book (there are more shares being offered than bid for), which may lead HFT algorithms to anticipate that prices will fall. Those algorithms may therefore "sell into" the spoofer's bid to buy 100 shares.

Analogous forms of deception in trading pits were often tolerated, sometimes even well regarded, as akin to successful bluffing in poker (interviewees MG and RJ). With the shift to electronic markets, attitudes toward spoofing shifted (Arnoldi 2016). Although some of the more libertarian of my HFT interviewees still defend spoofing, theirs is now a minority viewpoint. There is widespread hostility to spoofing in at least the larger, more firmly established HFT companies. While there have been cases in the past of spoofing by traders or groups of traders in some of these companies, they are now sharply aware of the legal risks they would run if their traders deployed an algorithm that spoofed. Indeed, HFT firms often incur losses as a result of spoofing; it is inflexible behavior by HFT algorithms that spoofers mainly exploit. Several of my HFT interviewees had reported spoofing to exchanges and regulators, and even acted as witnesses in subsequent legal action. As touched on in chapter 7, US law has changed in respect to spoofing, and some, though by no means all, of this legal action has taken the form of criminal prosecution of alleged spoofers, with at least one jail sentence as a result. (In one case, even the head of a programming firm that wrote an algorithm for a spoofer was prosecuted, albeit unsuccessfully.) Although only a tiny minority of alleged spoofers have faced criminal prosecution, and the prosecutions have not all resulted in convictions—proving intent, for example, can be hard—exchanges and regulators are now far more active than a decade ago in seeking to detect and punish spoofing.

Specialization, "Hardwiring," and an Ecology of Algorithms

Let me now return from the contested boundaries of legitimate algorithmic action to the central divide within it, between "making" and "taking." Nothing in principle stops a market-making algorithm—running as part of the extraordinary technical architecture described in chapter 5, and often informed by a reasonably sophisticated predictive model—from also taking, and my interviews reveal that there are, for example, algorithms that make if their price prediction is between the highest bid and lowest offer, and take if it is sufficiently far outside them. The blending of making and taking is, however, less pervasive than one might expect. Often, though certainly not always, trading groups and sometimes even entire companies specialize in one or the other. For example, those interviewees who were sufficiently senior in compartmentalized companies—those made up of separate trading groups—to be familiar with those groups' trading strategies reported that groups often focused either on making or on taking, but not both.

> I think there is just something that's so different about having to have an opinion all the time [a market-making algorithm has to constantly be making decisions about its bids and offers] versus occasionally having an opinion [a taking algorithm needs only to identify the intermittent circumstances in which taking will be profitable] . . . for some reason those two things can't really be married without somehow ruining an aspect of the other one (AG).

> It's ["making" and "taking"] like cars and trucks: they're just different disciplines. . . . Sometimes they'll cross but usually not, as a general observation (MG).

That there is often specialization in either making or taking is confirmed by the literature of financial economics on HFT. There can be large differences among companies in the proportions of their algorithms' trades that are making versus taking, differences that are broadly stable over time. It is unusual for a firm to mostly make in one month and take in the next.[19]

Why is there a degree of specialization in either making or taking? Interviewee AG, who as noted above has a senior role in a firm that has some groups that take and some that make, says, "It's almost like two very different . . . thought processes." Mathematically sophisticated taking requires what he calls "extreme quantitative analysis," in which "you tend to be looking at signals that are on the edge of statistical significance . . . trying to tease the signal out of a lot of noise." Market-making, on the other hand, was (as noted above) a well-established human practice, which provided a template for efforts to automate making, efforts that often did not initially involve extensive quantitative research. As several interviewees point out, it is easier to simulate and "back test" (test using stored market data) taking strategies, because they execute against bids and offers already in the order book, in contrast to making strategies, which add bids and offers to the order book. As a result, in making,

> you don't know [in advance] how your own trading influences the market . . . you need to experience the market in order to really understand it. . . . It's not so much I think that "making" strategies are incapable of "taking" or incapable of forming an opinion as to when you're supposed to cross the market [i.e., to "take"], it's just not inherently what they [specialists in "making"] do, so they're not as good at developing those alpha signals [quantitatively sophisticated predictors] as other people [specialists in "taking," for whom] that's their whole methodology, basically. (Interviewee AG)

"Cognitive" specialization of this kind in either making or taking can also be reinforced by the different technological requirements of the two activities. Large-scale market-making can be thought of as essentially an engineering enterprise. It requires a company to have a trading system that is not just fast (so as to achieve favorable queue position and—if not protected by the speed bumps discussed below—to avoid being picked off) but also extremely robust; market-making algorithms need to constantly be canceling stale bids and offers and replacing them with orders at slightly different prices. A firm that is market-making across many different shares and other financial instruments will have many different orders in the market simultaneously (a problem that, as discussed below, is at its extreme in options market-making), so for its trading system to freeze, even for a second or two, could be disastrous.

In contrast, as already discussed, takers often do not need such a fast technical system (although those whose main business is the picking off of stale quotes do require speed), and the demands on a taking system in terms of robustness are typically lower. By using immediate-or-cancel orders, a taking firm can minimize the number of orders it has in the market. Takers, we might say, can afford to concentrate on the mathematics of HFT, not on its engineering; makers need excellent engineering. Some market-making firms are also strong in quantitatively sophisticated price prediction—and my interviews suggest that the need for this has grown over time—but not all are specialists in this. So cognitive and technological specialization may explain why makers don't often seem to also be quantitatively sophisticated takers, and why the latter don't usually try to simultaneously be market-makers. Neither form of specialization would, however, prevent a predominantly market-making firm from practicing the simpler forms of arbitrage and the picking off of stale quotes. While my interviewees were often not explicit on the point, the interviews suggest that market-making firms do indeed do this, especially those with the fastest technology.[20]

Creating a technological system to facilitate market-making on a large scale can have lasting effects. In the earliest genuinely large-scale such system (not that of Automated Trading Desk, but the even larger-scale system deployed by one of the firms in the next wave of HFT), the priorities of making were in a sense hardwired or "baked in," reducing the capacity of the company's traders to write algorithms that would successfully "take."[21] The placing and cancellation of orders by the system was not under the direct control of the traders. The only straightforward way they had of influencing order placement—of, for example, encouraging the system to take—was by changing the formula that the system used to calculate the "theoretical value" of the financial instrument being traded:

> You didn't have a lot of control over order placement. You had control over valuation, and order placement was kind of implicit from that. So if you wanted to take, you had to create some cockamamie series of events that would cause you to say that the price is worth five cents more [than the current market price], which will cause the strategy to maybe take, you hoped. (Interviewee AF)

Even if the valuation formula input by a trader caused the firm's system to take, its inventory-management function would often lead it to eliminate the resultant trading position too quickly, before it became profitable:

> [I]f you're trying to do something different than the system was conceived and built [for] in the first place, you spend an awful lot of time and energy trying to stop it from doing what it wants to do. You get into

a position and the first thing it wanted to do was to place an order on the other side [to reduce inventory] . . . I want to hold [the position] for five minutes [until it becomes profitable]. No, you can't do that. It's not that you couldn't, but you'd be trying to rework the code . . . Very, very, very difficult. (Interviewee CE)

Such was the scale at which this company made markets that its many trading algorithms interacted with each other within the firm's own system, not just with other firms' algorithms via exchanges' order books. If one of its traders deployed an algorithm designed to take in the trading of a particular stock, it was likely that one or more of the firm's making algorithms would also be active in that trading. The HFT market-making firm therefore developed a software system to stop its algorithms from trading with each other on the exchanges on which they were active. If an order from a taking algorithm were, if sent out to an exchange, to execute against another of the firm's bids or offers that was already in the exchange's order book, that bid or offer would be canceled and the taking order not sent.

This firm's use of its internal self-trading-prevention software caused its HFT algorithms to interact with each other within its own system. Attempts to take, reports interviewee AF, had the unintended, emergent consequence of increasing the profitability of the firm's market-making algorithms. The latter would be to a degree protected from taking algorithms in the wider market by the fact that one of the firm's own taking algorithms might well cause the cancellation of a making order before it could be picked off, and so its making algorithms would be "run over" less often than would otherwise have been the case, boosting their profits. The firm's traders were rewarded according to the profitability of their algorithms, so they were therefore implicitly incentivized to continue to prioritize market-making, while those who sought to develop taking algorithms often found that the firm's self-trading-prevention system stopped those algorithms' potentially highly profitable taking orders from being dispatched. "[P]eople were just like, 'oh, my making strategy is doing very well.' The other guy is like, 'I'm never getting any fills [executions] in my removals [taking],'" says AF.

The Material Politics of Foreign-Exchange Trading

The way in which this market-making company's system shaped the relative success of its taking and making algorithms was inadvertent, but let me now turn to deliberate interventions in how algorithms interact. At the end of the chapter I will discuss interventions in the trading of shares and options, but in those markets at least overt interventions typically require the approval of regulators such as the SEC. Foreign-exchange trading is much more lightly regulated. As described in chapter 4, it is a transnational activity in a world in which (the European Union aside) most financial regulation remains national. So trading venues in foreign exchange can mount interventions without seeking regulatory approval, and such interventions are therefore common.

In the background of these material interventions in foreign-exchange trading is the challenge, discussed in chapter 4, mounted by HFT businesses to the incumbent foreign-exchange dealers, the biggest of which were (and mostly still are) major banks. The first widely adopted intervention in response to this challenge was an automated procedure known as last look, which became highly controversial. Its origins, in around 2005, were in banks' unhappiness at HFT taking algorithms profiting from the slow speed and technological fallibility of banks' market-making systems. Facing widespread complaints, those who ran electronic foreign-exchange trading venues began to offer banks' and other market-makers' algorithms a "last look": before the venue's system finalized a trade involving one of these algorithms, it would send the bank's system a message alerting it to the impending transaction, and give it a short period of time in which to reject it. When I first learned of last look, in interviews in 2013–14, interviewee AT told me that the typical last-look period granted to banks' systems was "[a]nywhere from five to ten milliseconds, up to a few hundred milliseconds, sometimes up to a few seconds."

Last look made what initially were highly profitable HFT taking strategies in foreign-exchange infeasible. For example, "Tri arb doesn't work, because of last look," said interviewee AY in May 2013.[22] The combined result of last look and the "turning off" by banks of HFT companies that I described in chapter 4 was a sharp relative decline—reported, for example, by interviewee FN—in the activity of HFT taking algorithms in foreign exchange, a shift also noted by Moore, Schrimpf, and Sushko (2016). Interviewee FW, who helped run one of the foreign-exchange trading venues in which the dealer/HFT conflict was particularly prevalent, recalls telling HFT firms that their approach had to change:

> So, by telling them [high-frequency traders], and speaking to them, and saying look, nobody [no dealer] is going to tolerate you just running them over [picking off their stale quotes] every time they have a blip in their trading system . . . in general a lot of them [HFT firms] . . . morphed into market-makers now [with] less predatory behavior.

Last look was thus part of a modestly successful effort by dealers and the managers of foreign-exchange trading venues to curb HFT algorithms employing taking strategies. Its legitimacy, however, was fiercely contested. Interviewee BB was typical of the high-frequency traders I spoke to who had come to the trading of foreign exchange from a background in shares or futures. He reports being incredulous when he learned of the practice: "How is that legal?" Even some in the foreign-exchange dealing community dislike having price quotations that appear to be firm but which can be backed away from. For example, during an interview with one dealer (XI), I was asking him about last look when one of his colleagues (FG) came into the room. My interviewee had just said, "Last look is a huge part of the FX [foreign-exchange] market." His colleague objected, "It's an abomination!" They then proceeded to debate between themselves:

XI: To a purist like [FG] I would agree . . .

FG: It is [an abomination]!

XI: It kind of is [but] for us at [a major dealer bank] to facilitate a high-frequency fund [which relies on dealers to grant it credit] . . . it seems right to me that they should get liquidity, but it shouldn't be on . . . terms where [the bank's] inner weaknesses [could be exploited].

Interviewees report that use of last look has gradually declined since around 2014. Pressure from regulators is one explanation. Although regulators have not sought to reshape the market structure of foreign-exchange trading in the way they did in US share trading, they have started to take action on specific issues. In 2015, for example, Barclays Bank settled a case brought by New York State's Department of Financial Services by agreeing to pay a $150 million penalty in regard to a set of allegations—whose validity remains contested[23]—concerning its use of last look (New York State Department of Financial Services 2015). There seems little doubt that the threat of similar hostile regulatory scrutiny and possible substantial penalties has discouraged use of last look. "During last-look window . . . you have private information [for example] that this client wants to sell," says interviewee CJ. It may be difficult for a dealer to show that this information has not been misused.

Last look was a direct material intervention in maker-taker interaction in response to dealers' complaints about taking by HFT algorithms. There were, however, also complaints about quote matching and other forms of making by these algorithms. Bids and offers, these critics alleged, "can disappear as quickly as they emerge, making market liquidity illusory" (Stafford and Ross 2012), and hampering the activities of banks' traders, especially those still using manual keyboards. "It's frustrating and it's harder to transact cleanly in the market," a trader told the *Financial Times*. "It's something that affects you every day" (Ross and Stafford 2012). In response, EBS, then the dominant foreign-exchange trading venue, modified its matching engines in 2009 so that, once entered, a making order could not be canceled within a so-called minimum quote lifespan of 250 milliseconds (a quarter of a second), roughly the reaction time of the fastest human beings.

A minimum quote lifespan (a frequent policy proposal by opponents of HFT) might appear also to expose market-making algorithms to a greater risk of being picked off by taking algorithms. There were, however, says interviewee GM, "ways the high-frequency guys got around it . . . what they used to do is totally feather the book all the way down the stack"—that is, enter bids not at the highest bid price but at lower prices (and offers at higher prices than the best offer price). If and when the market moved in such a way that an HFT algorithm's orders became likely to be executed, it could then if necessary cancel them without delay, because 250 milliseconds would most likely already have elapsed. "The MQL [minimum quote lifespan] was a bit of a PR thing," says GM. It was a "compromise," as EM puts it, with "manual traders who complain that those guys [automated traders] always outsmart them."

None of these measures ended foreign-exchange dealers' unhappiness at facing what they felt to be unfair competition from HFT firms, and that unhappiness intensified in 2011 when EBS—by then no longer owned by the dealer banks, which had sold it in 2006 to the London-based interdealer broker ICAP—decimalized, reducing the minimum increment of price by a factor of ten. As described in chapter 4, the new trading venues such as Hotspot had already done this, and (just as had happened in share trading) the long-established venues, EBS and Reuters, were losing business as a result, missing trades because one of the new venues would "price inside us by a tenth, or two-tenths or three-tenths" (interviewee GM).

EBS's decimalization, however, had the side effect (again, as in share trading) of making it easier for HFT firms to undercut dealers. Just as had happened when the foreign-exchange dealers had originally been faced with the potential dominance of electronic trading by Reuters (see chapter 4), a consortium of dealer banks was formed to set up a new trading venue to compete with EBS, Reuters, and the other existing electronic venues. The consortium's original names, Clean FX and then FX Pure, signaled its intention to "inoculate speed advantage" and "create a fair market where foreign exchange risk could be hedged without being 'taxed' by the HFT firms" (Taylor 2015). With the assistance of the interdealer broker Tradition, the consortium launched a new trading venue, ParFX, in April 2013.[24] ParFX partially reversed decimalization (increasing the minimum increment of price fivefold) and—unlike on other trading venues—the actual names of firms, not just identifier numbers, were disclosed to their counterparties after a trade was consummated. If a bank experienced what it considered to be "toxic behavior" by an HFT firm, it could then complain not just to ParFX, but also—perhaps very effectively—to the prime-broker bank that acted as the firm's sponsor.

ParFX's most influential feature, though, was randomization.[25] The implementation by ParFX's servers of each message to them from the servers of the firms trading on the platform is delayed, with the length of the delay varying randomly between a minimum of 20 and a maximum of 80 milliseconds. If you work for a trading platform, says interviewee FI, HFT firms always ask you to tell them the platform's response time. "If . . . you say it varies, that screws up their equation," he says. ParFX's randomization delays both new orders and (crucially, in terms of HFT market-making) also cancellations of existing orders. The goal of delaying the latter is to stop trading firms from adding a bid or offer to the order book and then "remov[ing] that order from the market without it getting dealt on. Like putting the bait in the water and getting it out before the fish gets a chance to bite. Not really fair on the fish is it, if you can do that consistently quickly?" (FI).

The creation of ParFX, by banks that had helped set up or been heavily involved in EBS, reinforced a sense that, in interviewee HB's words, "[EBS's] clients have revolted, [it had] lost tons of market share . . . tons of clients." Even before ParFX launched, EBS—"[u]nder pressure from the banks" (Zhou and Olivari 2013)—had already also partially reversed decimalization. In August 2013, EBS too introduced randomization, albeit in a different form than ParFX's: EBS's matching engines bundle orders (both making and taking) together into a batch, then execute them in a randomized sequence.[26] "[Y]ou need to make sure that all participants in the market have a fair shot in getting [a] trade," says interviewee HB, a supporter of randomization: "Otherwise, don't pretend this is a market."

Reuters—by then Thomson Reuters (following its 2008 takeover by the Canadian media company Thomson)—took measures similar to those of EBS, but the way in which it implemented randomization differed in an apparently small but consequential way.[27] Reuters added a module, described to me by interviewee GR, to its foreign-exchange trading system in 2016. The module examines incoming buy and sell orders for each of the currency pairs being traded, classifies them as either taking or making, and adds them to the corresponding buffer.[28] The first order to enter an empty buffer starts a timer that runs for three milliseconds (three-thousandths of a second), at which point the buffer is emptied by sending the bids or offers it contains to the matching engine in a random order.[29] Randomization stops the fastest market-making algorithm from always getting to the head of queues.

Importantly, though, the Reuters module does not place cancellations of orders in a buffer, but sends them to the matching engine immediately. This made the Reuters module (unlike, for example, the way ParFX and EBS had originally implemented randomization) a direct intervention in the interaction between making and taking algorithms—a form of asymmetric speed bump, in the terminology of share trading. Delaying taking while not delaying "cancels" gives substantial protection to market-making algorithms. If the market moves, they have three milliseconds (a long time, by HFT standards) to cancel their stale quotes before they are picked off. During the design of the module, the proposal not to delay "cancels" sparked heated debate within Reuters. Those who opposed the proposal argued that it turned the module into a form of "last look," which was already seen as a controversial procedure, and one that the Reuters platform had never employed (interviewee GR). The defenders of not delaying "cancels" argued—eventually successfully—that there was a crucial difference between their proposed design for the module and last look. Both measures protect making algorithms, but last look gives a making algorithm potentially profitable private information. The algorithm can reject an order that would have executed against one of its price quotations, and then perhaps take advantage of its private knowledge that the order might still be in the market, unfilled.

EBS also intervened directly in making-taking interaction, modifying its randomization procedure to protect makers. (The intervention seems to have been prompted by the fear that "taking" algorithms might employ price data transmitted by the soon-to-be-opened, ultrafast, and very expensive Hibernia Networks transatlantic fiber-optic cable; see Detrixhe and Mamudi 2015.) Originally, messages canceling orders were entered into EBS's batching and randomization procedure on the same basis as new orders were, but as Mark Bruce of EBS told the magazine *Euromoney*, that meant that "a window opens for additional takers to arbitrage the maker, with the odds of the maker successfully removing their quote significantly diminished" (Golden 2015). So EBS stopped imposing random delays on "cancels." EBS also made available to market-making firms a faster, more expensive version of its datafeed, EBS Ultra. "[A]vailable to EBS clients fulfilling certain criteria regarding liquidity provision [i.e., market-making]," the Ultra feed provided order-book updates every five milliseconds, rather than the standard ten (Bank for International Settlements 2018: 6, note 6).

Speed Bumps: Slowing Taking, Protecting Making

As the examples of "last look," the Reuters module, and EBS Ultra show, the protection of market-making algorithms is a persistent theme in the material politics of foreign-exchange trading. That form of material politics is also to be found in the trading of other financial instruments, most prominently shares, but also options (discussed at the end of this chapter) and futures.[30] There is no evidence in my interviews that exchanges intervene to protect making because they regard it as more moral than taking. Their fear, rather, is of "empty screens" (interviewee GI)—order books devoid of bids and offers—which make an exchange fatally unattractive to traders and institutional investors. Their intervention, though, is political, in the broad sense of the word. Precisely because there is a degree of specialization in either making or taking among trading groups and firms, interventions by exchanges that influence the interaction between making and taking have economic consequences for those groups and firms.

One way of intervening to encourage making is indeed directly economic: instead of charging firms whose liquidity-making orders are executed against, exchanges (especially in share trading) make small payments—"rebates"—to them. The first electronic trading venue on which HFT became prevalent, Island, paid rebates (see chapter 3). "[W]e need[ed] [liquidity-making] order[s] on our system," says interviewee AK, who was heavily involved in Island, "and it [was] important enough to us for us to pay someone to put [them] there."[31] As rebates became more prevalent, they sparked controversy, with their critics suggesting, for example, that payments of this kind, which often were retained by brokers rather than being passed to their clients, could distort brokers' decisions as to where to send their clients' orders for execution (for evidence consistent with this suspicion, see Battalio, Corwin, and Jennings 2016). Nevertheless, this pricing structure—takers being charged fees, makers being given payments by the exchange—has become predominant in US share trading.[32]

There is increasing attention, though, to supplementing the economic incentivization of "making" with directly material interventions. Their

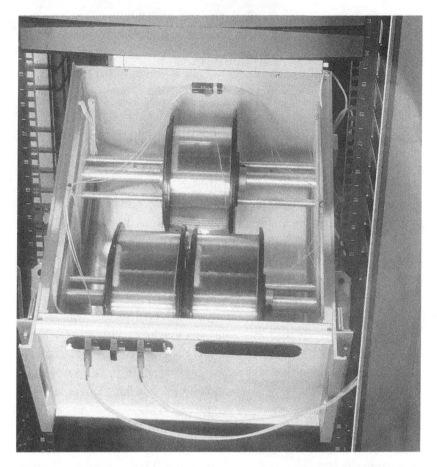

FIGURE 6.3. IEX's original coil, now in a glass case in its offices, 3 World Trade Center. Author's fieldwork photograph.

currently most prominent form is speed bumps. (That is delightful for any academic in my field. Bruno Latour, a social theorist and sociologist of science who has been a huge if indirect influence on the social studies of finance, uses the example of speed bumps in roads to explain what is meant by material politics. Rather than relying on moral injunctions or legal penalties to slow down traffic, speed bumps do so physically.)[33] The best-known speed bump in finance, highlighted in Michael Lewis's 2014 best-seller *Flash Boys* and shown in figure 6.3, is a 38-mile-long (61-kilometer-long) coil of fiber-optic cable installed in one of the share-trading datacenters (NY5) by the new US stock exchange, IEX. All incoming orders to IEX (and all market data from IEX) must pass through the coil, and the process is designed to slow them down by 350 microseconds. IEX's coil, though, is a less-than-decisive intervention in the interaction between making and taking algorithms, because it slows down both categories equally.[34] That did not, however, prevent controversy among market participants in the US over whether or not IEX's order-slowing coil should stop it from being able to register with the SEC as an exchange. (Eventually, and after IEX made substantial material changes to its system to assuage critics, the SEC allowed IEX's registration.)

The material politics of US share trading has not, however, ended with the SEC's approval of IEX's speed bump, which market participants refer to as a symmetric speed bump because of the way it slows both making and taking algorithms. At the time of writing, the current focus of controversy of that material politics is *asymmetric* speed bumps, which—like the Reuters module described above—impose delays on "taking" algorithms, while not delaying cancellations of orders by "making" algorithms, thus protecting the latter from being picked off. The first such proposal, in 2016, came from the Chicago Stock Exchange, which was small and somewhat peripheral to US share trading. The staff of the SEC initially approved the proposal, but Republican Commissioner Michael Piwowar opposed that decision, which was then put on hold. In April 2018, the Chicago Exchange was bought by the Intercontinental Exchange, owner of the New York Stock Exchange, and its proposal for an asymmetric speed bump was subsequently withdrawn.

The issue continued to be a live one, though, because each of the three "families" of US stock exchanges (the New York Stock Exchange, Nasdaq, and the Chicago Board Options Exchange or CBOE) owns multiple exchanges—the CBOE, for instance, owns four—which gives them a certain freedom to take just one of the exchanges they operate and experiment with modifying its market structure in the hope that a different material arrangement of trading will increase revenues. In June 2019, the CBOE proposed installing a four-millisecond asymmetric speed bump in one of the New Jersey exchanges, EDGA (SEC 2019a). Slowing taking orders by four milliseconds would enable making algorithms reliant on fiber-optic cables from Chicago to cancel stale bids or offers before they are picked off by taking algorithms using wireless links, but is beyond the maximum delay of one millisecond that, in the case of IEX's coil, the SEC ruled was acceptable.

The CBOE's approach to seeking regulatory approval was intriguing. It proposed that, even though the vast majority of the bids and offers in EDGA's order book would continue to be generated by electronic systems, they would be labeled electronically as manual quotations. This would deprive them of order protection under Reg NMS, the main regulations currently governing US share trading, but remove the requirement under the latter that immediate execution against those quotations be possible.[35] The CBOE's proposed asymmetrical speed bump provoked strong controversy. One of my interviewees told me that the head of a major trading firm had phoned the CBOE to warn it that the firm would cease trading on any of the CBOE's exchanges if the asymmetric speed bump was installed. That is hearsay, and I have no independent evidence of the alleged phone call, but the fact that my interviewee believed it had taken place is indicative of the sensitivity of the issue. In February 2020, the SEC rejected the CBOE's proposal, arguing that the exchange had not shown that slowing taking but not making was consistent with the requirements in the securities laws to treat market participants fairly (SEC 2020). IEX, too, submitted to the SEC in December 2019 a proposal to supplement its currently symmetric speed bump so as to offer a de facto asymmetric speed bump that would protect "making" orders from one of the most common ways in which they end up being picked off.[36] The fate of the IEX proposal is not known at the time of writing.

Let me end this discussion of speed bumps with the case of options, a class of financial instrument covered by the research but not discussed in any detail in this book. Making-taking interaction has particular salience in options because of their sheer multiplicity. For instance, while most corporations have a single category of shares, there may be dozens or even hundreds of different options on those shares. There are both calls (options to buy) and puts (options to sell), and sometimes more exotic options as well; different "strike prices" (the strike price of, for example, a call is the price at which the shares are bought if the call is exercised); and different expiration dates. In 2018, so interviewee OW told me, no fewer than 950,000 different options contracts were traded on US options exchanges. These exchanges want market-makers to quote prices not just for a small subset of the options on a given stock, but for all of them, leaving market-making algorithms particularly vulnerable when market prices change. They may need to cancel hundreds or thousands of stale bids or offers, while a taking algorithm can make a profit by finding just one stale bid or offer to execute against.

Options exchanges, as interviewee OY told me, "don't want the large market-makers to go out of business, certainly," which creates shared incentives. "There's a mutual benefit to working together," says OY. Perhaps the most important way in which options exchanges protect market-making firms is the provision to market-makers of a "purge port," a dedicated connection to the exchange that circumvents any other network traffic between it and the firm, and is therefore very fast. The purge port is used for so-called mass cancels, in which a single message from the firm's system cancels all its bids and offers in an entire class of options (all the options on Apple shares, for example). While ordinary cancels are normally implemented sequentially, a mass cancel is typically implemented by changing a single binary digit in each of the bids and offers, which renders them invalid, and therefore not executable, but is much quicker than a series of ordinary cancels, according to interviewees OX and OY. The matching engine can then remove the orders entirely without the risk that some will be picked off while it is doing so. Options exchanges also frequently offer market-making firms automatic mass cancels (without a cancel message from the firm's system) if, for example, a certain number of its bids or offers in a particular class of option are executed against without the firm's system responding by changing its quotes. This protects market-makers from potentially catastrophic system outages.[37]

Options exchanges can also intervene in making-taking interactions in less explicit ways. Sometimes, for example, making and taking orders are channeled into different typical material pathways through an exchange's computer system, with the pathway followed by taking orders slower. "Maybe they run the market-maker stuff on new hardware and they run some of these other order . . . gateways on older hardware," says OY. At least in the past, some exchanges had what were, in effect, different APIs (application programming interfaces) for making and taking orders. Interviewee AF, for example, cites one exchange that

> . . . had a quoting [i.e. making] API that you couldn't really remove [i.e. take] with, and then they had an order API for doing removal [taking], and there was a relational database on the order API [which journaled— i.e., recorded—the order] where it would take 100 millis[econds] for them to serialize it . . . and [goodness] knows what.

The "quoting" API used for market-making, says AF, was "two orders of magnitude faster" than the order API that a taker had to use.

Issues such as this serve as a useful reminder that the material politics of finance is not restricted to overt controversies such as those surrounding IEX's or EDGA's speed bumps, or to the rulings of regulators such as the SEC. Material politics can also be found deep in the inner workings of finance's black boxes, in features of exchanges' systems that may never become public but can nevertheless be consequential aspects of market structure.

7

Conclusion

In the early summer of 1381, with much of England convulsed by insurrections of the common people, the townspeople of St Albans stormed its great Benedictine monastery, whose abbot was their feudal overlord. By one of the strokes of fortune that connect us to the distant past, the monk who supervised the abbey's scribes and illuminators was the chronicler Thomas Walsingham, most likely an eyewitness. He records that the crowd demanded that the abbot release them from serfdom, broke into the abbot's prison, setting inmates free, and went on to a room close to the cloister called the Parlour. There they smashed the room's stone floor, taking fragments of it away with them.[1]

The explanation of the smashing of the floor lay fifty years previously. The then-abbot of St Albans had succeeded in prohibiting its townspeople from milling grain by hand, and, as the historian Marc Bloch put it, "[f]rom all over the town the millstones were brought in to the monastery . . . like so many trophies" (Bloch 1967: 158). The Parlour had been paved with the confiscated millstones, and half a century later that was still remembered and resented. Throughout medieval Europe, feudal lords often sought to suppress hand-milling and replace it with windmills or watermills, because they could exact fees for their use. The preference of their serfs and tenants for hand-milling—despite the physical effort involved—was equally long-standing. Even as steam mills were introduced, hand-milling continued. As late as the end of the 19th century, Bloch notes, villagers in Prussia were still using hand mills, and although their landowners no longer had the right to stop them, they still "felt obliged . . . to hide from strangers as they did so" (Bloch 1967: 159).

The Material Political Economy of Market Structure

The issues discussed in this book are esoteric compared to the milling of grain. They do not determine, at least directly, who eats and who does not. Nevertheless, the monks' confiscation of the St Albans millstones was a stark instance of what I mean by material political economy. First, the confiscation was a reordering of the material world. Second, it was a political act. Use of the legal system made the confiscation possible—the then abbot had "won the day by going to law" (Bloch 1967: 158)—and the powers and privileges that feudal overlords enjoyed likely framed that outcome and deterred resistance to the confiscation. Third, the confiscation was economically consequential, an intervention in what the previous chapters have referred to as market structure. If feudal lords could remove hand mills from their estates, they could ensure that their tenants had no alternative but to grind grain on the lord's mill, "subject, of course, to a respectable payment to the lord of the mill and the millstream," because "[i]t was no very difficult matter to prevent the construction of other watermills, windmills or even horse-driven mills on the lord's land" (Bloch 1967: 153).

In August 2019, a controversy erupted in the pages of the *Wall Street Journal* that, to an outsider, might seem almost as perplexing as the smashing of the Parlour's floor. It was sparked by the installation of two small, white, wireless antennas, each one foot in diameter, on the roof of the New York Stock Exchange's datacenter (Osipovich 2019a). The datacenter is a functional, modern building, not a historic landmark, and the antennas had been approved by the local zoning board with no dissenting votes.[2] That area of New Jersey is affluent, and its residents, as noted in chapter 5, are able to influence what gets built in their neighborhood, but—as described in that chapter—the datacenter is in a dip in the terrain, and so largely invisible from outside its grounds. It would be hard to even catch a glimpse of a couple of little antennas on its roof.

The objections to the antennas came in a telephone call and then letter to the regulator of US share trading, the Securities and Exchange Commission, from one of the world's most successful high-frequency trading firms, Virtu (described in chapter 1). The new antennas on the roof of the NYSE datacenter can send wireless signals to and from further antennas on an existing pole in the datacenter's grounds; that pole carries communication links to the other share-trading datacenters in New Jersey. A direct wireless link from the datacenter to that pole would eliminate 260 meters (about 850 feet) of "fiber tail"—the distance that a signal has to travel not wirelessly but more slowly, through fiber-optic cable—and could thus save nearly half a microsecond of transmission time (a microsecond is a millionth of a second).[3] Virtu's objection was that the application to the zoning board was for antennas to be used by a single communications provider "as selected by the NYSE" (Virtu Financial 2019b: 1). Virtu's fear, as paraphrased by the *Wall Street Journal*'s Alexander Osipovich, was that "trading firms will have to pay hefty fees to access the [new] antennas. . . . [T]here wouldn't be any cheaper providers that can offer the same superfast access," and the firm viewed that as "unfair." Without superfast access, said Osipovich, trading firms' algorithms "will be preyed upon by competitors that can act on market-moving information a split-second faster" (Osipovich 2019a).

The NYSE has not, in fact, gone ahead with the use of the rooftop antennas to speed transmission (see its letter to the SEC: King 2020); it is unclear whether Virtu's objections played a part in this. Neither, though, did that end controversy. The continuing dispute focused on the spatial advantage of the pole inside the grounds of the datacenter, which houses equipment used by IDS (the data-services affiliate of the Intercontinental Exchange, owner of the NYSE, in partnership with atmospheric-laser pioneer Anova Financial Networks) to transmit market data and to lease bandwidth to trading firms that enables their computer servers in the NYSE datacenter to communicate quickly with their systems in other datacenters. Other organizations "do not have access" to that pole (King 2020: 5), and instead must place their equipment on poles outside the datacenter's grounds that are just over 200 meters (about 700 feet) farther away from it.[4] Although the distance between the poles is by no means the only determinant of transmission speed (see chapter 5), it is an important factor.

It now seems that the cable linking the nearer pole to the datacenter will be coiled to remove its advantage, although there was disagreement over how much coiling was needed. That this dispute should have continued even against the backdrop of the coronavirus epidemic is a small but striking manifestation of issues of material political economy discussed in earlier chapters. Their political-economy aspect is clearest when explicit interventions are made in the material processes and infrastructures of trading, most often with the goal of protecting market-making algorithms such as Virtu's from being picked off by "taking" algorithms. As interviewee AF points out, such interventions influence "who makes what money," although the absence of intervention of course influences that as well. There are other aspects, too, of the material arrangements of trading that are also political, at least in the broad sense of the word. Take, for example, the (sometimes fiercely controversial) question, discussed in chapter 5, of whether "fill" messages should or should not be dispatched before the corresponding trade is reported on an exchange's datafeed. On an issue such as this, different firms whose algorithms act in different ways will have different economic interests, and can be expected to have different preferences, and furthermore such issues can have unintended effects on market structure. Recall interviewee DI's view that receiving fill messages early keeps competition alive by allowing market-making firms that are not the fastest to still make profits. More generally, even material phenomena that are essentially fortuitous can influence market structure, such as the effectively accidental fact (also discussed in chapter 5) that until 2010 the firm that had "gold line"—the fastest fiber-optic route from Chicago to New Jersey—was predominantly a market-maker.

The materiality of market structure goes beyond the technologies of trading such as exchanges' computer systems or the gold line. Also important are the systems for clearing and settling trades—that is, for registering them, guaranteeing them, processing them, and transferring money and the ownership of the securities or other assets being traded. Clearing and settlement are often ignored as mundane, back-office administrative matters, but they play the essential role of ensuring "the undisputed closure of financial transactions" (Millo et al. 2005: 23). Because of this, "[c]learing binds a market together," as interviewee CC puts it. If you cannot access a market's clearing system, as the Island-like Treasurys trading venue Direct Match, discussed in chapter 4, found it could not, you are effectively shut out from that market.

What is bound together materially by clearing and settlement, and how, are thus crucial. The most clear-cut example discussed in the previous chapters is the difference between futures (in which exchanges such as the Chicago Mercantile Exchange and Eurex usually own and control their own clearinghouses, making it hard for a new futures exchange to build momentum in the trading of a product already traded by one of those exchanges) and shares, especially US shares. As described in chapter 3, the existence of a single centralized, nationwide, easily accessible clearing and settlement system for US shares greatly facilitated the rise of new trading venues such as Island. Clearing—an everyday, undramatic process—is pivotal enough that, in the European Union, even national governments have become involved in conflict over how it should be organized.[5]

In the background to the contrast between US futures and shares in respect to clearing is the differences in the interaction—the "hinge," to use Andrew Abbott's terminology—in the 1970s between the political system and, on the one hand, futures exchanges, and, on the other hand, stock exchanges. In the case of futures, as described in chapter 2, the hinge was in a sense quite specific, and the resultant reforms were strongly influenced by futures exchanges. In the case of shares, as sketched in chapter 3, the "paperwork crisis" of the late 1960s created a substantially broader incentive for members of Congress to become involved, and the reforms that resulted were much less closely shaped by stock exchanges. One consequence of those different interactions with the political system is the big difference, discussed in previous chapters, between the signals (patterns of data that inform how algorithms trade) available to HFT algorithms trading shares and those trading futures. With most leading US shares traded on multiple exchanges, the fastest possible information on what is happening on those other exchanges is vital to HFT. Many financial futures, in contrast, are traded only on the Chicago Mercantile Exchange, making the flow of information to it from other datacenters often a little less important; more typically, it is the flow of data *from* the CME that is crucial.

The Politics of Information

As is indicated by the contrast between shares and futures, the material practices of HFT differ in different circumstances, and sometimes those differences in practices are political, either in the narrow sense of developments in the political system having been involved in generating them, or in the broader sense of the differences being influenced by or influencing the positions, power, status, or economic resources of different actors. Consider, for instance, the overall issue of the availability of information. Asked about how the early HFT firm Automated Trading Desk developed the mathematical models that informed its algorithms' trading, interviewee BT said:

> It's as if someone puts certain game pieces on the table, and it's like okay, I've got these pieces of data, let me look at all the different ways I might use them. And then here comes some new datafeed attribute . . . we have multiple exchanges as separate exchanges. Then we had more pieces [more "signals"] and we'd rearrange them [alter the models], and then here comes depth of book [fuller data on the bids and offers in electronic

order books, not just on the best-priced bids and offers] . . . and . . . that was even more complicated . . .

That quotation nicely captures two things. First, the information employed by an HFT algorithm in making its decisions to bid or offer is indeed material (a "datafeed attribute"), even if the form of its materiality is electromagnetic, rather than matter's solid state. What is processed by HFT algorithms is literally a signal, or a set of signals, as an engineer would use the term. Second, the availability of information—of BT's "game pieces"—is historically variable. BT's career in HFT had been long enough for him to have witnessed the gradual enriching of that information.

To an extent that is perhaps surprising, the existence and availability to HFT algorithms of signals (such as those listed in tables 3.2 and 4.4, or cited by BT in the above quotation) are the outcome of struggles over regulation and/or market structure. Let me not exaggerate; that is not the case for all of those signals,[6] but it is true of three of the main classes of signal employed in HFT in US shares: "futures lead," the outcome of the episodes discussed in chapter 2; and the two classes referred to in what BT said above ("fragmentation," or the signals that arise from the same shares being traded on multiple venues; and order-book dynamics, the signals made available by the processes, discussed in chapter 3, by which access to order books was gradually opened up). Signals of all three kinds—outcomes of past conflicts as they are—are now hardwired, so to speak, into the large technological system that US share trading has become. They are, we might say, material-*ized* political economy.

It is also important to note that there are "game pieces" that could be on the table but are not: information that could form an important set of signals for trading but is kept private to exchanges. There is a crucial difference between, for instance, the New York Stock Exchange's old paper order books, an example of which is in figure 3.1, which included brokers' names and firms' acronyms, and a modern electronic order book of the kind shown in figures 1.5 and 6.1. Orders in a book of this latter kind (prevalent in the exchanges that trade shares and futures and in the interdealer electronic trading of Treasurys and foreign exchange) are anonymous. Although the exchange's computer system keeps a record of which firm submits which order, that information is not included in the stream of update messages from which trading firms' computer servers construct their mirrors of the order book. Even anonymized identifiers of firms or trading accounts are not normally disseminated on exchanges of this kind. As a result, there is, for example, no straightforward way of determining whether a series of orders are all from the same firm or algorithm. (In practice, as described in chapter 6, trading firms can, sometimes at least, partially deanonymize order books, but doing that requires either intensive human scrutiny of patterns of trading—perhaps along with intelligence gleaned in informal conversation with employees of other trading firms—or the use of sophisticated machine learning.)

As emphasized in chapter 1, material political economy as advocated here complements, rather than replaces, other perspectives on finance, such as those that focus on phenomena of the kind that we more commonly think of as normative or cultural. Anonymity is an example of an issue where normative preferences are important. The anonymity of order books, at least in the trading of shares and futures, has accrued normative force. In 2017, for example, there was controversy about two sets of specialized data products sold to market participants by Nasdaq—at additional cost—that contained information not disseminated in its standard datafeeds. One of those specialized data streams was Nasdaq's Pathfinders service, which it advertised as "provid[ing] a real-time indication of what the 'smart money' is doing in a stock" (Nasdaq OMX 2009: 1).

> Using NASDAQ trade data, the Pathfinders data feed constantly monitors the buying and selling of market participants to identify "pathfinders" that are actively buying or selling a large volume of shares in a particular security, in the anticipation of a price increase or decrease over an extended period of time. NASDAQ does not reveal the identities of the Pathfinders but instead captures the sentiment of this group by indicating the number of Pathfinders bullish versus bearish and the total number [of] shares bought versus sold by Pathfinders. (Nasdaq OMX 2009: 2)

Although the Pathfinders datafeed thus preserved anonymity and gave only aggregate information, the aggregation of successive orders from the same firm was criticized as undermining the efforts of investors to "disguise their intentions [by] breaking up large orders into smaller ones so they aren't obviously coming from a large investor" (Stockland 2017). "[S]ome customers," said Nasdaq, "have recently posed questions regarding the types of information included in the product." Although Nasdaq did not regard those concerns as justified, it withdrew the package of products involved, citing low revenues from them and the cost of upgrading them (SEC 2017: 5).[7]

As the disagreement concerning Pathfinders shows, the norms surrounding electronic order books balance disclosure and nondisclosure.

That balance, and the material forms it takes (materiality, to repeat a point made in chapter 1, is not something separate from culture), again vary from market to market. In shares and futures, orders typically remain anonymous throughout. In professional foreign-exchange trading, in contrast, that full anonymity is hard to maintain, for the reasons discussed in chapter 4, which largely have to do with the absence of any full-fledged arrangements for central clearing. Indeed, the normative preference for anonymity in the trading of shares and futures is sometimes reversed in foreign-exchange trading, in which "name give-up" (full deanonymization after a trade) can be seen as praiseworthy transparency.

> [W]e have full post-trade transparency. Post-trade we give up not just the name of the executing broker and the prime [broker] bank, but also the client name . . . Our idea is that if you need to trade FX [foreign exchange] and you trade it in a responsible manner, in line with the system, then you should have no issue giving up your name post-trade. (Interviewee FI)

On foreign-exchange trading venues in which it is possible to learn at least counterparties' identifier numbers after each trade, those who have this information can do things that their equivalents in other, comparable markets cannot. In particular, they can often determine that deals with a specific counterparty systematically lose them money. As described in chapter 4, in foreign-exchange trading, a participant that discovers this—especially if it is a large and influential bank—can ask the administrators of a trading venue to change system settings so that this "predatory" counterparty loses the capacity to trade, at least with that particular participant. (Predatory and toxic are words that seem to be used often in complaints of this kind, words that have normative force.) If, as on some foreign-exchange trading venues, it is possible to discover counterparties' names and not just their identifier numbers, an aggrieved market participant can also contact the allegedly predatory firm's prime broker and request that it discipline its client, a threat that has force because the absence of central clearing of foreign exchange means that an HFT firm can access the mechanisms of professional trading only via a prime-broker bank.

What Algorithms Can and Can't Do

The availability of "signals" and other forms of information such as counterparties' identifier numbers or names is closely related to how trading algorithms can act and the constraints on algorithmic action. These too are political issues, in the broader sense of politics—and sometimes also in the narrower sense of the political system having been involved in the processes leading to these capacities and constraints. In foreign exchange, for instance, the combined result of refusals to trade, threats to expel participants from trading venues, and the granting to market-making algorithms of "last look" privileges (see chapter 6) has been a significant constraint on algorithmic action. It has become difficult to successfully pursue at least the simpler HFT taking strategies in foreign exchange, and there has been a consequent wholesale shift away from taking and toward HFT market-making.

Foreign-exchange trading is distinctive in the extent to which incumbents such as big banks are able to monitor and constrain the actions of HFT algorithms, but the latter's actions are never free from all constraint. As discussed in chapter 6, in any market organized around an electronic order book, trading algorithms act by placing, canceling, or modifying orders. One key constraint on these actions is present in all the markets discussed in this book, but to quite different degrees: it concerns what is in many respects the easiest way to make money in automated markets, spoofing. As described in chapter 6, spoofing (in at least its most basic form) involves the placing of large bids or offers that will, if things go according to plan, be canceled before they are executed but will cause HFT algorithms—and perhaps other algorithms as well—to anticipate a movement in prices and therefore to execute against other, smaller, orders that the spoofer has placed.

Although spoofing often was, and in some cases still seems to be, informally tolerated (Arnoldi 2016), there has been an increasingly energetic crackdown on it by market regulators and, in the US, even criminal prosecutions and at least one jail sentence. Among the effects of criminal prosecution, says interviewee BM, is to make it much harder for exchanges to informally tolerate spoofing. It would be too embarrassing if a spoofer to whom the exchange has been lenient were jailed. In the markets in which the crackdown has been most pronounced, such as in the trading of US shares and futures, exchanges now deploy automated systems to detect spoofing. Interviewee BM tells me that those systems quickly detect simple, traditional forms of spoofing such as the example given in chapter 6. Interviewee CJ reports that the activity has by no means disappeared, but it has, says BM, changed form. Sophisticated spoofers use multiple small orders (perhaps submitted from separate trading accounts) rather than a small number of big orders; they do not try to create huge, suspicion-inducing imbalances in the order book, but only more modest imbalances; and they try to evade exchanges' automated detection systems by operating across more than one exchange so that no one detection system can "see" the entirety of their activity.

The incentive to spoof is pervasive, but the extent of effort devoted to its detection and punishment varies across markets. There have been few reported cases of spoofers in sovereign-bond or foreign-exchange trading being punished, but that does not seem to be because there is little or no spoofing in those markets. In the case of Treasurys, for example, regulatory jurisdiction is split between the SEC, FINRA (the Financial Industry Regulatory Authority),[8] the Department of the Treasury, and the latter's market agent, the Federal Reserve Bank of New York. The effect of split jurisdiction is that determining the agency responsible for punishing spoofing can be unclear.

> AUTHOR: Who do you go to in the cash bonds [to report spoofing]?
> INTERVIEWEE BM: The cash you go to no one. No one really covers it.

The variable extent of monitoring for and punishing spoofing is only one example of a constraint that influences algorithms' actions. Those actions are directly constrained by the order gateways and matching engines of exchanges (or other trading venues). The case of US shares is particularly interesting in this respect, because governmental regulation of share trading is built into the exchange software that determines whether an order received from an algorithm or human trader is entered into an order book or rejected as invalid. As discussed in chapter 6, this has made one specific type of order—intermarket sweep orders—pivotal to success or failure in HFT, for example in helping market-making algorithms achieve favorable positions in the time-priority queue for the execution of orders. Exactly what such an order does need not detain us here—that is described in chapter 6—but what is worth emphasizing here is the regulatory and political process that gave birth to that class of order and gives it its centrality.

Intermarket sweep orders were, as outlined in chapter 6, created as part of the market regulator's (the SEC's) effort to bridge two sometimes conflicting priorities: first, to promote competition among exchanges and other trading venues, and second, to keep US share trading coherent without trying to impose a single nationwide consolidated limit order book, an approach that had already been judged by the SEC to be politically infeasible. As explained in chapter 6, pivotal to the SEC's 2005 Reg NMS (Regulation National Market System, the centerpiece of the current regulatory framework for US share trading) is order protection: the prohibition of, for example, an exchange allowing the purchase of shares when a better price is available on another exchange. The original rationale for intermarket sweep orders was the need to facilitate large-scale trading, for example by institutional investors, while still preserving order protection.

Order protection originally was (and may again become) an explicitly political matter. The five commissioners who head the SEC are political appointees, nominated by the President and approved by the Senate. No more than three of them can be members of the same party, and in practice it has been common for two to be Republicans and two Democrats, with a chair of the same party as the president. In 2005, under George W. Bush, the commissioners split on party lines over order protection. Two commissioners, Cynthia Glassman and Paul Atkins, both Republicans, argued that order protection was an unnecessary and probably harmful imposition on market participants. (The argument, expressed, for example, by interviewee EZ, was that instead of "prescriptive rules on order routing," it was "better just to deregulate. Nobody meeting their fiduciary duty of best execution is going to ignore a readily available better price.") Their two Democratic Party-affiliated colleagues, Roel Campos and Harvey Goldschmid, supported order protection. Reg NMS was adopted only because in the decisive vote on April 6, 2005, the SEC's chair, the Wall Street grandee William Donaldson (a Republican appointed by Bush, but "pretty patrician . . . he wasn't a deregulatory guy," says EZ), broke from party lines to support order protection and Reg NMS.

Order protection had had strong support within the staff of the SEC. Even some of these supporters, though, did not expect order protection to be necessary for long. As one regulator (interviewee RZ) puts it, "Reg NMS . . . was the route to get rid of the New York [Stock Exchange] manual market hold where they locked out any electronic competition," via the regulatory requirement to use the slow Intermarket Trading System. Once electronic competition was fully in place, says RZ, "most of the people that were on the [SEC] staff thought that we could probably get rid of the trade-through rule [order protection] in three years because it would've done its work already." Instead of that happening, though, Reg NMS became largely locked in place. To alter it fundamentally is dauntingly difficult, for reasons that are in a broad sense political, even if not "party political." "On every NMS issue," explains RZ, "it's a zero-sum game":

> There's winners and losers, and the people that have gained something fought to keep it [Reg NMS and order protection]. And the people that had lost something fought to change it. Then you had a succession of

[SEC] commissioners that were either too busy or just didn't understand it well enough to have the confidence to weigh into this brutal dogfight.

Even the dramatic change in US politics brought about by the election of President Trump had only limited impact on Reg NMS and its order-protection rules. Such changes as the SEC has proposed primarily affect other aspects of the regulations.[9]

Just as HFT's signals are hardwired into the technological system that US share trading has become, so Reg NMS's order-protection rules are programmed into exchanges' matching engines. Those engines mechanically reject orders that seem (given the information available to them) to conflict with those rules. The significance of intermarket sweep orders (ISOs) is that they partially circumvent this otherwise massive constraint on algorithms' actions. An algorithm that is able to use the electronic flag labeling an order an ISO is thereby able to get the relevant matching engine to process an order it would otherwise have had to reject. As explained in chapter 6, however, not all algorithms can use an ISO flag, and it is a potentially serious disadvantage not to be able to do so.[10]

Regulators, Politicians, and Lobbying

Governmental regulation is a variable influence on the conduct of HFT. That influence is at its strongest in the case of US share trading, with, as just discussed, regulatory order-protection rules programmed into exchanges' matching engines. Share trading, in both the US and Europe, has also been unusual in the extent to which regulation has encouraged competition between trading venues, competition that has helped force exchanges to adopt HFT-friendly material features and fee structures. It might have been expected that regulatory encouragement of competition would be pervasive. It fits well with, for example, the version of neoliberalism extracted by Michel Foucault from his reading of the German neoliberals, with their emphasis on the way in which competition "is absolutely not a given of nature. . . . [P]ure competition, which is the essence of the market, can only appear if it is produced . . . by an active governmentality" (Foucault 2008: 120–121). Yet the scope of this active governmentality in respect to the market structure of trading has been much more limited than one might have anticipated. As discussed in chapter 4, government agencies have, for example, been content to leave primary-dealer structures intact in sovereign-bond trading, and, similarly, have made few efforts to replicate in futures trading the measures that have encouraged competition between exchanges in share trading.[11] "Governmentality," in Foucault's sense, goes beyond direct regulation. It includes, for example, techniques of the self (internal self-disciplining and the construction of "entrepreneurial" selves), forms of knowledge (especially of "populations"), technical procedures, and more. In the episodes examined in the previous chapters, though, the presence or absence of action by state agencies to promote competition is an important factor.[12]

Furthermore, even in the case of US share trading, with its powerful regulator, the Securities and Exchange Commission, it would be quite mistaken to see regulation as simply an external, autonomous influence on market structure.[13] Interviewees who had been SEC officials describe how the agency is buffeted by finance-sector lobbying, by the fallout from financial crises and scandals, and by spasmodic surges of attention from the formal political system. As interviewee RF puts it, "[T]he ability of the [Securities and Exchange] Commission to move forward on major issues really does require . . . at least some segment of the [finance] industry to be supportive." In the case of the debate in the 1970s over proposals for a single nationwide consolidated limit order book, or CLOB, the segment of the financial sector that supported the CLOB was slender, and—as just noted—the SEC ultimately did not try to impose the huge change in market structure implied by the CLOB. The debate over the CLOB "cost me a promotion," says former regulator RI, who was seen as a supporter of the controversial system. The then chair of the SEC told RI that he had received telephone calls from finance-sector leaders making clear that RI's appointment to a more senior role would be unwelcome.

Reg NMS offers an interesting contrast with the CLOB. When Reg NMS was being drafted, says interviewee RY, politicians

> were very, very heavily lobbied [by the finance sector] and the SEC was under enormous pressure from certain members of Congress. Our feet were held to the fire in terms of what positions we were going to take.

The difference from the case of the CLOB, though, was that the finance sector was split much more equally over Reg NMS, giving the SEC greater freedom of action.[14] Furthermore, even though there were long periods (for example, the Reagan presidency) in which SEC interviewees report having felt unable to make major interventions in market structure, in none of the episodes examined in my research did the SEC appear simply to have been captured by finance-sector interests.

It is also wise not to take regulators' proposals for changes in market structure too literally. One tactic reported by SEC officials whom I interviewed was to propose a change that they knew would provoke strong finance-sector opposition (and would, therefore, not ultimately be implemented) in the hope of being able to make more modest changes. Several of them suggest that there was an element of this to the proposal for the CLOB. It helped make possible more limited initiatives such as the mandatory dissemination of transaction prices via the "consolidated tape," which began in 1975, and of the highest bids and lowest offers for shares traded on registered exchanges (disseminated by the Consolidated Quotation System, launched in 1978). To those familiar only with share trading, the presence of such systems may seem a normal, inevitable feature of all but the most rudimentary of financial markets. It is worth noting, though, that almost half a century on since the start of the mandatory dissemination of the prices and sizes of transactions in US shares, there is still no equivalent dissemination system for transactions in US Treasurys, with dealers vociferously protesting that it would make their hedging and unwinding of trading positions too difficult.[15]

My favorite example of regulators' tactical politics is what I think of as the battle of the asterisk (I particularly like it because it highlights the mundane economics of finance). The context of the battle was what became the SEC's order-handling rules, which were important in the rise of HFT (and in the demise of the dealer-client market structure of Nasdaq) because they resulted in prices on Island and the other new electronic share-trading venues set up in the 1990s—prices that were often set by HFT algorithms—becoming visible on Nasdaq's widely used screens. A former regulator, interviewee RH (who was central to the formulation of those rules), told me that his approach to circumventing finance-sector opposition to SEC market-structure interventions "was that if I wanted to achieve this" (making a hand gesture indicating a minor move), "I would propose this" (making a gesture signaling a larger change).

What started the battle of the asterisk was the difference between the minimum increment of price on Nasdaq's screens (an eighth and, later, a sixteenth of a dollar) and the increment on the new electronic venues, which in the case of Island was as little as 1/256th of a dollar. That meant—there seems to have been no dispute about this—that prices from the new venues would have to be rounded for display by Nasdaq. Prices on the new electronic venues were usually better than those of Nasdaq's official dealers by only small amounts, often, in the case of Island, simply by its minimum unit of price, 1/256th of a dollar. What interviewee RH proposed—the large change indicated by the second of his hand movements, though the change would not have appeared large to an outsider—was that when a price quote from a new electronic venue was rounded for display on Nasdaq screens, an asterisk should be added to indicate the rounding. His heart, he admits, was not in the proposal. It was a "[t]errible idea," but it served as a "distraction" and "consumed a lot of air in the room." The asterisks would have prompted market participants to search for marginally better prices on the new venues, and could easily have become a form of advertising for them, so there was fierce objection to them from incumbents. As another interviewee, RZ, puts it, "Nasdaq . . . said . . . we can't live with an asterisk." The SEC did eventually back away from imposing the asterisk, but—in RH's opinion, at least—because incumbents focused on stopping the asterisk, it became easier for the SEC to achieve what for him was the main goal: getting prices from the new electronic venues onto Nasdaq's screens.

At least in the episodes relevant to this book, the involvement of the formal political system in financial regulation was of two quite different kinds. The first, which seems pervasive, occurs when political figures are lobbied by specific financial interest groups and in turn seek to exert pressure on regulators. The second, much rarer but occasionally highly consequential, occurs when there has been a crisis or scandal whose effects are sufficiently widespread that members of Congress can envisage broader political rewards (and not simply campaign contributions) from being seen as reformers of the financial system. "Congress has an interest," says interviewee RY, "to the extent that their constituents have an interest." The episode of this kind that had the deepest effects on the evolution of algorithmic trading was the late-1960s' "paperwork crisis" and resultant bankruptcies of stockbrokers, the accompanying threat that large numbers of the general public would lose substantial amounts of money, and the resultant congressional reform efforts, culminating in the 1975 Securities Acts Amendments, which still form a major part of the legislative framework that gives the SEC its legal powers.

The near-catastrophic 2008 banking crisis prompted another phase of intense congressional involvement in reform efforts, but those efforts have not played a major part in the events described in this book, because their greatest effects were on one of the markets that I researched but (to prevent this book from becoming overcomplicated) I have not discussed: interest-rate swaps, in which efforts to practice HFT have to date largely been unsuccessful.[16] The legal crackdown on spoofing, touched on above, was, however, largely made possible by this post-2008 congressional reform effort. On the face of it, this is puzzling, since spoofing played no discernible role in the crisis, but widespread involvement of Congress in reform can create political opportunities for regulators to move on unrelated matters. As interviewee SD described to me, the Commodity Futures Trading Commission helped draft the sprawling 2010 Dodd-Frank Wall Street Reform and Consumer Protection Act, and—feeling its legal powers to act against spoofing to be too limited—the CFTC took advantage of the opportunity to include in the Act an explicit ban on spoofing in futures markets. The lawyers whom I interviewed were unanimous that this part of the Dodd-Frank Act has greatly facilitated the criminal prosecution of spoofers, and is thus in good part responsible for the crackdown on the activity.

The political system can, in addition, have effects that are structural rather than depending directly on lobbying efforts, on the temporary engagement of politicians motivated by crises and scandals, or on regulators' occasionally astute political tactics. Most important for the developments discussed in this book is the way the structure of congressional committees, especially in the Senate, underpins the divide in the regulation of US financial markets between the Securities and Exchange Commission (responsible for shares and other securities) and the Commodity Futures Trading Commission (responsible for futures trading). As described in chapter 2, proposals to merge the SEC and CFTC (or even simply to reorganize their responsibilities so that the regulation of share-index futures would move to the regulator of shares, the SEC) have always failed, even when originating from the normally influential Department of the Treasury. The Chicago Mercantile Exchange has maintained the emphasis championed by its leading figure in the 1970s and 1980s, Leo Melamed, on strong ties to Washington. But the ultimate underpinning structural factor appears to be that the CFTC falls within the jurisdiction of the powerful Senate Agriculture Committee, which (quite independently of its changing membership and party affiliations) appears consistently reluctant to agree to a loss of its authority. As discussed in chapter 2, the consequent difference in regulatory regime seems to underlie, at least to a degree, the historically most important (and still crucial) "signal" used by HFT algorithms trading shares: "futures lead."

Mundane Politics, Mundane Economics

It should, however, be emphasized that the explicit involvement of the political system in issues of market structure in finance is not the norm. We might say that politics of market structure is normally "local," not necessarily spatially but in the sense that the actors in that politics are mainly—perhaps exclusively—participants in the market in question.[17] A common form of that local politics, found across all the markets discussed in this book, is persistent jockeying for position between incumbents and challengers. (Social-science readers will recall the discussion in chapter 1 of field theory, which emphasizes precisely this aspect of markets.) Quite often, this jockeying centers on issues that are opaque to outsiders, such as tick size (the minimum unit of price) or access to a market's clearing system.

In other words, at stake in the mundane, local politics of finance is often, perhaps usually, its mundane economics, its routine, undramatic (but, in aggregate, substantial) money-making. That, to repeat, is why I regard the battle of the asterisk—a heated struggle over whether to label a price as having been arithmetically rounded—as something of a parable. It centered on a difference in prices that in many cases would have been less than half a cent, yet Nasdaq's dealers rightly saw the asterisk as a dangerous threat to their routine money-making.

I've already sketched in chapter 1 the mundane nature of the economics of HFT. Profit rates in HFT are usually low. My interviews suggest that the profit on a winning trade is often, indeed typically, a single tick (in the case of US shares, a cent per share), and even the most successful HFT algorithm does not win anything like all the time. Since most HFT trades are small—often involving, for example, as few as 100 shares—that makes the average profit on each trade undramatic in the extreme. HFT is remunerative only if very large volumes of trades are made. So those involved in HFT have to focus on the most mundane of economic matters—the fees and other costs of trading, the costs of technology and communications links, the expenses involved in clearing, and so on—because those costs can easily swamp the modest gross revenues from trading. It's easy for a researcher from academia, in which competition takes quite a different form, to underestimate how strongly issues of this sort can shape what goes on in an HFT firm. One of my earliest HFT interviewees struck me as having a certain quiet desperation about him. I thought during the interview that he was simply under time pressure, but not long after the interview his firm went out of business, and I now suspect that the swamping of revenues by costs had already begun when I spoke to him.

One successful HFT firm that I visited has a policy that all new recruits (PhDs included) have to start their career with the firm in the normally low-status activity of operations, which includes monitoring and managing the processes of the submission, execution, and recording of orders, and clearing trades—an experience that can help recruits develop an understanding not just of trading's potential profits but also of its routine costs. The structure of those costs can shape HFT deeply. On most exchanges, for example, fees are tiered; the more trading a firm does, the lower the fee rate. As several interviewees explained, it can therefore make sense for HFT algorithms to make a trade even when no profit is expected. To "scratch," as those involved would put it (to trade without making a profit but not incurring a loss), can be a useful outcome. It can keep the firm's aggregate volume of trading sufficiently high to qualify for a tier with a lower fee rate.

Let me repeat, one last time, that "mundane" does not mean trivial. Even something as simple as the tiering of fees is consequential. In many markets, HFT firms—once upon a time in the role of challenger—are now incumbents, and tiered fees can form a barrier to a new generation of challengers, because the scale on which an incumbent firm trades means that not only are its resources greater but its costs per trade are lower. Under some circumstances, indeed, scale can outweigh a modest speed disadvantage.[18] Furthermore, even small amounts of money, made many, many times over, add up to considerable sums. The economists Eric Budish, Robin Lee, and John Shim calculate that in US share trading, the annual total in 2015 of what they call "arbitrage rents"—the money at stake in the race that breaks out between making and taking algorithms when there is a substantial change in a relevant signal—was between $3.1 and $3.7 billion (2019: 40).[19] Separate work by Aquilina, Budish, and O'Neill, using a different methodology, produces an estimate of the size of the aggregate annual "prize" across stock markets globally of around $5 billion (Aquilina et al. 2020: 4).[20] There are currently no equivalent estimates for the other classes of financial instrument in which my interviews suggest that speed races of this kind are common—futures, Treasurys, listed options, and (perhaps to a lesser extent) foreign exchange—but the annual total across all types of financial asset globally is likely to be well in excess of $5 billion.

The estimate of a speed-race prize of $3.1-$3.7 billion annually in US share trading is around three times larger than the aggregate annual profits being made from HFT in US shares (see Meyer, Bullock, and Rennison 2018), which highlights another important facet of the mundane economics of HFT. As is clear from my interviews, the pie of HFT firms' gross trading revenues is in effect shared among those firms, the exchanges, and the suppliers of technologies, communications links, and other services necessary to HFT firms. Budish and his colleagues estimate that the "exchange-specific speed technology revenues" of the three main families of US equities exchanges—what those exchanges earned by selling fast data on changes in their order books, leasing cross-connect cables and access to wireless links that can transmit these data and algorithms' orders, and (in the case of exchanges that own or lease their datacenters) leasing space in those datacenters to allow trading firms' servers to be as close as possible to exchanges' matching engines—were between $675 and $790 million in 2015, and between $874 million and $1.024 billion in 2018 (Budish et al. 2019: 40). The level of costs of these kinds is an issue that several of my HFT interviewees complain about volubly, pointing out that it is their aggregate activity that largely generates the data for which they have to pay, while exchanges, in their turn, defend their charges vigorously. This overall divide is likely in the background of specific controversies such as the dispute, discussed at the start of this chapter, over poles and rooftop antennas.

The revenue that exchanges earn by selling fast data and access to the cables (and sometimes also wireless links) that carry them is in turn a constraint on the possible introduction by exchanges of the asymmetric speed bumps described in chapter 6, and even more strongly on their possible support for the change in market structure proposed by Eric Budish and his colleagues (Budish, Cramton, and Shim 2015; Budish, Lee, and Shim 2019). They propose a shift from continuous trading to very frequent but discrete auctions (perhaps as frequent as every millisecond; perhaps even every 50 microseconds), the rationale for which is discussed in a note.[21] Either measure would most likely reduce the incentive and/or need for extreme speed, but by doing so could also reduce exchanges' revenues. In consequence, measures of this kind are mainstream only in foreign-exchange trading (in which banks, with their generally slow systems, remain influential).

In the trading of shares and of futures, serious consideration of asymmetric speed bumps has so far been restricted largely to exchanges and/or products that are not central to global finance. That restriction, however, may not be permanent. This book (especially chapter 3) shows how a mutually reinforcing "hinge"—to use the term introduced in chapter 1—came into being between an approach to trading (HFT) and exchanges with a particular material and economic configuration. My interviews made amply clear that there are automated market-making firms of some size and scale that either economically cannot, or would prefer not to, pursue extreme speed. Will a similar hinge come into being between that approach to trading and exchanges with asymmetric speed bumps, their own versions of the Reuters module described in chapter 6, or even Budish-style frequent batch auctions? It is too early to tell, but it cannot be ruled out. One manifestation of the original hinge was HFT firms setting up or investing in HFT-friendly trading venues. In my most recent interviews I discovered that two automated market-making firms that dislike HFT's speed race have, analogously, invested in trading venues that have material features or rules that mitigate that race. (One of these venues is the new European exchange, Aquis, which does not have a speed bump—which, interviewee EA pointed out to me, could be problematic under Europe's "best execution" rules—but has taken a simpler route. It has an outright ban on "taking" by proprietary trading firms' algorithms.) Trading firms, and even in a sense algorithms, do not simply adapt to existing environments. They can change those environments, encouraging developments to which they are well adapted.

The material arrangements of trading are significant not just to traders. Very likely, the early stages of the transformation of trading examined in the previous chapters saved considerable amounts of money for the "end investors" in financial markets—in other words, for the pension funds, mutual funds, insurance companies, and ultimately private individuals that receive the income and capital gains from investment. Other things being equal, cost saving of this kind would be expected to be economically beneficial and welfare improving. (The proviso "other things being equal" is needed because trading becoming cheaper can have wider effects. For example, end investors or those who manage their assets may respond simply by doing more trading. More broadly, cheaper trading may encourage a fixation on short-term gains, which may have adverse socioeconomic consequences, but that is an issue beyond this book's remit.) In the case of US share trading, for example, competition among trading venues increased, fees fell considerably, and the reduction of the standard minimum increment of price from an eighth of dollar to a single cent made it possible for the new automated market-making firms to greatly reduce the previous generously wide spreads between the highest prices at which market-makers would buy shares and the lowest prices at which they would sell them. The changes—which took place in the late 1990s and early 2000s—almost certainly cut transaction costs; see, for example, the time series of estimated costs in Angel, Harris, and Spatt (2013: 23).

What is much less clear, though, is the extent to which transaction costs have continued to fall. For example, in Angel, Harris, and Spatt's data there is no consistent decline in costs after 2006. Perhaps, as Budish and his colleagues suggest, the increasing costs of HFT's speed races have begun at least partially to cancel out cost savings resulting from continuing broader improvements in information technology (Budish et al. 2015: 1555 and

1593–4). I know of no conclusive data on the issue, but it is surely an important one.

It is difficult, certainly, to avoid the suspicion that a financial system at the heart of which are speed races will spend excessively on the technologies of speed, and thus waste social resources. As described in chapter 5, even some of those whose businesses are built on those races are aware of that. It is striking, for example, that Virtu, despite being an enormously successful HFT firm, suggested, in its letter to the SEC complaining about the two new antennas, that the wireless speed race needs to be curbed:

> [P]erhaps it is time to offer fixed latency [transmission time] numbers from data center to data center. All providers could have circuits with the pairwise fixed wireless latency that connect between the major data centers and pay the same amount for that access. . . . Instead of spending money on eliminating the next microsecond, money could be spent elsewhere as firms compete on non-latency grounds. (Virtu Financial 2019b: 4)

It must be said, though, that there are other forms of waste in the financial system, such as highly paid investment managers' and other intermediaries' excessive fees for services of sometimes dubious value, which are almost certainly much larger than the costs of speed races (see Arjaliès, Grant, Hardie, MacKenzie, and Svetlova 2017). There are also many other important issues to consider about how the financial system is currently organized, including whether it creates incentives for corporations' senior executives to do things that boost their firms' share prices in the short run, even if they are damaging in the long run to the firm, its workforce, the general public, or the environment. But, as just discussed, the costs of speed races are not trivial. Furthermore, ordinary economic reasoning, and the model put forward by Budish et al. (2015), suggest that these costs are borne ultimately by end investors. In particular, market-making firms need to set their bid and offer prices so that the spread (the difference between the highest bid price and the lowest offer price) is sufficient to recoup their expenses and the losses that they incur when they are picked off, and the spread is a cost to the end investor.

The research I did was not designed either to determine whether HFT is economically beneficial or to produce policy recommendations (either of those goals would require a different methodology), but proposals such as Budish's frequent batch auctions or the Reuters module examined in chapter 6 do strike me as worth considering as ways of mitigating HFT's twin speed races: the race among making algorithms to be at the head of queues, and the race between making algorithms and taking algorithms trying to pick off their stale quotes.[22] In contrast, asymmetric speed bumps that simply slow taking algorithms mitigate the second of the two races, but less so the first.[23] I sympathize, too, with those, such as interviewee AF, who are uncomfortable with explicitly asymmetric interventions that, to quote him again, influence "who makes what money." The Budish proposal in particular has the advantage that it is not an overt intervention in favor of one category of market participant, even though if it were successful it should greatly reduce the revenue that can be earned by picking off.

From Lit Markets to Bilateral Relationships?

The costs of HFT's twin speed races are an incentive for firms or trading groups that specialize in market-making—even in HFT market-making—to shift emphasis from what participants call "lit" markets (i.e., markets in which there is an order book that is visible to participants) to private trading arrangements. Bilateral "systematic internalizer" relationships—in which HFT firms, rather than operating only in anonymous public markets, directly buy shares from, and sell shares to, clients whose identities are known—have been gaining momentum in European share trading (Cave 2019). Bilateral relationships of this kind also form a way in which HFT firms can profitably coexist with, rather than directly challenge, the incumbent big banks in foreign-exchange and Treasurys trading. Bilateral relationships with HFT firms are attractive to dealers as a way of unloading positions they have taken on in trading with clients (unloading that previously took place in the lit interdealer markets such as EBS, Reuters, eSpeed, and BrokerTec), while HFT firms are able to give dealers better prices because they are at much less risk than in more public markets of being picked off.

The absence of fear of being picked off is in part because dealers' systems are often slower than those of HFT firms, but it is also because excessive profit-making by either party in these bilateral arrangements is quite explicitly curbed. (Recall interviewee CA's remarkable statement, quoted in chapter 4, that his HFT firm's algorithms "will lock down [shut off automatically] if we've made too much [profit]. In other words, we'll stop trading with Goldman because we've made too much.") An economic sociologist like me is of course delighted to find trading arrangements in the midst of today's ultrafast electronic markets in which participants deliberately avoid making too much profit! This intellectual delight, however, may come at a cost. As the financial journalist Gillian Tett points out, "the 20th-century vision of democratic capitalism based around public markets" is eroding (Tett 2019). That erosion has many aspects, but among them—as yet little noticed—may be the gradual displacement of those markets by much more opaque networks of private bilateral relationships. As with "dark pools" in share trading, prices in those bilateral relationships are essentially derived from the more public markets, so the spread of such arrangements may undermine the very prices on which they depend.[24]

Unruly Materialities

This book has emphasized the "material politics" of finance. We shouldn't, however, over-simplify that politics by imagining that it concerns simply active, intentional human beings clashing over how passive matter should be arranged.[25] It would, for example, be a mistake to think of finance's large technical systems as either simply the outcome of human intentions or as fully under human control. Such systems can manifest behavior that is neither anticipated nor welcomed by the human beings who design and construct them. As a consequence, even interventions in the design of these systems that seem desirable (the frequent auctions proposed by Budish and his colleagues, for instance) should be approached with caution. Any intervention in a large, complex system can have unexpected effects, and it is therefore better to make such interventions in the form, at least at first, of limited, reversible experiments.

By far the best-known form of the unruly materiality of trading's large technical systems is "flash crashes": sudden, large, quickly reversed price movements. When one of these takes place, the finger of suspicion is often pointed, at least initially, at HFT (or, perhaps, at algorithmic trading more generally). The most dramatic such crash took place at 2:40 p.m. on May 6, 2010, with an abrupt drop of 6 percent in US share prices. A drop of that size in a few minutes is unusual indeed, but it had largely reversed by 3:00 p.m. It was accompanied, however, by gigantic fluctuations in the apparent prices of some individual shares. Shares in the global consultancy Accenture, for example, had been trading at around $40.50, but dropped to a single cent. Apple, in contrast, had been trading at around $250, and suddenly jumped to $100,000 (CFTC/SEC 2010: 83 and 86).

Identifying a single cause of an event like the 2010 flash crash may well be impossible (multiple factors may need to be present simultaneously for such an event to occur), and—despite a thorough official investigation (CFTC/

SEC 2010)—there is still no clear-cut, agreed-upon explanation. The trigger seems to have been the operations of a simple execution algorithm (not an HFT algorithm), which sold S&P 500 share-index futures, fast and on a large scale, in the Chicago Mercantile Exchange's datacenter, at that point still housed in Cermak, the datacenter described in chapter 5. But the havoc that broke out in the East Coast share-trading datacenters is hard to explain simply as a result of this trigger. Interviews with those trading on May 6 both by the official CFTC and SEC investigators and by Aldrich, Grundfest, and Laughlin (2017) suggest that the streams of data flowing into share-trading firms' systems that afternoon often failed automated data-integrity checks, leading those systems either to shut themselves down or to be shut down by their human supervisors. Seemingly normally priced orders thus emptied out from order books, with the result that incoming market orders—orders simply to buy or to sell at the best available price—were sometimes executed at bizarrely extreme prices such as one cent or $99,999.99.

Failed data-integrity checks plausibly exacerbated the effects of the big, fast, algorithmic selling that seems to have been the trigger. Aldrich and his colleagues report that one share-trading venue suffered delays in its reporting, to the systems that construct the official consolidated tape, of transactions in the SPY (the exchange-traded fund that is, as discussed in chapter 2, a stock economically nearly equivalent to the S&P 500 futures contract with which the flash crash began). HFT firms do not rely on the relatively slow official datafeed for their trading, but they do use it as a data-integrity check on the faster direct feeds that they purchase from exchanges. In a context in which prices were already falling fast, the intermingling of up-to-date and out-of-date SPY prices on the consolidated tape gave rise to apparent sharp price oscillations in the SPY, oscillations that were not present in the fast private datafeeds. It was this discrepancy, Aldrich et al. (2017) suggest, that led to the failed data-integrity checks. The SPY is a vital guide to the trading of other shares—especially, my interviewees report, for firms that cannot, or choose not to, pay the high cost of the fastest futures data direct from Chicago—and failed data-integrity checks on SPY transactions might thus have led to the widespread shutting down of automated share-trading systems and to the disorderly trading that took place in their absence. If that is correct, it is a fascinating example of individually prudent, rule-bound behavior (checking data integrity *is* prudent) generating potentially damaging, unruly, collective turmoil.

At the time of writing, there has been no repetition—even during the frantic pandemic-related trading in March 2020—of disruption to US share trading quite as extreme as in the 2010 flash crash. Osipovich (2020) attributes the greater robustness of stock-market infrastructure to the much enhanced attention to it that followed the flash crash, in particular the SEC's 2014 Reg SCI (Regulation Systems Compliance and Integrity).[26] At 9:33 a.m. on October 15, 2014, a different market—the market in US Treasurys—suffered an event broadly analogous to, although not as severe as, the flash crash: a brief upward price spike (very large by the standards of the Treasurys market), one that again quickly reversed, in this case within 12 minutes. Order books in the Treasurys interdealer market did not empty to quite the extent their equivalents in shares had done in 2010, but the unprecedented spike shook regulators. No clear trigger such as a specific large trade has been identified, but there is interesting tentative evidence of mutually reinforcing algorithmic "taking" trades, most likely informed by models that identify price trends and thus involve buying as prices rise and selling as they fall.[27] There is some evidence consistent with this mechanism—algorithms "mimicking their rivals" (Borch 2016: 371; see also Borch 2020) and influencing each other's trading—in the 2010 flash crash as well; see CFTC/SEC (2010: 48 and 56).

As in 2010, a thorough official investigation of the 2014 price spike in Treasurys was not conclusive, with the investigators admitting that "[t]he dynamics that drove continued trading at such volume during that short period of time remain an open question" (Department of the Treasury et al. 2015: 33). The Treasurys market was also badly disrupted in March 2020, but the crucial source of stress was not in automated trading per se. Rather, capital-constrained dealers could not absorb the large sales of Treasurys demanded by the unwinding of trading positions and/or sought by clients desperate to raise cash. The Federal Reserve Bank of New York had to intervene to make this possible, reducing dealers' holdings of Treasurys by purchasing huge quantities directly from them (Schrimpf, Shin, and Sushko 2020: 5), especially on Friday, March 13, at the end of a week of particular stress.

The 2010 and 2014 "flash" events, although quick, took place on a timescale perceptible to human beings, and involved substantial price movements. There is also evidence of much larger numbers of faster, smaller—although still quite abrupt—price fluctuations. Positing "a new machine ecology beyond human response time," the physicist Neil Johnson and colleagues suggest that these events might be caused by interactions within "crowds" of algorithms (Johnson et al. 2013: 1). One of my interviewees suggested one plausible mechanism, focusing on interactions among what are called volume-participation algorithms. These are execution algorithms designed to buy or sell a block of shares (or other financial instruments) by breaking up the block into smaller slices proportional in size to the fluctuating overall volume of trading in the stock in question.

> [T]hat's fine until you've got [for example] four [such algorithms] participat[ing] with . . . buy orders, so every time one of them prints [executes a trade], it causes all the other guys [i.e. the other algorithms] to print, which causes the first one to print, and the stock will just go "zhwoom" until they're all done [have bought the intended total of shares] and then it'll go "pffft" again, right? (Interviewee AD)

In order to exploit interaction of this kind, it is not actually necessary "to wait for that to happen," says AD. "We can go out into the market and we can pretend to be a load of these [volume-participation] algorithms, trading with each other, and then everyone else will see this behavior and they'll all jump in, right?" (A strategy of that kind would be described as a momentum-ignition strategy.) Research on patterns of interaction of this generic kind among trading algorithms is, however, still in its infancy. The most promising approach, being pursued by Christian Borch and colleagues at the Copenhagen Business School, is to incorporate into software agents the results of fieldwork among traders, and then study the behavior of such agents in a simulated financial market (see Borch 2020: 251–253).

There are, though, two definite causes of occasional abrupt movements in the price of particular shares or other financial instruments. One, apparently the more common, is simply human error (sometimes called "fat finger" error) in entering into execution algorithms the necessary parameters of price and, especially, total size of order. Rarer, but more relevant to this book, is the second cause: serious technical malfunctions of an HFT or other automated trading system. In chapter 3, we saw how a problem of this kind—the result of a mistake in a single character in a program—caused a financial loss to Automated Trading Desk that could have been catastrophic had the human trader involved not noticed it quickly and switched off the automated system involved. (As noted in chapter 3, the speed race was an important background factor, because it had led ATD to remove an automated risk control that previously would have stopped the errant algorithm's trading well before it came to the attention of its human supervisor.) Interviewee BK told me about a similar episode, in which an HFT firm that was a client of his "had a software problem, and their software went a bit nuts, and traded on all of the [foreign-exchange] platforms at the same time and maxed their credit limit on every single platform." What was most striking about this episode is that it did not simply cause large losses to the HFT firm, but also losses to its prime broker, a major bank, on a scale that—if the episode that BK reported corresponds to a similar one covered in the specialized press—caused the bank to cease being a foreign-exchange prime broker.[28]

The most serious of all the losses of this kind was incurred in 45 ghastly minutes on the morning of August 1, 2012, by Knight Capital (not an HFT firm per se, although it did have a substantial electronic market-making business). An upgrade to its trading software, occasioned by the launch by the New York Stock Exchange of a new system for the execution of orders from members of the general public, was, by mistake, not fully completed, and old software was not replaced on one of Knight's eight order-routing, share-trading computer servers. Unfortunately, Knight's new software reused an electronic "flag" that previously had launched the old system, so when the new software went live that old system, still physically present on that one server, inadvertently switched on, but with the function that kept track of its trading position deactivated. It took Knight's staff three-quarters of an hour to diagnose the problem and switch off the errant system, in which time that system had built up a $6.65 billion trading position, causing Knight a catastrophic loss of $460 million.[29] The firm was saved from bankruptcy only by an emergency takeover by the HFT firm Getco.

Jitter

Not all material unruliness, though, is necessarily a bad thing. One of the most mundane forms of unruliness in computer systems—such as the exchange systems that process incoming orders from trading firms and execute those orders—is "jitter": random or quasi-random fluctuation in the time taken to perform the same or similar operations.[30] The paradox of jitter is that, although it is widely regarded as a technical deficiency, jitter in an exchange's system may be beneficial to competition. "Jitter is an equalizer," as Stéphane Tyč of communications supplier McKay Brothers puts it (Tyč 2016). A speed advantage that's small relative to the jitter in an exchange's system is limited in its effects. If there's enough jitter, the second-fastest firm—and perhaps the sixth-fastest, or even the tenth-fastest—should "get the trade" often enough to stay in business and maybe generate sufficient revenue to make the investments needed to catch up on speed.

The software developers and engineers who design exchanges have made considerable efforts, often successfully, to reduce jitter. The most dramatic example is the Chicago Mercantile Exchange (CME). When I first started interviewing high-frequency traders on the CME, in 2012–13, they weren't complimentary about its systems. Suppose, one of them said in March 2012, that another firm's round-trip time (the time difference between its receipt of market data and the dispatch, in response to that data, of a new order or a cancellation of an existing order) was a millisecond, and his firm's was 0.9 milliseconds. If "the difference randomly [in processing time] that could occur on the CME side is 10 milliseconds . . ." said interviewee AJ, "what does it matter if I get down to 0.9?" Since then, however, the CME's systems have been redesigned completely. As touched on in chapter 5, they now incorporate FPGAs (field programmable gate arrays, described in that chapter). FPGAs are not just fast, but also highly deterministic, meaning they manifest only small amounts of jitter. Since the CME's redesign, the complaints about jitter that I heard in 2012–13 seem to have ceased. The case of the CME, furthermore, is exceptional only in the extent to which jitter has been reduced; it seems to have declined considerably throughout the markets in which HFT firms are active.

The trouble with a speed race is not just that it's costly, but that (as exchange systems become ever more deterministic) it can have a consistent winner or winners. A single firm, or a small number of them that are nearly always the fastest to respond to simple signals of the kind listed in tables 3.2 and 4.4, can consistently prevail. This process may be a factor in the consolidation of the HFT business that has taken place during the years in which I have been researching it. The list of HFT firms that have disappeared through merger includes Getco, Chopper, Infinium, Teza, RGM Advisors, and Sun Trading, as well as a number of less well known names. True, new entrants have emerged, but as far as I can tell only two of them, Headlands Technologies and XTX Markets, approach the scale of the firms that have disappeared. Consolidation in HFT in US equities is particularly striking. In 2019, the *Financial Times* reported that just two firms, Virtu and Citadel, "account for around 40 per cent of daily US trading flow" (Stafford 2019b). The newspaper didn't cite its sources, so the figure could be an exaggeration, but it would certainly be noteworthy if only two firms are now responsible for two-fifths, not just of HFT in US shares, but of *all* US share trading. If speed races in deterministic systems are contributing to outcomes such as this, that is another reason for considering fundamental alterations to the current material arrangements of trading.

Other Material Political Economies

High-frequency trading has, of course, some highly specific aspects. Its materiality, I've suggested, is Einsteinian, the materiality of a world in which the speed of light is a binding constraint and time is measured in billionths of a second. It is a world in which very specific spatial locations are there-fore crucial, and technological systems are designed and tuned to wring out every last nanosecond of avoidable delay. I can't think of any other economic domain that has quite these specific characteristics, at least in fully formed fashion.

I've been taking a material political economy approach, with a focus on how the material world is ordered, on the possibility of alternative orderings, on the often political nature of the issue of which of these orderings becomes real, and on the economic consequences of that issue. Those include appar-ently mundane economic consequences such as the capacity of intermediar-ies to exact fees and other individually small (but in aggregate large) amounts of money from other market participants. Is a material political economy approach applicable only to HFT, with its Einsteinian materiality, or might it be applicable to other spheres of economic life? I think it is more gener-ally applicable, and want to end this book by briefly discussing one sphere in which that is most definitely the case, and another in which I think the approach may be applicable (but in which further research is needed to know exactly how).

The sphere to which material political economy unequivocally applies is decentralized cryptocurrencies such as bitcoin and ethereum. (The issues are different for cryptocurrencies such as Facebook's proposed Libra, which, if it is launched, will be run, at least initially, in a centralized fashion; I don't propose to discuss those currencies here.) The issue that most clearly makes material political economy applicable is how to motivate at least a subset of the users of a cryptocurrency to check the validity of each transaction (including checking the validity of each other's checking) and take part in adding it irreversibly to the blockchain, the record of every transaction that has taken place. The solution adopted for bitcoin by Satoshi Nakamoto, its pseudonymous inventor, is known as proof-of-work. Roughly every ten minutes, all day, every day, bitcoin miners, as they are called (and I like the moniker's materiality) compete to be the first to find a hash of a block of transactions that is smaller than a certain target binary number (a hash is a cryptographic transformation by a predetermined algorithm). The reward for the winner is a set amount of newly created bitcoin. Since May 2020, the prize has been 6.25 bitcoins, at the time of writing worth around $60,000.[31]

Satoshi's original vision appears to have been that any bitcoin user could become a miner, simply by installing the requisite software on a laptop or other ordinary computer system. The analogy here with the milling of grain is actually close: the vision was, essentially, of hand-milling. Bitcoin's water and windmills turned out to be ASICs, application-specific integrated circuits, which are silicon chips designed for a specific purpose such as bitcoin mining. A mining ASIC is vastly more efficient for that purpose than an ordinary computer. There is no abbot of bitcoin who, like the abbot of St Albans, monopolizes bitcoin ASICs—although there is one dominant designer of them, the Chinese company Bitmain, which has some 90 percent of the market (Liu and McMorrow 2019), and the miners who use Bitmain's ASICs do tend to be organized in very large pools—but there has been deep unhappiness in the world of cryptocurrencies about the shift to ASICs. Indeed, bitcoin's main rival, ethereum, was designed to be, in the terminology of the field, ASIC resistant. The hashing algorithm for ethereum was designed to make it hard to develop ASICs that are much more efficient than ordinary computers in ethereum's equivalent of bitcoin mining.

Trying to make a cryptocurrency ASIC resistant is quintessential material political economy, reminiscent (as I've said) of the defense of hand-milling, even if in the case of ethereum the effort was less than fully successful. Efficient ethereum ASICs have been developed, although they haven't yet swept the board as fully as their bitcoin equivalents have. Another aspect of the material politics of cryptocurrencies is environmental. A back-of-the-envelope calculation of bitcoin mining's global electricity consumption at the beginning of June 2020 is 4.5 gigawatts, the equivalent of that of an entire small country.[32] (Ireland, for example, consumes around 3.1 gigawatts, as de Vries [2018: 804] points out.) In early June 2020, bitcoin transactions were averaging around 300,000 a day, which implies that each individual bitcoin transaction was consuming, at that point, around 360 kilowatt-hours, equivalent to leaving a 2-kilowatt domestic electric heater running full blast for just over a week.[33] Much, but not all, of that electricity comes from renewable sources. It is more than likely, for example, that the bitcoin mines in the high desert of Inner Mongolia (a major site of the activity) are powered, at least in part, by the cheap, plentiful coal-generated power available there.

Even bitcoin, though, remains esoteric. What is far from esoteric is the mainstream digital economy: Google, Facebook, Amazon, their huge Chinese equivalents, and so on. Facebook, for example, reports that by June 2020 over three billion people—nearly 40 percent of Earth's population—were using its systems (including WhatsApp, Messenger, and Instagram).[34] Precisely because of the numbers of users and quantities of data involved in the digital economy, the major participants in that economy have to deploy material megasystems. Google, for example, operates 21 huge datacenters globally, and Facebook 15.[35] Interviewee DH suggested to me that Google's crucial competence is the automated management of its giant assemblage of machines, so that servers that have failed physically can be identified and circumvented, while keeping the necessary computations and—especially—memory accesses fast enough that users do not encounter annoying delays. Something similar must also be true of Facebook. The automated management of megasystems of this kind is a different material task than HFT—a human user can readily tolerate a delay of around a second, while a millionth of that can be fatal in HFT—but no less material, and, because of the sheer scale of these systems, no less demanding.

There is, furthermore, an ever-present mundane economy of much of today's digital world, that of online advertising. Advertising is, of course, the dominant source of revenue for Google and Facebook. Unlike them, Amazon directly sells products and services on a mass scale, but for it too advertising is important. More broadly, vital activities in the wider society—most obviously, serious journalism—have come to depend strongly on revenue from online advertising. The giants of the digital economy, above all Google, exercise considerable sway over the parts of the advertising ecosystem that most strongly affect them, but that is not the case for smaller, less central companies, including, for instance, newspapers such as the *Guardian* and the *New York Times*. Just as in finance, online advertising often involves multiple layers of intermediaries, and advertising's intermediaries seem able to capture an even greater proportion of the flow of money than their equivalents in finance do. In 2016, for example, the *Guardian* experimented by buying advertising space on its own website, and discovered that in the worst cases as little as 30 percent of what it had paid found its way to the newspaper as revenue (Pidgeon 2016). The *Guardian*'s subsequent experience has been better (Davies 2018), but a recent study of UK online advertising suggests that when publishers that are not among the digital economy's giants sell advertising space on the open market, they typically receive only around 60 percent of what advertisers spend. The remaining 40 percent is swallowed up in fees and other payments to intermediaries (Adshead, Forsyth, Wood, and Wilkinson 2019: 13).

It is likely that the changing materiality of online advertising is connected to its intermediary-rich aspect. Most firms always needed an advertising agency to produce a TV ad (or a print ad of any sophistication), but the placing of that ad was a relatively simple, unhurried commercial transaction. In its early days, online advertising was also often relatively straightforward. Firms used to negotiate in advance the right to show an ad on a particular web page. Now, in what's called real-time bidding, a separate, individualized, automated auction can be triggered by each individual act of search or other opportunity to show an ad to a particular user, and what is known about the user (her/his location, gender, age group, hobbies, search history, etc.) is critical to the value of the opportunity. This information is often gathered—by cookies, pixels, and other material mechanisms—as the user's browser and computer, mobile phone, or other device interact with websites and apps.[36] Bids in each of these millions of auctions typically must be submitted in about 120 milliseconds, which is well beyond the capacity of a human bidder.

It is not surprising, therefore, that advertisers either seek intermediaries' expensive help to navigate the world of online advertising, or simply allow the field's giants, Google and Facebook, to implement advertising campaigns for them. (In online advertising, supply and demand are often not at arm's length. Facebook's system, for example, normally makes the decisions, on behalf of advertisers, whether to bid for an advertising opportunity on its platform, and if so how much to bid, and that is often the case for Google's system as well.) In the wake of the European Union's General Data Protection Regulation and the scandal surrounding the consultancy firm Cambridge Analytica (in which it became clear that access had been gained to information on tens of millions of Facebook users without their knowledge), user data is flowing between firms in this domain much less freely than in the early days of real-time bidding. However, while this can improve privacy, it may also further enhance the already considerable market power of the biggest companies with their huge data silos (CMA 2019).

It's striking how little the complex, fast-moving, material domain of online advertising—which is, to repeat, the foundation of much of the everyday digital economy—seems to be understood except by insiders. The research that is required to improve our understanding of it will have to open the black box, to invoke an old but still resonant slogan of the social studies of science and technology: it will need to reveal internal mechanisms that are normally hidden from view. This book has tried to do this for high-frequency trading and in the process, I hope, has shown that the idea of material political economy is a useful way of bringing to light processes that—though frequently obscure—are often deeply conflictual and have played and are playing a crucial role in shaping today's financial markets. Even a glimpse into the world of cryptocurrencies makes clear that it too is a domain of sometimes ferocious material politics. Given how pervasive online advertising is, its inner workings remain remarkably opaque. It's surely time for the searchlight of material political economy to be shone on that world too.

A Note on the Literature on HFT

By far the best-known book on HFT is Michael Lewis's 2014 bestseller *Flash Boys*, which combines first-rate reporting (such as his chapter on the laying of the new, direct Chicago–New Jersey fiber-optic cable, which I draw on in chapter 5) with hostility to HFT and its alleged "predatory strategies" (Lewis 2014: 172).[1] Other popular books dealing with HFT include Patterson (2012) and Steiner (2012). The former is particularly lively, and it contains a discussion of Island that conveys well the milieu from which it emerged. Vaughan (2020) provides a vivid account of spoofing of the kind discussed here in chapter 6, and much detail on the background to the most famous prosecution, that of the London-based futures trader Navinder Singh Sarao. There are also a number of "how to" guides to HFT, none of them genuinely detailed. Perhaps the best is Durbin (2010).

Starting in around 2010, financial economists began to produce what has become a large body of journal articles and working papers on HFT. A major early goal of this literature was to identify the effects on markets of the increased prevalence, especially in the US, of HFT and other forms of algorithmic trading. See, for example, the 2012 review (primarily based on this early literature) by the UK's Foresight Programme, which painted a broadly positive picture of what it referred to as computer-based trading as having reduced transaction costs and improved efficiency and liquidity—albeit with what the review cautioned was perhaps "greater potential for periodic illiquidity"—and with "no direct evidence" that HFT increased market volatility (UK Government Office for Science 2012: 11–12). Some of the underlying studies (such as the widely cited Brogaard 2010) indeed suggested that the presence of HFT can actually reduce volatility.[2]

More recent research on algorithmic trading in financial economics both differentiates HFT more clearly from other forms of algorithmic trading and focuses more strongly on the central divide within HFT between market-making and liquidity-taking strategies. A useful 2016 review by Albert Menkveld of the evolving literature (to which readers can turn if they wish to explore this literature in more detail) finds that "HFT market-making reduces transaction cost[s]," but also suggests that "HFTs are able to predict" and profit from the flow of what are often called the child orders that are generated by the execution algorithms that break up large orders from institutional investors into small parts. To the extent that this is so, this profit making will increase these investors' transaction costs (Menkveld 2016: 19 and 11–12).

Three particular contributions to the financial-economics literature on HFT especially influenced my research. One, referred to several times in the previous chapters, is the work by Eric Budish and colleagues (Budish et al. 2015 and 2019; Aquilina et al. 2020) on the interaction between HFT market-making and HFT liquidity-taking, the resultant speed races within HFT, the consequent capacity of exchanges to exact rent by charging high fees for fast data and the material means by which they are transmitted, and the overall costs—ultimately borne by end investors—of these speed races. The second was a report commissioned by the UK Foresight Programme from one of the earliest researchers on HFT, Jonathan Brogaard. In it, he drew on the wider literature of financial economics—and also, I suspect, on conversations with high-frequency traders—to discuss possible types of information used in HFT and likely sources of the activity's profitability (Brogaard 2011). That report helped me develop a series of prompts, particularly useful in my early interviews, that enabled me to get interviewees talking about the different classes of "signals" employed by HFT algorithms. The third was another article by Menkveld (2013), which drew on proprietary data to examine the trading of a large HFT market-making firm. His study suggested that the firm's attractively-priced bids and offers contributed to the new "Island-style" European electronic share-trading venue Chi-X's prospering as a challenger to long-established incumbent stock exchanges (see chapter 3). Menkveld's analysis helped me make sense of what my US interviewees were telling me about similar processes there, processes that I came to think of as forming a "hinge," in Andrew Abbott's sense (see chapter 1) between the fields, or ecologies, of trading and of exchanges.

Although the research for this book thus drew upon financial economics, it is of course a contribution not to that specialism but to the looser, more sociological domain referred to as the social studies of finance. Two strands of literature in that domain are particularly pertinent. The first is research by Fabian Muniesa, Susan Scott, Yuval Millo, Juan Pablo Pardo-Guerra, Devin Kennedy, and others on the shift from manual to electronic trading, including work on the contexts of this shift, such as by Walter Mattli.[3]

For instance, Muniesa provides (especially in Muniesa 2003) an especially in-depth study of how that shift played out on the Paris Bourse. His study was pioneering in its focus on the different ways in which trading can be automated, including differences in how the algorithms implemented in exchanges' matching engines prioritize and execute bids and offers, and thus bring together supply and demand, particularly in the generation of the trading day's most important prices, the closing prices of the stocks being traded, which are important to derivatives contracts, index-tracking funds, etc. To take another example, Pardo Guerra (2019) covers in depth the automation of share trading in the UK, which I have largely set aside in this book, and he also discusses crucial episodes in the US, including in particular one that I too examine in chapter 3: the controversy in the 1970s over the proposal to organize share trading around a single, nationwide electronic order book.[4]

The social studies of finance has produced a number of fine, ethnographically informed studies of the practices of trading, such as Knorr Cetina and Bruegger (2002a & b), Zaloom (2006), Preda (2013 and 2017), and Beunza (2019). Most work of this kind has focused either on face-to-face trading or on electronic trading conducted by human beings. However, a second strand of research in the social studies of finance that is immediately relevant to this book is a growing body of work that focuses directly on HFT. Most extensive is the research of Christian Borch and his group at the Copenhagen Business School, which included Ann-Christina Lange (who did particularly fine fieldwork on the topic) and now includes Bo Hee Min, Kristian Bondo Hansen, Daniel Souleles, Nicholas Skar-Gislinge, Pankaj Kumar, and Zachary David. They have, for example, examined similarities and differences between high-frequency traders and their pit-trading predecessors in the forms of their bodily engagement with markets and in how they manage their emotions (Borch, Hansen, and Lange 2015; Borch and Lange 2017). As in my fieldwork, they too find that men predominate in roles closest to trading—"We have not so far encountered a single female high-frequency trader" (Borch et al. 2015: 1094)—and, as noted in chapter 1, they also discovered that some firms are very strictly compartmentalized. For instance, in the main firm studied by Lange, she found most traders "sitting isolated at their desks, and, in some cases, even separated by walls. Most of the [high-frequency] traders that I visited had installed filters on their screens so that their codes could only be viewed when facing the screen directly" (Lange 2016: 237).[5] Souleles (2019) develops insights such as this into a fascinating, more general account of "the distribution of ignorance" in finance. As touched on in chapter 7, though, the most novel of all the strands of this group's work is their commitment to draw on their fieldwork to develop agent-based simulations of financial markets that will throw light on how trading algorithms interact (a goal prefigured in Borch 2020).[6]

Another researcher who has done extensive fieldwork among high-frequency traders is Robert Seyfert. In Seyfert (2016), he shows how anomalous sequences in market data (such as brief periods of unusually high volumes of rapidly canceled bids and offers) can be interpreted differently by different groups of actors who inhabit what he calls different epistemic regimes. The critics of HFT can view such episodes as manipulative "quote stuffing," perhaps designed to slow an exchange's system or confuse competing trading firms (for quote stuffing, see, e.g., Mattli 2019: 139–140), while traders themselves often view them as most likely caused by a technical malfunction.[7] Marc Lenglet and Nathan Coombs have investigated the often problematic fit between the rules and requirements of government regulatory bodies and the material practices of algorithmic trading, Lenglet drawing on ethnographic insights gained working for a large broker (and on subsequent interviews), and Coombs on an interview-based study of the implementation of Germany's 2013 *Hochfrequenzhandelsgesetz*, its law governing HFT (Lenglet 2011; Lenglet and Mol 2016; Coombs 2016). Most materialist of all these scholars, though—and in that sense closest to the approach taken in this book—is Alexandre Laumonier, with his remarkable investigations of the precise paths, especially in Europe, of HFT's microwave links; see Laumonier (2019) and his blog https://sniperinmahwah .wordpress.com/, which is widely followed by high-frequency traders. His work is drawn on in particular in chapter 5 above.

NOTES

Chapter 1: Introduction

1. See Pinder (1993).

2. Behind the storefront was a TV studio, set up by Island, which was used by Yahoo Finance for web broadcasts (interviewee BW). The set of panels looks like concrete but is "actually painted foam. You could pick it up with one hand. It is glued onto the facade" (email to author from Josh Levine, September 1, 2012).

3. Another, earlier, robotic device to strike a terminal's keys was designed by Timber Hill (primarily an options-trading firm) to automatically post bids and offers on Nasdaq, again to circumvent a ban on directly connecting a computer to Nasdaq's system; see Steiner (2012: 11–17). For the specific rationale of Nasdaq's rule, see chapter 3, note 11.

4. This definition of HFT reflects useful discussions of the point with interviewee BU.

5. Another important category of algorithm is that deployed by statistical arbitrageurs, who seek to profit from patterns of price movements that play out on longer timescales (minutes, hours, days, or even longer) than the near-term movements that are the focus in HFT. Statistical arbitrage first became large-scale in the 1980s, but initially the purchases and sales involved were not fully automated, while nowadays they usually are. A recent book by Greg Zuckerman (2019) vividly portrays one of the most celebrated statistical-arbitrage firms, Renaissance Technologies.

6. As Weisberger (2016) explains, retail brokers' standard procedure is to send "marketable" orders (those that can be executed immediately) to a wholesaler, while routing to exchanges only the minority of orders that are not marketable. SEC regulations forbid wholesalers from executing orders at prices worse than the best bid or offer on any of the exchanges, and wholesalers often offer so-called price improvement: prices better than those available on exchanges. HFT firms are prepared to pay to trade directly in this way against retail orders because it does not carry the same level of risk as trading on an exchange. In the terminology used in chapter 6, retail order flow seldom "runs over" or "picks off" an HFT algorithm. Trading with retail is therefore reliably, if modestly, profitable.

7. Virtu Financial (2019: 23); Stafford and Bullock (2017); Stafford (2019b).

8. At the end of December 2013, for example, Virtu's headcount was 151 (Virtu Financial 2014: 5).

9. Trading teams in compartmentalized firms often welcome the separation, not wanting others, even within the same firm, to profit from "their" ideas. Other reasons for strict compart-mentalization include avoiding concentrations of risk caused by teams imitating each other's trading, and persuading exchanges and regulators to allow one team's algorithms to trade with another's. This can easily happen accidentally, and such self-trading is normally frowned upon, because it can, for example, be used to create a manipulative "false price."

10. By no means all electronic trading venues are registered exchanges; Island, for example, was never an exchange. Aside from parts of this book in which the distinction is important, I will often for brevity simply refer to all exchange-like trading venues as "exchanges."

11. The burst was on the Securities Information Processor datafeeds (the official "consolidated tape"), which cover not just shares but options, and the nature of the latter creates very large message volumes. The peak rate measured by Exegy for the aggregate of the direct feeds from US stock exchanges and futures exchanges was 41.7 million messages per second, at 3:00 p.m. on May 30, 2019. See https://www.marketdatapeaks.net/rates/usa/, accessed May 19, 2020.

12. The most important such respect is simply the postulate that the speed of light in a vacuum is a fixed constant, and that no signal can travel faster than that. The need to apply special relativity is in other respects currently restricted by the fact that the datacenters in which HFT is conducted are all in fixed locations on what is a single and (for most relevant practical purposes) rigid body, planet Earth (see Einstein 1920, especially chapter 2; q.v. Angel 2011). If, however, as seems quite conceivable, a swarm of low-earth-orbit satellites starts being used for long-distance data transmission for HFT (MacKenzie 2019c), their clocks will need to be adjusted to take account of the special-relativity effect of the satellites' velocities. If HFT continues to speed up in the way that it has, point out Laughlin, Aguirre, and Grundfest (2014: 284), an effect from general relativity—that "clocks run at different rates depending on their location in a gravitational field"—may also eventually need to be taken into account even in terrestrial HFT.

13. A technical presentation by the futures exchange Eurex in September 2018 reported—on slides kindly passed to me by another of my interviewees—Eurex as having measured responses as fast as 84 nanoseconds. At the time of writing, that is the fastest that has been recorded quasi-publicly. However, my interviewee's report of 42 nanoseconds (for trading firms' systems in the datacenter of the Chicago Mercantile Exchange; see chapter 2) is perfectly plausible, although the technical difficulty of measuring time intervals that short is considerable.

14. Direct transmission through the earth, rather than on its surface, would be somewhat quicker: Laughlin et al. (2014: 296) calculate it would save around three microseconds on the crucial Chicago–New Jersey links. Achieving such transmission, however, would likely be technologically hugely demanding and very expensive.

15. The classic discussion of the shrinkage of space and time in postmodernity is Harvey (1989). Zook and Grote (2017) draw on the literature on HFT to discuss what they nicely call the "microgeographies" of global finance. Chapter 5 below takes the notion of microgeography rather more literally than they do, via a discussion of "fiber tail," explained in that chapter.

16. HFT firms' algorithms form part of their larger systems, making it difficult to unambiguously identify which aspects of the latter constitute an HFT algorithm. This was a major practical headache for attempts in Europe to regulate HFT algorithms. See Coombs (2016).

17. Perhaps the single best account of actor-network theory is Latour (2005), and the scholar who has done most to extend the perspective to the study of economic life is Michel Callon, most famously in his introductory chapter in Callon (1998).

18. For volume 1 of *Capital* viewed as what I would now call material political economy, see MacKenzie (1984). It is worth noting, however, that I see material political economy as what a sociologist would call a meso-level approach, while Marxism has classically been macro-level in its emphasis on overall modes of production such as feudalism and capitalism. For the wider literature on materiality, see Dourish (2017: especially chapter 2). Dourish's book is itself a useful contribution to that literature.

19. For collections of readings that illustrate this empirically, see MacKenzie and Wajcman (1985 and 1999).

20. See MacKenzie (2019d).

21. See, e.g., Bourdieu (1984, 1996, and 1997), Fligstein (2001), Fligstein and McAdam (2012), Kluttz and Fligstein (2016), and Abbott (2005 and n.d.). Kluttz and Fligstein define a "field" as a structured, meso-level domain in which participants orient themselves to each other. (A meso-level domain is one that does not encompass the entirety of a society, but is more than simply a

small-group interaction.) There is "something at stake" (often something specific to the domain), differential access to resources, "rules of the game," and structurally more favorable (and less favorable) positions. There is cooperation, competition, and sometimes conflict, the last of these at least potentially involving challenges to the rules of the game (Kluttz and Fligstein 2016: 185). Abbott's "ecologies," likewise, are field-like "set[s] of social relations . . . best understood in terms of interactions between multiple elements that . . . constrain or contest each other," just as the actors in a field do (Abbott 2005: 248). While, unlike the case of, e.g., Fligstein's fields, Abbott's definition of ecology is not explicitly meso-level, nearly all his actual examples are, and while Abbott (n.d.) distances his position from Bourdieu's version of field theory, it is less clear that there are any profound differences between Abbott's "linked ecologies" and Fligstein and McAdam's "fields . . . embedded in systems of fields" (Kluttz and Fligstein 2016: 186). MacKenzie (2018b) analyzes the development of HFT, especially in US shares, from a somewhat more explicitly field/ecology viewpoint than this book does.

22. For previous applications of Abbott's "linked ecologies" to financial regulation, see Seabrooke and Tsingou (2009) and du Gay, Millo, and Tuck (2012: 1090–93).

23. What I mean by the "mundane" political economy of finance is different from the "everyday international political economy" advocated by Hobson and Seabrooke, in their (entirely justified) attention to the actions of the "bottom ninety per cent" (2007: 12). The traders, dealers, and so on that I focus on are elite actors; my argument, in contrast to Hobson's and Seabrooke's, is that the mundane actions of these elite actors, and the economic consequences of those actions, have too often been neglected. For useful discussion of the mundane aspects of economic life, see Neyland, Ehrenstein, and Milyaeva (2018) and the other papers in the special issue of the *Journal of Cultural Economy* (11[5], October 2018). It is worth noting that the original usage of "mundane" was to identify a phenomenon as an aspect of the material world, not the spiritual realm. Had that meaning survived in today's everyday usage, which it has not, the entire perspective I'm taking could simply be called "mundane political economy," even if that might not help boost this book's sales.

24. What participants mean by "market structure" is similar to what financial economists (following Garman 1976) call "market microstructure"—i.e., "the process by which investors' latent demands are ultimately translated into prices and volumes" (Madhavan 2000: 205)—a field of study that is touched on briefly at the start of chapter 3. The literature in economics on financial-market microstructure is valuable, but is largely "depoliticized": although contributors to it are certainly aware that there is often intense conflict over market structure, that conflict, and especially its political aspects, is only occasionally the focus of their analytical attention. Exceptions to this include the impressive historical research on the changing structure of French financial markets conducted by the economist Angelo Riva and colleagues (see, e.g., Hautcoeur and Riva 2012).

25. Another exception is that most exchanges allow participants to submit "hidden" orders (which are not displayed in the order book) or "iceberg" orders (only a part of which is displayed). It is typical for exchanges' matching engines to place hidden orders behind visible orders in the queue for execution.

26. Crucially, HFT trades, interviewees report, are often statistically close to being independent from one another, bringing the law of large numbers into play. This means that even if the average profitability of the trades is tiny, the chance of, e.g., a losing day is negligible. Famously, Virtu experienced only one such day in the four years prior to its initial public offering (Virtu Financial 2014: 3; see Laughlin 2014).

27. I write "to a first approximation," because as well as trading on exchanges HFT firms are increasingly offering "execution services" to retail brokers (see above), institutional investors, banks, etc., and those services are often in competition with exchanges, diverting orders that might otherwise flow to those exchanges.

28. Phil Mirowski impressed on me 15 years ago the importance of what was then the recent process of "demutualization": the transformation of exchanges from member-owned entities to publicly listed corporations.

29. Philippon (2019: 210–213) updates his 2015 paper with new data, but the pattern that is revealed remains the same.

30. The unit cost of intermediation is the total cost of intermediation services divided by the total amount of those services. To calculate the total amount of intermediation, Philippon (2015) adds together the sums of money involved in four broad financial activities: the total amounts held in bank accounts and similar "safe" deposits; the money lent to firms and the value the market gives their shares; the money lent to households; and the total value of corporate mergers and acquisitions. He works out the total cost of intermediation by adding up the profits and staff salaries of the entire gamut of financial intermediaries: banks, investment-management companies, insurance companies (adjusting for their activities, such as health, buildings, and vehicle insurance, that are not financial intermediation), private equity firms, and so on. The lower line in figure 1.6 is Philippon's estimate of the unit cost corrected for the changing aggregate level of the difficulty of the task of intermediation. For example, investing wisely in start-ups involves more screening and monitoring—and is thus intrinsically more expensive—than buying the shares of established corporations with lengthy track records.

31. See, e.g., Tomaskovic-Devey and Lin (2011), who estimate the difference between actual finance-sector profits and employee remuneration in 1980–2008 and what would have been their totals if remuneration per employee, finance's share of the overall workforce, and its share of total profits in the US economy had either remained at their average levels for 1948–1980 or had followed the only slowly rising trend evident in those decades. It's obviously a far from conclusive way of proceeding, but the result (a total difference of $5.8–$6.6 trillion) is striking. For examination of the contribution of the finance sector to growing inequality in the UK see Bell and Van Reenen (2013); for the case of France, see Godechot (2012 and 2013).

32. As Kean Birch notes, in a stimulating analysis of rent from the viewpoint of science and technology studies, definitions of rent within economics tend to naturalize market processes and to conceptualize rent, in an implicitly normative way, as resulting from a distortion of those processes (Birch 2020: 18). That is arguably true even of Wolf's definition, but the latter is nevertheless helpful as a way of giving nonspecialists a sense of what the term means when used by economists.

33. BD learned this while setting up a new HFT firm: "Quite literally we interviewed hundreds of people to come in and guys would go up on the whiteboard and detail some of their thoughts on research and calculations that they thought were important, and sure enough they're pulling out some of the formulas we were using at [BD's previous HFT firm]. Pretty amazing."

34. In total, across all categories of interviewee (not just high-frequency traders), 35 people were interviewed twice, 6 interviewed three times, 3 interviewed four times, 1 interviewed five times, 2 interviewed six times, 1 interviewed seven times, and 2 interviewed nine times. Although most interviews were one-on-one, 34 were with two people, 12 with three people, 3 with four people, and 1 with five people.

35. As discussed above, algorithmic market-making inherits the legitimacy of a long-established human role, which may have facilitated my access to specialists in it, but I suspect that it is also the case that quite specific "secret sauce" plays a more salient role in liquidity-taking.

36. A difficult decision in categorizing interviewees was whether to include staff of automated options market-making firms as high-frequency traders. Some such firms—especially the Amsterdam-based firms—also conduct "classic" HFT, of the kind described in this book, in, e.g., shares, and even the options market-making firms that do not do this still have to place a huge priority on speed, and use much the same technologies as HFT firms do. Interviewees from the options firms, however, were often emphatic that they did not see options market-making as

HFT. (For them, "high-frequency trading" often seemed to mean "liquidity-taking" strategies of the kind described in chapter 6, against which they had to protect their algorithms.) I decided to respect this self-perception in table 1.1 by classifying options market-makers who do not practice "classic" HFT as among the "practitioners of other forms of algorithmic trading," a category that also includes, e.g., statistical arbitrageurs.

37. For example, Brogaard, Hendershott, and Riordan (2014: 2300–2302) show that HFT algorithms "take liquidity" on Nasdaq (execute against orders already in its order book) in response to order-book imbalances, by, for example, buying when more shares are being bid for (at the national best bid price) than offered for sale at the national best offer price. That imbalance is one aspect of the class of signal I call "order-book dynamics"; see chapter 3.

38. Melamed and Tamarkin (1996); Melamed (2009); Smith (1996); Weeden (2002); Cummings (2016).

Chapter 2: To the Towers

1. There is a useful cultural history of the divide between gambling and legitimate investing or trading in de Goede (2005). See also Preda (2009).

2. There is a video clip of Emanuel saying that at htps://www.youtube.com/watch?v=dBpAZ-ST5Ow, accessed April 6, 2019.

3. Falloon (1998: 247); Committee on Agriculture and Forestry, US Senate (1974: 27).

4. The Chicago sociologist Andrew Abbott uses the term "ligation" (in the sense of binding) to describe the simultaneous creation or reshaping of a profession—or, e.g., a regulatory body—and of a task over which it has jurisdiction (Abbott 2005: 248).

5. CME Eurodollar trader Ryan Carlson, who has documented the hand-signal language of futures trading pits, reports that arb emerged in the 1970s as pits began to trade financial futures, which often offered very short-lived arbitrage opportunities, for example to make an almost riskless profit by buying currency futures and selling the underlying currency. Such opportunities vanished too quickly to be exploitable by writing out an order on paper and having a runner take it to the pit. See https://tradingpithistory.com, from which the following summary of the main features of arb is taken.

6. As Carlson notes, price was "indicated at arms length away from the body and quantity is displayed close to the face. . . . Quantities of 1–9 are indicated at chin level whilst increments of 10s are indicated at the forehead" (https://tradingpithistory.com/hand-signals/basics/, accessed May 3, 2019).

7. In other words, the broker was indicating an urgent need to sell 10 futures contracts at a price the final digit of which was 5.

8. See Greising and Morse (1991). A decade later, there was still debate in the Chicago pits about how serious the violations had been. "[T]hey nail[ed] lots of people for doing Ginsey," one trader told me in November 2000. ("Ginsey"—I have not encountered the term outside the Chicago pits and my interviewees did not know its origins—involved a tacit understanding, sometimes proposed using a subtle hand movement, to circumvent the minimum unit of price by striking half of a deal at one price and the other half at the next permissible price.) This trader did not, however, deny that there was more serious malpractice: "They [the FBI agents] could have found lots of dirt, there's no question about it, but they did not know where to look."

9. See Barrett and Scott (2004) for an analysis of how issues of global time framed the shift to electronic trading of futures.

10. Melamed and Tamarkin (1996: 337–39); Melamed interview, 2012.

11. Melamed interview, 2012; Crawford (1994).

12. See the patent application for the Aurora system: Belden et al. (1990).

13. It seems as if the "fill" messages users received from the Globex system when one of their orders was executed did originally contain an identifier of the counterparty (Hicks 1998: 291), so the latter did not remain anonymous throughout. Interviewee BB tells me this practice ceased in around 2005, but I am not certain of that date; BD thinks it may have stopped before then.

14. For example, LIFFE's Automated Pit Trading system, launched in 1989, was—as its name indicated—an attempt to replicate a pit, albeit with a simpler visual interface than Aurora's, and no directly global ambitions. It was a closed network, says an interviewee (AR) who used it, "only available inside the M25 [the freeway encircling Greater London]." It usually operated as no more than a minor supplement to the pits, but did have occasional successes, for example being heavily used on the evening of Friday, October 5, 1990, when the UK Treasury suddenly announced, just as LIFFE's pits were closing, that the UK was joining the European Exchange Rate Mechanism (Kynaston 1997: 213). Its late-1990s replacement, LIFFE Connect, made no attempt to emulate LIFFE's trading pits, which (as noted below) closed in 1999–2000.

15. Melamed (2009); Melamed interview (2012).

16. The program was described in a brief history of the HFT firm Jump Trading, which was available on its website during the early phase of this research: http://www.jumptrading.com /about/history.aspx, accessed February 16, 2012.

17. http://www.jumptrading.com/about/history.aspx, accessed February 16, 2012.

18. See Millo, Muniesa, Panourgias, and Scott (2005).

19. Carlson's comments can be found at https://tradingpithistory.com/2016/09/mechanizing -the-mercs-eurodollar-pit/, accessed May 6, 2019.

20. See Kawaller et al. (1987: 1309) and Budish et al. (2015: 1570–71).

21. For the history of ETFs, see Ruggins (2017).

22. For the econometric evidence, see Laughlin, Aguirre, and Grundfest (2014), Budish et al. (2015), and Shkilko and Sokolov (2016).

23. Interviewees BQ and BV report a somewhat bidirectional relationship, with the SPY sometimes leading the ES. Aldrich and Lee (2018) put forward an interesting model of why there are occasions in which this is so, supported by econometric evidence in data from 2014; see note 27 below for further discussion.

24. The CME's system, interviewees reported, "box-carted" changes to the order book (aggregated them before sending out periodic updates), rather than disseminating them order by order as was the case with the Island system (discussed in chapter 3) and its descendants in share trading.

25. Random delay, even if not at all intended by the designers of an exchange's system, can affect market structure; see chapters 6 and 7. The CME's large pre-2014 "jitter" (random or quasi-random delay) was, in the terminology of chapter 6, "symmetric"—it did not selectively protect market-making algorithms—but it does seem to have given a systematic advantage to larger firms. They could afford to purchase multiple trading sessions and thus send orders or cancellations of orders to multiple "gateways" (see chapter 5) so as to discover which was processing messages most quickly. In this game of "gateway roulette" (interviewee CS's phrase), larger firms could thus purchase more "chips."

26. For econometric evidence consistent with what interviewees said about Treasurys, see Brandt, Kavajecz, and Underwood (2007). I know of no equivalent study in foreign exchange.

27. A third factor, focused on by Aldrich and Lee (2018), is the relative size of "ticks" (minimum increments of price) in the trading of futures and of shares and the consequence of tick size for arbitrage-like trading. ES ticks are 2.5 times larger than SPY ticks, which affects a crucial mechanism by which one market influences the other: a bid or an offer by a market-making algorithm in one market being executed against, and the algorithm then seeking to hedge the resultant risk (and perhaps make an arbitrage profit) by "taking liquidity" (see chapter 6) in the other market. If the ES moves and the SPY has not yet done so, this form of trading is likely to

be profitable, and it will transmit the change in price from the ES to the SPY. The SPY's smaller ticks, however, mean that it can move without the equivalent form of trading becoming profitable. Note, though, that even the apparently deeply technical factor of tick size is actually an issue of political economy. Other things being equal (which often they are not), market-makers prefer large ticks, because they earn their revenue from the difference in price between the highest bid and lowest offer, a difference that in many markets is restricted by competition to a single tick. In share trading, as touched on in chapter 3, the SEC, as a matter of policy, deliberately narrowed the standard tick size in share trading from the previous sixteenth of a dollar (6.25 cents) to a single cent. The much less interventionist CFTC has never sought to make equivalent changes to tick sizes in futures, which are often large.

28. Volumes of orders in the ES order book dropped considerably in 2018–19, report Osipovich (2019b) and Wigglesworth (2019), and were also low in the turbulent trading of March 2020 (Flood 2020). "The futures are significantly less liquid than they were," said interviewee OX in October 2018. Previously, "when a piece of news would break, the first thing that would happen is they would go trade the futures . . . if we were fast enough, we could see that, we could reprice our options." What had started to happen more frequently, OX reported, was that liquidity-takers would act immediately in the share-index options market. The reasons for the decline in liquidity in share-index futures are unclear. Liquidity typically deteriorates in periods of market stress, but does not seem to have been recovering as it once did when the stress eases, which might suggest some structural change. It is possible that market-making algorithms have become more vulnerable in share-index futures trading to being picked off by liquidity-taking algorithms (see chapter 6).

29. See Stafford (2017) and Meyer (2015).

30. Interviewees tell me that share-index futures tend to lead changes in the prices of the corresponding ETFs and the underlying shares in Europe as well as the US, but European countries do not have split regulation analogous to the CFTC/SEC divide. (The only European exception to "futures lead" that I have heard of is Switzerland, where I'm told that the pattern tends to be the reverse, because a small number of large, highly liquid shares dominate its stock market.) That "futures lead" exists in Europe without split regulation is, however, not a compelling argument against the US divide being of causal importance, because, as far as I can tell, Europe's new financial futures exchanges seem from the start to have adopted requirements for margin similar to those of the US exchanges they were emulating, thus building in to futures trading in Europe the same leverage advantage over shares. To my knowledge, European regulators have never challenged what I suspect has been taken to be a rather technical aspect of the trading of financial instruments.

Chapter 3: "We'll show you our book. Why won't they?"

1. For Whitcomb's work in this field, see, e.g., Cohen, Maier, Schwartz, and Whitcomb (1981).

2. In the first version of the equation that ATD used to predict share prices, the equation's coefficients were simply Whitcomb's informed guesses rather than statistical estimates, as they are in regression analysis.

3. In December 1967, the first woman, Muriel Siebert, gained membership in the NYSE, but the trading floor remained—and, as I've found on my visits to it, to a large extent still remains—predominantly male (for Siebert, see anon. 2013).

4. A limit order is an order to buy shares at up to a specific price, or to sell them at or above a specific price. For the controversy surrounding the CLOB, see Pardo-Guerra (2019: 248–300), Kennedy (2017: 905–907), and MacKenzie (2018b: 1660–1666).

5. For the capacity to glimpse the book, see SEC (1963: part 2, 77).

6. As far as I can tell, only one other electronic trading system was contemporaneous with Instinet, or may slightly have preceded it. One of the US regional exchanges, the Pacific Stock

Exchange, which had trading floors in San Francisco and Los Angeles, launched a system called Scorex in 1969. Its early history is unclear, but by 1980 it allowed small orders to be executed electronically at the best price being quoted on the Consolidated Quotation System, which disseminated the prices of the best bids and offers on US stock exchanges; see Seligman (1982: 531).

7. Adams, Behrens, Pustilnik, and Gilmore (1971: 1). For Instinet's origins, see Pardo-Guerra (2019: 228–235).

8. Originally, reports interviewee GN, Instinet users could see only the best (i.e., highest-priced) bids and the best (lowest-priced) offers, a restriction he attributes to a constraint imposed by regulators that ultimately reflected traditional financial intermediaries' desire to limit information disclosure. "The more information you give out," said GN, "the less money you make per trade." Later—the exact date of the change is not clear in my data—Instinet terminals displayed the full order book for each stock.

9. Instinet did continue to give institutional investors the capacity to mark their orders "I-ONLY," allowing only other institutional investors to see them (Instinet 1988: 12).

10. I borrow the term "fixed-role" from Aspers (2007) but employ it differently. For Aspers, a fixed-role market is one in which some actors are only sellers and others only buyers. In the fixed-role financial markets I am discussing, any actor can both buy and sell, but how he or she can do so is constrained.

11. An NASD rule barred market-makers from installing an automated system to update their quotes to reflect changes in other market-makers' quotes. According to interviewee EZ, who worked for the NASD in the 1990s, the rationale was to stop market-makers from evading their responsibilities by automatically "fading" their bids and/or offers, i.e., altering their quotes so that they would never be executed.

12. The first such SOES-trading operation (described in detail by Donlan 1988) was up and running within four months after the execution of SOES orders became compulsory.

13. Because Nasdaq was designed primarily to facilitate trading by telephone, it could not be anonymous. The firms displaying orders on-screen and those sending them via SOES were all identifiable, their telephone numbers were readily available, and in practice the identities of the leading individual "bandits" were well known to Nasdaq's dealers.

14. William Timpinaro et al. *v.* Securities and Exchange Commission, 2 F.3d 453 (US Court of Appeals 1993).

15. That "bandit" reasoning was of this general form, and was profitable, was later confirmed by quantitative analysis by Harris and Schultz (1998).

16. I had a very enjoyable lunch with Levine in October 2011, but he preferred to answer questions by email rather than be interviewed face-to-face. My colleague Juan Pablo Pardo-Guerra and I sent him these questions in two large batches, to which he responded in January and May 2012. Levine also made available to us a corpus of email messages he wrote to provide information for a *Wired* article about Island (Brekke 1999).

17. Email from Levine, January 27, 2012; Brekke (1999). Citron's role was primarily the business side of his and Levine's joint ventures, but he did some of the early programming and Levine testifies to his influence: "Pretty much everything I did was . . . shaped and guided by the long and deep arguments we would have" (email from Levine, May 21, 2012).

18. In using the term hacker ethos, Andresen was referring primarily to a specific aspect of hacker subculture—disdain for monetary reward—but I think the term is applicable to Island more generally. In respect to money, Andresen said, "There's that whole hacker ethos of 'I'm above money,'" but unlike many cases in which "they affect it because it's considered cool," he found it to be genuine in Levine's case: "I'd be like, 'Josh, here's your bonus check,' [and] he was like, 'Ah, give it to those guys.'" ("Those guys" were the programmers who had taken over much of the programming burden from Levine; email to author from Levine, September 1, 2012.)

19. See https://colin-scott.github.io/personal_website/research/interactive_latency.html, which gives an estimate of 23 nanoseconds for a level 1 "cache reference," using the technology of 1996 (accessed January 21, 2020). I am hugely grateful to interviewee AF for pointing me to this site, which is a wonderful resource for someone interested in computing's materiality.

20. A "two-phase commit" is the procedure by which a system writes information onto a disk or other form of memory and receives back a message acknowledging that the information has indeed been written.

21. Hendershott, Jones, and Menkveld (2011: 13). As they note, if 30 seconds elapsed without a manual update being disseminated, the NYSE's computer system would send out the update.

22. There is a useful history of the clearing and settlement of US shares in Wolkoff and Werner (2010).

23. Precisely because a centralized system for the clearing and settlement of share transactions was long established by the late 1990s, ECNs and HFT firms did encounter some difficulties in linking their systems to what for their technical staff were unfamiliar "old mainframe software and . . . big batch [discontinuous] processes" rather than fast, continuous processing (interviewee AF). Those difficulties were, however, more easily solved than the deeper issue in the trading of sovereign bonds, discussed in chapter 4, where it was in practice impossible for an HFT firm or new trading venue to access the relevant clearing system except via a big dealer.

24. As noted in chapter 1, order books are not visible in the "dark pools" that also trade shares; indeed, the invisibility of the order book is why they are referred to as dark. However, the very fact that these are regarded as a special category of trading venue (and one that quite commonly is the subject of suspicion) indicates that open order books have become normal. For the history of dark pools, see MacKenzie (2019d).

25. OTC is the abbreviation of over-the-counter, and refers to trading conducted by direct negotiation between the parties to a deal.

Chapter 4: Dealers, Clients, and the Politics of Market Structure

1. Data from https://www.sifma.org/resources/research/us-treasury-trading-volume/, accessed 25 May 2020.

2. I write "essentially" because a big and valuable client does have some capacity to negotiate with a dealer over price.

3. See Lenglet and Mol (2016) for the regulation, in European share trading, of direct market access. Many institutional-investment firms seem cautious about direct market access, sometimes for a mundane reason: fear of mistakes such as buying when they should have sold or vice versa (interviewee IA). If a broker-dealer firm is trading on their behalf and makes a mistake of this kind, it has to remedy it at its own expense.

4. The original 1960 list of primary dealers is available at https://www.newyorkfed.org/markets/primarydealers, accessed 27 January 2019.

5. Unlike the public reporting in corporate bonds, TRACE reports of Treasurys deals are private to regulators (only aggregate data are published), and reporting need only take place within one day, not 15 minutes as in corporate bonds.

6. The only European sovereign-bond HFT that I know of takes place on a relatively small scale on the Borsa Italiana, which has made "government bonds . . . tradeable electronically just like [shares] and . . . centrally cleared" (interviewee CR). Trading, though, is informed by prices in the interdealer market, which (bizarrely for HFT) sometimes must be gleaned via telephone calls.

7. Governments do of course intervene in foreign-exchange trading to influence exchange rates (although less often than in the past), but such interventions are typically conducted within existing market structures. During the past decade, government regulatory bodies have also started

to detect and penalize specific alleged "market abuses" in foreign-exchange trading, but without seeking to intervene in the overall way in which that trading is organized.

8. The objection was that what Reuters wanted to lease was not simply lines for its own use but lines that would be used by "third parties" (i.e., banks), thus encroaching upon the domain of telecommunications providers by itself becoming something of a provider. Eventually, in 1977, the relevant European organization, the Comité Européen des Postes et Télécommunications, was persuaded to allow third-party use if Reuters agreed to pay supplementary charges (interviewee FS).

9. For this research, see, for example, Knorr Cetina and Bruegger (2002a and 2002b).

10. As with other electronic trading systems of the epoch, such as Instinet and Globex, some users also circumvented the rule against "nonhuman things" by screen scraping as described in chapter 3, and it appears likely that the input to the Clackatron was generated in this way.

11. Knorr Cetina (2007: 713 and 718–721) discusses how traders interwove EBS and conversational dealing.

12. The traditional increment of price in foreign exchange was the "pip" ("percentage in point"). If, for example, an exchange rate moves from 1.1850 to 1.1851, that is a one-pip move. Decimalization was the change to a minimum price increment of a tenth of a pip.

13. As noted above, for repo and its political economy, see Gabor (2016). Brandt, Kavajecz, and Underwood (2007) find that the cost of repo financing seems to affect whether the Treasury futures market leads the market in Treasury securities or vice versa.

Chapter 5 "Not only would I lose my job, I might lose my legs too!"

1. The terminology of racks was inherited from US telecommunications, and even today rack sizes are usually defined in inches, not centimeters. A standard rack unit is 19 inches (48.26 cm) wide and 1.75 inches high, and a typical rack, or "cabinet," is 42 units tall (73.5 inches, or 1.87 meters). Power densities of about 15 kilowatts per rack now seem routinely achievable. See https://en.wikipedia.org/wiki/19-inch_rack and https://www.datacenters.com/news/understanding-the-interplay-between-data-center-power-consumption-data-center-en, both accessed November 26, 2019.

2. If the incoming order is an "immediate-or-cancel" order (see chapter 6), it will simply be canceled rather than added to the order book.

3. As noted in chapter 1, most exchanges allow users' systems to submit both "hidden" orders (which are not disseminated to other users via the market-data publisher system; such orders usually rank behind visible orders in the electronic queue for execution) and "iceberg" orders, which have a hidden part in addition to a part that is disseminated.

4. As noted in chapter 2, older systems (such as the original versions of the CME's Globex), which were designed with human users in mind, often aggregated multiple updates into periodic "snapshots" of the order book, a practice that my HFT interviewees disliked. (It makes it difficult, for example, for an HFT firm's system to keep track of exactly where its orders are in the queue for execution.) Gradually, this practice has been replaced by the "Island-style" procedure described in the text.

5. T-1 (Transmission System 1) was the original 1962 AT&T digital-transmission specification, which was later reimplemented for optical fiber. T-2 and T-3 are higher-capacity versions.

6. One interviewee, TO, tells me that a crucial component of the gold line was an old cable laid several years earlier by the pioneering Internet service provider UUNET. The cable's transmission capacity was limited, he tells me, and to save money UUNET had simply buried it in the soil, rather than laying it in conduits as was normal practice, but its route made it faster than the alternatives. I have, however, been unable to find independent confirmation of this.

7. In fact, because the location was so vital, Spread seems simply to have offered over $100,000, rather than the owners demanding that.

8. There was, as noted at the end of chapter 4, a second tier of subscribers who paid lower fees, and experienced a transmission time about a thousandth of a second slower than the premium. "There was literally a cabinet that the fiber just went around and around and around until it added a millisecond in . . . delay" (interviewee TO).

9. For a vivid account of the manufacture of glass fiber for fiber-optic cable, see Crawford (2019). While the refractive-index effect is the main reason why pulses of light move more slowly in fiber-optic cable than in a vacuum, those pulses also reflect many, many times from the fiber's walls (this takes the form of what in optics is called total internal reflection, and the resultant low level of attenuation is what makes it possible for optical fiber to transmit light signals for substantial distances without amplification). Although bouncing off the fiber's walls does not in itself slow the pulses, it means that (even though an optical fiber's core can be less than 10 microns—millionths of a meter—thick) the path followed by those pulses is not an entirely straight line. I am grateful to Greg Laughlin for clarifying this point.

10. There is a map of Pilosov's route in an insert in Laumonier (2019). One reason for going as far south as Pittsburgh was that it would make it easier to build an extension of the network to Washington, DC, which is where macroeconomic data crucial to financial trading are released. "It didn't happen for various commercial reasons," says Pilosov, but other firms did construct links from Washington to Chicago and New Jersey.

11. Pilosov tells me that with the exception of the reused Long Lines antenna (which was very heavy) his antennas were lighter than this, at around 150 pounds.

12. In 2018, Anova Financial Networks (whose millimeter-wave and laser links in New Jersey are discussed later in this chapter) acquired and improved an existing microwave link from Chicago. An entirely new link also appears to be under construction by specialist communications provider Scientel Solutions, but if so the identity of its client remains unclear.

13. There is discussion of ducting and other common causes of microwave fading in Manning (2009: especially 51–52 and 155–172). Also problematic, but more readily correctable, is "multipath propagation" (Manning 2009: 171–172). This occurs when, as Tyč put it, you "receive the same wave" more than once, because of reflection from the surface of a lake or layering of the atmosphere. Since these multiple waves will "interact [interfere] constructively at one point and destructively at another one," this problem can be circumvented, says Tyč, by having two antennas (on the same tower, but some distance apart) that both receive signals, with an automated control system that "pick[s] whichever signal is the best." This solution does, however, add somewhat to latency (delay).

14. BATS, the electronic share-trading venue mentioned in chapter 3, set up in 2005 by the HFT firm Tradebot, originally had its matching engines in NJ2, but they are now in NY5.

15. In Roald Dahl's children's book *Charlie and the Chocolate Factory* (Dahl 1964), Willy Wonka, the owner of the factory, hides five golden tickets in chocolate bars. Those who find them are allowed to tour the normally under-wraps factory and provided with free chocolate for the rest of their lives. Charlie, the impoverished boy who finds the fifth ticket, is made Wonka's heir.

16. As Persico explained to me, this switching is at the byte level (a byte is a unit of information made up of eight binary digits). The hybrid system can thus send part of a packet—a larger, structured unit of data—by laser, and part by millimeter wave.

17. The "Shannon limit" is named after the MIT electrical engineer and mathematician Claude Shannon, who did famous, fundamental work on information theory and the capacity of communications channels.

18. See Tyč (2018). Longer hops are possible because LMDS is lower in the frequency spectrum than E-band, and so less affected by rain. There are no other LMDS links in the relevant

areas with which McKay's signals might interfere, which makes it easier to install antennas in optimal, geodesic-hugging locations. I write "quasi-public" because these exchange datafeeds are commercial products.

19. In 2019, for example, the cost of a basic 1Gb (gigabit) per second connection to Nasdaq's system was $2,500 per month, while a 40Gb connection cost $20,000 per month (see http://nasdaqtrader.com/Trader.aspx?id=PriceListTrading2, accessed April 14, 2019).

20. See https://meanderful.blogspot.com/2018/01/the-accidental-hft-firm.html.

21. A packet's or message's "checksum" is a special datafield that contains an arithmetic function of the other binary digits in the packet. The receiving system checks for errors that have occurred in the transmission of those digits by calculating the same function of the digits it has received.

22. In the midst of the coronavirus-induced market turbulence of March 2020, Eurex postponed the requirement for its member firms to use the "discard" IP address, and at the time of writing has not yet reintroduced it. As interviewee GR points out, the requirement may only be a partial solution, because the switch in the exchange's system at which incoming messages arrive before being forwarded to an order gateway may still become overloaded.

23. A further speed advantage could potentially be obtained by designing an application-specific integrated circuit or ASIC, a silicon chip in which the circuitry to perform a particular computation is *permanently* hardwired. My interviews, though, revealed only rumors of the use of ASICs. That might be because those who use them do not want to reveal that fact, but it could be because HFT algorithms need to be changed quite often, and the design and manufacture of an ASIC is a slow and expensive process. One possible scenario (but one I cannot confirm) is for HFT firms to use ASICs for "feed handling" (the processing of exchange datafeeds, the formats of which are reasonably stable), while still using reprogrammable FPGAs for trading.

Chapter 6: How HFT Algorithms Interact, and How Exchanges Seek to Influence It

1. The first two of these actions can sometimes trigger a "self-match" prevention rule, which (as discussed later in the chapter) can cause the algorithm's action to cancel an existing order by another of the firm's algorithms, rather than leading to the submission of a new bid or offer.

2. It was hard to get HFT interviewees to say much about how their algorithms interacted with execution algorithms. The topic is sensitive because of accusations that HFT algorithms "sniff out" and exploit execution algorithms (see, e.g., Lewis 2014), but it is also often difficult for traders to know with any certainty with whom or with what their algorithms are trading. That difficulty is rather less in the case of the central mechanism described in this chapter—the "picking off" of the "stale" quotes of market-making algorithms—because only another HFT algorithm will usually have the speed to successfully pick off an HFT market-making algorithm.

3. Recall how Nasdaq dealers' avoidance of odd-eighth price quotes made this difference often as much as 25 cents as recently as the early 1990s (chapter 3).

4. Not all HFT firms seek to estimate theoretical value. Thus interviewees AI, AQ, AU, and BP reported that their algorithms' predictive efforts did not take this form.

5. In a minority of markets (such as the Chicago Mercantile Exchange's Eurodollar futures), the matching algorithm is "pro rata": executions are allocated in proportion to the size of executable bids or offers in the order book. Another complication is where exactly in an exchange's computer system the time of arrival of an order is recorded: for example, at the matching engine, or at the system's periphery, such as an order gateway.

6. Another strategy for achieving favorable queue position is to "feather" (interviewee GH) the order book with orders at multiple price levels. In the order book in figure 6.1, for example, an

algorithm might place bids to buy not just at $29.49 but also at $29.48, $29.47, $29.46, $29.45, and so on. This plainly does not help if prices rise, but if they fall, $29.48 (for instance) might become the highest bid price, so a preexisting bid at that price could become the head of the time-priority queue. The strategy of feathering—of entering bids and offers at multiple price levels—is certainly followed in HFT, by at least one of the world's leading market-making firms, and (as discussed later in this chapter) in foreign-exchange trading venues whose computer systems prevent orders from being canceled until after a certain time period (a "minimum quote lifespan") has elapsed. Interviewee BM's futures-trading firm, for example, also tried to achieve favorable queue position while avoiding the expense of extreme speed by placing orders at levels that were not the best price and then carefully tracking what happened to them as prices moved. Feathering, however, involves having more orders in the market than an equivalent firm that simply races to join a newly formed level would have. There is therefore a risk that if prices move sharply (perhaps because of news bearing on the financial instrument being traded, or because of "market-impact trading," the large-scale "sweeps" or "swipes" described later in the chapter), serious losses may be incurred, although having fast technology that enables orders to be canceled quickly reduces that risk. Another strategy—less risky but technologically still demanding—is for an algorithm to place bids and offers not at multiple price levels but only at what would often be called "level two." In the book shown in figure 6.1, this would involve bidding at $29.48 and offering at $29.51. Again, the hope is that prices move in such a way that what was previously level two becomes the highest bid price or lowest offer price and the algorithm's order is then at the head of the queue. This strategy is followed widely in futures trading, reports BM, creating a race to join a level as soon as price changes have made it level two. That race makes this strategy technologically quite demanding. (BM also points out that "when there is a race to level two, those orders still want the market to move away from them for a number of ticks before they become good." If it moves back immediately, "the order, even though it was placed quickly, would still not have great priority most likely since it would have been placed behind many other contracts.")

7. Trade throughs of exchange-listed stocks were banned prior to Reg NMS, but policing of the ban was not rigorous. It relied on complaints from the specialist or exchange that believed that he or it had been traded through; and the effect of a successful complaint was simply a modest compensation payment from the perpetrator to that specialist or exchange. Trade throughs seem to have been the main type of complaint that was automated by Archipelago's algorithmic complainer, "The Whiner"; see chapter 3. As an ECN rather than a registered exchange, Archipelago would not originally have enjoyed trade-through protection, but in 2000 it bought the share-trading license of the Pacific Stock Exchange, which meant that its price quotations for listed stocks should have been protected from trade throughs.

8. See the next paragraph for why a firm might wish to avoid accidental "taking."

9. "Crossing the spread" is another term for "taking," one that implicitly emphasizes that (other things being equal) taking is more expensive than making. For example, in the order book in figure 6.1 the cheapest bid that will "take" is at $29.50, while bids that "make" are at $29.49 or less.

10. Drawing on data from 2010, Madhavan (2012) reports that 28 percent of US share trading, and 21 percent of trading in exchange-traded funds, involved the use of ISOs; McInish, Upson, and Wood (2012) report higher incidences (40–45 percent) of ISO use in the trading of stocks in the S&P 500.

11. In September 2015, Latour Trading LLC (it has no relation that I know of to the theorist Bruno Latour but is a subsidiary—led by a former trader from the French bank Société Générale—of the leading US HFT firm Tower Research, hence "la tour" or "Latour") reached an $8 million settlement with the SEC for what appears to be entirely inadvertent noncompliance with Reg NMS in these respects. See https://www.sec.gov/news/pressrelease/2015-221.html, accessed July 29, 2019.

12. AE said this in December 2011. Since then, the capacity for trading firms to use ISOs has become more widespread, presumably reducing this "wealth transfer" among them. Unfortunately, though, I know of no quantitative data on the issue.

13. As Aquilina, Budish, and O'Neill point out, to be able to identify a race, it is necessary to detect not just actions by "winning" algorithms but also actions by "losing" algorithms, and the latter actions "*do not affect the state of the order book because they fail*" (Aquilina et al. 2020: 3; emphasis in original), which makes them invisible in order-book data. The relevant failed actions are intended "taking" immediate-or-cancel orders that are canceled because there is no longer an order in the order book that they can be executed against, and cancellations of "making" orders that fail because those orders have already been executed against. For details of their methodology, see Aqulina et al. (2020: 14–23).

14. The two races are interwoven, in that (as noted earlier in the chapter) an order at the end of the queue is more likely to be picked off than one at the front.

15. The random-forest technique was developed by Leo Breiman of the University of California, Berkeley (Breiman 2001).

16. The example of stigma he gave was the belief that "all you want to do is arb the cash and future all day," in other words, exploit short-lived price discrepancies between, for example, Treasury securities and Treasury futures.

17. There is a clear description of quote matching (and its risks) in Harris (2003: 248–50).

18. HFT algorithms have, of course, been improved over time to reduce the risk of their being fooled by spoofing. Although interviewees did not go into detail on these defensive measures, I suspect that the simplest forms of spoofing (such as the example in the text) would not nowadays usually deceive a sophisticated HFT algorithm.

19. See, e.g., Baron, Brogaard and Kirilenko (2012); Hagströmer and Nordén (2013); Benos and Sagade (2016). Benos and Sagade, for example, use regulatory data to classify HFT participants in the London Stock Exchange as "passive" (makers), "neutral" or "aggressive" (takers). "[A]ggressive HFTs take liquidity 82% of the time, whereas the passive do so only 11% of the time" (2016: 63).

20. As already noted, market-making algorithms can—and do—"take" unintentionally. When a fast market-making algorithm is changing its quote in response to a signal, it may well (unless it is using "post-only" orders) pick off the stale quotes of a slower market-maker. "You quote over somebody's else's quote . . . you bang in your two-sided bid and ask [offer], and it happens to cross somebody else's two-sided bid and ask . . . You . . . take" (interviewee OJ).

21. That the proportion of the firm's trading that was taking was indeed low is confirmed indirectly by Menkveld's (2013) econometric study, mentioned in the appendix on the literature and drawn on in chapter 3 in relation to Chi-X. As noted there, what my interviewees said about Chi-X makes it likely that the HFT firm on which Menkveld focused is the one discussed here. "[T]he vast majority" of its trades "are passive [i.e., making]," reports Menkveld: "78.1% in Euronext and 78.0% in Chi-X" (2013: 730).

22. "Tri arb," or triangular arbitrage, is the exploitation of fleetingly inconsistent patterns of prices in which, e.g., it is profitable to exchange dollars for yen, yen for euros, and then euros back into dollars.

23. See http://barclaysdfslastlooksettlement.com, accessed May 31, 2020.

24. There is a useful chronology, which I draw on here, of the recent development of foreign-exchange trading venues at http://edhoworka.com/a-brief-history-of-hft/, accessed October 16, 2019.

25. In a December 2012 *Financial Times* article, the economist Larry Harris argued that "[d]elaying the processing of all orders by a trivially small random time period of between 0 and 10 milliseconds" would help preserve competition among trading firms (Harris 2012). It is, however,

not clear from my interviews that the introduction of randomization in foreign-exchange trading was prompted by Harris's article.

26. Each batch contains the orders that have arrived in a period of 3–4 milliseconds (Tabb 2016).

27. Reuters was renamed Refinitiv in 2018, and, at the time of writing in 2020, is the subject of an agreed but not yet completed takeover by the London Stock Exchange.

28. There are separate buffers for "making" orders at different prices.

29. The randomization is by firm: all the orders in the buffer from the same firm are grouped, and only one of them is implemented before the algorithm moves to an order submitted by the next firm in the randomly ordered list of firms. The rationale is to prevent a firm from gaming the randomization and boosting the chance of execution of an order it wants to be executed by submitting large numbers of identical copies of it in the form of immediate-or-cancel orders. See Melton (2017).

30. In May 2019, the Intercontinental Exchange (ICE) gained the permission of the Commodity Futures Trading Commission to install a speed bump to slow "taking" orders in gold and silver futures by three milliseconds (Stafford 2019a). It is worth noting that the trading of these futures is dominated by the Chicago Mercantile Exchange (CME), and ICE appears to see the speed bump as a way of encouraging market-makers to build liquidity to help it become more competitive with the CME in the trading of these futures.

31. A human trader or algorithm that executed against an order in Island's order book was, as noted in chapter 3, charged a quarter of a cent for each share traded (Biais, Bisière, & Spatt 2003: 6), while the trader or algorithm that had originally placed that order was paid by Island a tenth of a cent per share for doing so. Initially, Island had offered an "order-entry rebate" that went to those who ran the trading systems from which orders were sent, so as, Josh Levine told me, to incentivize them to devote technical effort to implementing and supporting the technical interconnection. The rebate structure was later changed to that described above following Levine's thoughts about the "*price of immediacy*" (the cost to a trader who simply took up an existing bid or offer) and "*price of liquidity*," the cost to a trader who posted a bid or offer in the order book and thus gave other traders an implicit option, in the financial-market sense: the right but not the obligation to take up that bid or offer (email to author from Levine, May 21, 2012; emphases in original).

32. The most important exceptions to this payment structure are "inverted" exchanges (Nasdaq's BX; EDGA, originally set up the ECN by Direct Edge; and BYX, launched by BATS), which pay takers and charge makers. Such exchanges may attract takers (or brokers acting on their behalf) who want to take more cheaply. There have been fears that this may enable makers on inverted exchanges to gather useful early information about orders from institutional investors that brokers are in the process of executing, but I have no evidence of this. The most important effect of inverted exchanges on market structure, pointed out to me by interviewee AF, may simply be that they loosen the constraint placed on US share trading by the fixed one-cent minimum increment of prices, at least in the case of firms sophisticated enough to be able to operate strategically across exchanges (see also Chao, Yao, and Ye 2019). A fee or a rebate has the effect of marginally increasing or reducing the effective price of a purchase or sale. By choosing to bid or offer on an inverted exchange that pays rebates to takers, a market-making firm therefore can (at the cost of paying that exchange's fees) de facto slightly improve on the equivalent price quotes on conventional exchanges, which can (AF notes) make its queue position on those exchanges somewhat less important.

33. "Here is a simple example . . . the speed bump that forces drivers to slow down on campus . . . The driver's goal is translated, by means of the speed bump, from 'slow down so as not to endanger students' into 'slow down and protect your car's suspension.' The . . . first version appeals to morality . . . the second appeals to pure selfishness and reflex action" (Latour 1999: 187).

34. The main point of the coil is to inhibit a particular form of taking. Much trading on IEX is midpoint matching, in which trades are consummated at the midpoint of the highest bid price and lowest offer price on all the US exchanges. If a taking algorithm detected that the midpoint calculated by IEX's system was out of date, it might be able profitably to "take." However, the datafeeds that inform IEX's calculation of the midpoint do not go through the coil, so the midpoint is updated before any "taking" order has emerged from the coil.

35. A major political-economy aspect of Reg NMS was the restriction of order protection to orders that were "[i]mmediately and automatically" executable (SEC 2005: 37620), thus stripping protection from quotations available only on trading floors such as that of the New York Stock Exchange. Reg NMS, though, did not define what "immediately" means—in 2005, that no doubt did not seem necessary—but the controversy over IEX's speed bump forced the SEC to do so.

36. SEC (2019b); see also Bacidore (2020). IEX already employs a "crumbling-quote indicator" that detects, in the order books of other US exchanges, when a "level" of those books for a particular stock is emptying out, which often signals a coming price change. IEX proposes to introduce a discretionary limit order that would automatically be canceled and repriced by IEX's system when the crumbling-quote indicator suggests the order is becoming stale. Crucially, the data employed by the crumbling-quote indicator do not pass through IEX's coil in NY5, while a taking order designed to exploit a crumbling quote would have to do so. This makes the combination of the discretionary limit orders and the coil a version of an asymmetric speed bump that would protect those orders from being picked off, as Bacidore (2020) points out.

37. Among older measures that protected market-makers were quote-lock timers. These delayed the execution of "taking" orders for a set period (a quarter of a second seems to have been common, but OY reports sometimes as much as three seconds) to allow market-making algorithms time to cancel their quotes. These timers seem, however, no longer to be in use. Interviewee AF suggests that fast and sophisticated options market-making firms grew frustrated with quote-lock timers, because their algorithms' updated price quotes were often delayed until slower market markers "got out of the way," i.e., canceled the preexisting bids and offers whose presence had meant that the updated price quotes had triggered the quote-lock timer. OY reports that the original reason for introducing quote-lock timers was to encourage former floor traders to make markets electronically, but as electronic market-making systems became faster and more sophisticated the timers were eventually judged unnecessary.

Chapter 7: Conclusion

1. Walsingham's manuscript account, edited by Thomas Riley, was published as Walsingham (1869: see especially 293 and 309). See also Oman (1906: 93–94) and Bloch (1935); the latter was translated into English in Bloch (1967: 136–168; see especially 158).

2. See the zoning documentation annexed to Virtu Financial (2019b).

3. I take my estimate of saving in fiber tail from McKay Brothers (2020: 3).

4. For the dispute, see the comment letters to the Securities and Exchange Commission available at https://www.sec.gov/comments/sr-nyse-2020-05/srnyse202005.htm, accessed June 1, 2020. Again, I take the distance measurement from McKay Brothers (2020).

5. Europe's MiFID (Markets in Financial Directives) II regulations, in place since January 2018, include controversial new open-access rules governing clearing, rules that would end what are sometimes called the vertical silos in futures clearing, but these rules were put on hold until July 2020 because of Brexit. In December 2019, the Ministry of Finance of Germany (which hosts Eurex, Europe's leading futures exchange) was reported to be pushing hard to have the rules reconsidered during Germany's 2020 presidency of the European Union, and altered before they come into force (Wilkes 2019). A further postponement to July 2021 was granted, but this may

simply have been because of the coronavirus crisis; it is unclear whether the reported pressure played a role.

6. Consider, for example, changes in the prices of shares or other financial instruments that are correlated with the price of the instrument being traded. That class of signal could at most be asserted to be the outcome of a struggle in only a rather tenuous sense. It is true, though, that this correlation often arises from the classification of firms into economic sectors, because market participants often view firms in the same sector as being exposed to common risks and perhaps as having similar opportunities. For sociological analyses of the classification of firms, see Zuckerman (1999 and 2000) and Beunza and Garud (2007).

7. It is not clear why there had been only a small number of customers for Pathfinders. The rolling time intervals analyzed by Nasdaq's systems to identify such pathfinders were long by the standards of HFT (one minute, five minutes, and 60 minutes), and the messages alerting users of the datafeed to the aggregate activity of pathfinders were slow (dispatched, for example, in the case of one-minute intervals a full second after the end of the interval; Nasdaq OMX 2009). These features may have limited Pathfinders' attractiveness to HFT firms.

8. Founded in 2007, FINRA combined the previously separate self-regulatory functions of the National Association of Securities Dealers and the New York Stock Exchange.

9. In February 2020, the SEC proposed authorizing competing suppliers of the official "consolidated tape" of market data, and broadening the latter to include not just the highest bids and lowest offers but also the five next-best price levels. See https://www.sec.gov/news/press-release /2020-34, accessed June 2, 2020.

10. Although ISOs are the most salient example, exchanges also offer other specialized types of order to assist algorithms jockeying for advantage (especially favorable queue position) within the framework of Reg NMS's order-protection rules. The result is considerable complexity. Mackintosh (2014) counts 133 distinct types of order offered by US stock exchanges, but these can often be combined, creating a much larger universe of composite orders.

11. The main exception is the rules in Europe's MiFID II governing futures clearing; see note 5 above.

12. On governmentality, see Foucault (1991). It is noteworthy that while participants in financial markets do frequently espouse free-market, pro-competition views, those views do not usually translate into a warm welcome for measures that undermine privileged structural positions from which those participants benefit. Finance's mundane political economy can easily trump ideology.

13. There is a large body of literature on the influences on financial regulation. Examples include Goldbach (2015), Mügge (2006), Pagliari and Young (2016), Thiemann (2014), Thiemann and Lepoutre (2017), and Young (2015). I should acknowledge that the research underpinning this book was not designed to examine these influences in any systematic way; rather, I simply "worked back," starting with regulatory initiatives that are or were important to HFT and its evolution (including failed initiatives, such as the CLOB), and seeking to understand the processes that shaped these initiatives.

14. Interviewees report, for example, that the New York Stock Exchange, which had benefitted from the order-protection regime prior to Reg NMS, wanted to preserve it, while Nasdaq, which had not been subject to that earlier regime, did not want it extended.

15. Since July 2017, transactions in Treasurys must be reported to FINRA, the Financial Industry Regulatory Authority. FINRA, however, keeps these reports private, although in March 2020 it began to make week-by-week aggregate data available.

16. The Dodd-Frank Act of 2010 involved a major push to subject swaps to central clearing and to have them traded on exchange-like swap execution facilities, or SEFs (Ziegler and Woolley 2016). Interviewees from several high-frequency trading firms told me that they had therefore anticipated that swaps trading would become more "futures-like," and had made or were making

plans to extend HFT to swaps. These interviewees report, however, that regulatory difficulties and resistance by incumbents have largely preserved bifurcated dealer-client and interdealer markets. Although it does not seem to have been the main factor, in light of the above discussion of anonymity it is worth noting that the prevalence in swaps trading of post-trade "name give-up"—i.e., deanonymization—may have made clients such as hedge funds and other investment-management firms reluctant to take part in the interdealer markets more suited to HFT. They may have feared what a hedge-fund manager who spoke to Rennison (2014: 17) called retribution, from dealers on whom they depended, if they were discovered to be trading directly in those markets. Among firms with an HFT focus, only the big Chicago hedge fund Citadel has a substantial presence in swaps trading, and Citadel—with its extensive capital base and asset-management arm—is not a classic HFT firm.

17. Face-to-face exchanges such as the New York Stock Exchange, Chicago Mercantile Exchange, and Chicago Board of Trade used to be sites of spatially local politics, especially in relation to issues (such as the shift to electronic futures trading) on which traders were sometimes bitterly divided. Demutualization (the transformation of exchanges into listed companies) and the decline or closure of trading floors have largely, although not completely, removed this spatially local dimension.

18. An interviewee told me that at one point the HFT firm for which he worked "had 40 percent of all the FIX ports to Arca." (FIX is an electronic protocol that is "wordier" and therefore slower than Island's succinct Ouch, but nevertheless is widely used in finance. Arca, formerly Archipelago, was the ECN that, as described in chapter 3, was bought by the New York Stock Exchange in 2005.) That dominance of the "ports" meant, he says, that his firm's systems "appeared a lot faster to internal . . . individuals because they commanded so much exchange bandwidth." A firm that was faster, but that had not been able to afford as many ports, could beat it "on the first order," but its success with later orders would be constrained by the more limited bandwidth of its access to the exchange. So his firm could still beat its competitor on aggregate.

19. Budish et al. (2019) do not directly measure "arbitrage rents," but extrapolate from their more direct measure—but one that is still an estimate—of the "speed technology revenues" of the three main "families" of US stock exchanges, using a game-theoretic model of the interactions among trading firms and between those firms and exchanges.

20. See note 13 to chapter 6 for the key methodological innovation in Aquilina et al. (2020).

21. It may seem implausible that holding an auction every 50 millionths of a second could do anything to mitigate trading's speed race, but recall that, as noted in chapter 5, the three competing ultrafast Chicago–New Jersey microwave links have speeds that now differ (or soon will differ) by as little as a microsecond, and that the speed advantages in other aspects of HFT are now measured in nanoseconds. On those timescales, 50 microseconds is a long time. Consider an algorithm that is trading shares in one of the New Jersey datacenters, and imagine that it has the fastest link to Chicago. With today's material arrangements—in which a trade can occur at any moment in time— that algorithm will always have an advantage when share-index futures prices move. With Budish's proposal (even in its most frequent 50-microsecond form), the chance of a one-microsecond speed advantage being decisive is only 1/50. The rest of the time, a one-microsecond speed advantage is of limited use because many slower trading algorithms will be able to catch up before the auction takes place. (Trading firms that do not own microwave links can lease bandwidth on the McKay Brothers link, which is one of the ultrafast trio.) Note, however, that, as interviewee CJ pointed out to me, the possibilities of shifting from competition on speed to competition on price are limited in the many markets that are tick constrained (markets in which the normal difference in price between the highest bid and lowest offer is the minimum allowable increment in price). The choice of tick size is, as already noted, an example of mundane political economy, an apparent detail of the organization of a market that is in fact economically consequential.

22. Virtu's suggestion of fixed, equal wireless transmission times simply addresses a specific manifestation of these speed races, rather than their underlying causes.

23. As interviewees OX and OY pointed out to me, being protected by a speed bump from being picked off does somewhat reduce the disadvantage faced by an algorithm whose orders are at the back of queues, which is where much picking off happens.

24. As noted previously (see chapter 1), a dark pool is a private trading venue in which the order book is not visible to participants.

25. That, as readers familiar with the approach will be aware, would be an understanding wholly alien to the actor-network theory that is a crucial source of analytical attention to material politics.

26. After the 2010 flash crash, regulators also imposed tightened "circuit breakers" (pauses in share trading after extreme price moves, designed to allow human beings to do things like check whether there has been any news that might account for those movements and to give them the time to recalibrate and/or restart algorithmic trading systems), but it is impossible to be certain of the extent to which those circuit breakers—triggered, on a market-wide basis, four times in March 2020, and "[o]n some volatile days . . . hundreds of times" for individual stocks (Osipovich 2020)—helped protect automated markets.

27. Department of the Treasury et al. (2015: 23, 24, and figures 3.5 and 3.6).

28. My interviewee did not name either the HFT firm or the prime broker, but the episode closely resembles one that caused the Dutch bank Rabobank to close its foreign-exchange prime brokerage business in May 2014 (Szalay 2014).

29. My account of this episode is drawn from the investigation by the Securities and Exchange Commission (SEC 2013a).

30. I write "quasi-random" because it would be too narrow to think about this fluctuation as being caused only by stochastic aspects of the physical world, such as the heat-induced agitation of electrons. More broadly, jitter is speed fluctuation that a system's architects neither desire nor can fully control, and may not even fully understand.

31. For a fuller, but I hope still accessible, introduction to bitcoin mining, see MacKenzie (2019e). The best technical source that I know of on bitcoin is Narayanan et al. (2016).

32. My calculation follows the methodology of de Vries (2018). It begins with an estimate of the bitcoin network's total hash rate (in turn derived from the difficulty of the target and the average time taken to find an arbitrary parameter called a nonce [nowadays, usually two nonces; see MacKenzie 2019e] that generates a block hash that meets the target), and makes the assumption that all mining is done with equipment that is state-of-the-art in energy efficiency. It also assumes no electricity consumption for cooling. Those two assumptions mean that the estimate should be thought of as a lower bound on total electricity consumption. I took my rough estimate of the bitcoin network's fluctuating total hash rate (100 million TH/s) from https://www.blockchain.com /charts/hash-rate, accessed June 5, 2020. (A terahash or TH is a thousand billion applications of bitcoin's hashing algorithm.) The example of efficient equipment I used was Bitmain's S17e, which I assumed performed at the company's specifications (a hash rate of 60 TH/s and power consumption of 2.7 kW), taken from https://m.bitmain.com, accessed June 1, 2020.

33. I take the daily numbers of transactions from https://www.blockchain.com/charts/n -transactions, accessed June 10, 2020.

34. See https://newsroom.fb.com/company-info/, accessed June 5, 2020.

35. See https://www.google.com/about/datacenters/locations/, accessed June 5, 2020, and https://engineering.fb.com/data-center-engineering/data-centers-2018/, accessed November 3, 2019.

36. Cookies are small text files deposited in the browsers (and thus on the hard disks or memory chips) of the phones, tablets, or computers of those who visit websites, either by the

website owner's system (or, in the case of third-party cookies, by another firm). These cookies are included in subsequent request messages to the website from the user's browser, and thus serve as a record of the user's browsing. For an excellent analysis of cookies and their role in online advertising, see Mellet and Beauvisage (2019). In advertising, a pixel is a tiny transparent component of an ad that is copied into a user's computer, smartphone, etc., when that device loads the ad, and which then transfers information back to the advertiser and/or a data-gathering firm.

Appendix: A Note on the Literature on HFT

1. For a critique of *Flash Boys* by a former high-frequency trader, see Kovac (2014).

2. A good example of an early study—examining algorithmic trading as a whole, not HFT specifically—is Hendershott, Jones, and Menkveld (2011), who use electronic-message traffic on the New York Stock Exchange as a proxy for levels of algorithmic trading. They circumvent the problem of the endogeneity of traders' decisions to trade algorithmically rather than manually by examining the impact of a series of essentially exogenous events: the phasing in, by the NYSE, in 2003, in a series of steps planned well in advance, of automatic dissemination of changes to the prices of the best bid and offer in the NYSE's order book for a given stock. The resultant faster dissemination of data increased the attractiveness of algorithmic trading of the stocks covered by the rollout. (Changes in prices were previously input manually by specialists' clerks, who, as described in chapter 3, had difficulty keeping up at busy times.) Algorithmic trading, they find, "improves liquidity and enhances the informativeness of quotes" (Hendershott et al. 2011: 1).

3. See, e.g., Muniesa (2000a&b, 2003, 2005, 2007, and 2011), Scott and Barrett (2005), Barrett and Scott (2004), Pardo-Guerra (2010 and 2019), Castelle, Millo, Beunza, and Lubin (2016), Kennedy (2017), Mattli (2018 and 2019).

4. A useful more general—rather than "social studies of finance"—treatment of the history of electronic markets can be found in Gorham and Singh (2009).

5. It is also, for example, interesting to note that two traders interviewed for Lange and Borch (2014: 11) identify what I think can only be one of the mechanisms focused on in chapter 5, the tendency of "fill" messages to arrive before news of the corresponding trade on even an exchange's (especially the Chicago Mercantile Exchange's) fastest datafeed.

6. See the project website: http://info.cbs.dk/algofinance/, accessed June 6, 2020.

7. Quite unprompted by me, interviewee BT identified a plausible source of such episodes. He says that his HFT firm's algorithms could find themselves "right on a limit of a particular decision and kind of flip-flop around," placing orders at one price and almost immediately canceling them and replacing them with orders at a slightly different price. This did indeed lead to warnings from the trading venue in question, but BT says that programming algorithms so that they do not sometimes do this is highly demanding.

REFERENCES

Abbott, Andrew. 2005. "Linked Ecologies: States and Universities as Environments for Professions." *Sociological Theory* 23/3: 245–274.

———. n.d. "V: Ecologies and Fields." Available at http://home.uchicago.edu/aabbott/Papers /BOURD.pdf, accessed February 1, 2014.

Abolafia, Mitchel Y. 1996. *Making Markets: Opportunism and Restraint on Wall Street*. Cambridge, MA: Harvard University Press.

Adams, Charles W., Herbert R. Behrens, Jerome M. Pustilnik, and John T. Gilmore, Jr. 1971. "Instinet Communication System for Effectuating the Sale or Exchange of Fungible Properties between Subscribers." US patent 3,573,747, awarded April 6.

Adshead, Stephen, Grant Forsyth, Sam Wood, and Laura Wilkinson. 2019. "Online Advertising in the UK." Available at https://plumconsulting.co.uk/online-advertising-in-the-uk, accessed November 2, 2019.

AFME. 2017. *European Primary Dealers Handbook*. Available at https://www.afme.eu/globalassets /downloads/publications/afme-primary-dealers-handbook-q3-2017-3.pdf, accessed May 8, 2018.

Aldrich, Eric M., Joseph A. Grundfest, and Gregory Laughlin. 2017. "The Flash Crash: A New Deconstruction." Available at https://papers.ssrn.com/sol3/papers.cfm?abstract_id=2721922, accessed October 23, 2019.

Aldrich, Eric M., and Seung Lee. 2018. "Relative Spread and Price Discovery." Available at https:// ssrn.com/abstract=2772142, accessed May 6, 2018.

Anderson, Niki, Lewis Webber, Joseph Noss, Daniel Beale, and Liam Crowley-Reidy. 2015. "The Resilience of Financial Market Liquidity." Bank of England Financial Stability Paper 34. Available at https://www.bankofengland.co.uk/financial-stability-paper/2015/the-resilience-of -financial-market-liquidity, accessed January 10, 2018.

Angel, James J. 2011. "The Impact of Special Relativity on Securities Regulation." Available at https://assets.publishing.service.gov.uk/government/uploads/system/uploads/attachment _data/file/289020/11-1242-dr15-impact-of-special-relativity-on-securities-regulation.pdf, accessed September 17, 2019.

Angel, James J., Lawrence E. Harris, and Chester S. Spatt. 2013. "Equity Trading in the 21st Century: An Update." Available at https://www.q-group.org/wp-content/uploads/2014/01/Equity -Trading-in-the-21st-Century-An-Update-FINAL.pdf, accessed September 21, 2020.

anon. n.d. "The WATCHER guide." Available at http://josh.com/watcherm.htm, accessed January 27, 2012.

———. 1992. "EBS, Minex, Dealing 2000–2 Face Off in Battle of the FX Matching Systems." *FX Week*, June 5, 1992. Available at https://www.fxweek.com/fx-week/news/1541043/ebs -minex-dealing-2000-face-off-in-battle-of-the-fx-matching-systems, accessed May 22, 2019.

———. 1995–97. "WATCHER News Frame." Available at http://josh.com/wnews.txt, accessed September 21, 2020.

anon. n.d. 1999. "Chicago's Fallen Giants Make Progress of Sorts." *Euromoney*, December. Available at https://www.euromoney.com/article/b1320g6pzb11nc/chicagos-fallen-giants-make -progress-of-sorts, accessed September 21, 2020.

———. 2000. "Online Foreign Exchange: At Last, FX Online." *Economist*, August 19. Available at https://www.economist.com/finance-and-economics/2000/08/17/at-last-fx-online, accessed September 21, 2020.

———. 2013. "First Female NYSE Member Dies." Available at https://www.politico.com/story /2013/08/muriel-siebert-dies-at-80-nyse-095893, accessed September 21, 2020.

Aquilina, Matteo, Eric Budish, and Peter O'Neill. 2020. "Quantifying the High-Frequency Trading 'Arms Race': A Simple New Methodology and Estimates." Available at https://www.fca.org .uk/publication/occasional-papers/occasional-paper-50.pdf, accessed September 21, 2020.

Arjaliès, Diane-Laure, Philip Grant, Iain Hardie, Donald MacKenzie, and Ekaterina Svetlova. 2017. *Chains of Finance: How Investment Management Is Shaped*. Oxford: Oxford University Press.

Arnoldi, Jakob. 2016. "Computer Algorithms, Market Manipulation and the Institutionalization of High Frequency Trading." *Theory, Culture and Society* 33/1: 29–52.

Aspers, Patrik. 2007. "Theory, Reality, and Performativity in Markets." *American Journal of Economics and Sociology* 66/2: 379–98.

Bacidore, Jeff. 2020. "The IEX D-Limit Proposal: It's Good . . . But What If It's TOO Good?" Available at https://www.tradersmagazine.com/am/the-iex-d-limit-proposal-its-goodbut-what-if -its-too-good/, accessed January 13, 2020.

Baker, Charles H. 1908. *Life and Character of William Taylor Baker, President of the World's Columbian Exposition and of the Chicago Board of Trade*. New York: Premier.

Bank for International Settlements. 2018. "Monitoring of Fast-Paced Electronic Markets." September. Available at https://www.bis.org/publ/mktc10.pdf, accessed June 16, 2019.

Baron, Matthew, Jonathan Brogaard and Andrei Kirilenko. 2012. "The Trading Profits of High Frequency Traders." Typescript, November.

Barrett, Michael, and Susan Scott. 2004. "Electronic Trading and the Process of Globalization in Traditional Futures Exchanges: A Temporal Perspective." *European Journal of Information Systems* 13/1: 65–79.

Battalio, Robert, Shane A. Corwin, and Robert Jennings. 2016. "Can Brokers Have It All? On the Relation between Make-Take Fees and Limit Order Execution Quality." *Journal of Finance* 71/5: 2193–2238.

Belden, Glenn, John J. Brogan, Thomas C. O'Halleran, Burton J. Gutterman, John R. Kinsella, Michael B. Boyle, Alvin Chow, Bruce Phelps, and James White. 1990. "Simulated Pit Trading System." Patent Application PCT/US90/00877. Available at https://patentimages.storage .googleapis.com/f4/a3/bc/31949972ac3c07/WO1990010910A1.pdf, accessed October 14, 2019.

Bell, Brian, and John Van Reenen. 2013. "Bankers and their Bonuses." *Economic Journal* 124 (February): F1–F21.

Benos, Evangelos, and Satchit Sagade. 2016. "Price Discovery and the Cross-Section of High-Frequency Trading." *Journal of Financial Markets* 30: 44–77.

Berkowitz, Stephen A., Dennis E. Logue, and Eugene A. Noser. 1988. "The Total Cost of Transactions on the NYSE." *Journal of Finance* 43/1: 97–112.

Bernanke, Ben S. 2004. "The Great Moderation." Available at https://www.federalreserve.gov /boarddocs/speeches/2004/20040220/, accessed January 9, 2020.

Beunza, Daniel. 2019. *Taking the Floor: Models, Morals, and Management in a Wall Street Trading Room*. Princeton, NJ: Princeton University Press.

Beunza, Daniel, and Raghu Garud. 2007. "Calculators, Lemmings or Frame-Makers? The Intermediary Role of Securities Analysts." Pp. 13–39 in *Market Devices*, edited by Michel Callon, Yuval Millo, and Fabian Muniesa. Oxford: Blackwell.

Biais, Bruno, and Richard Green. 2019. "The Microstructure of the Bond Market in the 20th Century." *Review of Economic Dynamics* 33: 250–271.

Biais, Bruno, Christophe Bisière, and Chester Spatt. 2003. "Imperfect Competition in Financial Markets: ISLAND vs NASDAQ." Available at http://papers.ssrn.com/abstract=302398, accessed April 27, 2011.

Birch, Kean. 2020. "Technoscience Rent: Toward a Theory of *Rentiership* for Technoscientific Capitalism." *Science, Technology, & Human Values* 45/1: 3–33.

Blitz, James. 1993. "Foreign Exchange Dealers Enter the 21st Century." *Financial Times* September 13: 19.

Bloch, Marc. 1935. "Avènement et conquêtes du moulin à eau." *Annales d'Histoire Économique et Sociale* 7/36: 538–63.

———. 1967. *Land and Work in Medieval Europe: Selected Papers.* London: Routledge and Kegan Paul.

Blum, Andrew. 2012. *Tubes: Behind the Scenes at the Internet.* London: Penguin.

Borch, Christian. 2016. "High-Frequency Trading, Algorithmic Finance and the Flash Crash: Reflections on Eventalization." *Economy and Society* 45/3–4: 350–78.

———. 2020. *Social Avalanche: Crowds, Cities and Financial Markets.* Cambridge: Cambridge University Press.

Borch, Christian, and Ann-Christina Lange. 2017. "High-Frequency Trader Subjectivity: Emotional Attachment and Discipline in an Era of Algorithms." *Socio-Economic Review* 15/2: 283–306.

Borch, Christian, Kristian Bondo Hansen, and Ann-Christina Lange. 2015. "Markets, Bodies, and Rhythms: A Rhythmanalysis of Financial Markets from Open-Outcry Trading to High-Frequency Trading." *Environment and Planning D: Society and Space* 33/6: 1080–1097.

Bourdieu, Pierre. 1984. *Distinction: A Social Critique of the Judgement of Taste.* London: Routledge

———. 1996. *The Rules of Art: Genesis and Structure of the Literary Field.* Cambridge: Polity.

———. 1997. "Le champ économique." *Actes de la Recherche en Sciences Sociales* 119/Septembre: 48–66.

Brady Commission. 1988. *Report of the Presidential Task Force on Market Mechanisms.* Washington, DC: US Government Printing Office.

Brandt, Michael W., Kenneth A. Kavajecz, and Shane E. Underwood. 2007. "Price Discovery in the Treasury Futures Market." *Journal of Futures Markets* 27/1: 1021–1051.

Braun, B. 2018. "Central Banking and the Infrastructural Power of Finance: The Case of ECB Support for Repo and Securitization Markets." *Socio-Economic Review.* Early online.

Brekke, Dan. 1999. "Daytrading Places." *Wired* 7.07/July. Available at https://www.wired.com/1999/07/island-2/, accessed September 21, 2020.

Breiman, Leo. 2001. "Random Forests." *Machine Learning* 45/1: 5–32.

Brogaard, Jonathan A. 2010. "High-Frequency Trading and its Impact on Market Quality." Available at https://secure.fia.org/ptg-downloads/hft_trading.pdf, accessed September 21, 2020.

———. 2011. "High-Frequency Trading, Information, and Profits." Available at http://www.bis.gov.uk/foresight, accessed November 11, 2011.

Brogaard, Jonathan, Björn Hagströmer, Lars Nordén, and Ryan Riordan. 2015. "Trading Fast and Slow: Colocation and Liquidty." *Review of Financial Studies* 28/12: 3407–3433.

Brogaard, Jonathan, Terrence Hendershott, and Ryan Riordan. 2014. "High-Frequency Trading and Price Discovery." *Review of Financial Studies* 27/8: 2267–306.

Budish, Eric. 2016. "Investors' Exchange LLC Form 1 Application (Release No. 34–75925; File No. 10–222)." Available at https://www.sec.gov/comments/10-222/10222-371.pdf, accessed May 28, 2018.

Budish, Eric, Peter Cramton, and John Shim. 2015. "The High-Frequency Trading Arms Race: Frequent Batch Auctions as a Market Design Response." *Quarterly Journal of Economics* 130/4: 1547–621.

Budish, Eric, Robin S. Lee, and John J. Shim. 2019. "Will the Market Fix the Market? A Theory of Stock Exchange Competition and Innovation." Available at http://faculty.chicagobooth.edu/eric.budish/research/Stock-Exchange-Competition.pdf, accessed March 11, 2019.

Callon, Michel. 1986. "Some Elements of a Sociology of Translation: Domestication of the Scallops and the Fishermen of St. Brieuc Bay." Pp. 196–233 in John Law (Ed.), *Power, Action and Belief: A New Sociology of Knowledge?* London: Routledge & Kegan Paul.

———, ed.. 1998. *The Laws of the Markets.* Oxford: Blackwell.

Canales, Jimena. 2009. *A Tenth of a Second: A History.* Chicago: University of Chicago Press.

Castelle, Michael, Yuval Millo, Daniel Beunza, and David C. Lubin. 2016. "Where Do Electronic Markets Come From? Regulation and the Transformation of Financial Exchanges." *Economy and Society* 45/2: 166–200.

Cave, Tim. 2018. "MiFID II: Electronic Liquidity Providers, the SI Regime and the First RTS 27 Reports." Available at https://tabbforum.com/opinions/mifid-ii-electronic-liquidity-providers-the-si-regime-and-the-first-rts-27-reports/, accessed September 23, 2020.

———. 2019. "Meet Your (Market) Maker: Europe's ELP SIs Gain Ground." Available at https://tabbforum.com/opinions/meet-your-market-maker-europes-elp-sis-gain-ground, accessed November 6, 2019.

CFTC/SEC. 2010. "Findings Regarding the Market Events of May 6, 2010: Report of the Staffs of the CFTC and SEC to the Joint Advisory Committee on Emerging Regulatory Issues." Washington, DC: Commodity Futures Trading Commission and Securities and Exchange Commission, September 30.

Chao, Yong, Chen Yao, and Mao Ye. 2019. "Why Discrete Price Fragments U.S. Stock Exchanges and Disperses Their Fee Structures." *Review of Financial Studies* 32/3: 1068–1101.

Christie, William G., and Paul H. Schultz. 1994. "Why Do NASDAQ Market Makers Avoid Odd-Eighth Quotes?" *Journal of Finance* 49/5: 1813–1840.

Christie, William G., Jeffrey H. Harris, and Paul H. Schultz. 1994. "Why Did NASDAQ Market Makers Stop Avoiding Odd-Eighth Quotes?" *Journal of Finance* 49/5: 1841–1860.

Chung, Joanna, and Gillian Tett. 2006. "MTS Chief Hedges Bets on Global Expansion." *Financial Times*, October 19: 43.

———. 2007. "Hedge Funds are at the Gates of the Eurozone's Cosy Bond Club." *Financial Times*, March 13: 15.

CMA. 2019. "Online Platforms and Digital Advertising: Market Study Interim Report." UK Competitions and Markets Authority, December 18, 2019. Available at https://assets.publishing.service.gov.uk/media/5dfa0580ed915d0933009761/Interim_report.pdf, accessed February 9, 2020.

Cohen, Kalman J., Steven F. Maier, Robert A. Schwartz, and David K. Whitcomb. 1981. "Transaction Costs, Order Placement Strategy and Existence of the Bid-Ask Spread." *Journal of Political Economy* 89/2: 287–305.

Collier, Joe. 2002. "Lowcountry Firm among High-Tech's Best." *State*, August 26. Available at https://www.thestate.com/news/business/article14327990.html, accessed September 21, 2020.

Committee on Agriculture and Forestry, US Senate. 1974. *The Commodity Futures Trading Commission Act of 1974.* Washington, DC: US Government Printing Office.

Coombs, Nathan. 2016. "What Is an Algorithm? Financial Regulation in the Era of High-Frequency Trading." *Economy and Society* 45/2: 278–302.

Cowan, Ruth Schwartz. 1983. *More Work for Mother: The Ironies of Household Technology from the Open Hearth to the Microwave.* New York: Basic Books.

Crawford, Susan. 2019. "How Corning Makes Super-Pure Glass for Fiber-Optic Cable." Available at https://www.wired.com/story/corning-pure-glass-fiber-optic-cable/, accessed November 27, 2019.

Crawford, William. B. 1994. "CBOT Says Goodbye to Globex." *Chicago Tribune*, April 16. Available at http://articles.chicagotribune.com/1994-04-16/business/9404160076_1_globex-cbot-chicago-mercantile-exchange, accessed June 17, 2011.

Cummings, Dave. 2016. *Make the Trade: A Kansas City Entrepreneur Takes on Wall Street*. Kansas City, MO: self-published.

Dahl, Roald. 1964. *Charlie and the Chocolate Factory*. New York: Knopf.

Danner, Mark. 2017. "What He Could Do." *New York Review of Books* 64/5: 4–6.

Davies, Jessica. 2018. "GDPR Will Ultimately Be Good for the Industry: Guardian CRO Hamish Nicklin on 2019 Plans." Available at https://digiday.com/media/gdpr-will-ultimately-good-industry-guardian-cro-hamish-nicklin-2019-plans, accessed November 5, 2019.

de Goede, Marieke. 2005. *Virtue, Fortune, and Faith: A Genealogy of Finance*. Minneapolis: University of Minnesota Press.

Department of the Treasury, Securities and Exchange Commission, and Board of Governors of the Federal Reserve System. 1992. *Joint Report on the Government Securities Market*. Washington, DC: Government Printing Office.

Department of the Treasury, Board of Governors of the Federal Reserve System, Federal Reserve Bank of New York, Securities and Exchange Commission, and Commodity Futures Trading Commission. 2015. "The U.S. Treasury Market on October 15, 2014." Available at https://home.treasury.gov/system/files/276/joint-staff-report-the-us-treasury-market-on-10-15-2014.pdf, accessed September 21, 2020.

Detrixhe, John, and Sam Mamudi. 2015. "A New Fast Lane for Traders Spurs Plan to Thwart Exploiters." Available at https://www.bloomberg.com/news/articles/2015-08-13/a-new-fast-lane-for-traders-spurs-plan-to-thwart-exploiters, accessed May 28, 2020.

de Vries, Alex. 2018. "Bitcoin's Growing Energy Problem." *Joule* 2/5: 801–809.

Donlan, Thomas G. 1988. "Terrors of the Tube: Computerized Traders vs. Market Makers." *Barron's*, November 7. Available at https://professional.dowjones.com/factiva/, accessed September 21, 2020.

Dourish, Paul. 2017. *The Stuff of Bits: An Essay on the Materialities of Information*. Cambridge, MA: MIT Press.

du Gay, Paul, Yuval Millo, and Penelope Tuck. 2012. "Making Government Liquid: Shifts in Governance Using Financialisation as a Political Device." *Environment and Planning C* 30/6: 1083–1099.

du Gay, Paul, and Michael Pryke, eds. 2002. *Cultural Economy: Cultural Analysis and Commercial Life*. London: Sage.

Duhigg, Charles. 2009. "Stock Traders Find Speed Pays, in Milliseconds." *New York Times*, July 24. Available at https://www.nytimes.com/2009/07/24/business/24trading.html, accessed September 21, 2020.

Durbin, Michael. 2010. *All About High-Frequency Trading*. New York: McGraw-Hill.

Einstein, Albert. 1920. *Relativity: The Special and the General Theory*. London: Methuen.

Equinix. 2012. "Chicago's Financial Hub." Available at https://carlarweir.files.wordpress.com/2013/03/equinix-chicago_metro_report_6-26-2012.pdf, accessed November 8, 2019.

Eurex. 2020. "Introduction of a Framework to Confine Speculative Triggering and Recalibration of the ESU Fee Limits." Eurex circular 010/2020. Available at https://www.eurexchange.com/exchange-en/find/circulars/circular-1752276, accessed September 21, 2020.

Falloon, William. D. 1998. *Market Maker: A Sesquicentennial Look at the Chicago Board of Trade*. Chicago: Chicago Board of Trade.

Fligstein, Neil. 2001. *The Architecture of Markets*. Princeton, NJ: Princeton University Press.

Fligstein, Neil, and Doug McAdam. 2012. *A Theory of Fields*. Oxford: Oxford University Press.

Flood, Chris. 2020. "Costs to Borrow ETFs Jump as Volatility Spikes." *Financial Times* FTfm supplement, March 23: 2.

Foucault, Michel. 1991. "Governmentality." Pp. 87–104 in *The Foucault Effect: Studies in Governmentality*, edited by Graham Burchell, Colin Gordon, and Peter Miller. Chicago: University of Chicago Press.

———. 2008. *The Birth of Biopolitics: Lectures at the Collège de France, 1978–1979*. Basingstoke, Hants: Palgrave Macmillan.

Gabor, Daniela. 2016. "The (Impossible) Repo Trinity: The Political Economy of Repo Markets." *Review of International Political Economy* 23/6: 967–1000.

Galison, Peter. 2003. *Einstein's Clocks, Poincaré's Maps: Empires of Time*. New York: Norton.

Garman, Mark B. 1976. "Market Microstructure." *Journal of Financial Economics* 3/3: 257–275.

Godechot, Olivier. 2007. *Working rich: Salaires, bonus et appropriation du profit dans l'industrie financière*. Paris: La Découverte.

———. 2012. "Is Finance Responsible for the Rise in Wage Inequality in France?" *Socio-Economic Review* 10/3: 447–470.

———. 2013. "Financiarisation et fractures socio-spatiales." *L'Année sociologique* 63/1: 17–50.

Goldbach, Roman. 2015. "Asymmetric Influence in Global Banking Regulation." *Review of International Political Economy* 22/6: 1087–1127.

Golden, Paul. 2015. "FX Industry Divided on Randomization." *Euromoney*, November 12. Available at https://www.euromoney.com/article/b12kn5fbwc7j5g/fx-industry-divided-on-randomization, accessed September 21, 2020.

Goldman Sachs. 2014. 2013 Annual Report. Available at https://www.goldmansachs.com/investor-relations/financials/current/annual-reports/2013-annual-report-files/annual-report-2013.pdf, accessed September 17, 2019.

Gorham, Michael, and Nidhi Singh. 2009. *Electronic Exchanges: The Global Transformation from Pits to Bits*. Amsterdam: Elsevier.

Greising, David, and Laurie Morse. 1991. *Brokers, Bagmen, and Moles: Fraud and Corruption in the Chicago Futures Markets*. New York: Wiley.

Hagströmer, Björn, and Lars Nordén. 2013. The Diversity of High-Frequency Traders. *Journal of Financial Markets* 16/4: 741–770.

Harris, Jeffrey H., and Paul H. Schultz. 1998. "The Trading Profits of SOES Bandits." *Journal of Financial Economics* 50/1: 39–62.

Harris, Larry [Lawrence E.]. 2003. *Trading and Exchanges: Market Microstructure for Practitioners*. New York: Oxford University Press.

———. 2012. "Stop the High-Frequency Trader Arms Race." *Financial Times*, December 27. Available at https://www.ft.com/content/618c60de-4b80-11e2-88b5-00144feab49a, accessed January 31, 2020.

Harris, Lawrence E., and Venkatesh Panchapagesan. 2005. "The Information Content of the Limit Order Book: Evidence from NYSE Specialist Trading Decisions." *Journal of Financial Markets* 8/1: 25–67.

Harvey, David. 1989. *The Condition of Postmodernity: An Enquiry into the Origins of Cultural Change*. Oxford: Blackwell.

Hautcoeur, Pierre-Cyrille, and Angelo Riva. 2012. "The Paris Financial Market in the Nineteenth Century: Complementarities and Competition in Microstructures." *Economic History Review* 65/4: 1326–1353.

Hendershott, Terrence, Charles M. Jones, and Albert J. Menkveld. 2011. "Does Algorithmic Trading Improve Liquidity?" *Journal of Finance* 66/1: 1–37.

Hendershott, Terrence, and Pamela C. Moulton. 2011. "Automation, Speed, and Stock Market Quality: The NYSE's Hybrid." *Journal of Financial Markets* 14/4: 568–604.

Hicks, Alan. 1998. *Foreign Exchange Options: An International Guide to Currency Options Trading and Practice*. Cambridge: Woodhead.

Hobson, John M., and Leonard Seabrooke. 2007. "Everyday IPE: Revealing Everyday Forms of Change in the World Economy." Pp. 1–23 in *Everyday Politics of the World Economy*, edited by John M. Hobson and Leonard Seabrooke. Cambridge: Cambridge University Press.

Huth, John Michael. 2018. "A Clear Market Fairness Issue Requires a Clear, Collective Response." Available at https://www.realclearmarkets.com/articles/2018/02/14/a_clear_market_fairness_issue_requires_a_clear_collective_response_103150.html, accessed December 9, 2019.

Ingebretsen, Mark. 2002. *NASDAQ: A History of the Market That Changed the World*. Roseville, CA: Forum.

Instinet. 1988. "Customer Computer to Instinet Application Layer Specification, Version 2.6." May 6. In interviewee BT's private papers.

———. 2008. "Instinet Adds Chi-X Europe Equity Participants." Available at https://www.nomuraholdings.com/news/nr/europe/20080110/20080110.html, accessed July 23, 2019.

Jessop, Bob. 2009. "Cultural Political Economy and Critical Policy Studies." *Critical Policy Studies* 3/3–4: 336–356.

Johnson, Neil, Guannan Zhao, Eric Hunsader, Hong Qi, Nicholas Johnson, Jing Meng, and Brian Birnan. 2013. "Abrupt Rise of New Machine Ecology beyond Human Response Time." *Scientific Reports* 3/2627: 1–7.

Kawaller, Ira G., Paul D. Koch, and Timothy W. Koch. 1987. "The Temporal Price Relationship between S&P 500 Futures and the S&P 500 Index." *Journal of Finance* 42/5: 1309–1329.

Kennedy, Devin. 2017. "The Machine in the Market: Computers and the Infrastructure of Price at the New York Stock Exchange, 1965–1975." *Social Studies of Science* 47/6: 888–917.

King, Elizabeth K. 2020. Letter to Vanessa Countryman, Securities and Exchange Commission, May 8. Available at https://www.sec.gov/comments/sr-nyse-2020-05/srnyse202005.htm, accessed June 1, 2020.

Kluttz, Daniel, and Neil Fligstein. 2016. "Varieties of Sociological Field Theory." Pp. 185–204 in *Handbook of Contemporary Sociological Theory*, edited by Seth Abrutyn. Basel: Springer.

Knorr Cetina, Karin. 2007. "Global Markets as Global Conversations." *Text and Talk* 27/5–6: 705–734.

Knorr Cetina, Karin, and Urs Bruegger. 2002a. "Global Microstructures: The Virtual Societies of Financial Markets." *American Journal of Sociology* 107/4: 905–951.

———. 2002b. "Traders' Engagement with Markets: A Postsocial Relationship." *Theory, Culture and Society* 19/5–6: 161–185.

Kovac, Peter. 2014. *Flash Boys: Not So Fast. An Insider's Perspective on High-Frequency Trading*. N.p.: Directissima Press.

Kynaston, David. 1997. *LIFFE: A Market and its Makers*. Cambridge: Granta.

Lange, Ann-Christina. 2016. "Organizational Ignorance: An Ethnographic Study of High-Frequency Trading." *Economy and Society* 45/2: 230–250.

Lange, Ann-Christina, and Christian Borch. 2014. "Contagious Markets: On Crowd Psychology and High-Frequency Trading." Available at http://www.nanex.net/aqck2/Contagious.Markets.pdf, accessed January 31, 2019.

Lariviere, David Alan, Bernard Pieter Hosman, Pearce Ian Peck-Walden, Ari L. Studnitzer, Zachary Bonig, and Manmathasivaram Nagarajan. 2018. "Message Processing Protocol which Mitigates Optimistic Messaging Behavior." US patent application 2018/0183901 A1. Available at https://patents.google.com/patent/US20180183901A1/en, accessed March 23, 2020.

Latour, Bruno. 1999. *Pandora's Hope: Essays on the Reality of Science Studies*. Cambridge, MA: Harvard University Press.

———. 2005. *Reassembling the Social: An Introduction to Actor-Network-Theory*. Oxford: Oxford University Press.

Laughlin, Gregory. 2014. "Insights into High Frequency Trading from the Virtu Initial Public Offering." Available at https://online.wsj.com/public/resources/documents/VirtuOverview.pdf, accessed September 16, 2019.

Laughlin, Gregory, Anthony Aguirre, and Joseph Grundfest. 2014. "Information Transmission between Financial Markets in Chicago and New York." *Financial Review* 49/2: 283–312.

Laumonier, Alexandre. 2019. *4*. Brussels: Zones sensibles.

Law, John, and Annemarie Mol. 2008. "Globalisation in Practice: On the Politics of Boiling Pig-swill." *Geoforum* 39/1: 133–143.

Lemoine, Benjamin. 2013. "Les 'dealers' de la dette souveraine: Politique des transactions entre banques et état dans la grande distribution des emprunts Français." *Sociétés Contemporaines* 92/4: 59–88.

Lemov, Michael R. 2011. *People's Warrior: John Moss and the Fight for Freedom of Information and Consumer Rights*. Madison, NJ: Fairleigh Dickinson University Press.

Lenglet, Marc. 2011. "Conflicting Codes and Codings: How Algorithmic Trading Is Reshaping Financial Regulation." *Theory, Culture & Society* 28/6: 44–66.

Lenglet, Marc, and Joeri Mol. 2016. "Squaring the Speed of Light? Regulating Market Access in Algorithmic Finance." *Economy and Society* 45/2: 201–229.

Levine, Josh. n.d. "Island ECN 10th Birthday Source Code Release!" Available at http://www.josh.com/notes/island-ecn-10th-birthday, accessed August 13, 2012.

Levy, Jonathan Ira. 2006. "Contemplating Delivery: Futures Trading and the Problem of Commodity Exchange in the United States, 1875–1905." *American Historical Review* 111/2: 307–335.

Levy, Steven. 1984. *Hackers: Heroes of the Computer Revolution*. Garden City, NY: Anchor Doubleday.

Lewis, Michael. 1990. *Liar's Poker: Rising through the Wreckage on Wall Street*. New York: Penguin.

———. 2014. *Flash Boys: Cracking the Money Code*. London: Penguin.

Liu, Nian, and Ryan McMorrow. 2019. "Bitmain Civil War Breaks into the Open." *Financial Times*, November 8: 16.

Louis, Brian. 2017. "Trading Fortunes Depend on a Mysterious Antenna in an Empty Field." Available at https://www.bloomberg.com/news/articles/2017-05-12/mysterious-antennas-outside-cme-reveal-traders-furious-land-war, accessed November 24, 2018.

Lucchetti, Aaron. 2006. "Fast Lane: Firms Seek Edge Through Speed as Computer Trading Expands." *Wall Street Journal*, December 15. Available at https://www.wsj.com/articles/SB116615315551251136, accessed September 21, 2020.

Lucent Technologies. 1998. "True Wave® RS Nonzero-Dispersion Optical Fiber." Available at http://www.worldonecom.com/fibercable/truewave.pdf, accessed June 30, 2015.

MacKenzie, Donald. 1984. "Marx and the Machine." *Technology and Culture* 25/3: 473–502.

———. 2006. *An Engine, Not a Camera: How Financial Models Shape Markets*. Cambridge, MA: MIT Press.

———. 2014. "Be Grateful for Drizzle." *London Review of Books* 36/17: 27–30.

———. 2015. "Mechanizing the Merc: The Chicago Mercantile Exchange and the Rise of High-Frequency Trading." *Technology and Culture* 56/3: 646–675.

———. 2016. "Must Do Better." *London Review of Books* 38/9: 29.

———. 2017a. "A Material Political Economy: Automated Trading Desk and Price Prediction in High-Frequency Trading." *Social Studies of Science* 47/2: 172–194.

———. 2017b. "Capital's Geodesic: Chicago, New Jersey, and the Material Sociology of Speed." Pp. 55–71 in *The Sociology of Speed: Digital, Organizational, and Social Temporalities*, edited by Judy Wajcman and Nigel Dodd. Oxford: Oxford University Press.

———. 2018a. "'Making', 'Taking' and the Material Political Economy of Algorithmic Trading." *Economy and Society* 47/4: 501–23.

———. 2018b. "Material Signals: A Historical Sociology of High-Frequency Trading." *American Journal of Sociology* 123/6: 1635–1683.

———. 2019a. "How Algorithms Interact: Goffman's 'Interaction Order' in Automated Trading." *Theory, Culture & Society* 36/2: 39–59.

———. 2019b. "How Fragile is Competition in High-Frequency Trading?" Available at https://tabbforum.com/opinions/how-fragile-is-competition-in-high-frequency-trading/, accessed March 26, 2019.

———. 2019c. "Just How Fast?" *London Review of Books* 41/5: 23–24.

———. 2019d. "Market Devices and Structural Dependency: The Origins and Development of 'Dark Pools.'" *Finance and Society* 5/1: 1–19.

———. 2019e. "Pick a Nonce and Try a Hash." *London Review of Books* 41/8: 35–38.

MacKenzie, Donald, Daniel Beunza, Yuval Millo, and Juan Pablo Pardo-Guerra. 2012. "Drilling through the Allegheny Mountains: Liquidity, Materiality and High-Frequency Trading." *Journal of Cultural Economy* 5/3: 279–295.

MacKenzie, Donald, Iain Hardie, Charlotte Rommerskirchen, and Arjen van der Heide. 2020. "Why Hasn't High-Frequency Trading Swept the Board? Shares, Sovereign Bonds, and the Politics of Market Structure." *Review of International Political Economy*, early online.

MacKenzie, Donald, and Juan Pablo Pardo-Guerra. 2014. "Insurgent Capitalism: Island, Bricolage and the Re-Making of Finance." *Economy and Society* 43/2: 153–82.

MacKenzie, Donald, and Judy Wajcman, eds. 1985. *The Social Shaping of Technology*. Milton Keynes, England: Open University Press.

———, eds. 1999. *The Social Shaping of Technology*. Second edition. Buckingham, England: Open University Press.

Mackintosh, Phil. 2014. "Demystifying Order Types." Knight Capital Getco, September. Available at https://www.kcg.com/uploads/documents/KCG_Demystifying-Order-Types_092414.pdf, accessed October 1, 2016.

Madhavan, Ananth. 2000. "Market Microstructure: A Survey." *Journal of Financial Markets* 3/3: 205–258.

———. 2012. "Exchange-Traded Funds, Market Structure and the Flash Crash." Available at http://ssrn.com/abstract=1932925, accessed December 30, 2012.

Madhavan, Ananth, and Venkatesh Panchapagesan. 2000. "Price Discovery in an Auction Market: A Look inside the Black Box." *Review of Financial Studies* 13/3: 627–658.

Manning, Trevor. 2009. *Microwave Radio Transmission Design Guide*. Norwood, MA: Artech.

Marx, Karl. 1976. *Capital: A Critique of Political Economy. Vol. 1*. Harmondsworth, Middlesex: Penguin.

Mattli, Walter, ed. 2018. *Global Algorithmic Capital Markets: High Frequency Trading, Dark Pools, and Regulatory Challenges*. Oxford: Oxford University Press.

———. 2019. *Darkness by Design: The Hidden Power in Global Capital Markets*. Princeton, NJ: Princeton University Press.

Mavroudis, Vasilios. 2019. "Bounded Temporal Fairness for FIFO Financial Markets." Available at https://arxiv.org/abs/1911.09209, accessed May 28, 2020.

Mavroudis, Vasilios, and Hayden Melton. 2019. "Libra: Fair Order-Matching for Electronic Financial Exchanges." Pp. 156–68 in Association for Computing Machinery, *AFT '19: Conference on Advances in Financial Technologies, October 21–23, 2019, Zurich, Switzerland*. New York: Association for Computing Machinery.

McCormick, Liz. 2019. "The Treasury's Secretive Bond Whisperers Are More Crucial Than Ever." Available at https://www.bloomberg.com/news/articles/2019-01-29/treasury-s-secretive-bond-whisperers-are-more-crucial-than-ever, accessed September 21, 2020.

McInish, Thomas, James Upson, and Robert Wood. 2012. "The Flash Crash: Trading Aggressiveness, Liquidity Supply, and the Impact of Intermarket Sweep Orders." Available at https://papers.ssrn.com/sol3/papers.cfm?abstract_id=1629402, accessed September 21, 2020.

McKay Brothers. 2020. Letter to Vanessa Countryman, Securities and Exchange Commission, March 10. Available at https://www.sec.gov/comments/sr-nyse-2020-05/srnyse202005.htm, accessed June 1, 2020.

Meeker, J. Edward. 1930. *The Work of the Stock Exchange*, rev.ed. New York: Ronald Press.

Melamed, Leo. 1977. "The Mechanics of a Commodity Futures Exchange: A Critique of Automation of the Transaction Process." *Hofstra Law Review* 6/1: 149–172.

———. 1987. *The Tenth Planet*. Chicago: Bonus Books.

———. 2009. *For Crying out Loud: From Open Outcry to the Electronic Screen*. Hoboken, NJ: Wiley.

Melamed, Leo, and Bob Tamarkin. 1996. *Leo Melamed: Escape to the Futures*. New York: Wiley.

Mellet, Kevin, and Thomas Beauvisage. 2019. "Cookie Monsters: Anatomy of a Digital Market Infrastructure." *Consumption Markets & Culture*, early online.

Melton, Hayden. 2017. "Market Mechanism Refinement on a Continuous Limit Order Book Venue: A Case Study." *ACM SIGecom Exchanges* 16/1: 74–79.

Menkveld, Albert J. 2013. "High Frequency Trading and the *New Market* Makers." *Journal of Financial Markets* 16/4: 712–40.

———. 2016. "The Economics of High-Frequency Trading: Taking Stock." *Annual Review of Financial Economics* 8: 1–24.

Meyer, Gregory. 2015. "Political Clout Counts." *Financial Times*, November 19: 11.

Meyer, Gregory, and Nicole Bullock. 2017. "Algo Traders Look Beyond Need for Speed in Quest to Gain Competitive Edge." *Financial Times*, March 31: 28.

Meyer, Gregory, Nicole Bullock, and Joe Rennison. 2018. "Speed Bump." *Financial Times*, January 2: 9.

Millo, Yuval. 2007. "Making Things Deliverable: The Origins of Index-Based Derivatives." Pp. 196–214 in *Market Devices*, edited by Michel Callon, Yuval Millo, and Fabian Muniesa. Oxford: Blackwell.

Millo, Yuval, Fabian Muniesa, Nikiforos S. Panourgias, and Susan V. Scott. 2005. "Organized Detachment: Clearinghouse Mechanisms in Financial Markets." *Information and Organization* 15/3: 229–246.

Ministero dell'Economia e delle Finanze. 2017. "The Secondary Market for Italian Government Securities." Presentation to World Bank Conference, Washington, DC. Available at http://pubdocs.worldbank.org/en/625091493405007505/bonds-conf-2017-Davide-WB-conference-Italy-experience-on-ETPs.pdf, accessed January 2, 2019

Moloney, Niamh. 2014. *EU Securities and Financial Markets Regulation*. Oxford: Oxford University Press.

Moore, Michael, Andreas Schrimpf, and Vladyslav Sushko. 2016. "Downsized FX Markets: Causes and Implications." *BIS Quarterly Review*, December: 35–51.

Morgenson, Gretchen. 1993. "Fun and Games on Nasdaq." *Forbes*, August 16: 74–80.

MTS Group. 2003. *The Liquidity Pact: Enhancing Efficiency in the European Bond Market*. Originally available at http://www.mtsgroup/newcontent/news/d_new/the_liquidity_pact_mts.pdf, accessed November 1, 2007.

Mügge, Daniel. 2006. "Reordering the Marketplace: Competition Politics in European Finance." *Journal of Common Market Studies* 44/5: 991–1022.

Muniesa, Fabian. 2000a. "Performing Prices: The Case of Price Discovery Automation in the Financial Markets." Pp. 289–312 in *Ökonomie und Gesellschaft, Jahrbuch 16. Facts and Figures: Economic Representations and Practices*, edited by Herbert Kalthoff, Richard Rottenburg, and Hans-Jürgen Wagener. Marburg: Metropolis.

———. 2000b. "Un robot Walrasien: Cotation électronique et justesse de la découverte des prix." *Politix* 13/52: 121–154.

———. 2003. "Des marchés comme algorithmes: Sociologie de la cotation électronique à la Bourse de Paris." PhD thesis: École Nationale Supérieure des Mines.

———. 2005. "Contenir le marché: La transition de la criée à la cotation électronique à la Bourse de Paris." *Sociologie du travail* 47/4: 485–501.

———. 2007. "Market Technologies and the Pragmatics of Prices." *Economy and Society* 36/3: 377–395.

———. 2011. "Is a Stock Exchange a Computer Solution? Explicitness, Algorithms and the Arizona Stock Exchange." *International Journal of Actor-Network Theory and Technological Innovation* 3/1: 1–15.

Narayanan, Arvind, Joseph Bonneau, Edward Felten, Andrew Miller, and Steven Goldfeder. 2016. *Bitcoin and Cryptocurrency Technologies: A Comprehensive Introduction.* Princeton, NJ: Princeton University Press.

Nasdaq OMX. 2009. "Market Pathfinders Data Feed." Originally available at https://www.nasdaqtrader.com/content, accessed November 16, 2017.

New York State Department of Financial Services. 2015. "New York State Department of Financial Services in the Matter of Barclays Bank PLC, Barclays Bank PLC, New York Branch: Consent Order Under New York Banking Law." Available at https://www.dfs.ny.gov/system/files/documents/2020/04/ea151117_barclays.pdf, accessed September 21, 2020.

Neyland, Daniel, Véra Ehrenstein, and Sveta Milyaeva. 2018. "Mundane Market Matters: From Ordinary to Profound and Back Again." *Journal of Cultural Economy* 11/5: 377–385.

O'Hara, Maureen. 1997. *Market Microstructure Theory.* Oxford: Blackwell.

Oman, Charles. 1906. *The Great Revolt of 1381.* Oxford: Clarendon.

Osipovich, Alexander. 2018. "High-Speed Traders Profit From Return of Loophole at CME." *Wall Street Journal,* February 12. Available at https://www.wsj.com/articles/glitch-exploited-by-high-speed-traders-is-back-at-cme-1518431401, accessed December 9, 2019.

———. 2019a. "NYSE Antennas Spark High-Speed Trader Backlash." *Wall Street Journal,* August 8. Available at https://www.wsj.com/articles/nyse-antennas-spark-high-speed-trader-backlash-11565272102, accessed August 13, 2019.

———. 2019b. "Thinning Liquidity in Key Futures Market Worries Traders." *Wall Street Journal,* March 25. Available at https://wsj.com/articles/thinning-liquidity-in-key-futures-market-worries-traders-11553515200, accessed December 24, 2019.

———. 2020. "Post-Flash Crash Fixes Bolstered Markets during Coronavirus Selloff." *Wall Street Journal,* May 5. Available at https://www.wsj.com/articles/post-flash-crash-fixes-bolstered-markets-during-coronavirus-selloff-11588671000, accessed May 5, 2020.

Pagliari, Stefano, and Kevin Young. 2016. "The Interest Ecology of Financial Regulation: Interest Group Plurality in the Design of Financial Regulatory Policies." *Socio-Economic Review* 14/2: 309–337.

Pardo-Guerra, Juan Pablo. 2010. "Creating Flows of Interpersonal Bits: The Automation of the London Stock Exchange, c. 1955–90." *Economy and Society* 39/1: 84–109.

———. 2019. *Automating Finance: Infrastructures, Engineers, and the Making of Electronic Markets.* Cambridge: Cambridge University Press.

Patterson, Scott. 2012. *Dark Pools: High-Speed Traders, A.I. Bandits, and the Threat to the Global Financial System.* New York: Crown.

Patterson, Scott, Jenny Strasburg, and Liam Pleven. 2013. "Speedy Traders Exploit Loophole." *Wall Street Journal,* May 1: 1–2.

Persaud, Avinash D. 2006. "Improving Efficiency in the European Government Bond Market." London: ICAP and Intelligence Capital. Available at https://www.finextra.com/finextra-downloads/newsdocs/icapnov2006.pdf, accessed January 2, 2019.

Philippon, Thomas. 2015. "Has the US Finance Industry Become Less Efficient? On the Theory and Measurement of Financial Intermediation." *American Economic Review* 105/4: 1408–1438.

Philippon, Thomas. 2019. *The Great Reversal: How America Gave Up on Free Markets.* Cambridge, MA: Belknap.

Philips, Matthew. 2013. "How the Robots Lost: High-Frequency Trading's Rise and Fall." *Bloomberg Businessweek*, June 10–16. Available at http://www.bloomberg.com/bw/articles/2013-06-06/how-the-robots-lost-high-frequency-tradings-rise-and-fall, accessed January 18, 2016.

Pidgeon, David. 2016. "Where Did the Money Go? Guardian Buys Its Own Ad Inventory." Available at https://mediatel.co.uk/newsline/2016/10/04/where-did-the-money-go-guardian-buys-its-own-ad-inventory, accessed August 7, 2019.

Pinder, Jeanne B. 1993. "Downtown's Empty Feeling." *New York Times*, May 9. Available at https://www.nytimes.com/1993/05/09/business/downtown-s-empty-feeling.html, accessed July 14, 2019.

Preda, Alex. 2009. *Framing Finance: The Boundaries of Markets and Modern Capitalism.* Chicago: University of Chicago Press.

———. 2013. "Tags, Transaction Types and Communication in Online Anonymous Markets." *Socio-Economic Review* 11/1: 31–56.

———. 2017. *Noise: Living and Trading in Electronic Finance.* Chicago: University of Chicago Press.

Quaglia, Lucia. 2010. "Completing the Single Market in Financial Services: The Politics of Competing Advocacy Coalitions." *Journal of European Public Policy* 17/7: 1007–1023.

Read, Donald 1999. *The Power of News: The History of Reuters.* Oxford: Oxford University Press.

Rennison, Joe. 2014. "The Great Swaps Market Carve-Up." *Risk*, March: 14–18.

Roeder, David. 2004. "Eurex Chief Insists Exchange in U.S. for Long Haul." *Chicago Sun Times*, April 23. Originally available at http://www.highbeam.com, accessed January 11, 2012.

Ross, Alice, and Philip Stafford. 2012. "Rage against the Machine as Forex Traders Fight Back." *Financial Times*, July 12: 32.

Rowen, Harvey A. n.d. "The Securities Activities of the Subcommittee on Commerce and Finance of the Committee on Interstate and Foreign Commerce United States House of Representatives 1971–1975." Available at http://www.johnemossfoundation.org/h_rowen.htm, accessed June 13, 2016.

Ruggins, Sarah M. E. 2017. *Building Blocks: A Historical Sociology of the Innovation and Regulation of Exchange Traded Funds in the United States, 1970–2000.* PhD thesis: University of Edinburgh.

S&P ComStock. 1990. "Interrogation Mode Specifications, Version 1.0.0." August. In interviewee BT's private papers.

Salzinger, Leslie. 2016. "Re-Marking Men: Masculinity as a Terrain of the Neoliberal Economy." *Critical Historical Studies* 31/1: 1–25.

Scott, Susan V., and Michael I. Barrett. 2005. "Strategic Risk Positioning as Sensemaking in Crisis: The Adoption of Electronic Trading at the London International Financial Futures and Options Exchange." *Strategic Information Systems* 14/1: 45–68.

Schifrin, Matthew, and Scott McCormack. 1998. "Free Enterprise Comes to Wall Street." *Forbes*, April 6. Available at https://www.forbes.com/forbes/1998/0406/6107114a.html#18473b5d5300, accessed September 21, 2020.

Schrimpf, Andreas, Hyun Song Shin, and Vladyslav Sushko. 2020. "Leverage and Margin Spirals in Fixed Income Markets during the Covid-19 Crisis." Bank for International Settlements, Bulletin No. 2, April 2. Available at https://www.bis.org/publ/bisbull02.pdf, accessed April 20, 2020.

Seabrooke, Leonard, and Eleni Tsingou. 2009. "Revolving Doors and Linked Ecologies in the World Economy: Policy Locations and Practice of International Financial Reform." Available at http://wrap.warwick.ac.uk/1849/, accessed December 27, 2014.

SEC. 1963. *Report of Special Study of Securities Markets of the Securities and Exchange Commission.* Washington, DC: Government Printing Office.

———. 1971. *Study of Unsafe and Unsound Practices of Brokers and Dealers.* Washington, DC: Government Printing Office.

———. 2005. "17 CFR Parts 200, 201, et al.: Regulation NMS; Final Rule." *Federal Register* 70/124: 37496–37644.

———. 2013a. "In the Matter of Knight Capital Americas LLC, Respondent." Available at http://www.sec.gov/litigation/admin/2013/34-70694.pdf, accessed May 7, 2014.

———. 2013b. "Self-Regulatory Organizations; The NASDAQ Stock Market LLC: Order Approving a Proposed Rule Change to Establish a New Optional Wireless Connectivity for Colocated Clients (Release No. 34–68735; File No. SR-NASDAQ-2012–119)." Available at https://www.sec.gov/rules/sro/nasdaq/2013/34-68735.pdf, accessed January 17, 2017.

———. 2015. "Self-Regulatory Organizations; New York Stock Exchange LLC: Notice of Filing of Proposed Rule Change to the Co-location Services Offered by the Exchange (the Offering of a Wireless Connection to Allow Users to Receive Market Data Feeds from Third Party Markets) and to Reflect Changes to the Exchange's Price List Related to These Services (Release No. 34–76374; File No. SR-NYSE-2015–52)." Available at https://www.sec.gov/rules/sro/nyse/2015/34-76374.pdf, accessed January 17, 2017.

———. 2017. "Self-Regulatory Organizations; The Nasdaq Stock Market LLC: Notice of Filing and Immediate Effectiveness of Proposed Rule Change to Amend the Exchange Fees at Rules 7023, 7044, 7045 and 7048 to Withdraw Four Rarely-Purchased Products From Sale (Release No. 34–82302; File No. SR-NASDAQ-2017–126)." Available at https://www.sec.gov/rules/sro/nasdaq/2017/34-82302.pdf, accessed August 2, 2019.

———. 2019a. "Self-Regulatory Organizations; Cboe EDGA Exchange, Inc.: Notice of Filing of a Proposed Rule Change to Introduce a Liquidity Provider Protection on EDGA (Release No 34–86168; File No. SR-CboeEDGA-2019–012)." Available at https://www.sec.gov/rules/sro/cboeedga/2019/34-86168.pdf, accessed October 7, 2019.

———. 2019b. "Self-Regulatory Organizations; Investors Exchange LLC: Notice of Filing of Proposed Rule Change to Add a New Discretionary Limit Order Type (Release No. 34–87814; File No. SR-IEX-2019–15)." Available at https://www.sec.gov/rules/sro/iex/2019/34-87814.pdf, accessed September 21, 2020.

———. 2020. "Self-Regulatory Organizations; Cboe EDGA Exchange, Inc.: Order Disapproving Proposed Rule Change to Introduce a Liquidity Provider Protection Delay Mechanism on EDGA (Release No. 34–88261; File No. SR-CboeEDGA-2019–012)." Available at https://www.sec.gov/rules/sro/cboeedga/2020/34-88261.pdf, accessed May 29, 2020.

Securities Acts Amendments. 1975. "Public Law 94–29, 94th Congress, June 4." Available at https://www.gpo.gov/fdsys/pkg/STATUTE-89/pdf/STATUTE-89-Pg97.pdf, accessed December 20, 2016.

Seligman, Joel. 1982. *The Transformation of Wall Street: A History of the Securities and Exchange Commission and Modern Corporate Finance.* Boston: Houghton Mifflin.

Seyfert, Robert. 2016. "Bugs, Predations or Manipulations? Incompatible Epistemic Regimes of High-Frequency Trading." *Economy and Society* 45/2: 251–277.

Shkilko, Andriy, and Konstantin Sokolov. 2016. "Every Cloud Has a Silver Lining: Fast Trading, Microwave Connectivity and Trading Costs." Available at https://ssrn.com/abstract=2848562, accessed July 19, 2017.

Smith, Jeffrey W., James P. Selway, and D. Timothy McCormick. 1998. "The Nasdaq Stock Market: Historical Background and Current Operation." NASD Working Paper 98–01. Washington, DC: NASD Department of Economic Research.

Smith, Neal. 1996. *Mr. Smith Went to Washington: From Eisenhower to Clinton.* Ames: Iowa State University Press.

Smith, Robert Mackenzie. 2015. "Client List Reveals HFT Dominance on BrokerTec." *Risk*, October: 4.

Smith, Robert Mackenzie. 2016. "Clearing Hurdles." *Risk*, July: 42–44.

Souleles, Daniel. 2019. "The Distribution of Ignorance on Financial Markets." *Economy and Society* 48/4: 510–531.

Stafford, Philip. 2017. "Suitors Unlikely to Pick Up LSE or Deutsche Börse on Rebound." *Financial Times*, March 31: 28.

———. 2019a. "Futures Exchanges Eye Shift to 'Flash Boys' Speed Bumps." *Financial Times*, May 30: 25.

———. 2019b. "MEMX Turns Up the Heat on US Stock Exchanges." *Financial Times*, January 10: 25.

Stafford, Philip, and Nicole Bullock. 2017. "High-Speed Traders Fight to Keep Edge." *Financial Times*, April 26: 26.

Stafford, Philip, and Alice Ross. 2012. "Forex Brokers Curb Ultra-Fast Traders." *Financial Times*, July 11: 32.

Steiner, Christopher. 2012. *Automate This: How Algorithms Came to Rule Our World*. New York: Penguin.

Stockland, Eric. 2017. "Enough Is Enough." *Traders Magazine Online News*, November 14. Available at http://e.tradersmagazine.com/news/ecns_and_exchanges/enough-is-enough-116932 -1.html, accessed August 3, 2019.

Swanson, Steven D., and David K. Whitcomb. 2004. "Letter to ATD Shareholders." March 10. David Whitcomb, private papers.

Szalay, Eve. 2014. "Black Phoenix Glitch Highlights PB Dangers." Available at https://www.fx -markets.com/foreign-exchange/2346495/black-phoenix-glitch-highlights-pb-dangers, accessed June 20, 2020.

Tabb, Larry. 2016. "Speedbump Markets: Don't Get Burned." June 14. Available at https://tabbforum .com/opinions/speedbump-markets-dont-get-burned/, accessed September 21, 2020.

Tamarkin, Bob. 1993. *The Merc: The Emergence of a Global Financial Powerhouse*. New York: HarperCollins.

Taylor, Jack. 2015. "The Brit Beating the Forex Flash Boys in Less Time than the Blink of an Eye." Available at https://www.thetimes.co.uk/article/the-brit-beating-the-forex-flash-boys-in-less -time-than-the-blink-of-an-eye-2bct3mmmnl5, accessed June 10, 2019.

Tett, Gillian. 2019. "Family Offices Are Diving into New Markets." *Financial Times*, August 2: 11.

Thiemann, Matthias. 2014. "In the Shadow of Basel: How Competitive Politics Bred the Crisis." *Review of International Political Economy* 21/6: 1203–1239.

Thiemann, Matthias, and Jan Lepoutre. 2017. "Stitched on the Edge: Rule Evasion, Embedded Regulators, and the Evolution of Markets." *American Journal of Sociology* 122/6: 1775–1821.

Tomaskovic-Devey, Donald, and Ken-Hou Lin. 2011. "Income Dynamics, Economic Rents, and the Financialization of the U.S. Economy." *American Sociological Review* 76/4: 538–559.

Tyč, Stéphane. 2016. "Exchanges vs Networks: The Intensifying Competition between Determinism and Speed." Available at https://www.mckay-brothers.com/exchanges-vs-networks/, accessed August 12, 2019.

———. 2018. "Private vs Public Feeds: The Role of Transport." Available at https://www.quincy -data.com/trading-show-new-york-2018, accessed December 4, 2019.

UK Government Office for Science. 2012. "Foresight: The Future of Computer Trading in Financial Markets. Final Project Report." Available at https://assets.publishing.service.gov.uk /government/uploads/system/uploads/attachment_data/file/289431/12-1086-future-of -computer-trading-in-financial-markets-report.pdf, accessed December 28, 2019.

US Court of Appeals. 1993. "William Timpinaro, et al. v. Securities and Exchange Commission, 2F.3d 453." Available at https://law.justia.com/cases/federal/appellate-courts/F3/2/453 /615751/, accessed September 21, 2020.

Van Valzah, Bob. 2018. "Shortwave Trading." Available at https://stacresearch.com/system/files /resource/files/STAC-Summit-13-Jun-2018-Shortwave-Trading.pdf, accessed June 16, 2020.

Vaughan, Liam. 2020. *Flash Crash*. London: Collins.

Virtu Financial, Inc. 2014. Form S-1: Registration Statement under the Securities Act of 1933. Available at https://www.sec.gov/Archives/edgar, accessed August 6, 2014.

———. 2019a. 2018 Annual Report. Available at http://ir.virtu.com/financials-and-filings/annual -reports-and-proxies/default.aspx, accessed September 12, 2019.

———. 2019b. Letter to Brett Redfearn, Securities and Exchange Commission. June 25. Available at https://www.virtu.com/uploads/documents/Virtu-Comment-Letter-06.25.19.pdf, accessed January 26, 2020.

Walsingham, Thoma. 1869. *Gesta Abbatum Monasterii Sancti Albani, volume III, A.D. 1349–1411*. London: Longmans, Green.

Weeden, Donald E. 2002. *Weeden & Co.: The New York Stock Exchange and the Struggle over a National Securities Market*. N.p.: privately published.

Weisberger, David. 2016. "Measuring Execution Quality: The Blind Men and the Elephant." Available at https://tabbforum.com/opinions/measuring-execution-quality-the-blind-men-and -the-elephant, accessed December 29, 2019.

Whitcomb, David K. 1989a. "Letter to Prospective ATD Shareholders." June 12. David Whitcomb, private papers.

———. 1989b. "Letter to ATD Shareholders." November 11. David Whitcomb, private papers.

———. 1990. "Letter to ATD Shareholders." October 28. David Whitcomb, private papers.

———. 1995. "Letter to ATD Shareholders." January 5. David Whitcomb, private papers.

———. 2001. "Letter to ATD Shareholders." April 8. David Whitcomb, private papers.

Wigglesworth, Robin. 2019. "Subdued Volatility and Worsening Data Fuel Unease on Wall Street." *Financial Times*, June 15–16: 19.

Wilkes, Samuel. 2019. "Germany Scrambles to Shut the Door on Mifid Open Access." Available at https://www.risk.net/regulation/7196266/germany-scrambles-to-shut-the-door-on-mifid -open-access, accessed January 16, 2020.

Wolf, Martin. 2019. "Saving Capitalism from the Rentiers." *Financial Times*, September 18: 9.

Wolfe, Tom. 1988. *The Bonfire of the Vanities*. London: Cape.

Wolkoff, Neal L., and Jason B. Werner. 2010. "The History of Regulation of Clearing in the Securities and Futures Markets, and Its Impact on Competition." *Review of Banking and Financial Law* 30/1: 313–81.

Young, Kevin. 2015. "Not by Structure Alone: Power, Prominence, and Agency in American Finance." *Business and Politics* 17/3: 443–72.

Zaloom, Caitlin. 2006. *Out of the Pits: Trading and Technology from Chicago to London*. Chicago: University of Chicago Press.

Zhou, Wanfeng, and Nick Olivari. 2013. "EBS Take New Step to Rein in High-Frequency Traders." Available at https://uk.reuters.com/article/us-markets-forex-hft/exclusive-ebs-take-new-step -to-rein-in-high-frequency-traders-idUSBRE97M0YJ20130823, accessed September 21, 2020.

Ziegler, Nicholas J., and John T. Wooley. 2016. "After Dodd Frank: Ideas and the Post-Enactment Politics of Financial Reform in the United States." *Politics & Society* 44/2: 249–280.

Zook, Michael, and Michael H. Grote. 2017. "The Microgeographies of Global Finance: High-Frequency Trading." *Environment and Planning* 49/1: 121–140.

Zuckerman, Ezra W. 1999. "The Categorical Imperative: Securities Analysts and the Illegitimacy Discount." *American Journal of Sociology* 104/5: 1398–1438.

———. 2000. "Focusing the Corporate Product: Securities Analysts and De-Diversification." *Administrative Science Quarterly* 45/3: 591–619.

Zuckerman, Gregory. 2019. *The Man Who Solved the Market: How Jim Simons Launched the Quant Revolution*. London: Penguin.

INDEX

50 Broad Street, 1, 2f

Abbott, Andrew, 16
Abolafia, Mitchel, 19
actor-network theory, 14
advertising, online, 236–37
Aldrich, Eric, 229
Aldrich, Eric, and Seung Lee, 248nn23 and 27
algorithms, 4, 172–205, 213–17; defined,
    12–13; volume-participation, 230–31
Amazon, 236
Angel, James, 225
Anova, 155, 156, 159–60, 253n12
AOptics, 159–60
application-specific integrated circuits
    (ASICs), 254n23
Aquilina, Matteo, 183–84, 223, 256n13
Aquis, 225
arb, 43
arbitrage, 175; statistical, 243n5
Archipelago, 91, 96, 255n7
asterisk, battle of, 219–20, 222
Aurora, 50, 52
Automated Trading Desk (ATD), 28, 29,
    66–69, 77–80, 82–84, 90, 101–4, 176,
    210–11; staff roles, 84f

banks, 5, 103
Barclays Bank, 197
BATS (Better Alternative Trading System),
    96, 97
Biais, Bruno, and Richard Green, 110
bigs and littles, 54–55
bilateral relationships, 227–28
Birch, Kean, 246n32
bird droppings, 160
bitcoin, 234–35
Bloomberg FIT (Fixed-Income Trading),
    106–7, 110
Borch, Christian, 10–11, 231, 241
Brogaard, Jonathan, 240

broker groups, 46–47
BrokerTec, 105–6, 110, 113, 114, 115t, 165
Budish, Eric, 23, 223–24, 225–26, 240

C++, 167
cabling, 139–47, 165–66
Callon, Michel, 243n17
Cantor Fitzgerald, 111–13
Carlson, Ryan, 60, 247nn5 and 6
Cermak, 135–37, 136f
Chicago Board of Trade, 33, 35f, 36f, 37,
    59–60
Chicago Board Options Exchange (CBOE),
    203–4
Chicago Mercantile Exchange (CME), 29,
    32, 33, 37, 63–64, 232–33
Chi-X, 99–101, 240, 256n21
Christie, William, and Paul Schultz, 94
circuit breakers, 261n26
Citadel, 4, 104, 233, 260n16
Citigroup, 103–4
Citron, Jeffrey, 85, 250n17
Clackatron, 3f, 128
clearing and settlement, 209
CLOBs (consolidated limit order books),
    71–72, 97, 178, 218, 219
clock synchronization, 11, 187
coils, 258n34
Commodity Exchange Authority, 39
Commodity Futures Trading Commission
    (CFTC), 41–42, 133
cookies, 261n36
Coombs, Nathan, 242
Copenhagen Business School, 231, 241
coronavirus, 10
Cowan, Ruth Schwartz, 14
cryptocurrencies, 234–35
Cummings, Dave, 3–4, 29, 92

dark pools, 19–20, 116, 251n24
datacenters, 6–8, 135–39, 138f, 162–71